For

The Family Institute

FAMILY AND
MARITAL PSYCHOTHERAPY

By the same author

Family Therapy: the treatment of natural systems

FAMILY AND
MARITAL PSYCHOTHERAPY
A critical approach

Edited by
SUE WALROND-SKINNER

Routledge & Kegan Paul
London, Henley and Boston

First published in 1979
by Routledge & Kegan Paul Ltd
39 Store Street,
London WC1E 7DD,
Broadway House,
Newtown Road,
Henley-on-Thames,
Oxon RG9 1EN and
9 Park Street,
Boston, Mass. 02108, USA
Printed in Great Britian by
Thomson Litho Ltd
East Kilbride, Scotland

British Library Cataloguing in Publication Data

Family and marital psychotherapy.
    1. Family psychotherapy
    I. Walrond-Skinner, Sue
    616.8'915   RC488.5   78-40910

ISBN 0 7100 8981 3

CONTENTS

CONTRIBUTORS

DOUGLAS C. BREUNLIN, MSSA: Student Unit Supervisor, Family Institute, Cardiff.

BRIAN CADE, CSW: Course Tutor, Family Institute, Cardiff.

MICHAEL J. CROWE, DM, MRCPsych: Senior Lecturer, Institute of Psychiatry and Honorary Consultant Psychiatrist at Bethlem Royal and Maudsley Hospitals.

EMILIA DOWLING, MSc: Clinical Researcher, Family Institute, Cardiff.

NEIL FRUDE, BA, MPhil, PhD: Lecturer in Clinical Psychology, University College, Cardiff.

ANTHONY GALE, BA, FBPsS: Professor of Applied Psychology, University of Southampton.

GILL GORELL-BARNES, MA, MSc: Chairman, Family and Marital Course, Institute of Family Therapy, London.

PHILIP KINGSTON, BSc (Soc): Tutor in Social Work, Department of Extra-Mural Studies, University of Bristol; Associate Member of the Family Institute, Cardiff.

ANTHONY RYLE, DM: Director, University Health Service, University of Sussex.

A.C. ROBIN SKYNNER, MB, FRCPsych, DPM: Chairman, Institute of Family Therapy, London; Senior Tutor in Psychotherapy, Institute of Psychiatry, London; Honorary Associate Consultant, the Maudsley Hospital, London.

SUE WALROND-SKINNER, BA, DipEd, DipAppSocStud: Family Therapist, Bristol.

FOREWORD

A.C. Robin Skynner

During the mid 1970s a trickle of books on family therapy has grown
rapidly to a flood. The excitement previously aroused by the appearance of a new title has been replaced, for many of us, by an
apprehensive calculation of the time required to read so much material. Often they prove to be 'the mixture as before', and apart
from elementary introductory surveys of the field, they tend to fall
either into elaborations of the ideas of one particular school of
family therapy, usually ignoring the contributions of others, or new
collections of articles by different authorities, brought into physical proximity and giving the appearance of collaboration, but each
still written as if neighbouring chapters did not exist. The pleasurable shock of finding one's implicit assumptions made conscious
and challenged, one's mental horizons suddenly widening and deepen-
ing, and one's thought changing gear and moving into new and unfam-
iliar patterns is rare indeed, but the present volume is, I am del-
ighted to find, one of these exceptions.

It is a particular pleasure that it emanates from Britain and
that it exemplifies, in content and form, so many of the qualities
that have come to characterise the British family therapy scene.
While agreeing with the editor's belief that the details of recent
history are best left to the objectivity of future historians, it is
fair to say that, despite the hiatus in our exploration of this
field, due partly to John Bowlby (1) dropping his early experiments
in conjoint therapy in the late 1940s to concentrate on his research
into maternal deprivation, and to the fact that my own teacher,
S.H. Foulkes (2) (who was viewing and treating individual symptoms
as manifestations of the family system even earlier) turned his attention mainly to the 'stranger-group', the soil was nevertheless
rich and able to sustain rapid growth once development began.

From psycho-analysis, object-relations theory lent itself readily
to the conceptualisation of family interaction, and particularly in
theWwork of H.V. Dicks (3) and the Institute of Marital Studies, had
been brilliantly applied to the examination and treatment of the
marital dyad. The group-analytic concepts of Foulkes had anticipated many fundamental ideas of general systems theory, so that the
latter were half-recognised and readily embraced when they appeared.
Learning theory, and the behaviour modification approaches stemming
from it, were also highly developed and widely respected.

From these sources, Britain had already developed a sturdy, independent growth of family concepts and techniques before teachers
were imported from, or British practitioners trained in, the United
States.   But the field has since eagerly absorbed and sought to
integrate the variety of ideas and methods produced by North American colleagues with British ones, as this volume demonstrates.

To me, the most valuable feature of the British scene is its combination, at least so far, of basically affiliative (rather than oppositional) attitudes, and of good communication, between the different institutes and teams together with lively, constructive argument and respect for individuality and differences.   These are, in
fact, the first three criteria recently found to differentiate healthy from dysfunctional families, (4) and I believe they have facilitated, as this book shows, other characteristics of healthy family
functioning including creativeness, and capacity for co-operation
without need for conformity.

Thus we find here systems, communication, psycho-analytic and
behavioural approaches;   sociological, psychological and medical
perspectives;   as well as clinical, theoretical and research aspects
of the study and treatment of natural groups - ranging widely from
the supra-system of the community and related political considerations, through the extended and nuclear families to the sub-system
of the marital dyad and within that the intimate sexual encounter
from which all life stems.   Most contributors have succeeded in
combining and integrating several of these aspects, but the book as
a whole also gives the impression of a synthesis.   Many will find
it, as I did, an education in aspects of family theory and technique
distant from their original training.   And it is a tribute to the
editor, as well as the contributors, that despite its unusual variety and range it has remarkable unity and consistency, wearing its
impressive scholarship and research orientation lightly, and combining these with a clear, lively and most readable style.

A.C. Robin Skynner

NOTES

1 Bowlby, J. (1949), The study and reductions of group tensions in
   the family, 'Human Relations', 2, 123-8.
2 Foulkes, S.H. (1948), 'Introduction to group-analytic psychotherapy', Heinemann, London.
3 Dicks, H.V. (1953), Experiences with marital tensions seen in a
   psychological clinic in Clinical Studies in Marriage and the
   Family, 'Brit. J. Med. Psychol.', 26, 181-96.
4 Lewis, J. et al. (1976), 'No Single Thread: Psychological
   Health in Family Systems', Brunner Mazel, New York.

INTRODUCTION

Sue Walrond-Skinner

Family therapy can best be considered as a psychotherapeutic modality, embracing a variety of methods, each of these sustaining an array of techniques. The term modality refers to the character- istic orientation of the family therapist which underpins his thera- peutic practice, i.e. an orientation towards the interpersonal pro- cesses and behaviours occurring between the members of a natural psycho-social system, the family, and between the family system and its environment. All family therapists share this position and indeed claim to be family therapists precisely because they sub- scribe to this modal orientation. However, although family therapy is young in its development compared with individual psychotherapy, its practitioners can be distinguished from one another in terms of both the methods and techniques by which they operationalise their approach to the modality. We can begin to identify the early dev- elopment of 'schools' of practice, each working from what Ritterman (1977) has described as different 'pre-theoretical assumptions', as well as emphasising a somewhat different aspect of the theoretical framework supporting family therapy. Family therapy is not a homo- geneous enterprise and the contributors to this book, by the differ- ent approaches they take, argue the case for a technical and theore- tical ecclectism within the overall framework of a conjoint approach to psychotherapeutic intervention. Some effort to differentiate the developing methodological schools is therefore likely to be helpful in allowing practitioners to gain a more specific sense of their own identity within what otherwise can appear to be a confused and indeterminate field of practice. As Ritterman (1977, p. 29) comments, 'It is no longer sufficient to differentiate family ther- apy in general from other therapies. A method for distinguishing the unique contributions of the various models of family therapy is needed.'

I do not intend to address myself to so ambitious a task here but simply to comment on the work of others in this respect. Various attempts at differentiating schools of family therapy have been made - three of the best known being the GAP report (1970); Beels and Ferber's (1969) classification of therapeutic style; and Olson's (1970) rather more general classification of therapists in terms of the treatment unit they adopt. More recently, Guerin

(1976) has offered a descriptive study of the main groupings in the
field, delineating them as structural (Minuchin, Aponte, Montalvo);
strategic and/or communicational (Satir, Haley, Weakland, Fisch,
Watzlawick); dynamic (Ackerman, Bloch, Wynne, Framo, Boszormenyi-
Nagy); experiential (Kempler, Duhl); and differentiation purist
(Bowen, Fogerty).   Guerin (1976, p. 20) makes the interesting observation that, 'In 1970, the systems view was clearly a minority
point of view.   There were two major foci of its development in the
field - the work of the California communications theorists, derived
from Bateson, and the work of Murray Bowen.'   He goes on to comment
that now, by contrast, 'the systems approach has moved from the
periphery to the center of the field' (p. 21).   Guerin defines the
structural, strategic and Bowenian schools as systems based in contrast to the dynamic and experiential schools who derive many of
their ideas from psycho-dynamic, group analytic and gestalt therapies.   This strikes me as an unfortunate use of the word systems,
since family therapy *as a modality* derives its basic assumptions
either implicitly or explicitly from general systems theory.   A
more useful broad distinction seems to me to be between those
schools of family therapy which concentrate on assisting the family
group to change by acquiring some insight into areas of its dysfunction (dynamic, Bowenian and experiential schools), and those
schools of family therapy which concentrate on helping the family to
change its patterns of behaviour without increasing its awareness of
dysfunctional processes (strategic, communicational and behavioural).   The structural school bridges the two broad subdivisions,
for as Guerin (1976, p. 20) points out, Minuchin, its chief expon-
ent, 'shows the influence of Ackerman in his clinical aristry;
he also reflects the theoretical influence in recent years of Jay
Haley', and Guerin goes on to hope that, as a result, Minuchin 'may
well end up by bridging the ideologies in such a way that it will
allow therapists to move more comfortably back and forth' between
the two orientations.
   This is an important thought, for the development of these
schools of family therapy both helps and hinders the formation of
the modality's identity within the professional community.   It is
natural that as theoretical and clinical knowledge accumulates,
practitioners will group together to refine and develop a particular approach to the treatment of families which they find is both
effective and satisfying.   Moreover, this type of differentiation
between treatment methods enables us to move one step nearer to formulating a taxonomy of treatment approaches effective with different
areas of dysfunction and ultimately to clarify issues surrounding
the indications and contra-indications for using family therapy or
one of its subspecialities with different family types (Walrond-
Skinner, 1978).   The polarisation between methods can be a helpful
means of crystallising and sharpening the way in which we develop
clinical hypotheses regarding the suitability of an array of treatment techniques for an array of interpersonal problems, for, as
Haley (1962) comments, 'too much tolerance confuses the theoretical
and descriptive problem'.   But on the other hand, as Weakland
(1977, p. 46) points out, the whole enterprise of classification can
result in little more than a self-defeating exercise.   In discussing Ritterman's (1977) classification of pre-theoretical assump-

tions, he draws a distinction between descriptive characterisation and the rigidity of a classification system.

In my view, the proper and useful aim of attention to general premises and assumptions is to aid in *characterisation* not classification or categorization.   That is, the aim is to obtain a more accurate and organised positive description of what a given theoretical view involves, by clarifying what is basic but often only vague or implicit, so that its further theoretical and practical implications can be seen and evaluated better.

Likewise, descriptive characterisation of family therapists and their methods, rather than a classification of methods and a pigeonholing of practitioners, seems to me to hold out most hope of clarifying the different approaches in the field, without building rigid barriers between them.

Such descriptive characterisations need, of course, to be frequently updated.   Practitioners develop, grow and even change their allegiance quite dramatically from one approach to another.   Moreover, new faces appear on the scene.   Characteristically, each of the American accounts of family therapists and their methods described above implicitly assumes that the boundaries of the family therapy field are coterminous with the shores of the United States! For the sake of accuracy, some comments about the developing British scene may be in order.   So far as it is possible to be precise about these matters, family therapy in the formal sense is about 15 years old in Britain, but as early as 1949, Bowlby published a short, but extremely influential paper entitled The study and reduction of group tensions in the family.   In this paper, Bowlby described several conjoint family interviews, the material from which he then linked with his ongoing work with the individual.   1951 is another date that should be recorded in any brief history of the family therapy movement in Britain, for it marks a meeting between John Elderkin Bell and John Sutherland from which Bell developed his early work in the United States.   Bell (1961, p. 2) describes the incident as follows:

It was against this background of some urgency [a search for a more effective approach] that the method of treatment I have called 'family group therapy' was developed.   Its beginnings can be traced to London and August 1951, when I was visiting Dr. John D. Sutherland, medical director of London's Tavistock Clinic. In conversation one evening before dinner, Dr. Sutherland mentioned casually that Dr. John Bowlby of the clinic staff was experimenting in cases of problem children and adolescents with having whole families together for therapy.   Before I could ask for details, the topic of conversation shifted, and I took away a misapprehension of what Dr. Bowlby was doing.   I assumed he was using contact with the whole family as his sole way of meeting the problem child, or the problem adolescent, and was working out the treatment of the child through having the whole family come to each therapeutic session.

I discovered only much later through reading articles by Dr. Bowlby and a personal meeting with him, that the family approach he had used included only occasional conferences with the whole family.   These conferences were adjuncts within the typical mode of dealing with children and their parents where one therapist sees the child and another the adult (usually the mother).

But on the ship returning to the United States just after my visit with Dr. Sutherland in 1951, I began to think through the technical implications of meeting the whole family as a group. These small seeds were fertilised in 1959 by the publication of R.D. Laing's first book 'The Divided Self'.   Written when Laing was 28 years old, it was, as he described in his preface to a later edition (Laing, 1964) 'the work of an old young man'.   Schizophrenia and the schizophrenogenic process was described not as a biochemical or physiological disorder, but in terms of ontological insecurity deriving from the individual's prolonged experience of dysfunctional interpersonal relationships.   Laing followed this book with two others - 'Self and Others' (1961) and (with Aaron Esterson) 'Sanity, Madness and the Family' (1964).   In his writings Laing tried 'to depict persons within a social system or "nexus" of persons, in order to try to understand some of the ways in which each affects each person's experience of himself and of how interaction takes form.   Each contributes to the other's fulfilment or destruction' (Laing, 1961, p. 9).   Many other writings have followed, each depicting Laing's developing views of the part played by the family system in the aetiology and course of individual psychopathology. Laing's views do not take us far enough along the road to making the conceptual leap required in order to treat the family itself as the patient.   As Bartlett (1976, p. 58) has shown, 'He rarely includes the reciprocal action of the designated patient, much less the totality of the reciprocal actions of the family members as a system.' Nevertheless, Laing and his associates have been extraordinarily influential in developing an intellectual climate conducive to viewing psychological disorders from within a framework of dysfunctional interpersonal relationships.

At this point I had imagined that I would sketch out a brief history of developments in Britain in the 1960s through to the present day, mentioning the growth of the various centres and the many people from different professional disciplines which have contributed.   On reflection such a 'history' would be premature - and could hardly fail to be little more than my personal view of events. Suffice it to say that there now exist several institutes specialising entirely in the promotion of family psychotherapy, mostly in large conurbations such as London and Cardiff.   In addition there are numerous departments and agencies both in London and throughout the country where family therapy is being practised and taught. These include some of the main teaching hospitals but also many smaller units where family therapy is routinely used.   In Britain, the practice of family therapy seems to be spreading rapidly, not only within clinics and hospitals, but also within some of the statutory agencies.   In this way, family therapy skills are being made available to an increasing range of client groups.   This dissemination of enthusiasm and skill has been helped forward by the foundation in 1976 of an Association for Family Therapy, which is already seeking to provide support groups for interested professionals from different agencies.   As Skynner (1976, p. 383) points out:

The task of the seventies, already underway, is perhaps to apply this now well established knowledge on a broader scale, to discover its limits and indications, so that it can find its place within the broad spectrum of our treatment armamentarium throughout the helping services.

The contributors to this book focus mainly on three subspecial-
ties of family therapy - the treatment of the family group;   conjoint marital therapy;   and therapeutic work with broader networks
and intervention systems.   The book is introduced by a chapter by
Frude which reflects on the family itself and on the various meanings which we attach to this word.   Frude analyses various uni-
dimensional models of the family and differentiates 'family therapy'
from a whole range of 'therapies for the family'.   He redresses the
imbalance produced by some of the annihilistic approaches to the
family (Cooper, 1971) and highlights the positive impact and therapeutic potential of the family system for its members.   He traces
the development of the various approaches made by psychotherapists
to the family and by so doing, sets in context those family therapy
concepts which have become so firmly embedded within the family
therapist's knowledge base that their origins are liable to be lost.
In his section on the future of intimate relationships, Frude draws
attention to the increasing variation in relationship structures and
points out the challenge this holds for the family therapist.
'Individuals' family backgrounds and patterns of interaction will be
more heterogeneous and more fluid and the aims of therapy directed
at relationships will reflect this.'
    Kingston draws attention to inconsistencies in the way in which
family therapists working from a systems theory base all but
ignore the family's and the therapist's supra-systems.   He argues
that in some situations 'an intra-familial focus is certainly inadequate and may be almost irrelevant'.   He goes on to suggest that
family therapy should more properly be called 'systems problem-
solving' since both the words 'family' and 'therapy' conjure up a
partial and inaccurate picture of what should be the scope of a
systems worker's intervention.   Kingston reminds us that systems
include political systems and that a systems-oriented worker can
hardly avoid attending to the interface between family system and
environment if he is to remain true to his basic orientation.
Bloch (1977, p. 123) makes a similar point in a recent reflection on
the American scene:
    Contributions [by family therapists] to wider public understand-
    ing of the family and to the formulation of public policy con-
    cerning it have been minimal ... two concepts are important in
    regard to public policy matters: the interdigitation of family
    (however defined) and other social systems such as educational
    and health - care delivery systems, and the consequences of over-
    lapping membership for persons in the family in other groups such
    as the work system or age or gender groups.
Kingston calls for a much needed reorientation within the family
therapy movement; yet it is within the clinical sphere that the
systems revolution has been most needed, simply because other workers have been more willing to assume this task within the wider
community.   Moreover, the ultimate futility of 'radical non-inter-
vention' has been laid bare and the necessity for skilled psychotherapeutic work with individuals and families reaffirmed.   Family
therapists need to address themselves however to Kingston's challenge without abandoning their 'intensive attention to the structure
and function of the family as a psycho-social entity' (Bloch, 1977,
p. 123).

Gorell-Barnes picks up the theme proposed by Kingston and reminds
us that

The knowledge that physical aggression between spouses and between parent and child is more prevalent among those who are poor
and less well educated ... and the experience of continued living
with an awareness of their limited prestige and power in relation
to many aspects of the world outside the family, causes greater
frustration and bitterness when things go wrong within it.   As
therapists, knowledge of this kind must also remind us of the
continued task of developing a range of interventions that make
sense in terms of our clients' needs.

Her chapter tackles one of the most critical areas of psychopatho-
logy/environmental disorder that society and the helping professions
are faced with today - that of the violent family.   Whether the
violence is focused on child or adult, primitive levels of pain and
fear must necessarily be experienced by any therapist seeking to
treat the situation as a systems problem.   Gorell-Barnes includes
extended extracts of verbatim recordings of treatment sessions with
one family and illustrates her belief that the family therapist
needs to draw together ideas from both behavioural and psychodynamic
approaches to be effective in helping these families.

Similarly, Cade, while writing strictly from the point of view of
a strategic family therapist, nevertheless underlines the importance
of the use by the therapist of an empathic understanding of the
framework within which the family is operating.   And yet it would
be a misrepresentation to pretend that strategic family therapy does
not present a major challenge to the psychodynamically oriented
family therapist.   Working from the premise that the problem for
the family is its solution to the problem, the strategic family
therapist, as Cade points out, discovers that the solution to its
problem may well lie within the parameters of the problem itself.
Behaviour change is induced in order that the experience of the positive aspects of changed behaviour may produce continued behaviour
change.   Insight and 'personal growth' becomes redundant.   Yet, as
Dowling shows in Chapter 8, both the actual behaviours of family
therapists in sessions and the order and amount that they are used
are very similar even amongst therapists of widely different orientations.   Moreover, as I have shown in Chapter 9, students trained
within an entirely skills-centred strategic programme nevertheless
display a considerable amount of 'personal growth' after training.
Perhaps these paradoxical inferences might be satisfactorily explained so far as the strategic family therapist is concerned by
reflecting on a verse from the Tao Te Ching:

Less and less is done
Until non-action is achieved.
When nothing is done, nothing is left undone (Lao-Tsu, 1973).

Breunlin, in his chapter on non-verbal communication in family
therapy, offers a comprehensive review of interdisciplinary research
into non-verbal communication and he relates this knowledge base to
the three levels of systems organisation within the family - the individual, the dyad and the group.   Breunlin, in reflecting on the
dearth of literature relating to non-verbal communication applied
specifically to family therapy, suggests that this is because family
therapists are 'sensitive to the complexity of NVC in family therapy

and, therefore, have largely avoided NVC as an area of research'.
In the second half of his chapter, Breunlin discusses (a) the way in
which the family therapist can use the family's non-verbal communication in order to understand more fundamental levels of meaning in
the group, and (b) the many treatment techniques that family therapists have developed or adopted from other sources which rely primarily on non-verbal communication rather than on words. Many case
illustrations are given showing the way in which the family's nonverbal communication and the therapist's non-verbal techniques can
be used by family therapists working from either an 'insight' or a
'behavioural' orientation. Examples are given of an imaginative
use of the one-way viewing screen in therapy.

Ryle and Crowe provide thorough discussions of conjoint therapeutic work conducted with the marital dyad. Marital therapy is sometimes considered as a treatment modality in its own right and as
lying apart from family therapy. But clearly, when a systems approach to psychological and emotional disorders is adopted, the
marital dyad is conceived of and treated as a relationship
system using exactly the same basic orientation to treatment as when
the therapist works with a family group. The decision as to
whether or not the children should be included directly in the
treatment procedure when the marital couple present their problems
transactionally in terms of their relationship rather than displac-
ing their problems onto one or more of the children, can be considered to be either a technical issue or a matter of ideology. As
Ryle points out, there is at present 'little evidence in favour of
one or other course'. For most family therapists, however, it will
seem necessary from time to time to work with the marital pair without children or other family members being present. Ryle's chapter offers an account of the aims, approaches and techniques of marital therapy which should prove invaluable to the therapist approaching the marital dyad. Ryle's own treatment approach is founded on object relations theory, and he therefore works from within
the framework described earlier as dynamic. But like several of
the contributors to this book, he emphasises the usefulness of integrating models: 'The marital therapist of the future, whether
working with couples, or with groups of couples, can, with advantage, draw upon the work of all these schools, and should not, in my
view, abandon the contribution of any of them.' Ryle concludes by
describing some of his own research into the outcome of marital
therapy, using various forms of repertory grid technique, a research
methodology based on personal construct theory which holds out considerable promise for research into family and marital treatment.

Crowe's chapter complements Ryle's by examining the treatment of
sexual dysfunction with marital dyads. As Crowe points out,
'sexual dysfunction is almost always multifactorial in origin', yet,
as he goes on to show, probably the most pervasive and frequent
causes of sexual dysfunction are marital problems. In a study
which Crowe and his colleagues conducted into some of their own work
(Crowe, 1977), it was found that over 60 per cent of the
couples seen had marked or severe marital problems in addition to
their sexual ones. Thus, although Crowe carefully distinguishes
the multiple causative factors involved in sexual dysfunction, he
nevertheless views sex therapy as a part of family/marital relation-

ship work, rather than as a subspeciality in its own right, divorced from the psychotherapeutic process.   Crowe's clear factual descriptive statements concerning dysfunctional conditions, causes and treatment procedures will commend his chapter to the many family therapists who may experience some unease in handling this area of their psychotherapeutic work.   Crowe evaluates some of the outcome studies that have been conducted in this field and concludes his chapter with a section on training needs and opportunities.

Dowling offers an overview of co-therapy - a frequently used method of work utilised amongst practitioners from different orientations.   Its popularity probably stems from the intuitive self-protective needs of the therapist when confronted with the powerfulness of the family system.   Its pragmatic origins have not, however, prevented practitioners from capitalising on its therapeutic potential, as Dowling describes.   One of its most important side-effects seems to me to be the way in which it reduces the narcisstic and megalomaniacal tendencies that sometimes prevail in 'solo' work. Referring to Becker's (1971, 1973) discussion of the myth of the hero, Holt and Greiner (1976) point out that 'one of the most universal human problems involves the attempts of the individual to assert his narcissism and "cosmic significance", and to reject his mortality and fallibility by some heroic act' and they go on to comment that 'the single family therapist working with families is vulnerable to motives of heroism seen in his remarkable "cures" or "rescues" of families.'   The act of injecting a co-therapy relationship into the treatment process reduces these dangers.   Even so, co-therapy is no panacea, and Dowling discusses some of the pitfalls and difficulties inherent in the use of two therapists.   She concludes her chapter with a description of some research into the subject which she has conducted at the Family Institute, Cardiff.

Chapter 9 describes two types of training programme that are routinely used (with various modifications) in family therapy settings. The number of agencies and departments currently running full-time training programmes in family therapy is indicated in two surveys, one conducted by Framo (1976) and the other by Weiss (1976).   Both lists were almost entirely confined to centres within the United States, but additionally we can reckon on a considerably greater number existing, if British and European centres were to be included.   The effectiveness of this enormous investment in training has so far been almost entirely unmonitored.   Moreover, since training programmes of the two main persuasions frequently make untested assumptions about the other, it seemed valuable to try to examine the validity of some of these statements.   The research reported in this chapter was conducted at the Family Institute, Cardiff over a two-year period.

The final chapter by Gale, in common with much of Chapters 8 and 9, is devoted to research.   Gale reviews the problems of outcome research in family therapy from a vantage point that is outside the field - since he writes from a background of experimental psychology.   As Gale comments, the chapter is 'an attempt to summarise the main issues involved in the evaluation of outcome research in family therapy'.   It is a particularly important chapter, as 'it is argued that for a number of reasons, family therapy is in danger of going the way of all other therapies, unless steps are taken to curb blind

enthusiasm and to ensure a more rigorous approach.'   The chapter
sets out to provide a review of research reviews and then goes on to
offer a checklist of questions which could valuably be asked by the
researcher into family therapy.   The checklist is wide ranging, and
covers theoretical considerations, training methods, pre-treatment
characteristics of clients, treatment techniques, and the quality
and character of research itself.   Some glaring deficiencies in our
knowledge are highlighted.   For example, with regard to theory,
Gale concludes that 'no theory purporting to be relevant to family
therapy is precise enough or unambiguous enough, or general enough,
or, where necessary, specific enough, to help the family therapist
in any practical manner'.   The absence of any meaningful family
taxonomy is also underlined, together with the continuing and vexed
question of how one can both ethically and rigorously incorporate
adequate controls in one's outcome research.   Gale's constructive
critique strikes a realistic note:

> There is often little drama or romance in discovery and quite
> often the key lesson to be learned from research is that we must
> do the research better on the next occasion.   Unfortunately, as
> with a tedious opera, only the arias are memorable.

This collection of papers spans the spheres of practice, teaching
and research.   It seems important to keep these three areas of interest closely connected with one another, so that clinical practice
may benefit from the efforts of researchers, and research studies
can stay closely in touch with what actually happens in therapy.
Whatever its orientation, teaching needs to be firmly rooted in
practice;   but, at the same time, to remain open to the challenge
posed by new findings in the research field.   The book draws on a
representative sample of writers from different disciplines, different theoretical approaches and tackling different areas of interest within the field as a whole.   Two of the contributors are
not family therapists at all and were invited to participate in
order to bring a different and perhaps more objective perspective to
bear upon the subject.   It is a meal of different dishes which will
hopefully provide interest and stimulation for family therapists
working within different settings and from different theoretical
perspectives.

Various problems confront family therapists as they seek to
extend their practice of the modality in Britain.   Many of these
are alluded to in the various chapters of this book.   A few are
worth highlighting here.   First, let us examine the position of
theory.   The quality and developmental stage of family therapy
theory is worthy of continuous careful scrutiny.   Whether one con-
ceives of family therapy today as in a pre-theory (Stein, 1969) or
an anti-theory phase (Guerin, 1976) will depend much on which writer
one is reading at the time.   Some will agree with Whitaker (1976,
p. 156) regarding the 'chilling effect theory has on intuition and
creativity in general'.   Others would regard strong, unified and
well-conceived theoretical frameworks as an essential foundation for
the continued life and well-being of the modality.   Whether one
feels that the current stage of family therapy is in 'a healthy unstructured state of chaos' (Bowen, 1971, p. 162) or that 'theory
building is going along satisfactorily' (Bloch, 1977, p. 123).

depends largely upon the perspective from which one is viewing the field.   Moreover, our present-day cult of anti-intellectualism may teach us to emphasise the experiential therapies (be they for individual, family or group) without paying too much regard to their purpose or efficacy or even their ability not to damage.   This trend can also lead us to despise as mere jargon the development of a technical terminology designed to describe interpersonal rather than intra-personal experiences.   We are far from having such a language, but the attempt to achieve one seems worth making.   Every science or new field of endeavour needs a formal language that is specific to itself;   and whilst this can degenerate into the jargon of mystification, it can also provide the royal road to differentiation and clarification of meaning.

Second, various political dilemmas threaten to bedevil the development of family therapy in the future unless they are opened up for serious debate.   Some of these involve boundary issues regarding the type of personnel felt to be suitable to practice family therapy;   the standard of training and practice required of them;   and the way in which they should be rewarded.   Whether or not family therapy should be considered as a branch of psychotherapy is seldom discussed, but it is reasonable to assume that at some level both individuals and institutions are perplexed about this matter, sensing that important issues are at stake, even though being unclear as to what these might be.   If (as is usual) the terms family therapy and family psychotherapy are used synonymously, is the question of who should be allowed to practise it materially affected?   Those who are medically trained, be they psychiatrists or general practitioners, usually experience less guilt in claiming to practise psychotherapy than those who are not.   Indeed, social workers, till rather recently, defended themselves against their feelings of inadequacy in this matter by going to the other extreme and stressing the many differences between casework and psychotherapy.   Likewise (and probably for similar reasons), clinical psychologists who, again till quite recently, have tried to claim exclusive ownership of behavioural techniques, have stressed the differences between behaviour therapy and psychotherapy.   Do the professional disciplines transfer these attitudes experienced in relation to individual psychotherapy to the much newer field of family psychotherapy?   If so, are we likely to see some splitting off of specific fields of practice as being more suitably treated by family therapists with a medical background, whilst others are assigned to family therapists coming from non-medical professional disciplines?   Such a development would, I think, seriously vitiate some basic premises on which family therapy is grounded.

This problem intrudes most obviously when the person's basic professional discipline overrides the fact of his practising family therapy.   In other words, he is seen as a social worker/psychiatrist/clinical psychologist practising family therapy rather than as a family therapist coming from a background of social work/psychiatry/clinical psychology.   Such a position is, of course, a perfectly reasonable one to hold in our present youthful stage of development in Britain.   To abandon one's basic discipline too readily for the currently anomalous position of 'family therapist' is like stepping into a professional no-man's land, where there is as yet no

commonly accepted status, qualifications or salary structure.
Moreover, to emphasise the importance of the family therapist's
basic discipline allows us to rationalise the extraordinary discrepancies in financial rewards offered to professionals working side
by side, often in co-therapy treatment teams with family groups.
The salary differential which exists between psychiatrists, psychologists and social workers involved in other areas of the helping
professions may be justifiable in terms of different types and
lengths of training and different orders of therapeutic task.   But
it is hard to begin to see how practitioners from different disciplines, all working as family therapists, should be rewarded differently except in terms of their skill, responsibility and training as
family therapists.   The political challenge of family therapy in
this respect has been ably set forth by Haley (1975).

The third general problem worth highlighting can be stated in
summary as being how to put the humanity and humility back into the
family therapy movement, prone as it is to breeding somewhat narcis-
sistically inclined 'charismatic' leaders.   It seems hard for
family therapists to feel that remaining uncertain or puzzled is an
appropriate or useful position to adopt, except as a temporary phase
during the treatment process - and a phase through which they should
pass as quickly as possible.   Yet as Jung (1943) asserted many
years previously, 'Our whole life is unsure, so a feeling of unsure-
ness is much nearer to the truth than the illusion and bluff of
sureness.'   Some approaches seem designed to cut out much of the
confusion, mystery and uncertainty of life that exists for most
people most of the time.   Moreover, by placing such a high value on
openness, sharing, consciousness-raising and change, are family
therapists in danger of devaluing the reserving, conserving inward-
ness that characterises the spiritual core of the best of human experience?

Finally, it is my impression that, with a few notable exceptions
(Bowen, 1976; Paul, 1967), family therapists seem to find it hard
to address themselves to the most serious and certain of all life's
ventures - that of death.   No family which presents itself as in
need of family therapy can be without the experience of the dilemma
of death - for each of us carries within us the certainty of this
event.   The family therapy literature traditionally stresses
change, growth and integration - yet the knowledge and experience of
disintegration and death are just as real and important to the families with whom we work.   Whitaker (1977, p. 164), quoting Plato and
summarising 'a set of rules that will help keep the therapist
alive', ends by advising him to 'practise dying'.

The purpose of this book is constructive criticism.   Yet, when
all is said and done, the unique insight captured by the idea of
treating relationships rather than individuals remains unassailable.
Perhaps only those who have experienced the brutal intrusion into a
marriage of a psychotherapeutic relationship formed with one partner
to the exclusion of the other, can have a true understanding of the
profound wisdom and compassion of conjoint psychotherapeutic work;
just as only those who have tried to observe or treat a child divorced from his familiar background will realise the ultimate absurdity
of such an undertaking.   The inadequacies of family therapy as a
modality lie in the manner of its application and the shortcomings

of its practitioners, not in the validity of its fundamental philosophy.

It would be interesting to know, but hard to predict, whereabouts family therapy is in its life-cycle. Most therapies have a limited life. Family therapy has already lived beyond what might have reasonably been expected to be its normal life-span. This can give us cause to hope that it is well rooted in fundamental assumptions regarding the purpose and function of human existence in its social context. But the spring of creativity in the movement can always run dry, and careful scrutiny of possible flaws in theory, practice and evaluative technique is probably the best way to ensure the continued well-being of the modality. For example, the danger that family therapy may turn entirely into a technology sometimes seems to be a very real one - but the letter killeth and only the spirit gives life. The life of a treatment modality must be retained through the spirit of its theory and basic philosophy; its techniques are needed to enable the fulfilment of the theory in practice. Neither is effective alone.

REFERENCES

BARTLETT, F.H. (1976), Illusion and reality in R.D. Laing, 'Family Process', vol. 15, pp. 51-64.
BECKER, E. (1971), 'The Birth and Death of Meaning', Free Press, New York.
BECKER, E. (1973), 'The Denial of Death', Free Press, New York.
BEELS, C. and FERBER, A. (1969), Family therapy - a view, 'Family Process', vol. 8, pp. 280-318.
BELL, J.E. (1961), 'Family Group Therapy', Bookstall Publications, London.
BLOCH, D. (1977), Family therapy and public policy, 'Family Process', vol. 16, pp. 123-7.
BOWEN, M. (1971), The use of family theory in clinical practice, in Haley, J. (ed.), 'Changing Families', Grune & Stratton, New York.
BOWEN, M. (1976), Family reaction to death, in Guerin, P.J. (ed.), 'Family Therapy', Gardner Press, New York.
BOWLBY, J. (1949), The study and reduction of group tensions in the family, 'Human Relations', vol. 2, no. 123.
COOPER, D. (1971), 'The Death of the Family', Allen Lane, London.
CROWE, M.J. (1977), Sexual dysfunction today, 'Up-date', January.
FRAMO, J. (1976), List of family institutes and organisations offering ongoing training in family and marital therapy, 'Family Process', vol. 15, pp. 443-5.
GROUP FOR THE ADVANCEMENT OF PSYCHIATRY (1970), 'The Field of Family Therapy', vol. VII, Mental Health Materials Centre, New York.
GUERIN, P.J. (1976), Family therapy: the first twenty five years, in Guerin, P.J (ed.), 'Family Therapy', Gardner Press, New York.
HALEY, J. (1962), Whither family therapy?, 'Family Process', vol. 1, pp. 69-100.
HALEY, J. (1975), Why a mental health clinic should avoid family therapy, 'Journal of Marriage and Family Counseling', vol. 1, pp. 3-13.
HOLT, M. and GREINER, D. (1976), Co-therapy in the treatment of fam-

ilies, in Guerin, P.J. (ed.), 'Family Therapy', Gardner Press, New York.
JUNG, C.G. (1943), 'Collected Works', vol. 18, Routledge & Kegan Paul, London.
LAO-TSU (1973), 'Tao Te Ching', Penguin, Harmondsworth.
LAING, R.D. (1961), 'Self and Others', Penguin, Harmondsworth.
LAING, R.D. (1964), 'The Divided Self', Penguin, Harmondsworth.
LAING, R.D. and ESTERSON, A. (1964), 'Sanity, Madness and the Family', Penguin, Harmondsworth.
OLSON, D. (1970), Marital and family therapy: integrative review and critique, 'Journal of Marriage and the Family', vol. 32, pp. 501-38.
PAUL, N.L. (1967), The role of mourning and empathy in conjoint marital therapy, in Zuk, G.H. and Boszormenyi-Nagy, I. (eds), 'Family Therapy and Disturbed Families', Science & Behaviour Books, Palo Alto, Calif.
RITTERMAN, M.K. (1977), Paradigmatic classification of family therapy theories, 'Family Process', vol. 16, pp. 29-46.
SKYNNER, A.C.R. (1976), 'One Flesh: Separate Persons - Principles of Family and Marital Psychotherapy', Constable, London.
STEIN, J.W. (1969), 'The Family as a Unit of Study and Treatment', Rehabilitation Research Institute, University of Washington School of Social Work.
WALROND-SKINNER, S. (1978), Indications and Contraindications for the use of family therapy, 'Journal of Child Psychology and Psychiatry', vol. 19, no. 1.
WEAKLAND, J. (1977), Comments on Ritterman's paper, 'Family Process', vol. 16, pp. 46-7.
WEISS, H. (1976), List of family institutes and organisations offering ongoing training in family and marital therapy, 'Family Process', vol. 15, pp. 445-6.
WHITAKER, C. (1976), The hindrance of theory in clinical work, in Guerin, P.J. (ed.), 'Family Therapy', Gardner Press, New York.

Chapter 1

'THE FAMILY' AND PSYCHOTHERAPY

Neil Frude

There are several important areas of overlap between family studies and psychotherapy and there have been some particularly interesting recent developments. The term 'psychotherapy' is used here in a particularly wide sense, referring to any interactional treatment which aims to relieve emotional, behavioural or relationship dysfunctions or problems. In particular, of course, we will be concerned with those therapeutic techniques which focus on the individual within a family context or which treat the family as a unit. The problem area covered is wider than that of traditional psychiatry and includes personal and social problems such as truanting, marital conflict, difficulties in the forming or maintaining of relationships, and sexual dysfunction.

The task of this chapter is twofold. First, it will consider concepts of 'the family' as far as the various meanings may affect the approach of those concerned with family psychotherapy. Second, it will review briefly research evidence linking aspects of family life with personal and relationship problems and then attempt to set family psychotherapy in context as a method of treatment.

CONCEPTS OF 'THE FAMILY'

The question of what is meant by the term 'family' is a notoriously difficult one and has generally evaded a satisfactory answer (Stephens, 1963; Ball, 1972). Studies and discussions proceed in most cases unimpeded by a certain ambiguity in the use of terms, but the patterns and processes of family groups and family life may now be changing and diversifying in such a way that it will become increasingly important to be in a position to state explicitly how the term is being used. There are multiple perspectives used in family studies. 'The family' is studied by anthropologists, sociologists, psychologists, lawyers, etc., and within each discipline there are many alternative approaches. As in other fields of study, there has recently been a healthy interest in making explicit the implicit premises, frameworks, perspectives or images which necessarily shape the evident theories and practices in the area of the family (Hill and Hansen, 1960; Nye and Berardo, 1966; Broderick, 1971).

Nevertheless, the fundamental differences in what is referred to by
the term 'family' in different cases has not received adequate attention.   One possible explanation for the great difficulty in
finding any formulation which works as a definition might be that
there are several separate types of referent, and that we need to
consider not one meaning but several.

For one thing, we need to distinguish between, on the one hand,
the 'modal' or 'ideal' family embodied in universals such as 'the
Chinese family today' or 'the Christian family', and, on the other,
the real groups of people whom we might refer to as 'the Smith family' or 'the family next door'.   Another important distinction is
that between 'the family group' as a primary interacting group of
persons, and 'an individual's family'.   When we refer to an individual's family we often mean to include members of his family of origin, and of his family of procreation, and to include some in-laws
also.   Only very infrequently, however, will it be the case that
the membership of 'an individual's family' constitutes a primary
interacting group.   Thus, the two concepts, 'the family group' and
'the individual's family' need to be considered separately.

The family group

How can we define 'the family group', and how can we identify which
groups are, and which are not, families?   Various elements for a
definition come to mind - role structure, kinship, common residence
or 'household', affectional bonds, intensity of interaction, and so
forth.   It is apparent that between any two of these elements there
will be a degree of correlation or 'overlap' in terms of the real
relationships involved.   People who share a household tend to be
kin, and they tend to have strong affectional bonds.   But such
overlap is in no case perfect and the correlation between elements
differs from culture to culture, and is liable to change over time.
Any near equivalence of elements as criteria in identifying particular individuals as members of the same family is thus fortuitous.
Where the elements are not strongly related different criteria will
lead to different groups being identified, and it is therefore essential to specify the particular criterion used in establishing the
membership of a family group.

Can we, then, arrive at a satisfactory definition of the 'family
group' which would be appropriate to the family psychotherapist, and
to the psychologist and psychiatrist?   Clearly we may rule out certain elements as inappropriate.   Legal and kinship criteria do not
define 'interacting groups', and there seems no adequate formulation
of 'role structure' which would cover the childless couple, the
single-parent family, and egalitarian stable homosexual union, forms
of communal living, and other 'intimate life-styles' which may be
the concern of the psychotherapist either as a principal focus of
interest or as the 'background' to an individual with a problem.

It would seem that an interactional or relationship criterion is
necessary.   Very many specific alternatives are possible, and these
cannot all be elaborated here.   One possibility would be 'high frequency of emotional communication', with each term precisely defined
and suitable levels set.   Each individual would then have a number

of such relationships (or possibly none), and a 'nexus' of relationships (according to a pre-set level of 'sufficient interconnected-
ness') would be labelled a 'family group'.   Thus the pattern of
dyadic relationships would be scanned for sociometric type clusters.
There are a number of arbitrary points in such a procedure, in determining levels of frequency, 'emotionality of communication' and
'clustering' or 'nexus'.   These would be set by convention, possibly reflecting empirically determined 'natural breaks' in the distribution of collected data or shadowing present common usage of the
term 'family'.   One other important question concerns the time-
base, the period over which the 'interaction frequency' or 'emotional relationship' is to be assessed.   If this were too short then
family composition might be seen to change from day to day.   On the
other hand a limit is obviously necessary to preserve some degree of
sensitivity to changes over time.

Several properties of such a definition of the 'family group' are
apparent.   An individual may be in no 'family group' at all, or in
one or more than one at any particular time.   A common member in
two family groups does not convert them into a single group.   The
definition and the means for empirically 'deciding' family membership in any particular case have a common basis.   The concept of
family group implied is much the same as that of Burgess (1926):
'the family is a unity of interacting personalities' and of others
who have used the 'interacting groups' formulation (e.g. Turner,
1970; Handel, 1965) but it is more specific in terms of the distinction between family and non-family interacting unities.

It is not suggested, of course, that such a survey of relationships followed by a cluster type analysis should precede every
'family' experiment or therapy session'.   What is suggested, however, is that we need in principle to think in such terms when we
use the phrases 'family group' or 'family unit' or make decisions as
to group membership.   The further a particular group is from the
'modal' or 'conventional' the less is likely to be the overlap between 'elements' and the more the issue of membership is likely to
be problematic.

The methods of approach to the study of processes acting within
the family group are multifarious and are not specified or limited
by the defining process.   Thus we can study the family in terms of
exchange, transactions, communications, behaviour, or more structu-
rally in terms of roles, rules, themes, power structure, sociometric
structure and so on.   One of the key questions is how far there are
similarities in these processes or characteristics from family to
family.   If there are strong similarities then it is feasible to
make assumptions about a particular family on the basis of a familiarity with the ways of families in general.   On the other hand, we
may have to work to understand each family group without being able
to call on a generalisable fund of knowledge.   It has often been
claimed that the task of understanding a particular family is rather
like that of the anthropologist who has discovered a new tribe.
While the tribe will have certain unique rituals, taboos and myth-
ology, there are, nevertheless, likely to be themes and action patterns which they will share with other tribes and which will be
understandable and to some degree predictable from the anthropologist's prior experience and knowledge.

We would expect very few characteristics to be universal among families, but patterns might well emerge for families 'of a particular type'.   Numerous alternative typologies of family groups have been advanced, incorporating criteria of structure, functionality - dysfunctionality, role-centredness, social position, level of emotionality, diagnostic category and so forth.   Each of these has a limited sphere of relevance and the proliferation of often unrelated constructs used to differentiate families may be seen as a major impediment to the accumulation and integration of information and theory about family groups.   The area of similarities and differences between family groups is in need of empirical study and of conceptual clarification (Hill, 1971;   Burr, 1973).

It has often been suggested that families are in many ways like other groups and systems, so that it might even be possible to generalise from the actions and processes of non-family groups to those of specific families.   In particular, it has been claimed that a good deal may be learned about family processes from the observation of the 'ad hoc' groups used in experimental social psychological 'small group' research (Parsons and Bales, 1955).   But apart from the various obvious differences between these artificial groups and natural families there is now considerable evidence indicating a gross dissimilarity of communication processes in the two cases which makes it clear that there can be no easy equation of one with the other (e.g. Bodin, 1969;   Leik, 1963).

The individual's family

When we turn from 'the family group' to 'the individual's family' the focus of interest changes sharply and 'the family' is a background against which we attempt principally to understand the individual himself, his interactions and his reactions to others.   The collection of people who may be considered to constitute the individual's family do not necessarily all interact in the same family group.   There are similar problems of definition and membership criteria as with the family group and, as before, legal, kinship, or spatial criteria are not acceptable if we want to delineate those who are of special psychological importance to the individual.   An interactional or relational definition would work, as before;   we would need only to establish to dyadic links, without the additional 'cluster' stage.   An individual's family, then, would be all those people with whom he has a 'close relationship' or 'close interaction' according to some pre-set criterion of closeness.

Alternatively we could use a less 'mutual' criterion, such as the degree to which the individual 'feels close' or 'feels influenced by' or 'feels involved with' a particular other.   Such a phenomenological solution brings with it the usual methodological problems and would involve the possibility that 'the family' might include people who have died, pets and fictional or delusional characters. Nevertheless, such criteria seem likely to identify those who will have maximal emotional impact and influence, and would therefore be useful in enabling us to understand and predict the individual's reactions to 'interpersonal' events.

We would expect a degree of overlap between 'close kin' and an individual's 'family' selected on criteria of emotional closeness or dependence.   Some individuals will deliberately foster and maintain kin-based relationships, while others may place little importance on kinship.   There seem to be important cross-cultural differences affecting how highly individuals value kinship ties (Triandis and Triandis, 1965).   The high prizing of a blood relationship in the absence of a remembered interaction history is exemplified by those adults who feel an emotional need to seek out their biological parents even though they were adopted shortly after birth.

There are indications that individuals in Western culture may be becoming less kin-oriented.   In terms of the conception of an individual's family which has been suggested, this change would appear as a relative increase of non-kin on a list of 'significant others' or simply as a shrinkage in the size of such a list.   Demographic changes such as the decrease in the number of children couples have, increased longevity, and increased in divorce rates and of mobility would also affect the composition of such lists.   The question of how far kin relationships are being replaced by, for example, close peer friendships is of major importance.   There is good evidence that close relationships may be crucial in the precipitation or prevention of individual dysfunction and that the social isolate is psychiatrically at risk.   We have, nevertheless, little information as to those aspects of intimacy which are important or of the mechanisms involved.   Recently there have been some promising attempts to understand the growth of intimacy and of the conditions which foster it.

PSYCHOTHERAPY AND THE FAMILY

Several recent trends in the analysis of personal problems and the practice of psychotherapy have increased the degree to which 'the family', both in the sense of 'the family group' and of 'the individual's family', has been the subject of attention and involvement. There has been an increasing realisation of the importance of 'social background' to individual problems, and a willingness to look at the individual in a social context.   Research results continue to stress the importance of environmental and relationship variables in determining the origin and course of many types of personal illness and personal problems.   'Other people' are seen within various frameworks as a source of stress, disturbing communication, inappropriate reinforcement, unsuitable modelling, etc.   On the other hand, personal relationships have been shown to shield the individual from some problems and to help him to cope with others.

There has also been a trend towards accepting a view that problems are not necessarily always 'owned by' one individual or another but may occur in the relational spaces between people.   Thus a dysfunctional couple may be seen as two independently well-functioning individ als who are mismatched in their values or expectations or who are failing to interact together satisfactorily.   If relationships or systems are seen as dysfunctional in their own right then therapeutic attention may focus on those relationships or interactions rather than on the individuals.   The family psychotherapist clearly focuses on the dysfunctional relationships within the family

while the therapeutic focus for most therapists remains the individual, even if the family is involved as a background against which
that individual's problems are viewed.

Moreover, the notion of an intrinsically dysfunctional relationship is outside the range of the medical model or 'illness' approach
to problems. The 'mis match' model, according to which a problem
may be seen as a lack of fit between elements in a system (or between systems) without any necessary implication of individual dysfunction, is increasingly found in the literature. Illness and
disease concepts are obviously out of place in such cases; nevertheless, the term 'therapy' - with its overtone of pathology, 'cure'
or adjustment to a norm - often remains as a description of the
change process where 'modification' or 'development' might be more
appropriate.

Family involvement in the onset and course of individual dysfunction

An individual's relationships with other people, and especially with
close family members, greatly affect the problems and dysfunctions
which he has, his reaction to these problems, their chronicity and
the response to treatment attempts. Such a position has long been
accepted by many psychotherapists on the basis of their own experience, and a whole variety of explanations have been suggested.
Recent empirical evidence now strongly supports the position that
aspects of the immediate social environment can be of crucial importance in the onset and course of such problems.

It is probably true to say that clinical case-history evidence
has tended to suggest an overall picture of the family as a likely
source of stress, confusion and constraint, and of family life as an
obstacle course which the individual must try to negotiate. This
tendency has led some writers to present a generally negative view
of the family (Cooper, 1971). But if we sample more representa-
tively, then quite a different picture emerges. For example, despite the undoubted fact that in many cases marital problems are the
cause of an individual's depression or anxiety, adults who are married are less likely to suffer from a psychiatric illness than those
who are single, widowed or divorced (Crago, 1972). Those with
family and close friends are also on average more well-adjusted
(Srole, et al., 1962) and happier (Bradburn and Caplovitz, 1965) and
are less likely to commit suicide (Barraclough, Bunch, Nelson and
Sainsbury, 1974).

Evidence comparing the well-being, intellectual and emotional
development and symptom frequency of children raised in traditional
families and in other types of interactional situation suggests that
the family is also a particularly good social environment for the
child (Rutter, 1972; Pringle, 1975). This is not to say that
there can be no satisfactory substitute for the traditional family
group with regard to child-rearing, but only that the suggestion
that the family is on the whole a source of problems and constraints
for the child is not supported.

There are several alternative explanations for these findings.
Those adults who do not get married or who get divorced, and those
children who are not brought up in families, may be initially dif-

ferent from others, so that the evidence may not reflect the benefits of 'family' but prior personality and health differences between the types of people who tend or tend not to have such relationships.   There is, however, prima facie support for the notion
that the most common effect of family life on the number, extent and
effects of an individual's problems is one of prevention or treatment rather than of inception or aggravation.   Clearly, family relationships are not always 'good' for the individual; probably more
life problems arise from within the family than from any other
single source and many suffering adults or children may properly be
seen as victims of their parents or their marital partner or of the
interacting family group or the conflicting pressures of those
people with whom they are closely involved.

We must, however, be aware of any bias towards identifying problems as having a family source while not acknowledging that freedom
from problems may equally be attributable to processes within the
family.   For example, if interaction differences emerge between the
families of, say, delinquents and non-delinquents then this would be
as much in keeping with the hypothesis that families prevent children becoming delinquent as it would with the hypothesis that families cause delinquency.   'Clinical families' may in any case be a-
typical in some respects and there is danger in attempting to assess
the contribution of family factors to any personal problem area on
the basis of evidence gained from such clinical samples.

There are a number of suggestions as to how being part of a
family group or having a set of close relationships may promote an
individual's well-being and it is probable that a large number of
processes contribute to the overall effect.   Family members may
give emotional support and encouragement to the individual, and they
may provide a relatively constant definition of the 'reality' of
situations (Berger and Kellner, 1964).   Practical advice and guidelines for action may be given by intimates who feel they have a
right or a duty to do so, and the effect of this might be to confine
behaviour and attitudes within 'safe' prescribed limits.   In an
accepting interpersonal situation fears and anxieties may be expressed, and there is an opportunity to give affection.   There may
be motivation to function adequately or to remain healthy 'for the
sake of the others', and undertaking tasks as part of a group may
demand less of the individual.   As yet we have little sound evidence as to what human needs are fulfilled by social relationships,
or of the nature of those processes which may contribute to the
apparently beneficial effect of intimate relationships (Weiss,
1974a).

In addition to the possible dysfunction-prevention effect of
intimate relationships, it is likely that many of the same processes
will have a therapeutic effect on such problems as do exist.
Family relationships are likely to have many of the characteristics
that have been shown to constitute the effective counselling relationship (Truax and Carkhuff, 1967; Simonson and Bahr, 1974).   We
will consider this again later, when dealing with family members as
therapists.

The involvement of the family in the dysfunction or potential
dysfunction of the individual is thus ambivalent, creating or preventing problems, imposing or reducing stresses and making greater

or lesser demands on the vulnerable member.   There are a number of
separate ways in which we can consider this impact of the family.
We can examine those critical events related to family life, which
tend to produce emotional stress and illness - events such as the
death of a spouse or the birth of a handicapped child - and longer-
term stressors such as the presence of a chronically ill family
member.   In addition to this we can examine the particular patterns
of interaction within a family, from the point of view of the individual; we may identify particular dysfunctional interaction styles
- ambiguous communications for example, or inconsistent demands.
At a more general level we can assess the overall emotional atmosphere in the home, or the level of emotional involvement with the
individual, and then relate these to the presence of dysfunction or
its course and response to treatment.   Although these three types
of study obviously focus largely on aspects of the same phenomena
they have arisen out of somewhat discrete research traditions.
Each will therefore be considered separately.

1 Critical events   There is a large body of evidence showing that
life events such as a change of environment, the death of someone
close, the birth of a child, divorce, etc. stress the individual and
that this produces a vulnerability to illness of many kinds including heart disease, infections and depression.   There have been several attempts to draw up inventories of those events which are most
likely to stress the individual and such lists invariably include a
sizeable proportion of items concerning family members and family
relationships (Holmes and Rahe, 1967; Dohrenwend, 1974).

   Accounts are available of the effects of particular stresses such
as bereavement (Parkes, 1972; Birtchnell, 1970; Burton, 1974),
divorce and family break-up (Goode, 1965; Gregory, 1965), the birth
of a child (Dyer, 1963) and sudden family illness (Kellner, 1963).
Many of the stresses, however, are not discrete events or changes
and it seems that illness may be precipitated by a long history of
attempting to cope with a difficult life-style.   Thus the stress of
tending to a chronically ill cancer patient (Sheldon, Ryser and
Krant, 1970), to a handicapped child (McMichael, 1971; Burton,
1975) or to an old and infirm person (Townsend, 1957) might take its
toll only after accumulating for many years.   After recovering from
the initial shock of bereavement many widows and widowers fail to
adjust to life without the spouse, and loneliness becomes a chronic
stressor (Weiss, 1974b).   Stress may also result from more subtle
changes in the qualify of a relationship and from sustained patterns
of interpersonal action 'rarely verbalized and perhaps scarcely recognized' (Croog, 1970, p. 21).

   The dysfunctions which have been shown to be related to stress
include depression (Clayton, Halikas and Maurice, 1972; Hudgens,
1974), anxiety (Levi, 1972), psychosomatic disorders (Rees, 1976),
suicide and attempted suicide (Humphrey, 1974; Kiev, 1974) and
child abuse (Smith, Hanson and Noble, 1974; Gil, 1970) as well as
various symptoms and behaviour problems in childhood (Heisel et al.,
1973; Gersten et al., 1974).   There is good evidence, too, that
recent life events affect the course of a schizophrenic illness
(Birley and Brown, 1970).   Studies of psychiatric admission for a
variety of illnesses have revealed that there is a high incidence of
recent family events and crises (Morrice, 1974; Polak, 1967).

There is currently a great deal of theorising about the nature of the connection between stressful life-events and life-patterns and the illness or dysfunction with which they are linked.   That is, there is an attempt to go beyond the correlational evidence and to identify mechanisms leading to the dysfunction.   It seems likely that there is no one pattern that will emerge, but that different explanations will be involved for different types of problem.   Each single life-change affects many different aspects of the situation and alters the total picture.   The birth of a child, for example, will change the constellation of a family and the emotional relationships between the other members;   it will also change the nature of the tasks which must be accomplished, the roles which people fulfill, the financial situation and the future plans of the couple. The total impact which an event has on an individual includes the indirect effects which it brings about by changing various elements of the individual's total 'life situation' including costs and gains, expectations and beliefs, and constraints on action.

2 Patterns of family interaction   Many theories have been put forward which suggest that particular patterns of family interaction produce dysfunction.   The most notable of these have concentrated on the relationship between family processes and schizophrenia. Profoundly influential for family therapy was the concept of the 'double bind' developed by Bateson and his colleagues (Bateson et al., 1956;   Weakland, 1960).   This concept referred to a type of communication which was essentially contradictory and which was used in a social situation which demanded a response.   Thus there might be a contradiction between the verbal content of a message and the intonation or facial message accompanying it.   Typically the content of the double-bind message is concerned with highly emotive material and the relationship between the people involved is an intensely emotional one.   Bateson (1972) comments: 'To Jay Haley is due credit for recognising that the symptoms of schizophrenia are suggestive of an ability to discriminate the Logical Types', and this was simplified by Bateson, who added that the symptoms and etiology could be formally described in terms of a double-bind hypothesis.   Elements of this theory were adapted and incorporated into work by Haley (1964) and Laing (1961;   1965;   see critical appraisal by Siegler, Osmond and Mann, 1969) among others.   A critique of the double-bind concept has been provided recently by Olson (1972).   A whole technical approach to family therapy has been developed from these ideas, as Cade illustrates in Chapter 4.

Second, Wynne and his co-workers (Wynne et al., 1958) suggested that in families of schizophrenics there is typically a rigid adherence to stereotyped ideas about how a family should function and any actual deviation from such a pattern is reinterpreted or simply denied.   In families in which such 'pseudo-mutuality' prevails, it is argued, the free personal growth of the individual is sacrificed for the sake of maintaining appearances, and particular individuals are, by virtue of their position within the family dynamics, more vulnerable.   This notion of the inhibition of growth-enhancing spontaneity is found in the work of other authors, too (e.g. Jackson, 1957).

In a third theoretical formulation Lidz and others (Lidz et al.,

1957) suggested that there were two typical patterns of marital interaction in the families of schizophrenics.   In the first of
these, 'marital schism', there is overt conflict between the parents
including a good deal of fighting in which the child's loyalty is
contested.   In the second, 'marital skew', a disturbed parent-be-
comes dominant and the other accepts pathological child-rearing
patterns.

A large number of other ideas have been put forward and elaborated to explain how disturbed family interaction might produce schizophrenia, psychosomatic illness, and problems such as truancy and
delinquency.   It would be quite impossible even briefly to describe
these in the space available here.   It is probably true, however,
that the aetiology of schizophrenia has been the area which has produced the most influential theories and which has generated the most
empirical research.   For these reasons we will tend to concentrate
on the work of schizophrenia in this summary.

Arguments continue about the relative importance of non-quantita-
tive, naturalistic, clinical studies versus experimental quantified
research.   However, the theories mentioned here are essentially
testable and there has been a good deal of direct observation research comparing the interaction in 'disturbed' and 'normal' families.   A selection of such studies is presented in the collection
by Winter and Ferreira (1969).   These have involved the measurement
of such aspects of the outcome and process of interaction as 'disagreement', 'interruption', 'dominance', 'conflict', 'coalition',
'intensity of affect' and 'communication clarity' in a wide variety
of families.   The interaction is usually structured around specific
tasks which demand co-operation or decision-making, or which in some
way stimulate family communication.

The methodical difficulties in such studies are formidable, as
Gale points out in a later chapter, and there are so many variations
in the types of families used and in the procedures employed that
comparisons between studies are difficult to make.   Fortunately
there is good review literature in this area (Fontana, 1966;   Riskin
and Faunce 1972;   Jacob, 1975;   Hirsch and Leff, 1975).   These reviews indicate the serious shortcomings of many of the studies and
point out that few findings have been successfully replicated.

It now seems unlikely that there is a particular communicational
style which reliably characterises general communication within
families with a dysfunctional member and which can be identified
easily in interaction in the types of laboratory tasks so far
studied.   Such tasks typically generate only low emotional involvement and one alternative approach is suggested by the work of Rausch
et al. (1974) in which marital interaction patterns in simulated
high-conflict situations were examined.   Even if general 'style of
communication' turns out to be relatively unimportant in the generation of symptoms, the content of communication is likely to remain a
major focus of interest in the explanation of how problems arise.
Coercion, inappropriate reinforcement and imitation may all produce
dysfunctional behaviour or a dysfunctional attitude or relationship.
An analysis of the development of coercive control in married
couples, in exchange terms, has been put forward by Weiss, Hops and
Patterson (1973) and there are several accounts of how reinforcement
and imitation can produce symptoms (Ehrenwald, 1963;   Marks, 1969;

Patterson, 1973).   The interactions which produce the symptom may
be concerned with limited aspects of the relationship and may not be
typical of the whole relationship.   Areas of interaction which have
been shown to be involved in the origin of problems include sexual
behaviour (Masters and Johnson, 1970) and the management of a
child's eating and aggressive behaviours (Amdur et al., 1969; Patterson and Cobb, 1971).   Behavioural techniques of family intervention typically isolate specific areas for therapeutic attention
and are concerned with interaction in limited well-defined situations.

3 Emotional atmosphere   Instead of examining the impact of family
'events' or looking at the style or content of specific 'communications' or behaviours between family members, some researchers have
chosen to use broader variables which summarise the 'climate' or
'atmosphere' within a family.   We would expect a close relationship
between such a 'climate' and particular marital or parental interactions, but the former type of measure might be expected to represent more accurately the overall interactions and relationships
within the home.   There is a well-established research tradition in
which home climate is measured and then examined in relation to the
personality characteristics of the children in the family.   'Emotional atmosphere' can be measured along many dimensions, and when
correlations between several such measures have been subjected to
the mathematical reduction technique of factor analysis, they have
yielded, fairly uniformly across studies, two distinct factors of
'love vs. hostility' and 'autonomy vs. control' (Johnson and Medinnus, 1974;   Renson, Schaefer and Levy, 1968).
    Studies resulting from such analyses have indicated that there is
a strong relationship between aspects of family 'climate' and the
likelihood of childhood problems, such as refusal to eat, aggressiveness, and withdrawal (Symonds, 1939).   Such correlational data
is open to a variety of interpretations, and there has been an
interest in establishing the nature of such links in terms of less
'distant' variables (Hoffman and Lippitt, 1960).   There has also
been concern to understand the antecedents of particular parental
interaction styles;   maternal hostility, for example, has been shown
to be related to environmental stresses and frustrations, to a poor
marital relationship and to emotional maladjustment (Schaefer and
Bayley, 1973).   These same correlates have been found recently for
parents who physically abuse their children (Smith, Hanson and
Noble, 1974).
    Family conflict is related to individual dysfunction.   Marital
disorder and disharmony have been shown to be related to antisocial
behaviour and other childhood problems (Rutter, 1971) and are also
related to depression and attempted suicide (Hinchcliffe et al.,
1975;   Greer, Gunn and Koller, 1966) in adults.
    There has recently been a series of studies which suggest that
the emotional climate of the home is related to the likelihood of
relapse in psychiatric illness.   Brown, Birley and Wing (1972)
found that the level of emotion expressed by a key relative about a
schizophrenic patient at the time of admission was the best single
predictor of symptomatic relapse in the nine-month period after
discharge from hospital.   The research instrument used to obtain

the index of expressed emotion in this study was adapted by Vaughn
and Leff (1976a) and they were able to replicate the findings of the
previous study not only for schizophrenic patients but also for
those with a depressive neurosis (Vaughn and Leff, 1976b).   These
authors suggest that it might be possible to modify the emotional
involvement, hostility and critical behaviour of relatives.   The
influence of family factors on the course of psychiatric illness has
been clearly shown in these studies.   So far, however, the factors
involved have been only broadly indicated, and a more detailed examination of the family interaction processes involved is now needed.
The quality of the patient's marital relationship is also related to
prognosis for a wide variety of psychiatric illnesses including nue-
roses (Sims, 1975) and alcoholism (Orford et al., 1976).

4   The recognition and labelling of a problem   Dysfunctions often
arise insidiously, and the process of recognition, labelling and
'theorising' about the nature of the problem, its origin and likely
outcome will often involve discussions within the family (Ackerman,
1958;   Clausen and Yarrow, 1955).   There are often many ambiguities
concerning symptoms, and different family members may have different
perceptions of the problem and different motives and interests, so
that the process of coming to consensus may involve considerable
negotiation and bargaining.   Scheff (1968) has illustrated such a
phenomenon of bargaining over symptoms in psychotherapeutic interaction.   Likely to be of particular importance in family negotiation are those cases in which the 'ownership' of the symptom is in
doubt or where there is an issue of responsibility or blameworthi-
ness.   Thus in the case of a sexual failure each partner may blame
the other or claim that the other 'has the problem' or 'is abnormal'.   There is also evidence that couples may blame general relationship difficulties inappropriately on sexual dysfunction.   The
general need to 'account for' problems in a personally non-threaten-
ing way often leads to the attribution of blame or responsibility to
a convenient other person or to an aspect of person functioning
beyond one's own control.   An account of the use of 'stigmata' in
this way is given by Goffman (1964).   The phenomenon of 'scapegoat-
ing' within the family has been well described (Vogel and Bell,
1968) and Farber (1959) has provided evidence showing that couples
with a handicapped child may blame the child unjustifiably for their
own marital problems.   Such blame and attribution, however, is by
no means always the result of distorted perceptions.   An abnormal
child may well produce severe marital disharmony (Gath, 1977).
   In discussing a problem, the family or the couple generally construct a consensus theory about its nature and likely cause and outcome.   In some cases the deliberations within the family may parallel those between psychotherapists subscribing to different models.
Thus a couple may come to a mutual characterisation of a drinking
problem as an 'illness' rather than as a transgression or 'sin' and
this may remove 'blaming' and lead the individual to accept an illness role with its various costs and benefits.
   Thus, in addition to any process by which family interaction
shapes problematic behaviour itself, there is this interactional
process of negotiating the 'reality' of actions and symptoms.
This may be seen as a particular aspect of the mutual 'construction

of reality' which takes place between intimates (Berger and Kellner, 1964).   An additional influential view of the reality of a situation may come from a specialist or 'expert'.   Sometimes a mutually acceptable solution for family members may be challenged by such an outsider, who might then have the effect of bringing about a change of view or who might be ignored or devalued because of the strong consensus of the others.   Where there is disagreement within a family, or between a couple, then the therapist must often, in effect, enter into a coalition with one of the disagreeing factions (Clausen and Yarrow, 1955).   The family psychotherapist in particular is thus commonly placed in the position of judge or 'voice of reason' and asked to arbitrate over conflicting accounts of the reality or reasonableness of a position.

5 Treatment motivation and treatment outcome   The individual's symptomatology is typically a burden both to the client himself and to the rest of the family, and successful therapy will, in theory, therefore be universally welcomed.   Often, however, the identified client will find that the dysfunction brings reward - relief from work, attention and positive regard from others, distraction from other concerns, and so on - and in conditions of such symptom maintaining 'secondary gain', successful therapy may be especially difficult.   The individual's problem may also function positively for others, perhaps by shifting the balance of power, by providing an excuse for limited social functioning, or by giving someone the opportunity to play the role of 'selfless nurse'.

In addition it will be realised that in many cases presented for 'marital therapy' or counselling one of the partners may have no desire for the relationship to continue.   The consent of such a person to attend for guidance may be a deliberate strategy to indicate both his own 'reasonableness' and also the 'hopelessness' of the situation.   Such a person has a strong vested interest in the 'therapy' failing and being clearly seen to fail.   Indeed, his reason for attending is that it should fail.

Thus the interests of family members with respect to the seeking of effective treatment may be in accord or they may differ.   Such motivations may also critically affect the outcome of any treatment implemented.   Physical or chemical treatments will depend for their effectiveness on such factors as regular attendance, completion of treatment course, regularity in taking medication and adherence to dietary or exercise programmes, and all of these may be affected by the behaviour and attitudes of other members of the family.   Thus, in assessing the importance of family factors as a source of variation in the effectiveness of symptom relief or functional re-adjustment, it is essential to include a consideration of how such factors affect the recognition and formulation of the problem, the seeking of treatment and the reaction to treatment methods.   The decision about whether or not an individual's treatment is proving effective, and whether it is worth continuing, will often be taken by family members other than the client.   The problem shifts to a far greater order of complexity in family psychotherapy, where the family group as a whole is directly involved in treatment.   As with aetiology, treatment motivation and treatment outcome become entangled in the systems properties of the family group so that, paradoxically, when the identified client's symptoms begin responding to treatment successfully, other family members may begin to present with problems.

When the interests of different members of a family group are discordant then the therapist may be faced with a moral problem. An example will illustrate this.   A family may successfully readjust after the crisis of the birth of a severely handicapped child by institutionalising him and maintaining an emotional distance (Kershner, 1970).   Any treatment programme aimed at increasing the social responsiveness of such a child and which encourages regular interaction between family members and the child would then seem likely to disrupt the emotional well-being of the others.   Thus, the overall impact of the treatment cannot always be gauged on the basis of a change in the symptom focused upon or of changes only in the identified client.   Likewise, the therapist may have to come to terms with the notion of 'sacrifice' when the interests of one family member (for example an old person) are diametrically opposed to those of one or more of the other family members who 'need' her removal into an institution in order to function a-symptomatically.

The emergence of a problem or illness in an individual is likely to cause family disruption and to bring about some readjustment and reorganisation;   theoretical accounts of the adjustment of families to crisis have been provided by several authors (Koos, 1946;   Hill, 1949;   Parsons and Fox, 1952).   This readjustment may be so successful that there is then reaction when the removal of the original problem comes about.   Thus families of men who enter prison, or of an individual with a serious physical or mental illness, may find it difficult to cope with the eventual release from custody or successful treatment (Visotsky et al., 1961).

We are now in a better position to consider the main therapeutic approaches which can be taken both to the individual as a member of a family and to the family group as a whole.   In doing so, we can distinguish more clearly between what Wertheim (1973b) has called 'family member therapy' on the one hand and which includes the idea of using family members as therapists, as well as enlisting members of the individual's family in the treatment process and, on the other hand, 'family unit therapy' whereby the family group as a system is the focus of treatment.

Family members as therapists - the intra-personal level

Increasingly, therapists are involving members of a client's family as auxiliaries in treatment programmes, or are teaching family members, sometimes with the aid of classes or books, how to carry out their own treatment programmes.   Several factors lie behind this development.   Therapy is no longer seen as the sole prerogative of highly trained professionals, and there is no longer the assumption that the therapist will have a medical background.   The increased awareness of the importance of home and family factors in the creation and maintenance of personal problems has naturally led to the feeling that a treatment technique which directly confronts these effects is likely to prove more successful than one which is concentrated solely on interaction with the therapist.   Home-based programmes have high 'therapeutic density' - the ratio of treatment time to non-treatment time is high - and yet they are especially economical in terms of professional manpower.   And the implementation of such programmes has been made the more feasible by the development of several types of simply learned and managed effective treatment techniques.

The approach within which family member involvement in treatment has been most predominant is the behavioural.   Teachers and nurses have also been involved as therapists within this framework and recently the approach has come to include a variety of techniques in which the individual acts as his own therapist.   Family-based modification techniques have mostly involved parents as change agents for their children's behaviour (a review is given by Johnson and Katz, 1973) though modification by a marital partner has also been reported (Goldstein and Francis, 1969).   There are also several behavioural 'mutual contract' or 'family adjustment' treatments which will be considered later;   in this section we are concerned with those treatments where distinction is made between a family member or members as 'therapist' and another or others as 'client'.

A wide variety of specific behaviours have been modified in such programmes, including antisocial behaviour, phobias, speech dysfunction, seizures, self-injurious behaviour and oppositional behaviour in children, and lack of affectionate communication, money management problems and sexual dysfunction in marital partners.   Techniques used within the framework include operant control, modelling and behavioural contracts, as well as a number of specific physical sexual techniques.   One of the strengths of the approach is that the observation and measurement of change is generally easy.   There is a dense research literature and good evidence that such programmes may be highly effective in changing target behaviours.   It seems likely, however, that the total impact of the implementation of such programmes within a family will not be limited to the effect on the particular 'problem' behaviour under observation, so that ideally other factors likely to show beneficial or harmful side-effects should also be monitored.   The possible effects of such treatments on other aspects of the relationship between family members cannot be ignored simply because they are not easily scored.

Marital partners and parents have also been trained in the use of Rogerian counselling techniques (Ely, 1970;   Guerney, 1964;   Stover and Guerney, 1967).   In a good relationship between family members we might expect to find naturally high levels of those characteristics which have been shown to be related to effective counselling (Truax and Carkhuff, 1967).   There is good evidence that family members do often in an informal way act therapeutically towards one another (Blood and Wolfe, 1960;   Gurin, Veroff and Feld, 1960;   Komarovsky, 1962;   Nye, 1976), that they feel a duty to support others in this way and that both the helper and the helped believe that such interaction is therapeutically effective (Nye, 1976).   There has, however, been no systematic study of such intra-familial 'therapy' and little is known about the relative importance of various 'therapeutic elements' in such family interaction.   These may include the provision of models, help with problem solving, interpretation of difficulties, emotional support and the provision of a suitable interpersonal context for the expression of anxieties, anger and other feelings.   The help which family members give each

other is often related to areas of especial delicacy and intimacy
and will involve the keeping of confidences.   For these reasons it
seems likely that we generally underestimate the degree to which
natural therapy is taking place in other people's families, and in
our own.

The interpersonal level

As the whole family therapy movement has been instrumental in pointing out, many problems lie not 'within' any individual or individuals but in the relational spaces 'in between' people, and arise out
of a dysfunctional mismatch of behaviours, expectations or attitudes.   Thus one marital partner's need to receive affection may
not be satisfied by the degree to which the other expresses emotion.
Neither the level of need nor the degree of expression have to be in
themselves extreme for the difference to be a source of dysfunction
for the relationship.   Solutions to such problems may be found
either by focusing on a change in one or other of the individuals or
by working jointly with a couple to adjust or change aspects of
their mutual interaction.   Therapy for relationships has extended
the range of techniques in several areas and represents a major step
away from the traditional individual 'illness' conception of many
problems.   This has been an especially important development in the
area of sexual dysfunction.   (See Crowe, Chapter 7.)
     Interpersonal problems occur most frequently in the intense rela-
tionships between marital partners and between parents and their
children, and most therapies have concentrated on difficulties
within these.   Attempts at modifying the parent-child relationship
have generally concentrated on the 'parenting' function and have
perhaps been predominantly oriented towards the expressed wishes of
the parents.   Marital programmes have been more mutual affairs.
The numerous techniques which have been developed relate to many
different theoretical positions, though typically they have not been
'derived' from theory (Olson, 1970).   A review of outcome research
on marital therapy by Gurman (1973) suggested that across a heterogeneous collection of clients, therapists and treatment modalities
there was at least a 'moderately positive therapeutic effect'.
     Marital discord has recently become a major focus in the field of
behaviour therapy (Jacobson and Martin, 1976).   Such disturbance
has been analysed in terms of the mutual exchange of rewards and
costs and the reciprocation of aversive control strategies (Weiss,
Birchler and Vincent, 1974; Patterson and Hops, 1972), and there
has also been emphasis on the inconsistency and ambiguity or over-
selectivity of communication in discord situations (Stuart, 1975;
Friedman, 1972).   Therapeutic techniques developed within the
framework include teaching problem-solving strategies, and modelling, contracting and token economy methods.
     Behavioural approaches to sexual dysfunction in couples have been
very successful (Masters and Johnson, 1970; Lobitz and LoPiccolo,
1972).   Many such programmes involve co-therapists working with the
couple and giving them detailed instructions on specific techniques
designed to facilitate mutually satisfying sexual interaction.
Fantasy and role-playing are often involved along with physical contact procedures.

The systems approach and psychotherapy

The theory of 'general systems' has been most powerful in assisting
the theorist and therapist in making the step from the intra- to the
interpersonal, and we need therefore to consider its implications.
A system of linked relationships can be dysfunctional with or without any intrinsic problem within the individuals or within the
dyadic relationships of that system.

'Systems science' has had a rapid growth and has been applied to
a wide range of topics (von Bertanlanffy, 1968) including many
within the social sciences (Buckley, 1968; Kuhn, 1975).   There has
been considerable use of systems concepts in aspects of family analysis (Hill, 1971; Straus, 1973) and in particular in family psychotherapy (Jackson, 1970; Speer, 1970).   While systems theory includes highly specific mathematical formulations and enables us to
make specific predictions about empirical matters it also represents
a general framework of approach, so that familiar areas can be reviewed by a 'perceptual shift' to the systems perspective.   Systems
analysis is thus both a body of knowledge and a particular way of
organising knowledge (Kuhn, 1975).

A system is 'a set of elements standing in inter-relation among
themselves and with the environment' (von Bertanlanffy, 1968).
Some systems are essentially static organisations or 'patterns'.   A
genealogical 'family tree', a description of a modal kinship system,
or a role-structure analysis of a family illustrate this type of
system.   In contrast, in 'acting systems' there is dynamic interaction between elements.   A real family group analysed in terms of
communications or emotional interchanges is an example of an acting
system, and this is most commonly what is being referred to when the
term 'family system' is used in the context of psychotherapy.

Analysis of a system involves the consideration of interrelations
and interactions within the system boundary and between the system
and the environment.   The 'boundary' might conform to some physical
or functional characteristic but is essentially analytic.   The
analyst chooses the boundary to demarcate the system which he wants
to study.   Separate systems may interact and form part of a supra-
system.   On the other hand, elements of one system can be re-
analysed individually as complete systems.

There is, then, a hierarchy of systems and, with alternative approaches and descriptions, there are many different analyses possible at any one level of a particular hierarchy.   The relevant
hierarchy for psychotherapy would include specific systems within
the individual ('the ego', 'the autonomic nervous system' etc.), the
individual as a whole unit, the family group, and 'society' or 'the
culture'.   The same physical event, for example, may be formulated
in terms of different levels of this hierarchy, as well as in different ways at any one level.   One important aspect of the impact
of systems thinking on psychotherapy is this increased awareness of
the possibility of valid alternative formulations.   The selection
of one level of analysis rather than another is partly arbitrary,
though there are also some external criteria determining the relative appropriateness of rival descriptions.

Such reformulation is exemplified by cases in which 'individual

problems' such as aggressiveness, truancy or bedwetting are redes-
cribed in 'family system' terms.   In psychotherapy the 'family
group' has been the most common focus of interest for systems thinking.   However, systems vary in their characteristics and family
theorists who use the approach differ amongst themselves in several
important respects in how they see, or choose to analyse, the family
as a system.   A confusion between the analysis of the 'modal'
family and that of real family groups is apparent in many discussions in the literature.   For example, Hill (1971) speaks of a
family which lacks an occupant of a particular modal role position -
say, the fatherless family - as 'deficient in family structure'.
This involves reference to and comparison with an external averaged
pattern, while the idea of a deficiency in a real natural system
would seem to carry an assumption of a characteristic affecting the
working of the system, either internally or in interaction with
other systems.   A particular fatherless family may be in no way
deficient as an active system.

All natural systems are to some extent 'open' - they interact
with an environment.   The openness of systems differs considerably,
however, and some can more appropriately be treated analytically as
if they were closed.   Some family theorists choose to view the
family principally as a closed system and suggest that 'events
occurring within the family are likely to be better explained by
antecedent influences originating within the family than from external events' (Hill, 1971, p. 18).   On the other hand, most would see
interactions with the environment ('society', 'institutions', 'other
families' etc.), as well as externally imposed constraints, as vitally affecting the interaction within the system, and would thus
stress the open system nature of the family.

Undoubtedly families differ considerably in the degree to which
their actions are likely to be affected by environmental constraints
or input, and a particular family group might usefully be considered
open with regard to some areas of function and closed with regard to
others.   Looked at as an empirical rather than analytic issue the
openness of natural family groups will vary considerably, and to
best represent this system feature we need to think in terms of a
range of values on an open-closed continuum rather than of a single
modal value.

A similar argument holds for other areas of dispute about the
systems nature of 'the family'.   Is the family best conceptualised
as an undifferentiated system with any change in one element or relationship necessarily changing all the others, or should we think
in terms of relatively isolated subsystems within?   Another controversy concerns mechanisms of stability-maintenance and adapta-
tion, and this is of particular concern to those involved in family
psychotherapy.   Original systems formulations stressed the process
of homeostasis, by which functional and emotional levels are regulated to compensate for changes and to maintain stability.   Dysfunctions are seen by some to result from a failure of normal stab-
ilising processes and therapy is aimed at restoring homeostatic
function.   An alternative view is that homeostatic processes more
often produce dysfunction, and that therapy should aim at making the
family more easily able to change and adapt (Sonne, 1967; Speer,
1970).   Families in fact demonstrate both sorts of mechanism al-

though some may be categorised as either predominantly homeostatic
or adaptive (Wertheim, 1973a), and it seems that both processes may
be either functional or dysfunctional depending on the particular
circumstances.

It may, then, be inappropriate to try to specify too narrowly the
systems properties of 'the family', because families are likely to
differ widely in such characteristics.   There may be little that we
can assume about the dynamics of interactions within a particular
family without a knowledge of its individual system properties.
The degree of variation between families in systems terms is a
matter about which we have as yet little relevant empirical information.   Clinical evidence has pin-pointed certain patterns of common
systems dysfunction, and this now needs to be seen in the context of
a comprehensive picture of family systems and family system 'mechanisms'.

The relationship of problem formulation, aetiology and treatment

It seems often to be assumed that the formulation of a problem, the
theory of its origin or aetiology, and the nature of effective
treatment must all be closely interlinked.   For example, we might
formulate a case of truancy in terms of a 'family problem', then
suggest a way in which that symptom arose as a function of the
system action, and then finally arrive at a prescription for treatment involving conjoint therapy to bring about a change in those
problematic interaction patterns.   But in fact these three aspects
of a problem are not necessarily linked and the choice of treatment
need not depend on any particular theory about aetiology.   We can
reformulate the 'same' problem in a variety of ways;   we can, for
instance, look at an individual's physical handicap in terms of its
impact on the family group.   The reformulation of a problem in this
way does not of course imply that the handicap itself is a product
of group processes, or that a group approach to dealing with the
'family problem' - the impact of the handicap - will have any effect
on the handicap itself.

If a disease, or a legal problem, or poverty produces a family
crisis then this might be treated either by giving practical aid to
overcome the 'trigger' - we could give financial help, for example -
or else by attempting to modify the way in which the family reacts.
If a problem has arisen as a result of interactional processes it
does not follow that the only way to treat that symptom successfully
is by altering the family dynamics.   Again, problems which exist
solely in the relationship between two people may be effectively
treated not only by a therapy which focuses on the relationship
itself but also by one which changes one or other of the parties to
make the couple compatible.

So the optimal treatment for a problem cannot be necessarily
derived from a knowledge of what caused the problem.   Some processes are not reversible, and there are often many different paths to
the same goal.   Restructuring interactions within a family system
may not be the only or the best way to deal with a problem originating in particular interaction sequences of the family group.   On
the other hand, family intervention may have a range of effectiveness beyond those problems with a specific family system aetiology.

Effectiveness of techniques

The relative effectiveness of alternative methods of psychotherapy
has been the subject of considerable controversy (Eysenck, 1960;
Bergin, 1971; Gurman, 1973) and there are numerous methodological
difficulties in assessment.   One such problem is that of the criterion for therapeutic success.   Commonly, symptomatic improvement
of the identified client has been the criterion of choice, although
alternative and more complex formulae have also been developed
(Bergin, 1971).   Many therapists choose to reformulate a presenting
problem and may take the symptom as evidence of a more fundamental
dysfunction.   This presents a difficulty in assessing the effectiveness of therapy, for the criterion of 'mere' symptom improvement
is thus not seen by them as adequate to test the effectiveness of
their procedures.   In the report of the Group for the Advancement of Psychiatry (GAP, 1970), for example, it was shown that
adequacy of individual performance and symptomatic improvement were
of relatively little interest to family therapists and that they
concentrated on the improvement of communications and on empathy
and autonomy within the family group.

The debate over the most appropriate criterion is largely a product of different theoretical formulations of the nature of symptoms.   However, ease of measurement is a contributing factor to
the satisfactoriness of a criterion, and those who have taken the
position that effectiveness should be measured by symptom relief
have been able to point to the ease and reliability with which symptoms, especially behavioural ones, can be assessed.   It is perhaps
unfortunate that such a methodological consideration can have so
much influence on what is basically a theoretical issue.   However,
there is currently much interest in adopting procedures which will
enable family therapists to evaluate treatment outcome reliably in
terms of those variables which they believe to be important (Cromwell, Olson and Fournier, 1976; Phillips, 1973).   It will be interesting then to use these same measures to identify any changes in
'autonomy', 'empathy', and other areas of family functioning which
may result from family-based behavioural treatments.   Assessment of
the total impact of a therapeutic procedure must involve a large
number of variables; if we measure the change in just one variable
we are not then justified in believing that this change is the only
one that has occurred.

A knowledge of the relative 'average effectiveness' of a range of
therapies does not end the consideration of which one is most appropriate for a particular case.   Certain sizes, constellations or
types of family group may respond better to a particular technique,
for example, or there may be emotional features of a family which
contra-indicate the use of a certain approach.   The decision about
the optimal therapeutic approach depends also on the likely costs
and dangers of the procedures.   There is evidence that psychotherapy sometimes produces undesirable effects (Bergin, 1971; Gurman,
1973) and with some family intervention techniques there may be
over-optimism that a family is going to react adaptively rather than
maladaptively to the changes which the therapist promotes.   The
dangers of a possible deterioration after therapy are especially
evident in the case of those techniques in which stress or crisis is
deliberately increased.

The difficulties of establishing the effectiveness and dangers of family therapy techniques are formidable indeed, and tight studies with control over all relevant variables are impossible.   Samples of family groups with similar problems, constellations and system characteristics are not available and the matching of families is not likely to be achievable to any satisfactory degree.   These facts, however, do not merit the dismissal of the family therapeutic approach.   In the absence of scientifically sound evidence we are justified in working with techniques which merely 'seem' to work or 'might perhaps' work, hoping to develop both the techniques themselves and the means of testing their efficacy.

The 'plausibility' of family intervention techniques is fairly easy to establish.   There is good evidence, already quoted, of the crucial involvement of family interactions in (at least) the course of individual psychiatric illness, and many other personal problems are self-evidently a reflection of patterns of interaction within the family - marital violence being an obvious example.   From what we know about the effects of communication and feedback information on the performance and interaction of groups, it seems highly likely that a suitably 'influential' external agent might bring about a change in interaction patterns.   Given that the external agent, or therapist, has some accuracy in perceiving dysfunctional patterns, and some skill in bringing about adaptive changes, then the plausibility of family psychotherapy is established.   The case-history evidence of the effectiveness of specific techniques, together with some limited objective evidence (Wells, Dilkes and Trivelli, 1972; Gurman, 1973) further suggests that some effective intervention in such natural systems is not merely plausible but realisable. Logically, the development of a technique must precede its validation;   to demand proof of effectiveness prematurely will halt the development of any approach which builds on composite experience. Family therapy has already given rise to several interesting and useful techniques and is likely to lead to further major innovations.

The alternative to a purely technique-based development of therapy is to derive methods from theory.   In the field of family therapy, as in many other areas of psychotherapy, technique has tended to precede theory (Olson, 1970) and several very different theoretical positions may be used by different therapists to provide a rationale for a single technique.   However, even for those therapies in which rigid derivation from theory is claimed, as in behaviour therapy, the links may prove to be somewhat tenuous and the development of technique often outpaces the development of theory (London, 1972).   Caution must be exercised in drawing any conclusions about theory from the therapeutic success or failure of a 'theory-based' technique.   High effectiveness of a method does not prove the validity of any underlying theory, and the 'non-specified variables' in an intervention (including here contact with an agency, increased family 'self-consciousness' and so forth) may be sufficient to account for changes in family interaction which occur during the therapy programme.

It is easy to formulate a variety of problems in family system terms and to then consider whether a system intervention approach might be therapeutically effective.   There is, however, a danger of

being underselective and of trying to apply such techniques where
other methods would in fàct be more appropriate.   The 'average
effectiveness' of a technique is reduced when it is applied unsel-
ectively, as if it were a panacea.   There is a need to maximise .
the extent to which the choice of treatment reflects the nature of
the problem itself and the likely effectiveness of the methods
available, and to minimise the extent to which it depends on the
training and current orientation of the therapist.

THE FUTURE OF INTIMATE RELATIONSHIPS

The nature and composition of family groups is changing.   Demographic evidence shows how family size has decreased, how marital
stability has declined and how families have become less involved in
extended family networks.   Kinship structures are now less important than they once were (Farber, 1964), the value given to the
parenting function has declined (Bronfenbrenner, 1970) and the role
of women in society has undergone remarkable changes.   In addition
to these general developments, however, there is an increasing diversification of common family forms.   The composition, longevity
and interactional character of intimate groups covers a widening
range.   Technological, legal, social and attitudinal changes have
helped to create a situation in which there is more fluidity of
life-style, and in which more personal choice can be exercised.
There are more single-parent families, more divorces and more voluntarily childless couples.   More unmarried people are cohabiting,
attitudes towards homosexual relationships have become less res-
trictive and there is more experimentation with styles of communal
living.   The diffusion of such variants is bound to have an effect
on their acceptability and of their perceived viability for people
making choices about their own lives.   According to some theorists
such a positive feedback effect between the amount of variation and
the tolerance for variation is likely to lead to a sharply acceler-
ating diversity (Ramey, 1976) and most writers on the theme of
changing family patterns would agree that we have by no means already reached the end-point of this pluralism (Bernard, 1972;
Toffler, 1970).
    One of the effects of such diversification is to make the 'modal'
family less and less representative of real family groups;   fewer
actual groups conform to our single image of 'the family' as represented in general accounts of family structure and interaction.   As
the variation of forms increases it becomes essential to specify the
nature of a particular relationship or system of relationships, for
there is less chance that a particular relationship will conform to
the mode in any respect.   When some people refer to 'the breakdown
of the modern family' they mean simply the decreased regularity of
form.   Such a change, however, should not be equated with the
breakdown of individual family groups.   The societal change - increased diversity - may not represent any change in the average
functional viability of the individual units.   'Different' or 'diverse' are not simply interchangeable with 'dysfunctional'.
    Increased variation also suggests that the overlap between poten-
tial definitional elements - kinship, common residence, legal ties,

affectional closeness, etc. - will become less.   Some nuclear
groups will be founded on kinship, but others will not;   some will
inhabit a common residence and others will not.   It cannot be
assumed that the membership of a particular interacting group is
likely to be equally defined by different elements, and it therefore
becomes increasingly important to specify the meaning of such terms
as 'family group' and 'intimate relationship'.   The present ambiguity will be increasingly difficult to manage with the diversification of the phenomena to which the terms relate.

It is likely that with these widespread changes, the expectations
which individuals have of their relationships will also change and
diversify.   In many cases the life-style would be so different from
that experienced in childhood that the interactional patterns of the
family of origin would not provide any useful reference for current
patterns, so that familiarity with relevant norms would come indirectly through conversation with others living similarly, or
through the media.   With a decline of consensus about the 'ideal
family' a powerful source of reference and prescription will become
weaker.

The forecast changes in intimate life-style have been variously
seen as holding great promise for individual development and the release from conventional constraints or as a major source of danger
both to individuals and to the structure of society.   The impact of
such changes is difficult to predict or even to monitor.   We know
very little about how individuals' needs are fulfilled by their relationships with others or about the processes which make intimacy
so important.   The available evidence does clearly show that positively valued stable relationships are of crucial importance for the
well-being and happiness of many people.   The child is nowhere
better placed than in a stable nuclear network (Pringle, 1975) and
a well-functioning marital relationship is a significant factor in
the prevention and recovery process of many types of illness and
dysfunction.   Thus we could predict that the diversification of
life-style and the increasing instability of marital relationships
may lead to a sharp increase in the number and severity of problems
and of their resistance to treatment.

On the other hand it could be argued that since many intimate
relationships are 'poisonous', or at least constraining and stressful, any changes which allow for greater individual choice or for
easy escape might reduce the number of problems.   And since expectations as well as relationships will be changing, there are hazards
involved in any attempt to generalise about the effects of a trend
over time from any previous pattern.   However, it does seem likely
that one way or the other there will be a significant change in the
incidence and type of problems encountered in psychotherapy as the
pattern of relationships changes.

Although it is inconceivable that kinship should cease to be a
major factor in determining the composition of intimate groups and
those with whom the individual has his most significant relationships, the value placed on it might well decline.   Kinship-related
considerations frequently preserve a relationship and a sharp increase of instability and breakdown would probably be experienced if
their influence decreased.   Relationships between close friends,
for example, are generally not as stable as those between close kin.

Friendship is largely affected by current levels of mutual rewards and satisfactions and the intensity of current interaction (Altman and Taylor, 1973; Duck, 1973). Friendship bonds are often broken by an interruption to fairly continuous interaction; they are frequently not 'maintained over distance'. Friendships are also liable to break down after a prolonged period of one-sided dependency and there is generally less of a sense of duty than towards kin. The help and care given to family members by the others in time of need is partly dependent on the norm of duty and the consonant expectations of those concerned. The implications for the social services of any decline in such expectations are of enormous importance. It is possible, though it seems unlikely, that changes in the nature of other kinds of relationship - the neighbour or the friend, for example - would compensate for such a decline.

There are several important ways in which psychotherapy will be affected by changed patterns of relationships. Individuals' family backgrounds and patterns of interaction will be more heterogeneous and more fluid, and the aims of therapy directed at relationships and systems will reflect this. Any 'ideal family' image which now exists will be extended to include a variety of other forms, and there is likely to be an increase in the range of relationships seen as 'workable'. Fewer assumptions will be able to be made about such factors as task- and power-sharing and about the rights and duties which particular people feel towards one another. Psychotherapy with families will include many different kinds of group and will produce both a body of knowledge about each major alternative pattern and general formulations about personal relationships and corresponding natural systems. The viability of radically changing a system will increase. If there is societal 'approval' for many different sorts of system then the goal of therapy will more easily be able to reflect internal constraints and needs rather than being tailored to any modal image, common to family members and the therapist, of how 'families' are or should be.

REFERENCES

ACKERMAN, N.W. (1958), 'The Psychodynamics of Family Life', Basic Books, New York.
ALTMAN, I. and TAYLOR, D.A. (1973), 'Social Penetration: the Development of Interpersonal Relationships', Holt Rinehart & Winston, New York.
AMDUR, M.J., TUCKER, G.J., DETRE, T. and MARKHUS, K. (1969), Anorexia Nervosa: an interactional study, 'Journal of Nervous and Mental Disease', vol. 148, pp. 559-66.
BALL, D.W. (1972), The family as a sociological problem: conceptualisation of the taken-for-granted as prologue to social problems analysis, 'Social Problems', vol. 19, pp. 295-305.
BARRACLOUGH, B., BUNCH, J., NELSON, B. and SAINSBURY, P. (1974), A hundred cases of suicide: clinical aspects, 'British Journal of Psychiatry', vol. 125, pp. 355-73.
BATESON, G., JACKSON, D., HALEY, J. and WEAKLAND, J. (1956), Toward a theory of schizophrenia, 'Behavioural Science', vol. 1, pp. 251-64.

BATESON, G. (1972), 'Steps to an Ecology of Mind', Ballantine Books, New York.

BERGER, P. and KELLNER, H. (1964), Marriage and the construction of reality, 'Diogenes', vol. 46, pp. 1-24.

BERGIN, A.E. (1971), The evaluation of therapeutic outcomes, in A.E. Bergin and S.L. Garfield (eds), 'Handbook of Psychotherapy and Behaviour Change', Wiley, New York.

BERNARD, J. (1972), 'The Future of Marriage', World Publishing, New York; Penguin, Harmondsworth, 1976.

VON BERTALANFFY, L. (1968), 'General System Theory', Penguin, Harmondsworth.

BIRLEY, J.L.T. and BROWN, G.W. (1970), Crisis and life changes preceding the onset and relapse of acute schizophrenia: clinical aspects, 'British Journal of Psychiatry', vol. 116, pp. 327-33.

BIRTCHNELL, J. (1970), Early parental death and mental illness, 'British Journal of Psychiatry', vol. 116, pp. 281-313.

BLOOD, R.W. and WOLFE, D.M. (1960), 'Husbands and Wives: the Dynamics of Married Living', Free Press, Chicago.

BODIN, A.M. (1969), Family interaction: a social-clinical study of synthetic, normal and problem family triads, in Winter and Ferreira (1969).

BRADBURN, N.M. and CAPLOVITZ, D. (1965), 'Reports on Happiness', Aldine, Chicago.

BRODERICK, C.B. (1971), Beyond the five conceptual frameworks: a decade of development in family theory, 'Journal of Marriage and the Family', vol. 33, pp. 139-59.

BRONFENBRENNER, U. (1970), 'Two Worlds of Childhood', Russell Sage, New York.

BROWN, G.W., BIRLEY, J.L.T. and WING, J.K. (1972), Influence of family life on the course of schizophrenic disorders: a replication, 'British Journal of Psychiatry', vol. 121, pp. 241-58.

BUCKLEY, W. (ed.) (1968), 'Modern Systems Research for the Behavioural Scientist. A Sourcebook', Aldine, Chicago.

BURGESS, E.W. (1926), The family as a unity of interacting personalties, 'Family', vol. 7, pp. 3-9.

BURR, W.R. (1973), 'Theory Construction and the Sociology of the Family', Wiley, New York.

BURTON, L. (ed.) (1974), 'Care of the Child Facing Death', Routledge & Kegan Paul, London.

BURTON, L. (1975), 'The Family Life of Sick Children', Routledge & Kegan Paul, London.

CLAUSEN, J.A. and YARROW, M.R. (1955), The impact of mental illness on the family, 'Journal of Social Issues', vol. 11, pp. 3-65.

CLAYTON, P.S., HALIKAS, J.A. and MAURICE, W.L. (1972), The depression of widowhood, 'British Journal of Psychiatry', vol. 120, pp. 71-7.

COOPER, D. (1971), 'The Death of the Family', Penguin, Harmondsworth.

CRAGO, M.A. (1972), Psychopathology in married couples, 'Psychological Bulletin', vol. 77, pp. 114-28.

CROMWELL, R.E., OLSON, D.H. and FOURNIER, D.G. (1976), Tools and techniques for diagnosis and evaluation in marital and family therapy, 'Family Process', vol. 15, pp. 1-49.

CROOG, S.H. (1970), The family as a source of stress, in S. Levine and N.A. Scotch (eds), 'Social Stress', Aldine, Chicago.

DOHRENWEND, B.P. (1974), Problems in defining and sampling the relevant population of stressful life events, in Dohrenwend and Dohrenwend (1974).

DOHRENWEND, B.S. and DOHRENWEND, B.P. (1974), 'Stressful Life Events: Their Nature and Effect', Wiley, New York.

DUCK, S. (1973), 'Personal Relationships and Personal Constructs', Wiley, London.

DYER, E.D. (1963), Parenthood as crisis: a re-study, 'Marriage and Family Living', vol. 25, pp. 196-201.

EHRENWALD, J. (1963), 'Neurosis in the Family and Patterns of Psychosocial Defence: a study of Psychiatric Epidemiology', Hoeber (Harper & Row), London.

ELY, A.L. (1970), Efficacy of training in conjugal therapy, Unpublished PhD thesis, Rutgers University (quoted, Olson, 1970).

EYSENCK, H.J. (1960), The effects of psychotherapy, in H.J. Eysenck (ed.), 'Handbook of Abnormal Psychology', Pitman, London.

FARBER, B. (1959), Effects of a severely mentally retarded child on family integration, 'Monographs of the Society for Research in Child Development', vol. 24, no. 2.

FARBER, B. (1964), 'Family Organization and Interaction', Chandler, San Francisco.

FONTANA, A.F. (1966), Familial etiology of schizophrenia; is a scientific methodology possible?, 'Psychological Bulletin', vol. 66, pp. 214-27.

FRIEDMAN, P.M. (1972), Personalistic family and marital therapy, in A.A. Lazarus (ed.), 'Clinical Behaviour Therapy', Brunner/Mazel, New York.

GATH, A. (1977), The impact of an abnormal child upon the parents, 'British Journal of Psychiatry', vol. 130, pp. 405-10.

GERSTEN, J.C., LANGNER, T.S., EISENBERG, J.G. and ORZECK, L. (1974), Child behaviour and life events, in Dohrenwend and Dohrenwend (1974).

GIL, G.D. (1970), 'Violence Against Children', Harvard University Press.

GOFFMAN, E. (1964), 'Stigma: Notes on the Management of Spoiled Identity', Penguin, Harmondsworth.

GOLDSTEIN, M.K. and FRANCIS, B. (1969), Behaviour modification of husbands by wives, paper presented at the Annual Meeting of the National Council on Family Relations, 1969.

GOODE, W. (1965), 'After Divorce', Free Press, New York.

GREER, S., GUNN, J.C. and KOLLER, K.M. (1966), Aetiological factors in attempted suicide, 'British Medical Journal', vol. 2, pp. 1352-5.

GREGORY, I. (1965), Anterospective data following childhood loss of a parent, 'Archives of General Psychiatry', vol. 13, pp. 110-20.

GROUP FOR THE ADVANCEMENT OF PSYCHIATRY (1970), 'The Field of Family Therapy', New York.

GUERNEY, G.G., Jr (1964), Filial therapy: description and rationale, 'Journal of Consulting Psychology', vol. 28, pp. 304-10.

GURIN, G., VEROFF, J. and FELD, S. (1960), 'Americans View their Mental Health', Basic Books, New York.

GURMAN, A.S. (1973), The effects and effectiveness of marital therapy: a review of outcome research, 'Family Process', vol. 12, pp. 145-70.

HALEY, J. (1964), Research on family patterns: an instruments research, 'Family Process', vol. 3, pp. 41-65.

HANDEL, G. (1965), The psychological study of whole families, 'Psychological Bulletin', vol. 63, pp. 19-41.

HEISEL, J.S., REAM, S., RAITZ, R., RAPPAPORT, M. and CODDINGTON, R.D. (1973), The significance of life events as contributing factors in the diseases of children. III. A study of pediatric patients, 'Journal of Pediatrics', vol. 83, pp. 119-23.

HILL, R. (1949), 'Families under Stress', Harper, New York.

HILL, R. (1971), Modern systems theory and the family: a confrontation, 'Social Science Information', vol. 10, pp. 7-26.

HILL, R. and HANSEN, D.A. (1960), The identification of conceptual frameworks utilized in family study, 'Marriage and Family Living', vol. 22, pp. 299-311.

HINCHLIFFE, M., HOOPER, D., ROBERTS, R.J. and VAUGHAN, P. (1975), A study of the interaction between depressed patients and their spouses, 'British Journal of Psychiatry', vol. 126, pp. 164-72.

HIRSCH, S. and LEFF, J.P. (1975), 'Abnormality in Parents of Schizophrenics: a Review of the Literature and an Investigation of Communication Defects and Deviances', Oxford University Press.

HOFFMAN, L.W. and LIPPITT, R. (1960), The measurement of family life variables, in P.H. Mussen (ed.), 'Handbook of Research Methods in Child Development', Wiley, New York.

HOLMES, T.H. and RAHE, R.H. (1967), The social readjustment rating scale, 'Journal of Psychosomatic Research', vol. 11, pp. 213-18.

HUDGENS, R.W. (1974), Personal catastrophe and depression, in Dohrenwend and Dohrenwend (1974).

HUMPHREY, J.A. (1974), The process of suicide. The sequence of disruptive events in the lives of suicide victims, 'Disorders of the Nervous System', vol. 35, pp. 275-7.

JACKSON, D.D. (1957), The question of family homeostasis, 'Psychiatric Quarterly', supplement 31, pp. 79-90.

JACKSON, D.D. (1970), The study of the family, in N.W. Ackerman (ed.), 'Family Process', Basic Books, New York.

JACOB, T. (1975), Family interaction in disturbed and normal families: a methodological and substantive review, 'Psychological Bulletin', vol. 82, pp. 33-65.

JACOBSON, N.S. and MARTIN, B. (1976), Behavioural marriage therapy: current status, 'Psychological Bulletin', vol. 83, pp. 540-56.

JOHNSON, C.A. and KATZ, R.C. (1973), Using parents as change agents for their children: a review, 'Journal of Child Psychology and Psychiatry and Allied Disciplines', vol. 14, pp. 181-200.

JOHNSON, R.C. and MEDINNUS, G.R. (1974), 'Child Psychology: Behaviour and Development', 3rd edn, Wiley, New York.

KELLNER, R. (1963), 'Family Ill Health', Tavistock, London.

KERSHNER, J.R. (1970), Intellectual and social development in relation to family functioning: a longitudinal comparison of home vs. institutional effects, 'American Journal of Mental Deficiency', vol. 75, pp. 276-84.

KIEV, A. (1974), Prognostic factors in attempted suicide, 'American Journal of Psychiatry', vol. 131, pp. 987-90.

KOMAROVSKY, M. (1962), 'Blue Collar Marriage', Random House, New York.

KOOS, E.L. (1946), 'Families in Trouble', King's Crown Press, New York.

KUHN, A. (1975), 'Unified Social Science: a System-Based Introduction', Dorsey Press, Homewood, Illinois.

LAING, R.D. (1961), 'The Self and Others', Tavistock, London.
LAING, R.D. (1965), Mystification, confusion and conflict, in I.
Boszormenyi-Nagy and J.L. Framo (eds), 'Intensive Family Therapy',
Harper & Row, New York.
LEIK, R. (1963), Instrumentality and emotionality in family inter-
action, 'Sociometry', vol. 26, pp. 131-45.
LEVI, L. (1972), 'Stress and Distress in Response to Psychosocial
Stimuli', Almquist & Wiksell Periodical Company, Stockholm.
LIDZ, T. CORNELISON, A., FLECK, S. and TERRY, D. (1957), The intra-
family environment of schizophrenic patients. II. Marital Schism and
marital skew, 'American Journal of Psychiatry', vol. 114, pp. 241-8.
LOBITZ, W.C. and LOPICCOLO, J. (1972), New Methods in the behaviour-
al treatment of sexual dysfunction, 'Journal of Behaviour Therapy
and Experimental Psychiatry', vol. 3, pp. 265-71.
LONDON, P. (1972), The end of ideology in behaviour modification,
'Americal Psychologist', vol. 27, pp. 913-20.
MCMICHAEL, J.K. (1971), 'Handicap - a Study of Physically Handicap-
ped Children and their Families', Staples Press, London.
MARKS, I. (1969), 'Fears and Phobias', Heinemann, London.
MASTERS, W. and JOHNSON, V. (1970), 'Human Sexual Inadequacy',
Little, Brown, Boston.
MORRICE, J.K.W. (1974), Life crisis, social diagnosis and social
therapy, 'British Journal of Psychiatry', vol. 125, pp. 411-13.
NYE, F.I. (1976), 'Role Structure and Analysis of the Family Sage',
in cooperation with the National Council on Family Relations,
Beverly Hills.
NYE, F.I. and BERARDO, F.M. (1966), 'Emerging Conceptual Frameworks
in Family Analysis', Macmillan, Toronto.
OLSON, D.H. (1970), Marital and family therapy: integrative review
and critique, 'Journal of Marriage and the Family', vol. 32, pp.
501-38.
OLSON, D.H. (1972), Empirically unbinding the double bind: review
of research and conceptual reformulations, 'Family Process', vol.
11, pp. 69-94.
ORFORD, J., OPPENHEIMER, E., EGERT, S., HENSMAN, C. and GUTHRIE, S.
(1976), The cohesiveness of alcoholism - complicated marriages and
its influence on treatment outcome, 'British Journal of Psychiatry',
vol. 128, pp. 318-39.
PARKES, C. MURRAY (1972), 'Bereavement: Studies of Grief in Adult
Life', Tavistock, London.
PARSONS, T. and BALES, R.F. (1955), 'Family Socialization and Interaction Process', Free Press, Chicago.
PARSONS, T. and FOX, R. (1952), Illness, therapy and the modern
urban American family, 'Journal of Social Issues', vol. 8, pp.
31-44.
PATTERSON, F.R. (1973), Reprogramming the families of aggressive
boys, in C. Thoresen (ed.), 'Behaviour Modification in Education',
University of Chicago Press.
PATTERSON, G.R. and COBB, J.A. (1971), A dyadic analysis of 'aggres-
sive behaviours', in J.P. Hill (ed.), 'Minnesota Symposia on Child
Psychology', vol. 5, University of Minnesota Press.
PATTERSON, G.R. and HOPS, W. (1972), Coercion, a game for two: in-
tervention techniques for marital conflict, in R.E. Ulrich and P.
Mountjoy (eds), 'The Experimental Analysis of Social Behaviour',
Appleton, New York.

PHILLIPS, C.E. (1973), Some useful tests in marriage counselling, 'Family Coordinator', vol. 22, pp. 43-53.

POLAK, P.R. (1967), The crisis of admission, 'Social Psychiatry', vol. 2, pp. 150-7.

PRINGLE, M.L. KELLMER (1975), 'The Needs of Children', Hutchinson, London.

RAMEY, J. (1976), 'Intimate Friendships', Spectrum (Prentice-Hall), New Jersey.

RAUSCH, H.L., BARRY, W.A., HERTEL, R.K. and SWAIN, M.A. (1974), 'Communication, Conflict and Marriage', Jossey-Bass, San Francisco.

REES, LINFORD (1976), Stress, distress and disease, 'British Journal of Psychiatry', vol. 128, pp. 3-18.

RENSON, G.J., SCHAEFFER, E.S. and LEVY, B.I. (1968), Cross national validity of a spherical conceptual model of parental behaviour, 'Child Development', vol. 39, pp. 1229-35.

RISKIN, J. and FAUNCE, E.E. (1972), An evaluative review of family interaction research, 'Family Process', vol. 11, pp. 365-455.

RUTTER, M. (1971), Parent-child separation: psychological effects on the children, 'Journal of Child Psychology and Psychiatry and Allied Disciplines', vol. 12, pp. 233-60.

RUTTER, M. (1972), 'Maternal Deprivation Reassessed', Penguin, Harmondsworth.

SCHAEFER, E.S. and BAYLEY, N. (1963), Maternal behaviour, child behaviour and their inter-correlations from infancy through adolescence, 'Monographs of the Society for Research in Child Development', vol. 28, no. 3.

SCHEFF, T. (1968), Negotiating reality: notes on power in the assessment of responsibility, 'Social Problems', vol. 16, pp. 3-17.

SHELDON, A., RYSER, C.P. and KRANT, M.H. (1970), An integrated family oriented cancer care program: the report of a pilot project in the socio-emotional management of chronic disease, 'Journal of Chronic Disorders', vol. 22, pp. 743-55.

SIEGLER, M., OSMOND, H. and MANN, H. (1969), Laing's models of madness, 'British Journal of Psychiatry', vol. 115, pp. 947-58.

SIMONSON, N.R. and BAHR, S. (1974), Self-disclosure by the professional and paraprofessional therapist, 'Journal of Consulting and Clinical Psychology', vol. 42, pp. 359-63.

SIMS, A. (1975), Factors predictive of outcome in neurosis, 'British Journal of Psychiatry', vol. 127, pp. 54-62.

SMITH, S.M., HANSON, R. and NOBLE, S. (1974), Social aspects of the battered baby syndrome, 'British Journal of Psychiatry', vol. 125, pp. 568-80.

SONNE, J.C. (1967), Entropy and family therapy, in G.H. Zuk et al. (eds), 'Family therapy and disturbed families', Science and Behaviour Books, Palo Alto.

SPEER, D.C. (1970), Family systems: morphostasis and morphogenesis: or is homeostasis enough?, 'Family Process', vol. 9, pp. 259-78.

SROLE, L., et al. (1962), 'Mental Health in the Metropolis: The Midtown Manhattan Study', vol. 1, McGraw-Hill, New York.

STEPHENS, W.N. (1963), 'The Family in Cross-cultural Perspective', Holt, New York.

STOVER, L. and GUERNEY, B.G., Jr (1967), The efficacy of training procedures for mothers in filial therapy, 'Psychotherapy: Theory, Research & Practice', vol. 4, pp. 110-15.

STRAUS, M.A. (1973), A general systems theory approach to a theory of violence between family members, 'Social Science Information', vol. 12, pp. 105-25.
STUART, R.B. (1975), Behavioural remedies for marital ills: a guide to the use of operant-interpersonal techniques, in T. Thompson and W. Dockens (eds), 'International Symposium on Behaviour Modification', Appleton, New York.
SYMONDS, P.M. (1939), 'The Psychology of Parent-Child Relationships', Appleton-Century-Crofts, New York.
TOFFLER, A. (1970), 'Future Shock', Random House, New York.
TOWNSEND, P. (1957), 'The Family Life of Old People', Routledge & Kegan Paul, London.
TRIANDIS, H.C. and TRIANDIS, L.M. (1965), Some studies in social distance, in I. Steiner and M. Fishbein (eds), 'Current Studies in Social Psychology', Holt, Rinehart & Winston, New York.
TRUAX, C.B. and C. CARKHUFF, R.R. (1967), 'Towards Effective Counselling and Psychotherapy: Training and Practice', Aldine, Chicago.
TURNER, R.H. (1970), 'Family Interaction', Wiley, New York.
VAUGHN, C.E. and LEFF, J.P. (1976a), The measurement of expressed emotion in the families of psychiatric patients, 'British Journal of Social and Clinical Psychology', vol. 15, pp. 157-65.
VAUGHN, C.E. and LEFF, J.P. (1976b), The influence of family and social factors on the course of psychiatric illness: a comparison of schizophrenic and depressed neurotic patients, 'British Journal of Psychiatry', vol. 129, pp. 125-37.
VISOTSKY, H.M., HAMBURG, D.A., GOSS, M.E. and LEBOVITS, B.Z. (1961), Coping behaviour under extreme stress: observations of patients with severe poliomyelitis, 'Archives of General Psychiatry', vol. 5, pp. 423-8.
VOGEL, E.F. and BELL, N.W. (1968), The emotionally disturbed child as the family scapegoat, in N.W. Bell and E.F. Vogel (eds), 'The Family', Free Press, New York.
WEAKLAND, J.H. (1960), The 'double-bind' hypothesis of schizophrenia and three-party interaction, in D.D. Jackson (ed.), 'The Etiology of Schizophrenia', Basic Books, New York.
WEISS, R.L., BIRCHLER, G.R. and VINCENT, J.P. (1974), Contractual models for negotiation in marital dyads, 'Journal of Marriage and the Family', vol. 36, pp. 321-30.
WEISS, R.L., HOPS, H. and PATTERSON, G.R. (1973), A framework for conceptualizing marital conflict, a technology for altering it, and some data for evaluating it, in L.A. Hamerlynck, L.C. Handy and E.J. Mash (eds), 'Behaviour Change: Methodology, Concepts, and Practice', Research Press, Champaign, Illinois.
WEISS, R.S. (1974a), The provisions of social relationships, in Z. Rubin, 'Doing Unto Others', Spectrum (Prentice-Hall), New Jersey.
WEISS, R.S. (1974b), 'Loneliness', MIT Press, Cambridge, Massachusetts.
WELLS, R.A., DILKES, T.C. and TRIVELLI, N. (1972), The results of family therapy: a critical review of the literature, 'Family Process', vol. 11, pp. 189-207.
WERTHEIM, E.S. (1973a), Family unit therapy and the science and typology of family systems, 'Family Process', vol. 12, pp. 361-76.
WERTHEIM, E.S. (1973b), Family therapy and its social implications, 'Australian and New Zealand Journal of Psychiatry', vol. 7, pp. 1-9.

WINTER, W.D. and FERREIRA, J. (eds) (1969), 'Research in Family Interaction', Science & Behaviour Books, Palo, Alto, California.
WYNNE, L., RYCKOFF, I., DAY, J. and HIRSCH, S. (1958), Pseudo-
mutuality in the family relations of schizophrenics, 'Psychiatry',
vol. 21, pp. 205-20.

Chapter 2

THE SOCIAL CONTEXT
OF FAMILY THERAPY

Philip Kingston

This chapter is an attempt to understand some of the environmental
pressures upon families and family therapists and to suggest ways in
which these can be worked with so that the needs of families can be
met more effectively.   It outlines the reasons why this is of interest to the author;   considers some of the environmental forces
upon families;   considers similar forces upon therapists;   outlines
some dilemmas with which therapists are faced;   and suggests some
strategies for dealing with these.

As no one writes from an unbiased position it seems appropriate
to state some of the personal and professional factors which influence my views.   Like many others who become involved in family
work, the personal experience of problematic family situations has
been an important motivation.   Such situations are usually described in terms which suggest that the problems arise solely within
the family, but my perception is that it is also necessary to consider transactions between the family and its outside world before
being able to make a more rounded sense of the subjective experience.   Professionally, my academic background in sociology and the
experience of working with a broad range of problems, first as a
probation officer and later as a social worker in a children's
department, has led me to see family therapy within the context of
other kinds of systems intervention.   Because of my particular professional experience, much of the material for this chapter is drawn
from the dilemmas of the social worker who practises as a family
therapist within a government department.   This has given me a
special interest in the relationship between the social control
function of the helping professions within society and the practice
of family therapy.   This particular perspective is rarely reflected
in the writings of therapists, probably because the original development of family therapy was mainly in the United States in settings
which emphasized a voluntary approach by the client/patient and a
contractual element between the family and the helper.   Its transfer from these settings to government-sponsored ones raises major
ethical, legal and technical issues and requires considerable
thought.   However, there is little evidence yet to show that thinking on these issues is occurring.   The enthusiasm with which family
therapy has been greeted in Britain is immense: the mid-1970s has

seen a burgeoning of training courses and conferences which attempt
to develop knowledge and skills, and in 1976 a flourishing Association for Family Therapy was formed.   The enthusiasm is understandable, for family therapy provides theories and methods which appear
to fit some of the life and work experience of practitioners.   The
view of many involved in clinical practice is that it is more effective than many other approaches, and some American research (at
least with regard to certain categories of clients) confirms this
view (for example, Pittman, 1973).   In addition, many of the values
associated with family therapy, such as interpersonal honesty, individual growth, responsibility for one's own behaviour and appropriate caring for others are seen as congruent with some of the more
generally held values of the helping professions.

One general consideration underpins much of the detail of this
chapter, namely that, although family therapists appear to use systems concepts as their main theoretical base, their use of them is
open to criticism on two counts.   First, concepts which refer to
the relationship between the unit and its environment are used extensively when considering the individual in the context of the
family, but are used in extremely limited ways when considering the
family in relation to its context.   The second is that criticisms
of a systems framework by sociologists are almost entirely absent in
the literature of family therapy.   For example, concepts relating
to social systems were developed on the basis of an assumption that
there was an agreement or consensus of interests amongst the parts
of the system.   Gouldner (1975) comments on an aspect of this view
which is contained in the writings of Talcott Parsons and Robert
Merton.   He states that they regard the functional usefulness of
part of a system as being reciprocated by the functional usefulness
of the whole for the part.   However, if the a priori assumption
concerning a consensus of interests is incorrect, then in reality
such reciprocity may not exist and a priority of interests will be
established by those with most power.   This has relevance to some
current views of battered wives and battered babies where the recipient of the violence is also seen as receiving some psychological
gain from it.   Without denying that view as offering a partial explanation, it seems more plausible to conclude that the interests
of the person(s) expressing the violence are the ones which predominate.   Family therapists are in fact becoming much more interested
in power differences within the family, and some of those involved
in an approach known as 'strategic therapy' (Haley, 1973) have
utilized the idea of 'down-power' to describe the desperate efforts
made by a person whose formal or physical power is low, to assert
himself in some way, however bizarre this way may be (Silverstein,
1976).   The application of this idea to power differences within
the family is encouraging but it is yet to be explored in relation
to such differences between the family and other social institutions.

A number of family therapists have attempted to work with the
family in the context of its neighbourhood and in its relationships
with other institutions, but they are the exception rather than the
rule.   The crucial area which I believe they and most other family
therapists leave unexplored is the power and authority of the therapist, particularly the legal, professional and organizational power

and authority to intervene in the family's environment.   Yet none
of us can move very far into the family therapy field without
running into these issues.   For example, at a case conference an
educational psychologist presents the situation of a child with
school difficulties in which it becomes increasingly clear that the
problems of the child are created more by the head teacher of the
school than by the parents.   Alongside this recognition there
develops an atmosphere of embarrassment amongst the other professional workers involved in the case, as they struggle to avoid such
a conclusion, sensing the power dilemma in which they are automatically caught if the head teacher is recognized as part of the therapeutic unit.   The recognition initially brings with it a painful
sense of impotence; but relief too may flow from this wider and
more realistic view of the composition of the treatment group, since
inevitably, more effective strategies become available.   Much of
the difficulty stems from the fact that the first definition of the
problem is automatically made in terms of family causation rather
than involving an open exploration of causation in a variety of systems.   Moreover, the family therapist's view of the treatment unit
is often so narrowly focused that current economic and societal
trends, such as the unemployment level amongst school-leavers,
appear to be almost disregarded as factors worth considering when
evaluating the appropriateness of the treatment modality.

A startling example of this narrowly focused vision occurred at
the Annual Conference of the Association for the Psychiatric Study
of Adolescents held in Britain in 1975, the theme of which was 'The
Adolescent and his Family'.   The conference was held at a time when
the mass media were giving wide publicity to the fact that the unemployment level amongst school-leavers was higher than it had been
for forty years (half of the 250,000 July school-leavers were still
unemployed in the autumn).   No mention was made of this, yet
amongst the people it would most affect were those being worked with
by conference participants.

THE ENVIRONMENT OF FAMILIES

Despite a considerable amount of supporting sociological evidence
for the existence of a complex relationship between the family and
other social institutions there are many family therapists who do
not take this relationship sufficiently into account.   I will refer
briefly to three aspects of this relationship, namely the impact of
occupation, of major societal changes and of social stratification.

Occupation

There is evidence which shows that, in quite direct ways, some occupations have a marked effect upon the structure and processes of the
family.   For example, Tunstall's study of fishermen analyses the
impact of an occupation which involves men in being away from home
for two weeks in every three and the problems arising from rapidly
alternating role-allocation between husband and wife.   One of Tunstall's findings was that the divorce rate amongst these men was

twice that of other employed men in the same region.   To regard
marital problems as purely intra-familial in origin would be widely
to miss the mark, for as Tunstall concludes 'the fisherman's marriage is shaped by his occupation' (Tunstall, 1962).   Another example of the impact of occupation is contained in a study of coal-
miners.   This study shows the way in which a dangerous occupation
creates a situation where the relationships of the men involved necessarily contain high levels of interdependency and closeness.
This closeness is at such a level that family relationships become
secondary, even during the miners' leisure time.   This is to a
point where 'the whole life of the miner, under the influence of hi
group of friends, inhibits any display of tenderness and love in
sexual relationships' (Dennis et al., 1969).   Both these studies
show a direct relationship between occupation and family structure
and processes.

Major societal change

Unfortunately sociological analysis at a macro-level does not easily
lend itself to such clear-cut understandings of the relationship between the family and other social institutions.   But that such a
relationship exists is portrayed in the analyses of the impact of
World War II upon the structure of the family, by Fletcher (1966) in
Britain and Lipman-Blumen (1975) in America.   Lipman-Blumen shows
that there was a decrease in the age of marriage, an increase in the
number of women working, an entry by women into occupational roles
previously held by men, and an increase in divorce rates (Lipman-
Blumen, 1975).   Fletcher confirms that a similar increase in
divorce rates occurred in Britain and concluded that 'few people
seem to realise how extensively the major wars of our time have disturbed human relationships at the most intimate level' (Fletcher,
1966).
    A less dramatic but continuing and very important aspect of Brit-
ish and American life in recent years is the consistently high percentage of people who are unemployed.   Some of the impact of unemployment upon family life is described in Unemployment, Family
Structure and Social Disorganization (National Advisory Commission
on Civil Disorder, 1968).   The authors conclude that:
    If men stay at home without working, their inadequacies constant-
    ly confront them and tensions arise between them and their wives
    and children.   Under these pressures, it is not surprising that
    many of these men flee their responsibilities as husbands and
    fathers.
    Again the point of these illustrations for family therapists is
that an intra-familial focus is certainly inadequate and may be
almost irrelevant.

Social stratification

One of the central aspects of low social class is that it correlates
with a number of material factors which are thought to be relevant
to physical, emotional and intellectual development.   This is shown

in the extensive research programme of the National Child Development Study into 16,000 children born in 1958. Davie et al. (1972, p. 57) state that 'The results have demonstrated clearly the relationship between poor housing amenities and overcrowding on the one hand and on the other hand educational performance and social adjustment in school ...'. Utilizing the same sample, Wedge and Prosser (1973) applied three criteria which, when present together were described as representing 'social disadvantage'. These were low income, poor housing and atypical family composition (such as one-parent family or a large number of children). There were significant differences between this category and the remainder of the sample. Whilst one in every nine of the socially disadvantaged children were received into the care of public agencies, this happened to only one in a hundred amongst the rest of the sample; and the experience of chronic illness or disability amongst socially disadvantaged fathers was four times that of non-disadvantaged fathers.

Ferri's (1976) research into the one-parent families in the NCDS sample notes that the school attainment and social adjustment of the children in these families compared unfavourably with the rest of the sample and concluded that '... their relatively poor showing owed much more to the disadvantaging circumstances associated with one-parent status (such as poor housing and financial hardship) than to the fact of being brought up by a lone mother or father.'

This kind of evidence indicates that with many families who are designated as being of lower social class it is essential that the helping professions place an increasing emphasis upon intervention into environmental conditions.

Of relevance here is the fact that a very high proportion of the population served by the helping professions, at least in Britain, are of low social class. For example, the research by Nursten and colleagues (1972) into the clients of all social workers in Bradford found that the social class (where known) of the chief economic supporter of client families was disproportionately either lower class or unemployed. This was especially so with regard to problems involving children. Childcare officers and education welfare officers had only 1 per cent of clients in classes I and II (Registrar-General's classification) whilst family service unit workers and moral welfare workers had none. This latter situation was also true of the probation service. Social workers in other settings, namely mental health, child guidance and medical social work had about 6 per cent of their clients in these two classes.

Wedge and Prosser (1973) also note the very high rate of involvement of their 'socially disadvantaged' group with social workers. Although they consisted of only 1:16 of the population, they accounted for 2:5 of those who were involved with children's departments and the probation service.

That disadvantage is not all one-way is shown by another of Davie et al.'s findings that allergic conditions like asthma, eczema and hayfever (which are known to be partially associated with stress) (Sim, 1974, pp. 283-98) were approximately twice as high in class I as in class V. Other indicators of stress, such as suicide rates, are also known to be higher in classes I and II (Sim, 1974, p. 692). In this context the perceived association of the helping professions

with low social class clients may have the effect of inhibiting
middle and upper class families from seeking help with their pain
and in recognizing some of its social origins.   Some evidence that
the personal social services are perceived as inappropriate for
these classes is contained in the research by Glastonbury and colleagues (1972) into community perceptions about the consumers of
such services.   A random sample of the population in South Wales
were asked the question 'Who uses personal social services?'.   Just
over 50 per cent held the view that the users of such services were
either the poor, the feckless or lazy, or those who could not manage
their own affairs.   These attributes do not fit with the usual
stereotype of upper- and middle-class families and the findings support the view that such families experiencing interpersonal problems
may have considerable difficulty in obtaining a source of help which
is acceptable to them.

Clearly, families within any society are placed in radically different social contexts, the effects of which play a crucial role in
the aetiology of their problems.   Distinctions need to be made between those whose stresses are related to the demands of cultural
expectations and those who experience considerable material disadvantage and social stigmatization.   In both situations therapists
need as much to develop the knowledge and skills necessary for intervention outside the family boundary as they currently do within
it.

THE ENVIRONMENT OF THERAPISTS

There are three aspects of the family therapist's environment which
require consideration: the therapist's family, employing organization and professional discipline.   In selecting these three aspects
it is of course important to bear in mind that they are not discrete
entities but act as channels between the family therapist and a
still wider social context.   In other words these aspects of the
environment are themselves influenced by broader social pressures.

The therapist's family

As a member of a family the therapist is subject to some of the same
influences that were outlined in the preceding section.   But the
analogy cannot be taken far because the environment of therapists is
normally different from that of the majority of clients.   These
differences occur particularly in relation to guaranteed income
level, educational and professional background and social status.
If we use Perlman's (1972) distinction between people who are only
able to meet their survival needs and those who are secure in these
basic needs and thus able to consider self-realization needs, it is
likely that therapists are amongst the latter.   But solutions to
self-realization needs may sometimes prove elusive.   For while
therapists learn things from their work which are central to the
lives of all families some of these may, paradoxically, be experienced as least shareable within their own family.   This is because
such sharing may represent a considerable threat to the collusive

relationships already established.   Further, they may, like some of
the potential middle-class clients referred to earlier, find it difficult to acknowledge a need for help, or to find such help should
they seek it.   In fact there is a very real possibility of therapists being stigmatized if they seek such help, although I think
stigmatization is much more likely in Britain than in the United
States.   The climate there is such that Framo (1975) is able not
only to comment objectively on the high incidence of marital problems amongst therapists but is also able to refer to his own experience of receiving family therapy.   This, together with similar
openness such as in Whitacker's (1972) acknowledgment of personal
psychotherapy, offers a climate in which it may be easier for other
therapists to express their need for help in their struggle to grow.

Employing organizations

It is necessary first to refer to important differences between the
United States and Britain with regard to the organizational aspects
of the helping professions.   In Britain most people who practise
family therapy are employed within state organizations, whilst in
America many more are self-employed or employed by private organizations which may or may not be in receipt of funds from the state.
Whilst most of the references in this section are British, the ideas
they contain have a clear, if more indirect, relevance to the American setting also.
    It is important to consider the extent to which employing organ-
izations are expressions of social control.   One of the facts of
life for people in the British helping professions is that almost
all their members are employed by state organizations such as the
National Health Service, local authority Social Services Departments
and the Probation and After-Care Service.   These organizations are
directly influenced by politicians, who in turn respond to the
formal power of the majority or to the informal power of elites and
pressure groups.   It would, in this situation, be surprising if the
employees of these organizations were not under pressure to uphold
the norms of these categories.   The laws under which psychiatrists
and social workers function contain clear powers for controlling
people (HMSO, 1948 and 1959) and whilst these may apply directly to
only a part of their work, they inevitably influence all relationships between these professions and their clients.   Even where
their work is not underpinned by the law, these professions are
still involved in attempting to change social situations.   One
would imagine that the direction of such change would be a matter of
vital interest, yet Barbara Wooton's comments referring to social
work and written in 1959 could almost stand unaltered today:

    If the purpose of social casework is to encourage in others at-
    tributes and behaviour conformable to particular norms, then the
    obligation to examine those norms and to make them explicit be-
    comes imperative.   Of this, however, in the literature of social
    work there is as yet little sign.
The inclusion of control as an aspect of these professions does
not mean the exclusion of caring and responsibility.   Rather it
acknowledges that the role of the helper who is based in a state

organization is a highly ambiguous one.   Neither does the inclusion
of control signify something which is necessarily unacceptable or
unjust.   All societies have systems of control and what is important is that they are open to rational examination, especially to
the question: 'Is the control system functional for everybody, or
for a part of society only?'   It may be that this question is more
in the open in Britain than it is in the United States, where the
relationship between the helping professions and social control is
more blurred.   To take another example from social work, a recent
and very influential American social work text by Pincus and Minahan
(1973) contains no reference to social control when listing the purposes of social work but later includes it as a function of social
work practice.   It does not appear to relate to their list of purposes and seems to be brought in almost as an unfortunate side-
effect.   In the literature of family therapy whilst the term is
conspicuous by its absence, the reality to which the term refers is
often uncomfortably present, a point to which I will return under
'Dilemmas of the therapist'.

Whatever the organizational setting of the family therapist she
faces one common problem, namely the lack of legal power to intervene in systems.   This contrasts sharply with the presence of
powers to intervene with individuals.   The helping professions have
in general worked within a model which regards the causes of a person's symptoms as within the person.   To change this tradition is
difficult enough but it becomes almost insuperable when one takes
into account the fact that the traditional individualistic view of
aetiology is in fact underwritten by statute.   It is individuals,
not families or other systems, who are committed to mental hospital
or placed on probation.   And however much the helping professions
begin to take the view that an individual's symptom is functional
for a system, they have almost no legal basis upon which to follow
this through.   Thus, when these professions become involved in
family or other social systems they do so on the authority of their
knowledge, skill and personal values, not by the power of the law.

There is another major complication which arises from being employed by organizations which have powers over individuals, namely
that the organizations are a party to the process which labels those
individuals.   For the professional to switch to a systems focus
after she has taken part in affixing the label of individual pathology seems not only impracticable but unethical.

It is usual for members of different helping professions to be
employed in the same organization and for a definite status and executive hierarchy to have developed between them.   In most situations, the traditional hierarchy has been psychiatrist, psychologist, social worker and nurse, in that order.   There seems no doubt
that this hierarchy is being threatened by a family approach.
Haley, in his penetrating satire on Why a mental health clinic
should avoid family therapy (1975) points to the conflicts which
develop within an organization when a systems approach is introduced.   He notes that these arise from differences in theories,
diagnoses and methods of initiating change and that they are particularly painful because previous status distinctions between professions no longer hold.   The ability to be a successful family therapist does not depend upon one's professional discipline but appears

to rest much more upon being comfortable within a group setting, prepared to respond actively within it and able to understand and apply systems concepts rather than those of psychodynamic theory. Its concepts and methods are relatively new to all professional disciplines, so previous status differentials based upon believed expertise have been challenged.   The focus upon the family group brings with it a need for common skills, making the previous situation of complementary skills an anachronism.   This in turn makes nonsense of the considerable pay differentials which exist between the professional disciplines involved.

Even where the hierarchical levels occur within the same professional discipline, considerable conflict can arise from the introduction of a systems approach.   How, for example, do those in senior administrative posts cope with family therapists when the latter are involved in areas of work which the former have no competence to supervise;   and which the therapists themselves have no formal power or authority to enter?   What problems arise when systems ideas, developed in work with families and small groups, are applied by staff junior to other groups, such as at staff meetings and committees?   The conflicts and tensions suggested by these questions may appear to be entirely intra-organizational in origin. However, if the analysis of the relationship between social control and employing organizations is accurate, it is likely that these conflicts reflect those occurring between different interest groups in the wider society.

Professional discipline

The discussion of organizations has inevitably overlapped with comments about the helping professions, simply because, in Britain, the roles of state employee and helping professional normally coincide. The failure to grasp this fact adequately can lead to a major misperception of the professional role.   Johnson offers a useful analysis of this role when he suggests that 'a profession is not an occupation but a means of controlling an occupation' (Johnson, 1972).   He outlines three ways in which occupations are controlled, namely by colleagues, by patronage and by state mediation.   In modern societies, patronage occurs when the principal clients of the professionals are large-scale corporations, as is increasingly becoming the case with the profession of accountancy.   In this situation the aims and values of the professional are likely to be heavily influenced by the patron.   A similar influence occurs when the state intervenes in the relationship between the suppliers and recipients of services.   In both these situations control by other members of the profession may become less meaningful.   If one applies these ideas to the helping professions it seems clear that patronage and state mediation are major forms of control.   Patronage exists because central and local government departments have a virtual monopoly over employment opportunities;   state mediation exists because a legal basis has been established for many of the tasks and relationships with which the helping professions become involved.   One aspect of this analysis is that it gives a curious reversal to the usual meaning of the words 'client' and 'patient'.

Normally the terms refer to those individuals who have sought the professional's services and with whom the professional has face-to-face contact.   However, when seen in the light of the notion of patronage it may be equally appropriate to view the large-scale central and local government employees as clients, at least of the profession as a whole if not of the individual professional.   However unacceptable this view might be it does point to the considerable influence of the state when compared with that of colleagues.

There is probably a tendency to see the influence of other institutions, especially political ones, as being restricted to the actions and behaviour of the profession.   However, Bitesky (1973), writing about social work, and Pearson (1975), writing about psychiatry and social work, have argued that this influence extends into the theories used by the professions as the basis of their work. In the influence of political power in determining the theoretical development of social work, Bitesky traces the way in which changes in theories have accompanied changes in the social and economic milieu of social work.   He concludes that:

> Political influence manifests itself by its cumulative and pervasive effect on the theoretical superstructure and the value system of the profession.   And, because this process occurs unbeknownst to the social workers (since the profession has tended to minimise the interconnections between the theoretical framework and politics) the profession may find itself in the position of forwarding alien political objectives under the impression that these goals are congruent with the needs of its clients and the values of the profession.

Bitesky is here calling for the development of a greater political awareness, presumably in the belief that influence can be two-way. Inasmuch as the helping professions frequently deal with situations which are bothering and troublesome to others in society, they are likely to have some influence on the definition and treatment of such problems, even if this involves criticism of, and intervention in, other institutions.   In addition some of the traditional values of the professions push their members in this direction, as for example those concerned with autonomous decision-making, personal responsibility for actions and the commitment to meet the needs of others before one's own.   These values, when related to the developing knowledge about environmental pressures, leave many therapists with the belief that they fail in their responsibility if they do not translate this knowledge into action.

Professional associations have normally included amongst their functions the setting of standards of service and the protection of clients.   Whether the family therapist comes from a background of medicine, social work or psychology the interpenetration of her role with that of government employee makes these aims somewhat awesome. For the profession becomes concerned not just with the face-to-face work with clients but with the quality of work of the whole department, the adequacy of the resources it commands and the extent to which it colludes with other systems in not meeting clients' or patients' needs.

DILEMMAS OF THE THERAPIST

Knowledge about social influences on behaviour places family therapists in two principal dilemmas.   The first is that, whilst such
knowledge might indicate the necessity to change other systems,
therapists have limited power to effect such change.   Second, although collaboration with other systems may be necessary to bring
about changes in the family, the cost of such collaboration may be
the therapist's involvement in a process of control.
    Since the helping professions have become 'big business', ques-
tions have, rightly, been asked about their effectiveness in alle-
viating human problems.   Whilst some researches indicate effectiveness a substantial number do not.   In 1971 a conference was
held at Fordham University to assess the reasons for these differences.   The conclusions were complex but can be summarized as follows: that effective interventions occurred when clients and helpers were agreed upon the task to be tackled and set time-limits to
their work together; that ineffective interventions occurred when
the helpers attempted to work within face-to-face systems even
though it was apparent that the cause of the problems lay outside
these systems.   Contributors to the symposium regarded poverty,
racial and social class discrimination, sub-standard housing, unemployment, poor education, facilities and different kinds of social
stigmatization as being amongst such causes, and attested to 'the
futility of attempting to resolve our major social problems through
micro-system intervention' (Mullen, Dumpson et al., 1972).   This
view may have considerable significance in explaining the high drop-
out rate from family therapy of families of low socio-economic circumstances (Slipp et al., 1974).
    It is to the credit of family therapists that much of their
approach is within the time-limited and target-focused framework.
In addition, a small but important minority have not only ventured
into wider systems but have developed exciting methods of intervention.   Amongst these are the network therapists, Speck (and
Attneave, 1973; and Rueveni, 1969), Attneave (1969) and Rueveni and
those like Auerswald (1971), Garrison (1974) and Erickson et al.
(1974), who work with the family and representatives of other systems.   However, what is largely unexplored in the writings of those
who work across the boundary between the family and outside world is
the authority by which they intervene.   Those who have developed
network therapy appear to cope with their lack of authority by
having the nuclear family both convene the network and collect the
fee.   Others manage by inviting representatives of other systems to
attend, with no reference being made to the sanctions which might be
applied if these representatives decline the invitation.   The
missing housing manager or DHSS representative may in some situations be more significant than the missing family member.
    Perhaps the most striking feature of accounts of work across the
family boundary is the absence of a political perspective; or sometimes, the presence of a desperate attempt to be apolitical.   Auerswald (1971) noted the despair of many who grasp the interrelatedness of social problems 'because without the support of those in
positions of power, they cannot get on with the task' (p. 265).
The logic of this is that politicians become an important target for

therapists and families, but for some reason Auerswald took a different view, namely that therapists should become 'post-political'
and so avoid 'the trap of politicization' (p. 266).   What he
appears to mean by this is that they should take a view which recog-
nizes the interrelatedness of everything.   However, he then seems
to move to a different dimension by assuming that this recognition
leads to an overcoming of sectional interests and factions.   Auerswald is deeply aware of an ecological view of human problems; his
apolitical stance is, therefore, puzzling because it seems that
politics is, par excellence, the occupation which has to take an
ecological perspective.   Intervention in any system, including the
family, is always a political intervention inasmuch as it is aimed
at changing or maintaining the balance of power or the distribution
of resources.   In this sense to attempt to be post-political is in
fact to be pre-political.

The political nature of family-system intervention becomes more
clear if we compare it with intervention in other institutions.
For example, two research studies into paranoia, one pointing to
family processes as a source of pathology and the other pointing
more towards work and community processes, appear to have been
treated very differently by the helping professions.   Lemert (1962)
has described the ways in which people become labelled as paranoid,
not only within their families, but also within their work organizations and community relationships.   His study outlined processes
within colleague groups which are immediately very familiar to those
who work with family groups.   Schatzman (1971) wrote a fascinating
critique of Freud's analysis of Daniel Schreber in which he offered
a different understanding of Schreber's paranoia by placing it
within the context of his family.   Schatzman was able to do this
because he had access to a number of books on the subject of children's education which had been written by Schreber's father.
These suggested that if Schreber senior had followed his writings in
his own child-rearing methods, then his son had good reason to show
paranoid responses.   Here we have two papers describing some similar processes in human groups; yet the practical implications of
Schatzman's paper are likely to be acceptable within the helping
professions whilst those of Lemert's paper are not.   This appears
to be because families have much more limited ability to withstand
intervention by therapists than do work organizations.   Ackerman
(1971) commenting on Schatzman's paper wrote that 'the implications
of Schatzman's contribution are in some respects revolutionary'.
No doubt this is so to a degree but compared with the implications
of Lemert's paper, it is a muted revolution, whose society-wide outcomes are extremely limited.

There are few publications by family therapists which are concerned with the problems of specific occupational groups, so it is
not possible to generalize about the extent to which family therapists use such knowledge as they have regarding the impact of this
aspect of the family's supra-system or whether such intervention is
aimed primarily at family change or organizational change.   One
article describes work with the families of servicemen (Frances and
Gale, 1973).   This analyses the particular stresses created by
military life, such as constant moves, separation and the close
spatial and relationship links between work and leisure, but focuses

entirely upon the families when attempting to resolve the problems. There is no discussion of the possible development of changes in the families' military environment.   In a business organization setting, Culbert and Renshaw (1972) describe work with couples where the husband's employment necessitated considerable travel.   The stresses on family life were recognized by the organization's management who arranged a seminar in which couples could work at these issues.   Whilst the main emphasis was upon each couple's problem-solving attempts this research indicated a very positive outcome both for the couples and for the organization, and offers some optimism for similar approaches elsewhere.   However, a crucial aspect of this study is that the work was initiated by the organization's management and does not, therefore, represent an initiative taken from the outside by a systems therapist.

Some of the most impressive work in the family therapy field with low socio-economic families has been undertaken by Minuchin and his colleagues.   Their imaginative ideas and approaches, coupled with much skill and perseverance, are essential material for anyone who is interested in following their lead in this area.   Whilst recognizing the impact of forces arising from outside the family boundary the early work of this Philadelphia school of family therapy focused chiefly upon the family system itself.   'Our study and this book were largely limited to family interaction, though we are aware of the importance of extra-familial factors' (Minuchin et al., 1967, p. 5).   Minuchin and his colleagues emphasized the need for modifications in the family's 'communicational, behavioural and cognitive styles' before their ability to use new sources of material and educational help can develop (p. 30).

Others express the opposite view, as for example, Wilson (1974) in her study of materially deprived families.   She concludes that the lack of a minimum financial basis for living and its associated material environment may be a more immediate area to rectify because 'the realities of life in the slum forces parents to adopt methods of child-rearing they do not approve'.   It is difficult to evaluate either of these views on the evidence provided because Minuchin et al.'s study has been criticized on the grounds of inadequate control comparisons (Wells et al., 1972) whilst Wilson's study, although showing a significant correlation between poor child-rearing practices and lack of material resources, does not show that the latter is a causative factor.   Fortunately, an either/or choice between intra- and extra-family intervention is made increasingly redundant by a systems approach to problems.   What becomes important are the powers and resources of the different systems and what changes have to occur in both if targets are to be achieved.   This approach is well illustrated by the more recent work of the Philadelphia school, especially with regard to a combined intervention in school and family systems (Aponte, 1976).

The dilemma which arises when there is a disjunction between the therapist's knowledge and her perceived lack of power to implement that knowledge leaves many therapists with an ongoing crisis of conscience.   The enormity of the task when compared with the power of the person and role may be experienced as overwhelming.   This seems to lead some writers into moving away from the logic of their thinking.   Auerswald's reaction against involvement in politics may be a poignant example of this.

In a review of major trends in family therapy, Ackerman (1970)
listed nine such trends; seven were concerned with intra-familial
situations, one with multiple family therapy and one with eco-psy-
chiatric and network therapy.   Although the last of these was in a
minority on his list, he indicated his belief in its importance.
Referring to developments like street psychiatry, storepoint psychiatry and the use of lay-citizens in helping roles he stated that the
significance of such changes 'cannot be underestimated'.   In the
context of the rest of the paragraph it seems clear that he meant to
write that the significance of such changes 'cannot be *overestima-*
ted'.   To risk an interpretation, if someone of Ackerman's stature
was sufficiently ambivalent about the outcome of his logic to make
this slip of the pen, it should be no surprise if the rest of us
experience the same problem!

To turn to the dilemma which arises when therapists become involved with processes of social control, I want to consider what
happens when the presence of control is either not seen or not ack-
knowledged.   Zuk (1972), for example, describes a family in which
the boy refused to attend school and how, in treatment, the parents
enlisted the therapist onto their side against the school.   The
therapist decided that this was unhelpful in achieving the child's
re-attendance and decided to assume a go-between role instead,
namely 'to assist the parties in their dispute'.   However, what
transpired appears to be a series of highly controlling moves by the
therapist, some directed against the parents, some against the
child.   For example:

The school authorities were informed by the therapist that he believed the boy was ready to return to school and that they should
institute their regular procedures to secure his return.

The parents were told that 'further absence of the boy from
school would definitely result in his placement in a disciplinary
institution'.

The parents were recommended to call the police if the boy failed
to attend.

The detention officer of the juvenile detention centre to which
the boy was taken 'was encouraged by the therapist to use his full
authority to discipline the boy'.

Zuk's summary of the processes in this case refers to the therapist being initially perceived as an agent of the family, then as an
agent of the school.   'Finally he was able to convince the family
he was acting as a "third force", a mediator between the family and
the school authorities.'

It seems likely that this mystification of the nature of the relationship is unhelpful to families.   However, I doubt whether
Zuk's way of dealing with this is very different from others of us
in similar situations.   The emotional tendency to polarize care and
control is a very strong one and difficult to overcome, especially
if one sees oneself only as a caring agent and others as having only
a controlling function.

The example just given refers to the therapist's involvement with
other institutions which have controlling functions.   It is equally
important to consider the therapist's own employing organization inasmuch as it exerts control over the lives of patients or clients.
There appears to be a considerable dearth of literature in this

area, an absence which is of particular concern to the large number
of people who are based in organizations where this is an important
element.   My own involvement as a consultant to probation officers
using family therapy allows me to draw two tentative conclusions on
the basis of that experience.   First, for many children and adolescents there appears to be a vacuum in the exercise of adult power
and authority in their families.   A special skill of the family
therapist in this setting is to avoid pressure to fill the vacuum
and instead to enable the other adults to exercise their roles more
effectively.   Second, the power of the probation officer can give a
means of entry to a family which, whilst initially coercive, can
lead to a contract to work on issues which are useful to the family.
Whilst the bringing together of care and control in the same role is
a source of tension it seems that it can lead either to creativity
or to oppression.

The two dilemmas outlined in this section are linked to a third
which can be stated in this way: if family therapists want to influence other systems they require power; but the very systems they
want to change are those which can lessen their power.   It is for
this reason that there are limits to the extent to which institutions can be criticized and changed; for whilst logic might dictate
a change in other institutions, the people representing those institutions are likely to respond in ways which protect them against
change.   This suggests that family therapists can make little
impact unless they are a part of a wider current of change.   What
seems essential in working at this dilemma is to keep a balance between the extremes of, on the one hand, losing credibility and the
power which goes with it, or on the other, being in 'bad faith' by
completely accepting the ability of others to define one's role.

SOME STRATEGIES FOR CHANGING THE RELATIONSHIP BETWEEN FAMILIES AND
THEIR ENVIRONMENT

Theory

The commonsense approach to changing a relationship normally starts
by accepting that there is some agreed definition of what is to be
changed.   Such a definition is assumed to be real, in the sense
that it accurately describes what the relationship is.   However, we
are now becoming more aware that not only does the definition describe the relationship; it also, in subtle ways, prescribes it.
It follows that if we redefine the relationship then the relationship itself will change.   Many workers in the family-therapy field
are making exciting and effective use of this notion (e.g. Watzlawick et al. (1974)), but as yet little has been written about it regarding the family/environment relationship.   Before turning to
practical strategies, we need to consider some aspects of current
theory and its effects upon practice.

Systems concepts do not of themselves lead to an assumption that
pathology or dysfunction are created in a particular part of a sub-
system/system/supra-system.   The removal of the supra-system
appears to be based upon the arbitrary assumption that the nexus of
pathology is the family system, rather than its environment.   I

think this assumption occurs because the family is in fact made much more accessible than other institutions in terms of the therapist's power to intervene.   The arbitrary denial of pathology in other institutions seems a good example of Bitesky's thesis that theory can be used unwittingly to support particular power bases within society.

An outcome of removing the environment is that a number of the concepts used in general systems theory appear to become less applicable when used in family therapy.   Amongst these are the ideas of energy exchange (Carter and Anderson, 1974), equifinality (Janchill, 1969) and decider subsystem (Miller, 1965).

Normally the concept of energy exchange has a central place in systems theory, so its relative absence in the writings of family therapists is surprising.   Where energy is referred to, it is usually seen as the release of energy which is already available within the family.   Where it is recognized that energy is needed from outside (even if only to release the inside potential) it is usually manifested in the form of the therapist.   Energy in the form of material and emotional resources from within the community is rarely included.   An article by Forder (1976),however, offers a model which broadens this perspective by including the resources and relative power of the different systems involved in a transaction.

The principle of equifinality refers to the fact that the same end result can occur from intervention in different parts of the subsystem/system/supra-system.   This principle becomes incapable of application if the environment is excluded simply because the possibility of family change occurring from environmental change is excluded with it.

The decider subsystem is that part of a system which has executive power over other parts, as for example, the brain in human beings.   The exclusion of the supra-system in relation to the family limits the application of this concept to subsystems within the family.   This latter application has been made in an appropriate and thoughtful way by a number of family therapists, especially Minuchin (1972) and Skynner (1976) so that a sensible hierarchy of parents and children is established.   However, a helpful pin-pointing of the decider subsystem within the family tells us little about the situation at the next level in the hierarchy of a social system;   namely what is the decider subsystem within the complex of subsystems known as institutions, of which the family is one amongst many?   Unless the situation at both these levels is clarified there is a danger that the recognition of a decider subsystem within the family may lead to a belief that the same subsystem has control over events outside the family boundary.   For example, some parents may be expected to carry responsibility for children without having the material, emotional or intellectual resources to do so; the emphasis on parental power and responsibility may then serve to mystify the fact that actual power is vested elsewhere.

This virtual absence of some basic systems concepts from the repertoire of family therapists may lead to their being unaware of, or at best taking a minor role in, attempts to develop more general resources and policies for families.

The under-use of some concepts inevitably has the effect of others being mis-used or over-used.   This imbalance can be hidden

by some of the innately powerful methods used in therapy.   I refer
particularly to the bias which may arise from an emphasis on the
'here-and-now', and techniques like sculpting.   Whilst both have
great potential for helping families, they can only do so if the
causes of the problem are within the people present.   I think it
is probable that the emotional impact of these techniques can cover
over the absence of others who are vital to the problem.   By definition, a 'here-and-now' approach can only pick up what happens between the people present;   and the tangles and pain shown by sculpting can only be with those present.   Both may serve to hide the
fact that greater conflicts exist between the family and people outside it.   To return to the example of the boy who refused to attend
school (Zuk, 1972), one wonders what might have happened if all the
parties mentioned, including the therapist, had been brought together and been sculpted and worked with in the present by another
therapist.

There is another, less tangible, imbalance which arises from some
of the current usage of systems concepts.   This is the belief that
'Why?' questions are irrelevant.   It is clear that 'How?', 'When?',
'Where?' and 'What?' are basic and relevant questions when considering the workings of a system.   Equally, the exclusion of 'Why?'
where it seeks a historical explanation which is of little use in
practice seems appropriate.   But if, with that particular bath
water, we throw out the baby of human purposiveness and responsibility, we may fall into the trap of retaining the more mechanistic
questions and excluding the moral ones.   One certainty in family
therapy, as with any method of intervention, is that it is not
value-free.

Amongst the values which appear to underlie family therapy are:
holding families together so as to provide a secure base upon which
the child's self-image can develop;   and enabling parents to be individuals within an ongoing bonded relationship.   These values
point to different interests amongst family members and may reflect
conflicts which are inevitable within human groups.   These conflicting interests are normally resolved by the family members who
hold most power, but it is likely that family therapy, by a process
of consciousness raising, may alter the distribution of power both
within the family and between the family and other institutions.

I have used the term 'family therapy' throughout this chapter
without examining the ways in which the term itself affects what
family therapists do.   To return to the idea that language both
describes and prescribes, it is worth focusing a little more upon
the prescriptive aspect.   I believe that the term 'family therapy'
implies that pathology lies within the family.   To widen that to a
more realistic view of pathology, it becomes necessary to use a term
like 'systems therapy';   and because the word 'therapy' tends to
imply that the problems are inside an entity rather than between the
entity and its environment, I would prefer the broader term of
'problem-solving'.   Thus, 'systems problem-solving' appears to be a
term which may move us forward on a realistically broad front so
that society-wide goals can be articulated and the means to their
achievement distributed in a rational way throughout different institutions.   This reconceptualizing of 'family therapy', together
with the extension of the use of systems concepts to the social en-

vironment should change definitions of pathology.   Individual and family pathology would remain a possibility; but the pathology of other individuals and institutions would also become one.

Practice

Strategies to bring about change in the relationship between families and their social environment can be classified into two main kinds, (i) those which link up with current power systems in society and (ii) those which generate new sources of power.   Families and therapists are, theoretically, able to develop each of these, but in fact it appears that therapists have moved towards establishing links with current power systems, whilst families have moved in the direction of creating new power systems.

1 Strategies which link up with current power systems   Hoffman and Long (1969) have carefully described the ways in which a family's problems were exacerbated by the unco-ordinated actions of two helping agencies.   A number of therapists have attempted to work in a more co-ordinated way by bringing together not only the family but also representatives of the different agencies.   Although working in different settings, Garrison (1974), Auerswald (1971) and Erickson (1974) all describe the setting up of some kind of intersystems meeting, involving, for example, the police, social work departments, employers and priests.   The openness of the meetings is impressive, with the family and other people being able to voice their perceptions of the problems, and with tasks being allocated amongst the parties present through a process of contract-making.   It seems a particularly helpful way of enabling families to participate in decisions about their own lives, to avoid being labelled and to combat the inept or unjust use of power.   Garrison notes the importance of arranging the first meeting at the point of crisis, when motivation in all parties is high, and before the identified problem becomes transmuted into a heavily labelled person.
     These ideas seem to have special relevance to helping professionals who work in situations of social control.   First, the idea of contract-making helps to make clear what is open for negotiation and what is not; it distinguishes between the legal duties and the range of other roles which the person might take.   Second, the openness of the meeting may help distinguish between the oppressive and beneficial use of power.   Control which is based upon caring can have beneficial results, as Sainsbury's (1975) study of the work of a family service unit shows.   It seems that concerned control may give the security which is necessary for maturing processes to occur.   Third, the importance of combating immediately the labelling process cannot be overestimated.   This suggests that the most crucial point in intervention is often the first meeting, before the helper participates in labelling the person; at the social enquiry report stage for probation officers and other social workers; at the point of request for hospital admission for hospital personnel. A good description of such work is contained in Scott (1973).
     Working within current systems does not, of course, simply mean the co-ordination of information and the collaboration of effort.

This would imply that all institutions and groupings had similar ends.   When the helper enters the world of conflicting interests she is more likely to be needing advocacy skills than the more fam- iliar collaborative ones; and perhaps more important, the personal courage to put them into action, and the sense to recognize that only by combining forces with others will any action get far.   This last point directs one towards the importance of associations for people with similar interests.

A comprehensive list of practical strategies is contained in Sunley (1970).   He outlines approaches which range from the forma- tion of client associations to direct contact with officials and legislators.   Many members of the helping professions would be at a loss in using these approaches and most would have as much need of consultation/supervision in their attempts to develop them as they have had in developing the skills used within the family boundary. Video-tapes of meetings with families are commonplace; those of meetings with housing managers, DHSS officials, senior agency staff and politicians are probably non-existent.   Yet for therapists to learn about their responses to people in these latter roles is es- sential if their skills in these situations are to develop.

2 Strategies which develop new power systems   One of the striking features about the family as a social institution is that it does not have a representative voice.   This means that it is in a weak position to promote changes on its own behalf.   Since the 1960s, however, there has been an explosion of self-help organizations, some of which are set up on the basis of family structure; for ex- ample Gingerbread and Mothers-in-Action exist to help one-parent families.   Others, whilst apparently set up to meet the needs of individuals, yet have the effect of bringing together families with similar problems; for example disabled adults in the disablement income group; and unemployed and other adults in receipt of state benefits, in claimants' unions.   Of importance is that these organ- izations are not just providers of mutual help; they have overtly political aims and operate as pressure groups.   Many of these or- ganizations are critical of the helping professions which they see as controlling and withholding resources.   The latter, for their part, are ambivalent towards these organizations, especially when they level criticism at the departments which employ them.   What these organizations are forcing the helping professions to do is to recognize that the problems of clients are not just personal and technical, but moral and political as well.   Inasmuch as the hel- pers acknowledge this, they are likely to give their support to such organizations, either directly or by encouraging others to initiate them.   But as with most of the strategies being suggested, their actions will be based upon professional authority rather than stat- utory obligation.

Amongst the most powerless families may be those who are already on the caseloads of departments.   In this situation, the department becomes an important part of their environment and the development of power by these clients may initially be perceived as a threat to the department.   That this can be a positive development is illus- trated by Gibbs and Thorpe (1975) in their description of work with a group of parents, all of whom had children in public care.   Their

'feelings of inadequacy and powerlessness in relation to both their
children and the public authorities were clearly evident' but by the
end of the meetings the authors were able to note 'the increasing
confidence of group members to make constructive criticism and suggestion for the formation and amendment of the department's policies
concerning natural parents'.   This setting up of a multi-couple
group with common problems vis-a-vis their environment could obviously be repeated on a wide scale, yet such methods remain comparatively rare.   Again, it is worth noting that most of the work
with multi-family and multi-couple groups has been directed towards
attacking intra-familial pathology, rather than the difficulties
which may obtain between a group of families and a part of the wider
community (Framo, 1973; Laqueur, 1972).   Whilst this method
appears to give considerable help to families, presumably those
whose environments are relatively benign, there seems no reason why
a shared understanding of, and action in respect of, common environmental problems could not be an appropriate focus too.

The other major development in creating new power systems is in
the work of the network therapists.   I regard these as new because
although a system is present before intervention, it is there in a
very fragmented form and becomes potent and supportive only after
intervention.   Attneave (1969) has described the aim of network
therapy as 'mobilizing the family, relatives and friends into a
social force that counteracts the depersonalizing trend in contemporary life ...'.   The moving account of the session described by
Attneave and Speck (1973) leaves no doubt about the method's ability
to counteract this trend.   There are as yet few people with the
necessary skills to work in this way but it seems likely that their
results will encourage others to try.

By now some family therapists reading this will perhaps have concluded that they are being asked to do everything.   They may wonder
whether there is not already an appropriate differentiation of functions in approaches to social problems, with some members of the
helping professions aiming at intra-personal change, some at interpersonal change, some at the development of material support and
some at changes within communities.   I think they would be right in
seeing the importance of appropriate boundaries between different
tasks; and perhaps the essential distinction to make is between the
inevitable limits on skills and functions on the one hand, and the
possibility of a much more wide-ranging perspective on human problems on the other.   Boundaries can be defined as either barriers or
as links.

I want to end this chapter by rounding out two views of the ther-
apist/family relationship.   Minuchin (1972) has described how, when
the therapist leaves the family, the family is left with her ghost.
Haley (1975) has noted the surprise of the family therapist upon
discovering that she is part of the system she is observing.   It
logically follows from these analogies that the therapist must be
left with the ghost of the family; and eventually, for most of us,
be left with the ghosts of many families, some of which experienced
interpersonal pain but many of which experienced social stigmatization and material deprivation.   And, whilst it is a surprise to
find that one is part of the family system one is working with, it
may come as an even greater surprise to discover that one was always
a part, however distant of that family's environment.

REFERENCES

ACKERMAN, N. (1970), Family psychotherapy today, 'Family Process', vol. 9, pp. 123-6.
ACKERMAN, N. (1971), Commentary on Schatzman's paper, 'Family Process', vol. 10, p. 212.
APONTE, H. (1976), The family-school interview: an eco-structural approach, 'Family Process', vol. 15, pp. 303-12.
ATTNEAVE, C. (1969), Therapy in tribal settings and urban network intervention, 'Family Process', vol. 8, pp. 192-210.
AUERSWALD, E. (1971), Families, change and the ecological perspective, 'Family Process', vol. 10, pp. 263-80.
BITESKY, R. (1973), The influence of political power in determining the theoretical development of social work, 'Journal of Social Policy', vol. 2, pp. 119-30.
CARTER, I. and ANDERSON, R. (1974), 'Human Behaviour in the Social Environment', Aldine, Chicago.
CULBERT, S.A. and RENSHAW, J.R. (1972), Coping with the stresses of travel as an opportunity for improving the quality of work and family life, 'Family Process', vol. 11, pp. 312-37.
DAVIE, R., BUTLER, N. and GOLDSTEIN, H. (1972), 'From Birth to Seven', Longman, London.
DENNIS, N., HENRIQUES, F. and SLAUGHTER, C. (1969), 'Coal is our Life', 2nd edn, Tavistock, London, p. 229.
ERICKSON, G., RACHLIS, R. and TOBIN, M. (1974), Combined family and service network intervention, 'Social Worker' (Canada), no. 41, pp. 276-83.
FERRI, E. (1976), Growing up in a one-parent family, 'Concern', no. 20, p. 10.
FLETCHER, R. (1966), 'The Family and Marriage in Britain', Penguin, Harmondsworth, p. 136.
FORDER, A. (1976), Social work and system theory, 'British Journal of Social Work', vol. 6, pp. 23-42.
FRAMO, J.L. (1973), Marriage therapy in a couples' group, in D. Bloch (1973), 'Techniques of Family Psychotherapy: A Primer', Grune & Stratton, New York.
FRAMO, J.L. (1975), Personal reflections of a family therapist, 'Journal of Marriage and Family Counselling', vol. 1, pp. 15-28.
FRANCES, A. and GALE, L. (1973), Family structure and treatment in the military, 'Family Process', vol. 12, pp. 171-8.
GARRISON, J. (1974), Network techniques: case studies in the screening-linking-planning conference method, 'Family Process', vol. 13, pp. 337-53.
GIBBS, J. and THORPE, R. (1975), The natural parent group, 'Social Work Today', vol. 6, pp. 386-9.
GLASTONBURY, B., BURDETT, M. and AUSTIN, R. (1972), Community perceptions and the personal social services, 'Policy and Politics', vol. 1, pp. 191-211.
GOULDNER, A. (1975), Reciprocity and autonomy in functional theory, in A. Gouldner (1975), 'For Sociology', Penguin, Harmondsworth.
HALEY, J. (1973), 'Uncommon Therapy', W.W. Norton, New York.
HALEY, J. (1975), Why a mental health clinic should avoid family therapy, 'Journal of Marriage and Family Counselling', vol. 1, pp. 3-13.

HMSO (1948), Criminal Justice Act 1948, sec. 6(1), Her Majesty's Stationery Office, London.

HMSO (1959), Mental Health Act 1959, sec. 26(1), Her Majesty's Stationery Office, London.

HOFFMAN, L. and LONG, L. (1969), A systems dilemma, 'Family Process', vol. 8, pp. 211-35.

JANCHILL, M.P. (1969), Systems concepts in casework theory and practice, 'Social Casework', vol. 50, pp. 74-82.

JOHNSON, T.J. (1972), 'Professions and Power', Macmillan, London, p. 45.

LAQUEUR, H.P. (1973), Multiple family therapy: questions and answers, in D. Bloch (1973), 'Techniques of Family Psychotherapy: A Primer', Grune & Stratton, New York.

LEMERT, E. (1962), Paranoia and the dynamics of exclusion, 'Sociometry', no. 25, pp. 2-20.

LIPMAN-BLUMEN, J. (1975), A crisis framework applied to macro-sociological family changes: marriage, divorce and occupational trends associated with World War II, 'Journal of Marriage and the Family', vol. 37, pp. 889-902.

MILLER, J.G. (1965), Living systems: basic concepts, 'Behavioural Science', no. 10, p. 193.

MINUCHIN, S. (1972), Structural family therapy, in G. Caplan (1972), 'American Handbook of Psychiatry', Basic Books, New York.

MINUCHIN, S., MONTALVO, B., GUERNEY, B. Jr, ROSMAN, B. and SCHUMER, F. (1967), 'Families of the Slums', Basic Books, New York.

MULLEN, E. and DUMPSON, J. (1972), Concluding note, in E. Mullen, J. Dumpson and Associates (1972), 'Evaluation of Social Intervention', Jossey-Bass, San Francisco, p. 252.

NATIONAL ADVISORY COMMISSION ON CIVIL DISORDER (1968), Unemployment, family structure and social disorganization, in 'Report of the National Advisory Commission on Civil Disorder', Bantam Books, New York.

NURSTEN, J., POTTINGER, J. and ANDERSON, M. (1972), 'Social Workers and Their Clients', Research Publication Services, London.

PEARSON, G. (1975), 'The Deviant Imagination', Macmillan, London.

PERLMAN, H.H. (1972), Once more, with feeling, in E. Mullen, J. Dumpson and Associates (1972), 'Evaluation of Social Intervention', Jossey-Bass, San Francisco.

PINCUS, A. and MINAHAN, A. (1973), 'Social Work Practice: Model and Method', E.E. Peacock, Itasca, Illinois.

PITTMAN, F. (1973), Managing acute psychiatric emergencies: defining the family crisis, in D. Bloch (1973), 'Techniques of Family Psychotherapy: A Primer', Grune & Stratton, New York.

SAINSBURY, E. (1975), 'Social Work With Families', Routledge & Kegan Paul, London; Boston.

SCHATZMAN, M. (1971), Paranoia or persecution: the case of Schreber, 'Family Process', vol. 10, pp. 177-212.

SCOTT, R. (1973), The treatment barrier, 'British Journal of Medical Psychology', no. 46, pp. 44-67.

SILVERSTEIN, O. (1976), Contribution to a study day at Cardiff Family Institute, June 1976.

SIM, M. (1974), 'Guide to Psychiatry', 3rd edn, Churchill Livingstone, Edinburgh.

SKYNNER, A.C.R. (1976), 'One Flesh: Separate Persons', Constable, London.

SLIPP, S., ELLIS, S. and KRESSEL, K. (1974), Factors associated with engagement in family therapy, 'Family Process', vol. 13, pp. 413-27.

SPECK, R. and RUEVENI, U. (1969), Network therapy - a developing concept, 'Family Process', vol. 8, pp. 182-91.

SPECK, R. and ATTNEAVE, C. (1973), 'Family Networks', Pantheon, New York.

SUNLEY, R. (1970), Family advocacy: from case to cause, 'Social Casework', vol. 51, pp. 347-57.

TUNSTALL, J. (1962), 'The Fishermen', MacGibbon & Kee, London, p. 164.

WATZLAWICK, P., WEAKLAND, J. and FISCH, R. (1974), 'Change: Principles of Problem Formation and Problem Resolution', W.W. Norton, New York, pp. 92-108.

WEDGE, P. and PROSSER, H. (1973), 'Born to Fail?', Arrow Books, London.

WELLS, A.R., DILKES, T.A. and TRIVELLI, N. (1972), The results of family therapy: a critical review of the literature, 'Family Process', vol. 11, pp. 197-8.

WHITACKER, C. (1972), A longitudinal view of therapy styles where n = 1, 'Family Process', vol. 11, pp. 13-15.

WILSON, H. (1974), Parenting in poverty, 'British Journal of Social Work', vol. 4, p. 241.

WOOTON, B. (1959), 'Social Science and Social Pathology', Allen & Unwin, London, p. 283.

ZUK, G. (1972), 'Family Therapy: A Triadic Based Approach', Behavioural Publications, New York, pp. 59-61.

Chapter 3

INFANT NEEDS AND ANGRY RESPONSES
A look at violence in the family

Gill Gorell-Barnes

Aggression is one of the instinctual drives basic to man as one
species of animal. It has a positive developmental function and it
is also used to defend aspects of life held vital to the preservation of the species or the self. In family life the destructive
potential of the aggressive drive, and the way aggression is channelled within the family, is largely determined by the conscious
process of the older family members. In all families, however,
there are moments when these conscious processes - and the ideal intentions of the adult members - slip or are provoked; and adults
experience their more primitive feeling and display more childish
behaviour than they themselves consciously approve. These moments
are the subject-matter of this chapter.

Intra-familial violence is a recurring feature of the family
system in Western society, despite the cultural commitment to familial non-violence. Reviews of empirical evidence and relevant
theory in the United States (Goode, 1971; Steinmetz and Straus,
1974) and smaller scale but telling work in this country (Newsom and
Newsom, 1976) leave no doubt that violence is a common, rather than
a rare feature of family interaction. Recent research has elucida-
ted structural features of family life that are correlated with disturbance in children; and Rutter and his colleagues (Rutter, 1975;
Rutter et al., 1975; Yule et al., 1974; Rutter and Madge, 1976)
have gone further in linking family features with social and environmental factors affecting the overall probability of increase in
family disturbance and stress. It is now increasingly recognized
that the expression of feelings through violent behaviour is not
attributable to a single cause and cannot usually be treated in isolation from a host of other social and emotional factors. Bentovim
(1976) links the relationship between the world inside and outside
the family in a developmental approach to the problem of family violence. Carter (1974, 1977, 1978) argues the relationship between
community experience and family experience in a more sociological
approach to violence as it can become institutionalized within a
family. The wide awareness of these interconnections is also expressed in the recent report from the Select Committee of the House
of Commons on Violence in Marriage and Violence in the Family (HMSO,
1974-5, 1976-7).

The forms that the expressions of violence take will of course differ, according to class and culture, as will the stress experienced by each family in its dealings with the outside world.   The knowledge that physical aggression between spouses and between parent and child is more prevalent among those who are poor and less well educated, reminds us that some families have fewer alternative resources of any kind that will help them find ways of redressing a balance that has gone wrong.   They also have fewer alternative sources of pleasure, and the experience of continued living, with an awareness of their limited prestige and power in relation to many aspects of the world outside the family, causes greater frustration and bitterness when things go wrong within it.   As therapists, knowledge of this kind must also remind us of the continued task of developing a range of interventions that make sense in terms of our clients' needs.

THE DAILY STRUGGLE

In this chapter I am concerned with small daily aspects of behaviour in family life.   These are the experiences that are generated by living closely and intimately with a number of people at different developmental stages, who have different ideas about approaching every daily task with which family members are confronted.   Family life is marked by the frequency and intensity with which very intimate and personal exchanges take place around small and relatively uninteresting events like finding a pair of matching socks;   which parts of the body should be cleaned, and who should put the rubbish out at night.   It is these repeated experiences of the struggle for control, over objects, over others, and over oneself, that form the basic material of our work with families.   If we concentrate on this, on the formation and preservation of a sense of control of self in daily interaction with others, we can see that the psychological theories informing external behaviour and management, and those concerned with internal feeling and emotional management, come together and can more frequently be used to the benefit of families seeking help if they are used in conjunction with, rather than separately from, one another.

The daily exchanges of family life that provide the initial and repeated experience of intimacy for children and on which they are likely to model their own parenting behaviour in future years (Rutter, 1975) also contain daily and repeated experiences of violence in greater and lesser degrees.   The Newsoms' studies of parents and children in Nottingham (1963, 1968, 1976) give us many vivid anecdotes illustrating aggression between children and parents in normal families, in which the parents themselves see the lapse into violence as a regrettable fall from the standards they expect of themselves, but justify it as an essential part of socializing a child.

These lapses occur for many reasons in all families where parents find a child refusing to accept standards and limits that they regard as desirable or essential.   What is variable is the degree to which parents are prepared to negotiate and to forgo their own viewpoint in order to look afresh at the controversy in terms that

include the child's point of view.   For some parents, any challenge
by a child is felt as a very central threat to their own identity as
an adult and as a person with knowledge and authority;   and the
vital issue becomes not a fair resolution of the discussion in hand,
but the maintenance of the balance of power within the family.
Where a child is experienced as looming too large in his bid to run
things his own way or to impose his own sense of what is right,
parents may become intent on restoring their own essential image of
themselves which is felt to be under threat.   The quickest route to
this goal is a show of strength.

CARVING UP THE TERRITORY

In encounters between family members, issues of personal space and
defensive boundaries are paramount.   In animals territory is an
issue to be fought through to victory or death (Lorenz, 1966;
Ardrey, 1967).   In family life death, luckily, is rarely the outcome of such struggles although the high incidence of murder between
family members (accounting, for example, for one third of all mur-
ders in New York City in one year) has been well documented (Palmer,
1972;   Bard, 1971).
     In adults, and especially between spouses, confrontations about
personal territory play a crucial part in daily relationship.   The
negotiations around preserving these vital and subjectively defined
images of self are often veiled, although they are beginning to be
more honestly and openly discussed in the women's pages of news-
papers and magazines.   In time, such open discussion might provide
some more helpful stereotype of the male/female relationship and the
fights involved in marriage than that presented in popular televi-
sion.   For example, in an episode of 'Kojak' viewers were tempted
to condone one of their clean-limbed cops turning crooked, because
of his wish to buy his newly wed nubile wife a fur coat and a house
in a desirable suburb - a plan she explicitly rewards with instant
sex and the promise of 'a family'.   A neat insertion for potential
family therapists among the viewing public was the information that
the 'hero's' father had wanted to do the same for his mother (although he had never managed the fur coat), thus suggesting first,
that the cop could not help his actions because he was already conditioned, or at least pre-programmed, by his family to behave in
this way;   second, that it made it all right, because sons should do
at least as much if not more than their fathers did in their time;
and third, that the odds are especially stacked against cultural
minorities in New York City (of which the cop was one) for exploring
other forms of giving and receiving within a marital and sexual relationship.   A popular example such as this is valuable in counter-
acting the idea that 'bargaining' is only a feature of pathological
marriages.
     Arguments over possessions and entitlements in family life can
become life and death struggles about each person's experience and
display of their own personal identity.   Having the right to pos-
sessions and gifts is one way for a wife to define or mark out her
own estimated value to herself and to her husband.   If she feels
'naked' unclothed and equates this with being unloved rather than

loved, her boundaries and her sense of herself as a person of worth
are threatened.   One way in which popular myth often creates a
stereotype at the expense of the truth is in imagining that this
wish for recognition and care within the family circle is chiefly
the prerogative of women, while men 'traditionally' can get their
needs for recognition met in the world outside.   Families are char-
acterized by their varying capacity to cope with regressive needs,
as well as with developmental ones, and the expression of the basic
infant needs of each member will all become an issue at some time
(although hopefully not all at the same time).   The everyday recognition of these is sought through daily boundaries that mark out
each person's individual life-space.   The ways in which each person's wish not to be intruded upon by other family members are known
and marked.   These vary from family to family, but are there and
are respected to some extent within all families.   Daddy likes the
chair with the high back, the brown mug (known to the children as
Daddy's special mug) and the chunky marmalade, and hates having his
razor used by the women in the house.   Susan likes to be last in
the bathroom so that she will not be teased or bullied about how
much time she takes; will not wear her school shoes because she
thinks they are 'surgical' and hates having her records borrowed
without being asked.   John is not happy without his string, his
five-bladed penknife and an acknowledgment that Sunday afternoon is
always to be spent at the cycling club; and Sarah refuses to wear
her shoes at all (partly misunderstanding her sister Susan's pro-
test), has to have the tall stool, pour out her own cornflakes, milk
and sugar and have instant access to her 'sucky' whenever crossed in
battle.   Such boundaries, if respected, are vital steps to children's achieving successful autonomy within the family group.   What
is confusing for the group is that the boundaries are not static but
are continually open for redefinition and renegotiation, so that
some time has to be spent at regular intervals checking out how and
where things have changed, for different members of the family.

INVADING THE BOUNDARIES

Where a bid for conformity to others or for individual freedom from
others cuts across another's private space, the degree to which the
resulting argument can be modulated will relate to the degree of
threat felt by the person who believes their private space is either
not being acknowledged as of enough importance (record-listening
time is as important as homework time or washing-up time) or where
they feel it is being actively invaded.   (Mother's make-up is being
used and left messed up; Dad's clean car has been climbed all over;
the contents of John's pockets have been thrown away when his trou-
sers were washed, rather than left on the table in his room;
Sarah's latest drawing was just used to light Mum's cigarette from
the stove.)   Between small children, invasions, sorties and forays
occur all the time and retaliatory moves are expected as part of the
permitted exploration of boundaries.   Whether a less forgivable or
less manageable violence and invasion is feared (as in the child who
cringes at the adult approach) will relate to the previous experience of the child and will condition both his freedom to explore and

stake out new ground, and his ferocity in self-defence when in-
fringements occur on his own territory.

Most parents have enough strength to survive daily the boundary
breaking of exploring infants; the infinite range of risk that
children of different ages bring to light and the many attacks upon
themselves that such exploration and risk-taking involve.   But each
person will have a limit that is conditioned by his own history and
experience.   In some families the history of violence is sufficiently open and prolonged for any professional involved to understand the reasons that lie behind apparently exaggerated reactions
to minor interchanges, where small incidents appear to be experienced as major violations.   For example, Flynn had repeatedly witnessed his father denigrate and strike his mother for her disorganization.   When small he was very close to his mother, but, after
father left home and as he grew towards adolescence, he increasingly
received the reproaches and criticism that had in former days been
directed towards his father.   He found very slight reproaches very
difficult to bear and responded in the fiercest terms calling his
mother a 'bitch' and a 'slut'.   In the second interview, recounting
a violent exchange over whether he could mend his bike in the front
hall, he had picked up a chair to hit her.   He talked of his fear
of 'smashing' his mother one day.

The experience or in-built family knowledge of previous catas-
trophies, also affects the capacity to cope with minor incidents.
Mrs N rang the Social Services Department in an hysterical state,
demanding the instant removal of her foster child because she had
cut him with a knife while peeling vegetables.   Her sister, the
mother of this boy, was a prostitute and had been in prison for the
manslaughter of her other infant at under a year (according to one
account by injuring him with a spoon).   Mrs N had only been able to
maintain the fostering situation by divorcing herself completely
from her sister and all she stood for in terms of their joint childhood in which they had both been sexually exploited and experienced
some physical violence.   The reminder of violence and damage represented in the knife wound which she had perpetrated, punctured her
own self-image as the coping one of the family and did, in fact,
render her incapable of caring for her nephew, as it released a
stream of reminiscence and fear of violence that she had previously
held at bay.

EXPLORATION AND CHALLENGE

Adults expect attack from children and children expect attack from
adults.   The child's need to explore, to reach out and make his
own sense of things, can be seen from very early days as an attack
by anxious parents; and children, knowing their own parents, soon
learn at what point to expect retribution.   With experience, they
may learn to take avoiding action at the right moment, so that a
mother can praise her child for his forethought in warning her,
rather than clamp down on him in a rage for some destructive event
that has taken place.   Two-year-old cries of 'there's going to be a
flood' alerts a mother to the sequence of behaviour that has been
taking place in the bathroom in the unusually quiet five minutes

preceding the shouts, and if correctly timed means she can praise
him for calling her before the water reaches the top of the basin
rather than shouting at him for putting the plug in and turning both
taps full on.   Although these actions may have contained many intentions other than flooding her bathroom, the sight of water pour-
ing under the door onto the hall carpet is likely to obliterate the
adult desire to understand these if she has already framed the event
as an intended attack on her own rules.   A child on his own may
continue on a destructive course in the teeth of all the evidence
about his eventual defeat or self-injury because his absorption in
the intention and performance of what he is doing is more powerful
than his concern about others at that point.   If there is more than
one child involved a more conscious setting up of an alternative set
of desirable norms may swiftly be reinforced, the children's subsystem having more immediate power, and usually providing its members with more immediate reward and reinforcement, than the adult
one.   Sometimes adults collude in this.   Many adults have turned a
blind eye at six o'clock on a Sunday morning as the raiding party
creeps downstairs towards the biscuit tin, but when the same act is
performed just before Sunday lunch it may invite wrath.   Whether
issues of exploration, experiment and plain rule-breaking are seen
as attacks depends on both time and context.   A private challenge
may be more leniently dealt with than a public one.   Something
spilt or broken in the best room provokes greater anger in a parent
who tries to preserve a space or good family front as a representation of the coping aspect of themselves which is shown to visitors,
than something spilt or broken in the kitchen, a family room where
more 'mess' is permitted.   The fierceness of the retribution may
alternatively be tempered by the presence of other people.   Many a
mother tempted to hit her child in the supermarket has been forestalled by his display of noisy tears and self-conscious cries of
'don't hit me, Mummy'.   The most frightening kind of family violence is perhaps that which takes place between two people without
witnesses (or between two adults where the only witness is a child)
in which the event nominally under debate is in fact serving as a
vehicle for quite other feelings.

SECOND-LEVEL VIOLENCE

In many of the briefly violent exchanges between parents and children another area of personal territory is invaded of which the individual is not consciously aware.   It is expressed in such ordinary phrases as 'he gets in my hair' or 'she gets under my skin'.
It means that the current piece of intrusive behaviour has linked
into a prior set of irritations or annoyance which the parents themselves sometimes cannot define, but which they know instinctively
makes them on edge.
   Sometimes a small trigger can set off a response that contains
violence quite disproportionate to the offence, and a sudden out-
burst of rage or accumulation of pent-up feelings will occur.   This
can happen between any two people in relation to a particular recurrent situation (for example, potty training) or it can happen as
part of a recurrent family tableau.   A favourite tableau, for

example, is Sunday lunch, traditionally an inter-generational gath-
ering, or Christmas.   Others can be family outings or family holiday planning meetings.   The exploding member may attribute his rage
to some abstract entity like a 'tough day at work', or to a bad
week, or to a difficult year;   but sometimes there is no reason he
can give to account for what is happening.   It usually marks the
stage where a 'second level' of anger begins, which is related not
to the current family situation but to previous situations where the
individual has felt under attack and has not been able to preserve
his sense of self sufficiently to respond and counter-attack appropriately so that the row could be finished at the time and the associated strong feeling worked through and completed.

A simple example might go as follows:
Two-year-old: 'You've got a bleed.'
Mother: (furious silence)
Two-year-old: 'Where does it come from?'
Mother: (stonily) 'My finger.'
Two-year-old: 'How did you do it?'
Mother: 'Cutting your bloody orange' (assignment of blame).
Two-year-old: 'No you didn't, you did it cutting your toast'
(refusal to accept blame or attribution of guilt).
Argument can now go either way:
Option A Mother: (laughs ...) 'I know it's not your fault I cut
myself, don't worry.'
Option B Mother: 'I don't know why you can't have cornflakes
like everyone else instead of making me cut an orange and cut
myself' (attribution to child of wish to injure parent).
'Just like your father and his bloody coffee every morning when
we all have tea' (wish to enlarge scale of battle and provoke
spouse).
Father: (reading paper) 'What's that?'
Mother: (shouts) 'I've cut my finger and you don't even care.'
Two-year-old and four-year-old together: 'Don't shout at poor
Daddy.'
Mother: 'Nobody cares if I hurt myself, you all gang up on me.'

In this extract, the move from simple discussion about an event
(a cut finger) has moved into the full scale paranoia of family war-
fare.   If the second option of dealing with anger (i.e. enlargement
rather than closure) chosen by mother is the preferred mode the
parents adopt, the children will grow up with a complex and confused
experience of blame, guilt and unresolved anger in relation to many
everyday experiences in which they feel themselves accused without
clearly understanding the basis for their guilt.   A backlog of unresolved anger and guilt exists in the family pool and is available
to be brought in when triggered by any fresh stimulus.   The confusion will probably be held in each member, but be experienced and
acted out differently.   For example, Julia originally presented for
help suffering from acute phobic anxiety which prevented her from
leaving the house.   In the course of work with her the symptomatology of other family members was brought to the sessions in turn.
The primary problem she described was the murderous fighting between
her parents, which only she, the youngest child, could prevent.
Her parents related this problem back to an absence of parents in
their families of origin with a multiplicity of competing siblings

on one side of the family (thirteen in all) and a drunken father and
a mad brother on the other.   Father had regular psychosomatic
attacks that kept him off work for long periods.   Mother had mi-
graines and nervous skin conditions and worked as a cleaner although
she had trained as a nurse.   Subsequently, Julia's sister suffered
from depression (and made two suicide attempts) and her brother
wrote long goon-like scripts about mad and violent families which he
sent to therapy sessions via Julia, although he would never come
himself.

The unifying factor for the family in Julia's early adolescence
was her 'illness' which continually prevented the parents from
splitting up and the brother and sister from leaving home.   Julia
grew more independent over time, attended school, passed her 'O'
levels and held down a job, finally differentiating herself from her
parents to the extent that she said she was going to leave home and
share a flat with a friend.   This precipitated many parental scenes
of recrimination and reproach about her ingratitude in thus 'attacking' the family who had stuck together so long 'for her sake'.   She
presented clinically with fears that the world was drying up and
would split apart.   Some brief focal work on the relationship between family pressures, her own legacy of guilt and her current
anxieties relieved her fears and she made longer term, more realistic plans to work her way out of the family, and to preserve herself.

THE EXPERIENCE OF ATTACK

The concept of the attack which is internally anticipated is one
familiar in psychoanalytic theory.   Winnicott (1971), who as a
paediatrician and a psychoanalyst has always bridged theories relating to behavioural interaction with those relating to internal
(psychic) functioning, wrote brilliantly and simply on babies learning to observe the parental mood and adjust their own behaviour accordingly.   'Some babies, tantalized by this type of relative maternal failure, study the variable maternal visage in an attempt to
predict the mother's mood, just exactly as we all study the weather.
The baby quickly learns to make a forecast: "Just now it is safe to
forget the mother's mood and to be spontaneous, but any minute the
mother's face will become fixed or her mood will dominate, and my
own personal needs must then be withdrawn otherwise my central self
may suffer insult"' (p. 113).

While it is not possible to validate or invalidate psychoanalytic
hypotheses about early infant experience, the work of those observing infants in various controlled settings (Richards, 1975;   Richards and Bernal, 1974;   Schaffer, 1971) lends scientific respecta-
bility to the idea that children from very early on are capable of
responding to minute changes of mood as reflected in the behaviour
of those around them and are correspondingly influenced in their own
response.   Leboyer's film of the way birth itself is handled,
'Birth without violence' attempts to show that the way the infant
reacts and relates to its mother straight after birth is affected by
the birth process itself.   Melanie Klein's profoundly influential
work on the infant's experience of persecution by others relied pri-

marily on the belief that the instinctual drives contained by each
infant were too much for him to bear alone, so that all infants had
no option but to discharge their impulses onto those who were responsible for their daily care.   For example, where the baby felt
persecuted by its own hunger, the psychic mechanism for dealing with
this would be to see the mother (or care giver) as the persecuting
agent, for witholding the food that would relieve the tension in the
infant.   The responsibility for the pain - the state of hunger - is
thereby located in others and divorced from the baby.   The way
these others handle the infant's feelings of rage (manifested for
example by crying, screaming, kicking, biting or ultimately refusing
the proferred nipple or bottle) and demonstrate their preparedness
to take responsibility for the rage and the pain in their handling
of the infant, affects the infant's subsequent capacity to cope with
stress.   The tenuous interplay between a caregiver and an infant
under stress shows how crucial a variable responsive handling is, in
the infants' subsequent behaviour.   A bottle offered in a way that
makes it a desirable object to suck or hold, is clearly experienced
over time quite differently from a bottle that is elusive, because
it is propped up and continually slips over or from one that is positively attacking in the way it is shoved into the mouth.   Infants
that are abused in other ways also often have laceration marks
around their mouths from bottles too forcibly injected.

Sometimes parents do not have the energy or the capacity to meet
children's primitively expressed needs well enough for the child to
develop a sense of trust in others.   Consequently, subsequent behaviours - the development of self-containment, the capacity to control more violent expression of feeling in the belief that needs
will be met before they become too painful, do not develop readily.
Rather than contenting themselves with self-satisfying interim
arrangements like sucking thumbs or blankets, babies who do not have
much faith in those around them, make a great deal of fuss to ensure
that their presence and their needs are not forgotten.   Unfortunately, in a situation where parents are already finding infants'
demands too great to bear, this extra demonstration provokes further
retaliatory feelings.   Where physical abuse occurs, parents are
often attempting to stop a noise that they perceive as an expression
of need too great for them to manage.

Studies undertaken in Britain (NSPCC, 1969; Oliver and Taylor,
1973; Scott, 1973; Ounsted et al., 1974; Smith and Noble, 1974)
suggest that families where child abuse is most likely to occur are
those where there is least protection from the acting out of violence either from the external structure beyond the boundary of the
family unit or in terms of parental histories and their own interna-
lized resources.   Families are more likely to be younger than average, with unstable or non-existent marital or sexual relationships,
poor work records and of low I Q.   Parents are more likely to be
isolated from their families of origin (by choice) and often as a
result of disturbed parenting in their own youth.   They are also
likely to be isolated from their neighbours and to make poor con-
tacts with professional services.   Additional hazards are a history
of mental disorder or a criminal record.   The infants themselves
are often premature or underweight and have some kind of defect or
need for special care, which means they are more than averagely

demanding - often to parents that have less than average coping ability or external resources to draw on.   The implications of these factors for therapy and management highlight issues relating to intervention touching upon violence in all families;   and particularly to the question of how adequate containment is to be set up to help parents feel that some real recognition of their desperation is being offered, while more ongoing work to enable them to manage ' their feelings better is being done.

While I do not intend to enter into detailed discussion of management where child abuse is the focus of intervention here, perhaps two contra-indications for therapy should be included.   Smith and Noble (1974) defined the factors that contra-indicate therapy and indicated a need for removal as being where the parents have a personality disorder, and a record of one or more crimes and deny that they have battered a child.   Scott (1973) summed up the prototype of the family most at risk of killing a child as being where young, deserted and unhappy women associate with young psychopathic and criminal men and have babies that they do not want.

Parents who 'batter' continue to be discussed in the Press as though their response is beyond the range of normal human experience, but in my view child abuse is more relevantly seen by the professional as an extension of the bad feeling experienced to some degree by most parents, although the way the feeling is responded to is the crucial variable that needs detailed attention and detailed management.   The twenty-four-hour-a-day commitment of a mother without help to a pre-school child is more intense and of greater potential stress than most human relationships.   Where a mother has herself not had an adequate emotional experience of mothering in childhood the normal demands of the young child and his seemingly endless quest for new satisfaction and stimulus can seem like a reproach that she has not done enough, or an attack upon the attempts that have been made to meet his needs.   Either way, it can seem a confirmation of inadequacy, and the child's behaviour is taken as having a negative meaning so that normal dependency is reacted against with anger and with fear.   Rather than viewing parents who act out their violence as being different from others, it is more helpful to view them at the end of the spectrum of normal, but only recently identified, maternal distress.   (Brown et al., 1975; Richman, 1974.)   The envy, love and hate that mothers feel for their children on multiple levels fluctuate between feelings rooted in their own experience of childhood, and their phantasy of what both childhood and parenting should be, and is affected by the current settings available to them to check out their experience with other mothers in a similar position (Gorell-Barnes, 1975).

Parents who have known inadequate care themselves constantly envy their children at levels which are sometimes open and explicit ('Oh look at him in his pram, he'll never have it so good again') and at more dangerous levels of expecting proportionate returns of care from their child.   Many parents are angry and hurt that their children are not grateful for the care they receive.   They weigh the luck of the child against their own experiences, and as parents trying to do better than their own parents, they usually feel the child has all the luck.   Sometimes they expect from the child the unquestioning love a young child expects to get from its parents and

because the child insists on being a child, and making his own
search for individuality and independence (which necessarily involves both challenging and moving away from as well as towards), parents may take this as a rejection.

Where the parents' destructive, as opposed to healthy, anger intrudes is where this move away is experienced as a recreation of an
earlier experience of being rejected by a parent.   In his childhood
phantasy the rejection took place because of something wanting in
him as a child or something actively bad that he did which caused
his parents to send him away or mistreat him.

When children become parents, their own children are initially
seen as a possible fresh start for their own self-esteem.   New
hopes of not being found wanting by others, but of being the good
parents that they never had themselves, are frequently expressed by
all parents, not only those who abuse.   If the child is seen to
'reject' their advances (by crying, refusing to eat, soiling in the
wrong place), this action may be experienced as compounding and confirming already existing inadequacies in the adult, and the child is
a ready target for the expression of feelings of inadequacy and
rage.   The projection of an unloving grandparent onto the child and
the acting out of the angry and retaliatory feelings that had their
origin in the parents' feelings about their own parents occurs in
numerous accounts of child abuse (Court, 1973; Renvoize, 1974).
It is an exaggerated expression of what most parents feel to some
degree but are usually able to repress or to control.   Babies are
the most vulnerable to attack psychologically as well as physically
because they have not yet formed an identity of their own, and are
therefore, for many parents, objects to fill the slots in parental
phantasy.   What can get put into a baby is the sum total of the
parent's experience of never having been adequate to cope or able to
please.

Parents get a second chance for growth through the care they
offer their children.   As they see their children respond to care
and thrive, it makes them as parents feel good inside.   In the
early days of life, the single-minded ruthlessness of babies if
their needs are not met is more than some mothers can manager.
Many forms of infant care reflect this in a minor way, like the use
of pacifiers to stop screaming at all costs; the habit of propping
the baby up with its own bottle rather than holding it while it is
fed; the old style of ignoring the infant in between the regulation
four-hourly feed (preferably leaving it in a pram far enough away
not to be heard) that was advocated in the thirties and is still
current among many middle-class families today.   (It is a privile-
ged form of ignoring babies as it relies on adequate physical
space.)

As children develop, however, other routines develop in which the
infant has a richer variety of input.   The routines that have to be
gone through many times a day, or many times a week, begin to carry
a particular kind of meaning and emotional loading on both sides.
The management of sleeping and waking, of breakfast, of dressing, of
washing, and cleaning teeth and hair brushing, can all be opportunities for the development of exploration, social skills and increasing self-confidence and autonomy, or they can be arenas for bitter
fights about whose autonomy is threatened, who is controlling whom

and who holds the ultimate authority in each situation.   Depending
upon how these daily acts of caregiving are carried out, each member
will feel nourished, cherished, happy in his own skin and as though
he has a valued place in family life; or ignored, abused, trampled
on and as though he has to fight to get some of the existing family
resources.   The management of space was a crucial issue in the
family from which the following extracts are taken.   Mother's inability to manage the caretaking boundaries of her family any longer
related to her own final loss of parental attention and care at the
age of fourteen, when she was considered adult and went out to work.
From then on she received minimal care from her brother and his
girlfriend.   Her mother had died four years earlier and her father
was intermittently at sea and mainly drinking when at home.   She
had looked after her own four children adequately prior to their
adolescence, despite a very erratic relationship with her authoritarian and abusive husband.   He had continually pursued other
women, but had obviously provided a sense of caring in different
ways for each of the children.   Mother left him because of his violence towards her.   He had also been violent to his son for being
too close to his mother.

After father left, the eldest daughter Anthea, aged thirteen, at
that time took on the paternal role of helping mother control the
youngest siblings.   More authority devolved on Anthea when her
mother found a boyfriend, Stuart.   His presence radically upset the
family system at the most profound levels and threatened both individuals and subsystems within a group that had previously been manageable.   His unsuitability as a sexual partner for their mother
and his intrusion into her body and their lives, aroused the children's anger at levels that were both explicit and forbidden.   He
was only five years older than Anthea (being eighteen years younger
than mother) and was seen by the children as a rival and favoured
elder sibling who, in addition to other privileges, got away with
breaking all the sexual taboos.   He was seen by mother as like her
eldest brother when she herself was adolescent and in her attempts
to please Stuart and recapture this earlier period of life when she
described herself as feeling free and not 'hemmed in' by her children's demands, she abnegated much of her real parental role (thus
threatening the children further and increasing their demands on
her).   Stuart was not as clever as the children and, feeling threatened, in his turn tried to assert his right to their mother with
threats towards them.

His presence in the house was experienced as an invasion and a
defilement.   The children refused to eat with him - ostentatiously
washing anything he might have touched, and they expressed their
sense of violation by actively attacking areas in the house where
they thought sexual encounters had taken place, slashing the sofa
and mother's bed and fouling her wardrobe and the drawers where her
clothes were kept.

The family was referred when the violence to the home appeared to
be getting out of control.

In the first extract below, Stuart is seen by mother as attempting to defend her.   Erroll and Diana are trying to get mother to
face the extent to which they feel he has acquired a place in the
house and is attacking them.   Mother is trying to conceal this from

everyone, including herself, either by denying the amount of time
Stuart is there, by saying that it is in the past or by saying she
has to forfeit her right to her home in order to see him.   Arguments about territory are out in the open but each person can only
hear himself.

The extract includes: Mother, Diana 15, Erroll 14, Louise 8,
Social Worker and Family Therapist.

First interview

Erroll: to Mother.   You've left out all the good bits you know.
Family Therapist: What are the good bits?
Erroll: He used to - well he said once - he said something about
hitting Diana because she didn't like him coming to the house
before and then he started to get violent and everything and he
said he was going to lay that strap on her.
Mother: No, no.
Erroll and Diana: (together) Oh yes he did.
Erroll: With a little metal thing on the end.
Mother: No, no, you see what happened was I said to Diana ...
Family Therapist: With a buckle on it?
Erroll: - Yeah - but (to Mother) he told you to attack her and
you approached her and that's when she threw the bottle over
there.
Mother: No, you see you've got to listen to this point - I said
to Diana give me the glass and I'll go and wash it up, but it
went in my eye there and cut me and it was all blood.
Family Therapist: Whose blood - who was holding the glass?
Mother: Diana was - she sort of turned round and there was blood
here and blood there - there was blood all over the place - see,
well I nearly passed out 'cos I had such a shock, and Stuart got
one because he said he'd never seen anything like it before.
Family Therapist: (to Diana) It sounds as though you're sitting
on some very strong feelings there with a far away look on your
face as though you're trying to keep cut off from it all.

Mother: Yes, well you don't like to bring it up again, it's all
in the past.
Family Therapist: Well, I don't know - it's in the present, I
think.   Isn't it because of some very strong feelings that you
have all come here together.   They are not really feelings that
have gone away, have they?
(All say 'mm')
Mother: Well you see they keep calling me all sorts of names ...
we broke for a while - he went away and they still carried on
just the same.
Diana: That's because he was staying at the house.
Mother: He wasn't staying at the house.
Diana and Erroll: (together) Yes he was, he was staying at the
house, don't tell lies - once he stayed for a whole week.
Mother: Not a whole week.
Diana and Erroll: (accusing) Yes he did
                                         a whole week

                              don't tell lies
                              he did stay a whole week
                              he stayed a whole week
                              a whole week
                              don't tell me because I know it's
                              true

Mother: He came to see me in the days and went home in the
evenings.
Diana and Erroll: Don't tell lies he was there all the time, he
was, he was there all the time.
Mother: No he was not.   He does not stop in my place.
Diana: Yes he does, a week ago he said 'well shall I stay then
or shall I go', just to provoke us, to upset us.
Mother: Well, I don't let him stay in my home, right?   And I
can't right? because I've got children right?
Diana: Oh shut up.
Mother: I don't stop in my own home - I'm forced to go out of my
home, because of you, right?

In Extract two mother describes how things had changed.   At one
point in the interview she put this down to the children's age, although later on in the second interview she also spoke of the change
as related to Stuart's presence in the home.   Both these factors
were clearly crucial in the eruption and management of the violence.

Extract two

Mother: Well they were all right at first and they're all right
sometimes as long as you do what they want - you understand - I
mean they can be - Anthea was very happy.   She used to go to
work and Diana, I don't know - had her little ways of going on
and well, Erroll, he was always more difficult because of course
he's a boy and he's difficult to control because he's a boy.
Family Therapist: Everybody talks as though things were all
right once and then things started to go wrong.
Mother: As they grew older, yes, as they get bigger.
The way mother had increasingly involved Anthea in an attempt to
control the anger expressed by the two middle children, without recognizing the effect this was having on Anthea, led to Anthea's self-
admission to a mental hospital in the week prior to the first interview.   The two extracts that follow show the way Anthea had to move
between being her mother's ally in order to get any personal recognition at home and her counter-wish to challenge and attack mother
for her behaviour and for putting Stuart so centrally in her life to
the exclusion of the children and any real recognition of their
needs for love and care.   Mother's pitiless use of Anthea is demonstrated by the way she cannot empathize or enter into her feelings,
as a separate person at all.   Half way through Extract Three Anthea
moves from any attempt at trying to establish her own feelings, into
a coalition with mother against the middle two children and finds
her own familiar family identity in attacking them for attacking (in
very specific ways) their mother's space.   Louise (8) joins in the
fight to defend her middle brother and sister and is attacked in

turn.   Anthea ends by reassuring her mother that the preceding dis-
integrative sequence has not been her fault at all.

Extract three

(Extract includes Anthea 16, Diana 15, Erroll 14, Louise 8, Social
Worker and Family Therapist)

> Social Worker: Anthea has understood how everyone had felt -
> she's sometimes tried to control them and sometimes tried to keep
> the bad feelings at home - who has Anthea had to support her?
> Mother: Well Anthea could talk to me, 'cos I'm her mother.   A
> sort of mother and daughter affair.
> Social Worker: I think we should ask Anthea if that's how she
> sees talking with you, or whether she sees it as giving you sup-
> port.
> Mother: Well she can lead her own life, Anthea.   Last year she
> was going to work.   She was going here and there and that was
> all right - but you see I did speak to her about these two and
> how I can't control them - you see I can't - when they pick some-
> thing up and hit me with it, what am I to do?
> Diana: (interrupts) that's Erroll you're talking about.   Erroll
> Erroll, say you're talking about, Erroll - talking about him.
> Mother: (failing to get the point) Yes.
> Family Therapist: So you said to Anthea you couldn't control
> them, did you - and you hoped in some way that she might help
> you?
> Mother: (backtracking) I know that she couldn't help me, in what
> way could she help me?   I've got a home to keep and I've got a
> boy - they keep doing damage, breaking things (Anthea gets up and
> wanders around), tearing things.   When I tell them they tell me
> I'm mad;   I'm imagining things - they're telling me I'm mad....
> Are they trying to send me mad or what? (rising desperation)
> Family Therapist: Is that what you think?
> Mother: Yes, that's what I think ... so that when I go out and
> see somebody or I'm quite happy, they go upsetting me.   I
> couldn't stop in me own house, I had to go out and that's why
> they were left and then they moaned because they were left ...
> because I got a load of abuse from them I left them.   They gave
> me a terrible time.   They cut up my clothes with scissors -
> right....   There's filth in my wardrobe.
> Diana: (interrupts fiercely) That's Erroll.
> Mother: Yes well they did ... all these nasty things.
> Erroll: (interrupts desperately) Not me, I never done that,
> you're blaming me for things I didn't do.
> Anthea: You cut her dress up.
> Erroll: No, I didn't, I never even touched it.
> Anthea: (rising intonation) You cut that beautiful dress up, yes
> you did, you cut it up, it was beautiful - you did, don't deny
> it, it's the truth, you cut it up, it was beautiful, it came from
> a jumble sale, it was a beautiful dress and you cut it up the
> pair of you (pointing finger).
> Diana: He (pointing) cut it up, I didn't.

Anthea: Well at least you admit it now, don't you.
Diana: Yes.
Anthea: (sarcastically) About time you did face up to facts,
dear.
Diana: Oh shut up.   You're 'dear' and all.
Mother: (joining incantation) Yes that's what you did, that's
what you did between the two of you.
Anthea: Admit, admit that's what you did - admit the person you
are, admit, admit.
Diana: (rising) Oh shut up you stupid brat (walks out into next
room).
Anthea: (to Erroll) Admit, you admit (throws water at him).
Erroll: (hurls book at her, social worker restraining).
Erroll: I'll kick your head in, you bitch.
Mother: They were threatening me between the two of them: that
they'd get their father to beat me up.
Louise: (to mother) Oh shut up, you cow.
Anthea: Louise, Louise.
Louise: (to mother) Oh shut up.
Mother: they took me clothes and silk dress and threw it down
the stairs, they grabbed me purse and threw it all down - I had a
terrible time with the two of them ... (faded).   And I couldn't
even enter the door because of the two of them.
Louise: That's a lie, that's another lie.
(Anthea throws water at her)
Louise: F... off you f...... bitch, f... off.
Family Therapist: Is this what you have to do at home, Anthea,
move in to protect your mother?
Mother: Maybe I shouldn't have said those things.
Anthea: (faintly) No, it's all right, Mum, it's not your fault.
In Extract four, Anthea abandons her coalition with mother and
takes up the position previously held by Diana and Erroll.   She engages her mother in a long attempt to recognize responsibility for
her own life and, in a desperate struggle to get her to take back
the negative projections by which all the children felt they were
attacked and dominated, she tries to get mother to own her own identity by starting with her name.

Extract four

(Extract includes Anthea, Mother, Family Therapist)

Family Therapist: You feel the children have got bigger than
you?
Mother: Yes.   When they were younger I could hold them to me
but I can't now because they've got different ways of thinking,
different ways of going on.
Family Therapist: Well, maybe we're going to have to find some
way of helping you to feel you've got a role, that you're still
important to the family.
Anthea: (to mother) Look at yourself, speak for yourself for a
change.
Family Therapist: Anthea very much wants you to get some help
in your own right.

Mother: Yes, but ....
Anthea: Look at yourself - you're not helping yourself, you're moaning about everyone else - think of yourself for a change. Stuart's no good for you - he can't help you - you've got to help yourself.
Mother: Yes, all right, but what can I ...?
Anthea: Say something about yourself - what can you say about yourself - find something - what is your name, let's start with that, what is your name.
Mother: That's irrelevant.
Anthea: No, it is not irrelevant, it is a highly important issue - what is your name?
Mother: (remonstrating) Anthea.
Anthea: It's not Anthea, what is your name?
Family Therapist: (softly) Will you answer her?
Mother: Moira - right ....

In the final extract which is three interviews later, mother is talking with her two youngest children about her own experience at Erroll's age. In the dialogue that has been established, mother and son are trying to exchange their different perspectives.

Extract five

(Includes Mother, Erroll, Louise, Social Worker, Family Therapist)

Mother: Well I was very much on my feet and I didn't get upset about all these things that they get upset about - I went to work.
Erroll: Well it was different wasn't it: your mum didn't have another bloke, did she?
Family Therapist: She didn't have a mum.
Mother: Well, you know, I was living with my brother's girl-friend.   I had my dad but I didn't often see him.
Family Therapist: I think, Erroll, you are trying to say there are things you experience that she doesn't understand.
Erroll: But she had the countryside and everything - we have all streets and everything - it's different - they could go out and forget things - we don't have anything like that.
Mother: But when we were teenagers, we couldn't expect anything of anybody because we had to work - we couldn't go off into cor-ners and cry and have tempers, because we couldn't get our own way - we had to work because we had to live and we couldn't live if we didn't go to work.
Family Therapist: (confirming) There was nobody to cry on.
Mother: No, that's what I mean I'm telling them.   It's all very well, I want this, I want that.   What if they had nobody?   What would they do?   Where would they go ... what did I have to do? It's all very well locking yourself up in your own room, but at some stage in life you've got to stand on your own feet.
Social Worker: What did you do?
Mother: Well, I had my brother but he was here, there and every-where; I didn't really see him and I had my father, but he wasn't much use, too busy thinking about what to drink next ...

so I mean ... he was very jolly and all ... but he didn't have any time for me.

In this family a lot of time was spent discussing the moments when violence occurred - the build-up of violence, the ways in which the explosion took place and the feelings of each of the partici- pants in their interaction. In all normal family interaction cen- tred around small daily behavioural sequences, a very small change in the sequence, made from an accurate and empathic understanding of the process, its interactive nature, and the promoting and reinforc- ing factors involved, can diminish or even prevent the escalation. This is more likely to be heard and acted upon if the therapist has already to some degree achieved a shift in the family's perspective on the problem and some internal relabelling of the behaviour.

In this family, for example, Erroll and Diana's anger with mother was linked to their concern, their love and their wish to be big enough to look after her. A relabelling of many of their actions had to be achieved or believed by mother so that by re-experiencing the love behind their despair she could discover her own. A lot of time was spent making the children and mother listen to each other; and checking out that all the detail of each person's point of view had been heard. Then each one was asked to respond to the messages that they had previously cut out, ignored and interpreted as hos- tile. More than one kind of emotional exchange was thus initiated. Something that took place in the session, for example a good moment when a joke was shared, or when a positive caring statement was made, was used as a reinforcer or talisman for them all to take away as a concrete symbol of this different level of dialogue to bring to mind next time a quarrel was initiated. The moments just referred to were symbolized by a 'rat' and a 'coat' although there is not space here to define why. The intention was to initiate changes in the normal interactive sequence that led to the build-up of a vio- lence which was based on well-known patterns of exchange, by insert- ing new sequences of thought which would break the previous pattern of highly subjective and selective listening that trapped each person inside his own angry experience.

In all families who bring violence as a part of their problem to therapy the behavioural changes that are initiated early on, if suc- cessful, decrease the tension that is preventing the family from working effectively on the underlying causes. This is a positive way for the therapist to provide a 'holding' situation in which mem- bers learn to 'hold' their own violence before they begin to under- stand its causes. The more precarious the situation, the more vital is this early input of a therapeutic boundary around the family. Anxiety may be a valuable asset in exploration, learning and change; but the degree of the anxiety is a crucial factor. Too much produces an explosion (perhaps even provoked by the thera- peutic encounter) or a 'cutting off' from the topic in hand, disown- ing it as 'no longer relevant' and therefore not available for exam- ination and possible change.

One of the most difficult problems when beginning work with any family is knowing their capacity to contain and work with their more violent and angry feelings. Where there is a known history of vio- lence towards one another the therapist has to be particularly aware that his presence, his interventions and the situation of his meet-

ing together with them may in itself provoke rage.   I have found it
helpful over the last year, as I gained confidence, to share my
awareness of this fact with the family;   and to indicate that I
accept that as part of my responsibility to them.   I will check out
how the sessions are affecting the family balance on a regular
basis.   This may only be necessary for the first few sessions, as
family members themselves can readily respond to the idea of cause
and effect and rapidly let the therapist know if they are feeling
'mucked about'.   This monitoring of their own violent behaviour
also begins to bring it out from the realms of the feared (and
therefore often denied) part of their consciousness into some more
conscious area.   The fact that violent actions can be recorded, reported back and discussed openly in time begins to make it seem as
though they might become manageable.   While it is perhaps unnecessary to state well-known therapeutic principles, it does seem to me
crucial that families who fear a violence that is constantly breaking through the fear should be respected from the point of view of
pace.   Techniques oriented towards swift change, or powerful experiential exercises, should be avoided.   Until there is some containment within the therapeutic interaction, and the family themselves
demonstrate their awareness of this, risks are foolish.

Similarly, sessions should end with each member as much
in charge of himself as is possible, rather than ending in an open-
ended way that may leave some members fragmented and unable to
manage.   This is particularly important with regard to the parents,
as they are the ones who have to do the real-life parenting of their
own children in between sessions where they may have found themselves feeling particularly vulnerable and subject to persecutory
feelings.   The fact that some checking out is done in this way at
the end of a session does not prevent work continuing to take place
within the family group in between sessions.

This topic of the early interplay between family and therapist
cannot be further developed here;   but it is worth remembering that
it is particularly within situations of violence that the earliest
and most primitive feelings are stirred.   If the recognition of
these multiple levels of feeling, where hate and love are often very
close to one another, is expressed by the therapist on behalf of the
family early on in family sessions, this expression can itself be
experienced as a recognition, and the beginning of useful containment by a family at exploding point.   For example, Mr Gray and his
wife presented with their runaway daughter (the middle of three), in
a state of frozen rage.   Father said that his daughter would have
to go, that there was no longer any room at home for her, and that
he would wait while the family therapist telephoned the children's
home to arrange for her reception into care.   He added that the
police knew how he felt and that the therapist could ring them for
further details.   On further enquiry he said that he had been up to
them to hand in some household items for safe custody, as he feared
injuring his daughter with them, when he found her.   While his rage
was acknowledged, this behaviour was responded to by the therapist
as being a very caring action on his part;   one which was demonstrating a sense of responsibility and love towards a child which he
wished to protect from some of his strongest emotional feelings.
The therapist expressed to Fiona her sense of her as being a child

who was loved very much indeed.   This early recognition of the mixture of feelings involved allowed some dialogue to begin, which had
a successful outcome.

Throughout work with this family, love, hate and violence were
expressed as almost interchangeable emotions by a father who sat
rigidly and almost impassively while uttering statements of great
verbal force.   His wife and three daughters, by contrast, were
rarely still;   the children performing the most extraordinary acro-
batics in a calculatedly uninhibited fashion throughout some of the
sessions.   In their home the contrast between their overactivity
and his passivity was even more marked.   The therapist went there
by invitation, and it was there that work began on examining in
detail the sequences that led up to explosive bursts of violence in
which father would throw Sheila (the elder daughter) across the room
or storm out of the house in rage.   One example of this kind of examination of a small but regular incident of family life is given in
detail below.

For nearly two hours the discussion was focused on Sunday lunch.
Father came from a straight, strict working-class family with little
money, where the solidarity of the family was very highly valued and
Sunday lunch was the particular symbol of that solidarity.
Mother's background was more ambiguous and as the discussion progressed she became more involved in trying to recreate the Sunday
scene with the help first of the blackboard, and then with the
people in the room playing members of her family of origin, sitting
round the lunch table.   She arrived eventually at the realization
that she had spent much of her later childhood preoccupied with the
relationship between her father, her mother and a third woman in the
household whose status was not clear.   She was always wanting to
know something more precise about this, but knew questions were
taboo.   The children, of whom there were four in all, were expected
to conform to the fiction that 'auntie' was father's sister.   She
recreated the seating positions in which father sat between the two
women and the four children were ranged round the bottom of the
table facing them.   Later she found out that auntie was father's
mistress and mother of the two other children, whose real mother,
according to family lore, was in fact dead.   She and her brother
had been brought up by this 'auntie' as her mum worked full time,
and she felt primarily attached to 'auntie' as though she were, in
fact, her mum.

Mrs Gray had brought her own daughters up not to ask questions,
or challenge rules on the 'never mind why ... just do as I say'
principle, which actually conflicted with her own very lively en-
quiring mind.   She would, in fact, often undermine her own authority, or cancel out father's once he was out of the house and in many
ways actively encouraged the girls to challenge those aspects of the
family system which she herself had experienced as repressive, but
believed were essential in 'growing up'.   She liked the girls to be
lively and sexually aware and had taken herself along to the sex education classes offered to the children at the primary school, feeling she knew nothing because it had been too dangerous to ask as a
child.

Concentration on this one event - a regular family mealtime in
which family tensions of more than one generation were exposed,

freed Mrs Gray from some of her unrecognized anxiety and internal
preoccupation.   She could then confront the current situation more
effectively and help father cope more realistically with some of his
extreme feelings towards his daughters' sexuality and the fact that
they were growing up and away from the family.   She was perceptive
enough to change the way in which she had encouraged her daughters
to explore some of the areas that were taboo for her at the same
age, in a manner that was directly provoking to her husband.   The
family moved on to examine father's fear that when the girls grew up
there would be nothing left for him but the coffin and the grave, a
view which mother challenged with some more sympathetic offering of
herself as wishing to understand him and meet some of his needs for
liveliness and play.

This use of another family member as the one who is provoked into
question or experiment outside the overtly permitted limits of the
family system and who is then punished for the attempt, has been extensively discussed by Zinner and Shapiro (1972, 1974).   The psychoanalytic concept of projective identification as these writers
have defined and discussed it is extremely valuable in working with
families where violence is a frequent theme.

It relates to the work of Melanie Klein referred to earlier and
in particular to her analysis of the need of infants to displace
certain unmanageable feelings into their caretakers.   Where these
feelings have been badly handled by caretakers, so that they have
not become manageable by the children in turn, the child will continue to try and find someone else to take responsibility for them.
The same mechanisms of splitting off and projecting the feelings
into others in the family will continue into adult life and this
often recreates the problems left unresolved from the parents'
family of origin, in the relationship between them and their children.   The point that Zinner and Shapiro make so valuably is that
because of the dependency, the imbalance of power and the close
daily intimate contact and knowledge of how to manipulate one another that family members possess, a parent can evoke feelings in
others, especially in their children, that do in fact lead to behaviour that then conforms to their unconscious and inner needs, such
as the more open expression of violent feeling.   The child may
begin to act out a part the parent wants or needs him to play in
certain situations, even though overtly there may be quite strong
prohibitions against him doing so.

Work with the small daily details of family behaviour attempts to
examine such unconscious current needs as they manifest themselves
in the ordinary process of living together.   The tasks of everyday
life have to be performed, and the way in which they are performed
is the variable that affects the healthy development of children in
the current family;   that reflects the problems left over from the
past and that may precede the problems of the future.   By looking
at daily behaviour and the feelings it provokes in different family
members, the destructive operation of an unconscious need can be
spelt out in language that is given by the family itself and therefore more easily understood by them.   For me it is also the beginning of an attempt to integrate approaches developed in family therapy, directed primarily towards changing behaviour but using psychoanalytic theory.   In relation to violence and its management in

family life the issue of space is one that recurs in both langua-
ges; that of the internal world of emotion and imagination and the
behaviour that takes place in the external environment of the home
itself, its floor space and furniture, its rooms and doors, and the
sense that is made of these by the people who live in it.   Their
interaction and the freedom they give each other for individual ⁻
movement affects each person's internal world in turn.   Imagination
and behaviour continually interact, reflected in the play of the
growing child.   Examining, testing out and building on the extent
to which play can become interplay; the experience of imaginative
exchange without the fear of invasion or attack by another, in the
ordinary course of daily events, has been suggested in this chapter
as a way of approaching work with families under stress.

ACKNOWLEDGMENTS

I would like to thank Linda Binnington, David Campbell, John Eveson
and Tessa Jowell - the group with whom these ideas were originally
discussed.

REFERENCES

ARDREY, R. (1967), 'The Territorial Imperative', Collins, London.
BARD, M. (1971), The study and modification of intra-familial violence.   Originally printed in The control of aggression and vio-
lence, reprinted: S. Steinmetz and M. Straus (1974).
BENTOVIM, A. (1976), Disobedience and violent behaviour in children:
family pathology and family treatment I and II, 'British Medical
Journal', vol. 1, pp. 947-9; vol. 1, pp. 1004-6.
BROWN, G., BHROLCHAIN, M. and HARRIS, T. (1975), Social class and
psychiatric disturbance among women in an urban population, 'Socio-
logy', vol. 9, no. 2, pp. 223-53.
CARTER, J. (1974) (ed.), 'The Maltreated Child', Priory Press,
London.
CARTER, J. (1977), Strengthening the individual, in 'The Challenge
of Child Abuse' (ed.), A.W. Franklin.
CARTER, J. (1978), Is child abuse a crime? (for publication panel of
Proceedings RSM Conference).
CENTRAL COUNCIL FOR EDUCATION AND TRAINING IN SOCIAL WORK (1977),
'Non-accidental injury: A case example in Social work with children
and their caregivers', CCETSW publications.
COURT, J. (1973), Some reflections on non-accidental injury to chil-
dren, 'Social Work Service', vol. 3, pp. 3-11.
GOODE, W.J. (1971), Force and violence in the family, 'Journal of
Marriage and the Family', vol. 33, pp. 624-36.
GORELL-BARNES, G. (1975), Living up to the image of ideal mother-
hood, 'New Psychiatry', vol. 2, p. 2.
HOUSE OF COMMONS SELECT COMMITTEE ON VIOLENCE IN THE FAMILY, Volume
One, 'Violence in Marriage' (1974-5); Volume two, 'Violence in the
Family' (1976-7), HMSO.
LORENZ, K. (1966), 'On Aggression', Methuen, London.
NEWSOM, J. and NEWSOM, E. (1963), 'Infant Care in an Urban Commu-
nity', Allen & Unwin, London.

NEWSOM, J. and NEWSOM, E. (1968), 'Four Years Old in an Urban Community', Allen & Unwin, London.
NEWSOM, J. and NEWSOM, E. (1976), 'Seven Years Old in the Home Environment', Allen & Unwin, London.
NSPCC: Skinner, A. and Castle, R. (1969), 'Seventy-eight Battered Children: a Retrospective Study', NSPCC.
OLIVER, J. and TAYLOR, A. (1973), 'Severely Illtreated Children in North East Wiltshire', DHSS Library.
OUNSTED, C., OPPENHEIMER, R. and LINDSAY, J. (1974), Aspects of bonding failure: the psychopathology and psychotherapeutic treatment of families of battered children, 'Developmental Medicine Child Neurology', vol. 16, pp. 447-56.
PALMER, S. (1972), 'The Violent Society' (pp. 40-9), New Haven, Connecticut: College and University Press, reprinted in S. Steinmetz and M. Straus (1974).
RENVOIZE, J. (1974), 'Children in Danger', Routledge & Kegan Paul, London.
RICHARDS, M. and BERNAL, J. (1974), Why some babies don't sleep, 'New Society', vol. 27, pp. 509-11.
RICHARDS, M. (1975), 'The First Year of Life', Cambridge University Press.
RICHMAN, N. (1974), The effects of housing on pre-school children and their mothers, 'Developmental Medicine Child Neurology', vol. 16, pp. 53-8.
RUTTER, M. (1975), 'Helping Troubled Children', Penguin, Harmondsworth.
RUTTER, M., COX, A., TUPLING, C., BERGER, M. and YULE, W. (1975), Attainment and adjustment in two geographical areas, 'British Journal of Psychiatry', vol. 126, pp. 493-509.
RUTTER, M. and MADGE, M. (1976), 'Cycles of Deprivation', Heinemann Educational, London.
SCOTT, P. (1973), Fatal battered baby cases, 'Medicine, Science and the Law', vol. 13, p. 3.
SCHAFFER, H.R. (1971), 'The Growth of Sociability', Penguin, Harmondsworth.
SMITH, S. and NOBLE, S. (1974), Social aspects of the battered baby syndrome, 'British Journal of Psychiatry', vol. 125, pp. 568-82.
STEINMETZ, S. and STRAUS, M. (eds) (1974), 'Violence in the Family', Dodd, Mead & Co., New York.
WINNICOTT, D.W. (1971), Mirror role of mother and family in child development, in 'Playing and Reality', Tavistock, London.
YULE, B., QUINTON, D., ROWLANDS, A., YULE, W. and BERGER, M. (1974), Some factors accounting for area differences, 'British Journal of Psychiatry', vol. 152, pp. 520-33.
ZINNER, J. and SHAPIRO, R. (1972), Projective identification as a mode of perception and behaviour in families of adolescents, 'International Journal of Psycho-analysis', vol. 53, pp. 523-30.
ZINNER, J. and SHAPIRO, R. (1974), The family group as a single psychic entity. Implications for acting out in adolescence, 'International Journal of Psycho-analysis', vol. 1, pp. 179-86.

Chapter 4

THE USE OF PARADOX IN THERAPY

Brian Cade

A woman, defined as 'inadequate' and as having been 'chronically depressed' for some years, was referred for therapy.   Drug treatment, electro-convulsive therapy, and some sessions of individual psychotherapy had had virtually no effect.   Her husband did not work, staying home to look after the running of the house, though continually berated for his laziness by his wife.   The woman was rarely out of bed before midday, did little housework or cooking, spending much of her time lying on the settee in a housecoat, complaining of a variety of ailments.

The family was visited in its home shortly before one Christmas. The house was untidy, the kitchen piled up with dirty dishes, the children grubby.   The woman was slumped on the settee, the husband hovering nervously behind her;   the children peeped out from behind pieces of furniture.   The session was a difficult one, with the woman ceaselessly bemoaning her fate, asking what she had done to deserve 'this depression thing', every now and again becoming agitated and occasionally hurling obscenities at her husband, and, on one occasion, at the children.   She saw no reason for the therapist having been sent to see her;   there was nothing he could do.   If 'proper doctors' had been unable to do anything, how could he help? Talking was not the answer.

'And as for Christmas;   you can forget f...... Christmas. There'll be no Christmas in this bloody house!'

I expressed considerable concern over her state of health, saying that I was extremely worried about her.   I expressed shock at how early she was attempting to get up each day for a woman in her condition.   Under no circumstances should she be up before at least three o'clock in the afternoon;   if necessary she should remain in bed all day.   As for housework and cooking, these were to be done by the rest of the family;   the woman was solemnly warned that she was not to attempt such tasks.   I went on to express admiration at the brave attempts made by the woman to be a good wife and mother. I, however, agreed with her decision not to tax herself by trying to make something of the festive season.   The rest of the family would have to forgo Christmas for this year;   it would be a travesty to attempt to be cheerful at a time like this.   She was forbidden to worry about presents, decorations or about trying to arrange any

special food for Christmas day.   There would be other Christmases
to enjoy later on.   The rest of the family were asked to do all
they could to allow the woman to rest and to work through her depression, which they were not to let her try to avoid facing.   I
arranged to see the family again early in the New Year, commenting,
as I left, that I would not be so insensitive or cruel as to wish
them a happy Christmas, and sympathising with the husband and the
children for the sacrifices they would have to make.

On the following morning the woman was up at 8.30 and making
breakfast.   She tidied the house from top to bottom, then took the
children down to the shops to buy toys, decorations, and the Christmas foodstuffs, including a turkey.   On my next visit the family
reported that it had been the best Christmas they had had for years.

A man sought help, having found himself increasingly unable to maintain an erection.   This was causing him considerable distress and
creating some tension in his relationship with his girlfriend.
They were seen conjointly and the man told he needed to learn how
to control the behaviour of his penis more effectively.   As the
first step towards his learning this control, the girl was asked,
that night, to try all she could to make him excited.   He was instructed to try to prevent his penis becoming or staying erect.   He
failed.

Zen masters have, for centuries, known the power of paradox in helping individuals break free of frameworks within which they are
trapped.   Using the principle of 'extracting a thorn with a thorn'
(Watts, 1962, p. 187), dilemmas are used to resolve dilemmas.
Through the use of Koans, the Zen master helps his students resolve
the confusion caused by their attempts to find answers to existential problems.   He prescribes confusion by posing an unsolvable
problem, solvable only by the final realisation and acceptance of
its unsolvability.   The student may be asked to rediscover the
essence of himself before his conception and birth, and to supply
some proof of the discovery;   he may be asked to contemplate the
sound of one hand clapping.   (These examples and others can be
found in Watts, 1962.)   Continually frustrated by his master's refusal to accept any of his attempts to 'answer' the problems, en-
lightenment comes only with the discovery that it is the search
itself which has become the problem and which is blocking movement.

To excape from his confusion, the student must step outside his
normal problem-solving frameworks.   Within these conceptual and
existential frameworks, his attempted solution to the confusion
caused by his pursuit of the unknowable is normally more pursuit of
the unknowable, leading to more confusion, and so on.... Only
after the student has stepped outside these frameworks is he free to
move on.

This chapter will consider the treatment of a wide range of symptomatic behaviours through the deliberate use of paradox on the part
of the therapist.   A paradoxical prescription or prediction, if
correctly constructed, leaves no loophole for an individual or
family but to change sometimes seemingly entrenched patterns of behaviour, i.e. to step outside the problem-solving frameworks within
which they have become trapped.

Underpinning this author's use of the technique lie certain basic assumptions about relationships, the development of problems and about problem resolution.   In my development of this approach much is owed to the work and ideas of Gregory Bateson, Jay Haley, Paul Watzlawick and his colleagues at the Mental Research Institute, California, and to the work of Milton Erickson.   In the writings of the three former can be found extensive theoretical examinations of the effects and uses of paradox.   Bateson et al. (1956) looked at the paradoxes that arise from a confusion in logical typing and the problems that arise from an inability to classify correctly different levels of communication.   Haley (1963) has looked at the paradoxes implicit in all therapeutic relationships, and at the ways in which symptoms can be used in the struggle over the issue of control in relationships.   Watzlawick and his colleagues (1974) have further developed the implications of the theory of logical types (Whitehead and Russell, 1910) together with group theory from the field of mathematics, to develop a way of viewing the meaning of change and further to develop ideas on the pragmatic effects and the therapeutic uses of paradox.   Milton Erickson has been a continual source of inspiration.   His approach to therapy and his genius for devising therapeutic strategies, often paradoxical in nature, continue to have a widening effect on the field of psychotherapy.   The reader is referred to a collection of the writings of Erickson edited by Haley (1967) and also to a work by Haley (1973) which further discusses Erickson's work and ideas.   This chapter will not attempt to repeat what has already been so effectively presented, but will concern itself mainly with the pragmatics of using the technique, with as many clinical examples as space will allow.

From birth, each of us learns from the significant others upon whom we are dependent what is considered 'safe' and what is considered 'unsafe' in relationships.   We learn what levels of intimacy and of differentiation are considered tolerable and we learn or develop behaviours that help us keep within the boundaries of what we consider safe.   We choose to make relationships, particularly our more intimate relationships, from amongst those whose abilities to tolerate intimacy and differentiation exist at a similar level to our own, even though the behaviours through which this level of tolerance is communicated and protected may be very different.

Every relationship, in respect of the various functions of that relationship, involves the negotiation of rules for how it is to proceed, and, at a higher, level, meta-rules that govern the making, monitoring and changing of these rules.   Rules and meta-rules are negotiated largely through non-verbal channels outside the participants' awareness.   (See Breunlin, Chapter 5.)   An important function in all relationships involves the avoidance of those degrees of intimacy and differentiation that are considered unsafe by the participants.   Behavioural sequences are evolved that allow such areas to be avoided;   symptomatic behaviour can become one tactic within such sequences with the protection of self and/or others as the goal.   The symptom bearer denies to himself and others that he or she has power over these behaviours, and then, at a higher level, also denies that denial.   For instance, a couple can evolve a rule which dictates that when the demands of the relationship become too threatening, one member will become sick and the other take on the

role of caretaker.   Either partner can take either role.   The
meta-rules which, at a higher level, govern such a rule, can forbid
awareness of, comments on or changes in it, with attempts to do so
denied, or defined as mad or bad.   Haley (1963) has looked at how
symptoms can be used as tactics in the defining and redefining of
relationships.

Attempts, from within a system, to produce changes in the rule-
governed sequences that have been set up to avoid 'unsafe' areas,
will invariably meet with the meta-rules that, at a higher level,
contradict, thus producing an inevitable impasse.   Thus a wife can
overtly be demanding change in a husband's behaviour, yet outside of
her (or his) awareness, be blocking or forbidding that change
through a whole complex of non-verbal communications.

Bateson et al. (1956, p. 259) tell how:

A young man who had fairly well recovered from an acute schizophrenic episode was visited in the hospital by his mother.   He
was glad to see her and impulsively put his arm around her shoul-
ders, whereupon she stiffened.   He withdrew his arm and she
asked, 'Don't you love me anymore?'   He then blushed and she
said, 'Dear, you must not be so easily embarrassed and afraid of
your feelings.'   The patient was able to stay with her only a
few minutes more and following her departure he assaulted an aide
and was put in the tubs.

On the surface, both mother and son propose changes (i.e. to
allow a greater degree of intimacy) but non-verbally both exchange
behaviours carrying messages from the meta-level demonstrating that
such intimacy is 'unsafe' and forbidden.

To recapitulate, all relationships involve the negotiation of
rule-governed behavioural sequences, which can include symptomatic
behaviour.   These help the participants to avoid levels of emotional involvement considered by them to be 'unsafe'.   Meta-rules exist
which, at a higher level, govern the evolving, monitoring and changing of such sequences.   The therapist's power derives from his
being an outsider to this system and thus unconstrained by its rules
and, more important, by its meta-rules, thereby allowing him freely
to comment on and to attempt to change them.

When an individual or a family comes to a therapist, two levels
of message are always present, though at any point one may be more
in evidence than the other.   At one level is the request for help,
with its implicit or explicit statements about a wish for change;
at a second level exists a more covert and unconscious intention to
thwart the therapist's attempts to bring about change.   This second
level of message will be a function of the meta-rules that govern
and restrict change within the area of functioning within which
problems have arisen.   When the therapist actively employs this intention to thwart him by explicitly requesting that there be no
change, he can create an unresolvable dilemma.   Counter to the expectations of the individual or family, the therapist requests symptomatic and associated behaviours.   Thus to carry on acting symptomatically is to co-operate with the explicit demand of the therapist
yet to stop acting symptomatically is to obey the demand for change
that is implicit in the therapeutic situation.   As pointed out by
Watzlawick et al. (1967, p. 237):

The symptomatic behaviour is no longer spontaneous;   by subject-

ing himself to the therapist's injunction the patient has stepped
outside the frame of his symptomatic game without end, which up
to that moment had no meta rules for the change of its own rules.
Something done 'because I can't help it' and the same behaviour
engaged in 'because my therapist told me to' could not be more
different.

A twenty-year-old girl had become almost completely withdrawn.
She complained that her brain was 'melting', her body becoming increasingly numb.   She spent all day lying in her bedroom, her
parents hovering around experiencing both helpless despair and impotent rage.   The girl was refusing to eat or to move, alternately
crying to her parents for help, then begging them to leave her to
die.   I expressed admiration for the girl's struggle in the face of
such distress, and ordered that she should not be expected to leave
her room.   The parents were to remain in constant attendance and to
ensure that she stayed there except at meal-times when she was to
join them, though it was not expected that she would eat.   She was
forbidden to attempt to read or listen to music (both activities
that she had previously enjoyed enormously) even though she might
find that thoughts of doing so would pop into her head.   She was to
resist such thoughts.   She might even find that a desire to go out
for a walk would enter her head;   this was to be most strongly resisted at this stage.   It was important that she should remain
quiet and attempt to 'get in touch with her feelings of despair and
anger'.   (A previous therapist had defined her symptoms as a function of repressed angry feelings towards her over-protective parents
and so the same formulation was used to justify the instruction.)

After a few days the father phoned to say that the girl had begun
to read and to listen to some of her records again.   She was eating
'like a horse' and had even been out for a short walk.   She had
spent little time in her room and had begun to engage in conversa-
tions again and to make plans for the future.   (Typically, in response to her improvement, together with the occasional outbursts of
anger towards her parents that accompanied it, the parents pressed
for re-hospitalisation, a response that I should have better anticipated and was, in this case, unable to resist.)

This example, together with its outcome, highlights two important
aspects of the use of paradox.   The first is almost axiomatic for
family therapists;   symptomatic relief without a change in the functioning of the system within which the symptom is a necessary 'survival' behaviour, will usually result in either a rapid regression
or in symptom exchange.   The second has been highlighted by Watzlawick et al. (1967, p. 242):

> The choice of the appropriate paradoxical injunction is extremely
> difficult and ... if the slightest loophole is left, the patient
> will usually have little difficulty in spotting it and thereby
> escaping the supposedly untenable situation planned by the thera-
> pist.

(In this case, for 'patient' read 'family'.)   In the above example
I had failed to allow for the probability of the girl's outbursts of
anger and the inevitability of the parents' response to it.   To
have predicted it, maybe to have prescribed it, together with expressions of concern over how difficult it was going to be for them
to cope with it, might have forestalled their eventual response
until the next therapy session.

Problems can arise between people where one party demands of the other a spontaneous response.   For example, the woman, who continually demands of her husband that he 'grow up and be more of a man' faces him with the dilemma that, to do so, he must obey his wife and thus underline her power over him.   The wife who demands a greater show of love from her husband but indicates that such displays will only be accepted if he makes them because he 'wants' to, has trapped him (and herself) in a 'be spontaneous' paradox that will almost inevitably lead to further doubt and pain.   The parent who demands willing respect from his children can only expect their disobedience.   At an individual level, the man in the second example at the beginning of this chapter had trapped himself in a 'be spontaneous' paradox as he tried harder and harder to do voluntarily what can only be involuntary, the maintenance of an erection.   The more he failed the more he became determined to make it happen and thus the more he failed.   He succeeded at the point at which he tried not to maintain an erection under circumstances in which it would normally be impossible to avoid it.   Similarly, an orgasm is a natural and spontaneous phenomenon that becomes less likely to occur the more urgently it is sought after and 'worked at'.

A man with chronic insomnia sought help.   He was instructed that night to take to bed a writing pad and a book that he was not interested in.   For the first half-hour he was to read the book.   For the next hour he was to turn off the light, lie down, but keep a close eye on the luminous hands of the alarm clock.   During that hour, after periods of 17 minutes, 33 minutes and 51 minutes, he was to turn on the light briefly and make a note of the time on the writing pad.   After the hour had passed he was to read from the book for a further half-hour, then to repeat the previous exercise but to note the time at a different set of specified intervals. This pattern was to continue all night if necessary and each night for as long as necessary.   In the fact of a task whose execution needed him to stay awake under circumstances that would normally make it almost impossible to do so, he was able to get a reasonable night's sleep for the first time for months.

Usually symptomatic behaviour in families is part of a total pattern of behaviours on the part of all members, that both contributes to and maintains the current situation.   The therapist, when constructing a paradoxical intervention, must be careful to involve all the significant participants, requiring them, as part of the task, to continue, or increase, the behaviours that seem central to the development and maintenance of the symptom.   The therapist has to decide which system is centrally involved in the maintenance of the problem and the construction of his strategy is of a different order of complexity than when using paradoxical prescriptions with individuals, as the following example will illustrate.

A woman defined as having low self-esteem and suffering from frequent and debilitating attacks of anxiety was referred for help. The behaviours that seemed associated with these attacks were prescribed, with a particular time of day to be set aside for concentrated worrying.   These interventions produced little change until the therapeutic frame was widened to include the husband.   It soon became apparent that he was over-protecting his seemingly helpless and inadequate wife and was thus thwarting any attempt on her part to act more responsibly. An intervention was framed that required him to redouble his vigilance and to do much more for his 'helpless' wife. The situation improved, with the couple presenting a more 'equal' relationship, the wife being more able to cope with housework and with the children, the couple beginning to go out together socially as husband and wife. They were soon seeking advice from me on how to deal with their teenage daughter who had suddenly become difficult to handle, staying out late at night, answering back, refusing to help around the house. The frame was widened again and a rule became apparent that required one of the women in this triangle to be a problem, thus allowing the relationship between the other female and the male to be a relatively harmonious one. The girl was instructed to 'help' her parents by 'testing' any signs of harmony between them by behaving badly. This would allow them to see whether they were able to act together to solve the problem that she thus posed. From this point on the situation began to stabilise.

Surprising as it may seem, it is very rare for a paradoxical task not to be accepted, even though the behaviour that the therapist prescribes often must seem to the individual or family to be quite absurd. For example, a woman sought help for what she described as 'shop phobia'. For some time she had been unable to remain in the smallest of shops for more than a few moments before being sick or fainting. She described how, when approaching any shop, a humming would begin in her ears and she would start to sweat; for months, friends or other family members, had to do her shopping for her.

I told her how important it was that I see exactly what happened when she went into a shop. Only then could I make an accurate diagnosis of what might be wrong. I drove the woman to the city centre and began to approach a small tobacconist's shop. As we drew nearer to the door I told the woman she should be experiencing the humming noises in her ears by now and her skin should be beginning to feel clammy. She was not to try to avoid these feelings. Once inside the shop, I directed her to the less crowded part so that she would be able to faint without being stepped on. Although anxious, the woman reported that she had not experienced any of her usual symptoms. This fact was dismissed as unimportant and I reiterated the importance of my seeing the complete range of symptomatic behaviour.

After visiting several shops, each somewhat larger and more crowded than the former, the woman had still not experienced her usual symptoms. I expressed mild annoyance and took the woman into the city's largest department store. This, I said, would be her greatest test; here she was unlikely to last long before succumbing. I described how I was going to leave her and go into the next department to buy some books for my children. As soon as she felt she was going to be sick or to faint, she was to scream. I would hear her and know that she needed me and would be with her in a matter of seconds. Fifteen minutes later, I returned to find the woman buying some perfume for a teenage daughter's Christmas present. The woman was seen two years after the above experience. She was Christmas shopping alone in the crowded toy department of that same large department store.

In a paper delivered to the American Association for the Advancement of Psychotherapy in New York, Frankl (1973, p. 139) described his use of 'paradoxical intention' in situations where anticipatory anxiety produced precisely that situation that is most feared by the individual. He described how 'the pathogenesis in phobias and obsessive-compulsive neuroses is partially due to the increase of anxieties and compulsions caused by the endeavour to avoid or fight them'.

Frankl (1973, p. 141) tells of a school play in which 'one of the characters was a stutterer, and so they gave this role to a student who actually stuttered. Soon, however, he had to give up the role because it turned out that when standing on the stage he was completely unable to stutter. He had to be replaced by another boy'. He goes on to tell of a woman who had suffered for eleven years from attacks of palpitation with marked anxiety and fears of a sudden collapse. Her therapist 'advised her to tell herself at such a moment: "My heart shall beat still faster. I will collapse right here on the sidewalk!"' Furthermore, the patient was advised to seek out deliberately places which she had experienced as disagreeable, or even dangerous, instead of avoiding them. Two weeks later, the patient reported: 'I am quite well now and feel scarcely any palpitations. The fear has completely disappeared.'

Central to this approach to therapy is the relabelling of behaviour in a positive rather than in a negative way. For instance, a man's frequent blackouts were defined as evidence that he was struggling almost too hard to get better; his system needed a rest from this struggle and the blackouts were his body's way of forcing him to relax. The therapist implied that he would be pleased to hear of continued blackouts, as this would be further evidence of the intention to improve. From having two or three blackouts each day, the man went ten weeks without a further recurrence following this intervention.

Palazzoli and her colleagues at the Centro per lo Studio della Famiglia, Milan (1975, p. 289) have commented:

A family which comes to us in crisis is a family prey to the terror of change, which is seen as a threat to the cohesion of the group. Defining ourselves as favouring this change means increasing the level of panic and therefore creating a monolithic coalition against the change and those who favour the change. Through the positive connotation of all observed behaviours, we instead declare ourselves to be allied to the homeostatic ideal of the family.

A couple's constant argument over the disciplining of their children was defined as evidence of their love and of their determination to be good parents. They were invited to redouble their efforts and to argue more frequently until resolution was reached. To have defined their arguing negatively, however subtly, would only have served to make the couple more resistant (even though they might have seemed interested in the therapist's interpretations or even grateful to have been shown the error of their ways). The positive connotation placed on their arguing helped the couple become more available for change and, in fact, they argued less and became more consistent in their handling of the children.

Weakland et al. (1974, p. 156) have suggested that:

Redefining behaviour labelled 'hostile' as 'concerned interest',

for example, may be therapeutically useful whether or not either
label is 'true', and that such truth can never be firmly established.   All that is observable is that some labels provoke difficulties, while others, achievable by redefinition, promote adjustment and harmony .... If the therapist's redefinition of an
action or situation is not openly challenged - which can usually
be arranged - then the meaning and effects of that behaviour have
already been altered.

'The Tibetan Book of the Great Liberation' (Evans-Wentz, 1969, p.
232) declares that 'As a thing is viewed, so it appears'.   If the
way in which an action or situation is viewed can be changed, then
meaning is changed and thus also the potential consequences of meaning in terms of behaviour.

A couple were constantly 'checking up' on their thirteen-year-old
daughter's behaviour, defining her as aggressive, surly and untrust-
worthy.   The therapist did not experience the girl as particularly
disturbed, and felt that a feedback loop had developed in which her
behaviour was caused by the parents' constant vigilance as much as
their vigilance was caused by her behaviour.   The girl was told by
the therapist, during a conjoint session with the girl and her parents, that she was to make attempts to 'trick' her parents over the
next two weeks.   She was to do a number of things that she knew
would please them, but she was not to let them know what it was she
had done.   The parents, meanwhile, were to make every attempt to
detect what those things were and to note them down.   However the
girl was not to 'let on' and was even to deny it if, in fact, the
parents did guess correctly.   Set within a framework of 'tricking'
her parents, the girl was willing to accept a task requiring her to
please them.   The parents were not asked to lessen their constant
vigilance (which had earlier been defined as concern) but, in fact,
to increase it.   However, from the time of their accepting the
task, the meaning of that vigilance changed, as they were now looking carefully for evidence of their daughter's 'good' rather than
'bad' behaviour.   Whether the girl undertook the task or not hardly
mattered in that her normal behaviour patterns contained enough non-
confrontive or even co-operative acts, normally unnoticed, to satisfy the parents that a change was occurring.

Palazzoli et al. (1975, p. 289), talking about the giving of a
paradoxical prescription to the members of a family system, comment
that:

> This becomes possible only when we have been able to avoid any
> moralistic judgement of the single members of the group, drawing
> dividing lines between the good and the bad ... it is the posi-
> tive connotation which permits us to place all members of the
> family on the same level, in that they are all complementary in
> regard to the system and especially to the type of self-correc-
> tive organisation, or game, which is going on in the system.
> From this point, it is possible to take a further step with the
> prescription to all the members of the group of exactly those be-
> haviours which perpetuate the dysfunction, thus rendering their
> continuation impossible.

A couple had not been out for an evening together for fifteen
years.   They blamed the disturbed behaviour of their now sixteen-
year-old son for this.   He was described as violent, destructive,

and an incessant bully towards his younger siblings.   He had been
'professionally' diagnosed at various times, as having a personality
disorder, or as being 'schizoid', or 'psychopathic'.   If they were
to go out and leave him in the house there was no knowing what they
would find on their return.   Their children, however, including the
sixteen-year-old, found it immensely amusing that I should be considering suggesting that their parents went out together.   They
could never do it!   Before they reached the front door, one of them
would find a reason to criticise the other and, in no time, they
would be arguing and the outing would fail.   The children were
clearly suggesting that it was something inherent in the parents'
relationship that caused this rather than their concern about the
sixteen-year-old's behaviour (in fact, normally, the rest of the
children needed little encouragement to blame the sixteen-year-old
for all the troubles in the family).

The couple were praised for their concern over the children and
for the unselfish way in which the children's welfare was always
considered more important than their own pleasures.   This was the
unavoidable lot of responsible parents, particularly those with difficult children, and meant, of course, that it became easy to forget
how to enjoy themselves together.   Naturally, to go out together
without being sure that all was well at home would be an irrespon-
sible act and one that would cause them considerable feelings of
guilt which was, they were told, why they became so irritable whenever they tried to go out together.

I asked the parents to consider separately and privately, over
the next two weeks, where they would like to go if they did go out.
They were not to go out, but to think about going out, and for
twenty minutes or so, during the fortnight, were to try to find time
to discuss their ideas together.   They were told that they were
wise to be wary about going out and that I felt such arrangements
should not be made in haste and without full consideration of possible problems.   They were forbidden actually to plan an outing together at this stage.   The children were asked to help by making
sure their parents did not 'jump the gun'.   If they seemed to be
planning an outing, they were to be reminded of how unpredictable
the sixteen-year-old was.   In fact, he could be of most help to his
parents by continually reminding them, over this period, how difficult, even crazy, he might become if left unguarded.

At the next session, the mother triumphantly reported an enjoy-
able trip she and her husband had made to a local theatre.   The
children had posed no problems at all; the sixteen-year-old had
even prepared a hot drink on their return.   They were planning a
further outing later that week.   I expressed guarded pleasure but
cautioned continued wariness, repeating much of what I had said in
the previous session.

Where a family or an individual shows considerable resistance to
change, particularly where the well intentioned and more traditional
attempts of a succession of therapists to help have been thwarted,
as was the case in the above family, I normally caution against
change, deliberately attempting to frustrate it, and, where positive
change occurs, as in the above example, express increased concern
and make further moves to frustrate it.   (It is important here to
point out that neither the resistance nor the intention to thwart

the therapist, on the part of the family, are normally conscious
processes but stem from that level of rules that governs rules about
change and invariance.)

A single mother with a young child was referred for therapy.
She was described as being of 'low self-esteem', was grossly over-
weight, dressed shabbily and her hair was generally unkempt.   Her
house was ill kept, the walls dirty and she rarely went out except
to her part-time office cleaning job.   She had had no contact with
her parents for some considerable time and felt that they had rejected her.   Her son, five years of age, was failing to achieve what
his school considered to be his potential.   She had received supportive therapy over a considerable period of time with no significant change.

The therapist and her supervisor, discussing the case before the
first interview, felt that to attempt to improve this woman's image
of herself would constitute more of the same approach that had so
far failed to produce change.   It was decided to change direction
and that, however much the woman 'put herself down', the therapist
would 'put her down' a little further.

As therapy began and the woman began to describe how much of a
failure she was, the therapist agreed with her but suggested that
she was holding some things back.   The woman bemoaned her size and
appearance, and the therapist agreed that she was not a pretty
sight.   The woman pointed to the state of the house and the therapist agreed that it was in a terrible condition.   The woman talked
about her reluctance to go out other than to work, and the therapist
agreed that it must be difficult for her to go out without feeling
that people were looking at her, such was her size.   At the end of
the first session the woman angrily protested that it was the therapist's job to listen, not to agree.   The therapist nodded in a
concerned manner then advised the woman that the one thing she
could depend on was that the therapist would be completely honest
with her.

The therapist continually advised the woman against change, particularly in respect of going out or contacting her parents.   The
woman became increasingly angry at the therapist, calling her a
'catty bitch' and vowing that she would 'show that cow'.   In the
face of the woman's tidying up of the house, her trip in to town to
buy some new dresses, her trip to a hairdresser, her evening out at
a work's dance, her making contact with her parents and finding them
accepting of her, her plans for further social evenings, the therapist remained pessimistic and continued to prescribe caution and to
suggest no action.   At the end of therapy (seven sessions) the
woman said to the therapist, 'I thought you were a cow, but you've
really helped me'.   Six months after the end of therapy, the woman
was still maintaining her progress, was moving to a better house and
was losing weight.   During the follow-up interview she identified
the therapist's 'honesty' as that which had been the most useful
feature of the therapy and commented, after a short pause, 'and by
God, was she honest!'

It is important that the therapist should never take responsibility for changes occurring through the use of paradox.   Central to
the success of such maneouvres is the fact that improvements occur
in spite of, and as a reaction against, the therapist's predictions

and prescriptions.   For the therapist to claim responsibility would
be self-defeating and would risk a rapid relapse.   Generally, the
therapist should greet news of improvements with caution and with
incomprehension.   Warnings about the possible temporary nature of
such rapid changes and the probability of a relapse are more likely
to sustain the improvements.

> Talking of Erickson's work, Haley (1973, p. 31) comments that
> one of his more graceful procedures is to say ... 'I want you to
> go back and feel as badly as you did when you first came in with
> the problem, because I want you to see if there is anything from
> that time that you wish to recover and salvage.'   When done
> effectively, the directive to relapse prevents a relapse ....

For example, a couple in marital therapy were constantly arguing
bitterly and had thwarted all of my attempts to get them to discuss,
at a rational level, even the most minor of issues.   Finally, I
told them that they had absolutely no idea of how to argue.   To
call their pathetic bickering 'arguing' was a complete misuse of the
word.   They would never be able to resolve any issue and hence,
stop arguing, until they had learnt more effectively how to argue.
For the next three weeks the couple were instructed to seize every
possible opportunity for a disagreement and to use it to argue long
and bitterly until they had begun to learn to break, what I called,
the 'resolution barrier'.

At the next session, the husband said, 'You know, it's funny ...
we've not had any arguments ... we've had quite a few discussions;
you know, about things ....'

I expressed concern, talked about temporary lulls, restated the
importance of the couple's learning how to argue properly, and re-
imposed the task.   Over the next few sessions, spanning three
months, the couple continued to report an improved and calmer relationship while I continued to express concern, puzzlement and repeatedly imposed the same task.   At the end of therapy, I remained
sceptical about the changes, and warned the couple not to be surpri-
sed if the 'temporary lull' finally came to an end.   (An important
feature in this case was that both less arguing and more aguing had
been defined as signs of an improvement in the relationship.)

Communication through metaphor or the use of parables can be extraordinarily effective in dealing with issues, the open discussion
of which would result in denial or a massive increase in resistance.
In this way issues can be discussed and reframed, and outcomes suggested, predicted or prevented in ways which are hard for a family
or an individual to deny or resist because it is not their problem
that is being talked about.

Haley (1973, p. 27) gives an example of Milton Erikson's use of
metaphor:

> dealing with a married couple who have a conflict over sexual re-
> lations and would rather not discuss it directly, he will ap-
> proach the problem metaphorically.   He will choose some aspect
> of their lives that is analogous to sexual relations and change
> that as a way of changing sexual behaviour.   He might, for ex-
> ample, talk to them about having dinner together and draw them
> out on their preferences.   He will discuss with them how the
> wife likes appetisers before dinner, while the husband prefers to
> dive right into the meat and potatoes.   Or the wife might prefer

a quiet and leisurely dinner, while the husband, who is quick and direct, just wants the meal over with.   If the couple begin to connect what they are saying with sexual relations, Erickson will 'drift rapidly' away to other topics, and then he will return to the analogy.   He might end such a conversation with a directive that the couple arrange a pleasant dinner on a particular evening that is satisfactory to both of them.   When successful, this approach shifts the couple from a more·pleasant dinner to more pleasant sexual relations without their being aware that he has deliberately set this goal.

A couple were resisting an open discussion of their sex life and the subject shifted to the discussion of another area of contention, the decorating of the house.   Asked how they went about this task the wife explained, 'I do the stripping, he gets on with the job, then I clear the mess up after him'.   It was obvious to the therapists that the wife had, with that statement, made a clear comment on how she had come to view the sex act as a chore.

A couple with an 'agorophobic' sixteen-year-old daughter insisted that their marriage was perfect, almost idyllic.   The therapist, absentmindedly reminisced about a boy he had known at school, twenty years before, who had suddenly refused to leave the house.   He commented on how a doctor then had suggested that the boy had been trying subconsciously to draw attention to his parents' seeming lack of interest in each other.   The couple expressed a polite interest in this story and almost immediately went on to discuss how their lives had been completely taken up with caring for their children and how they now did very little together outside their role as parents.

Haley (1973, p. 28) gives a further example of Erickson's work, in the story of a young hospitalised patient who called himself 'Jesus'.   He paraded about as the Messiah, wore a sheet draped around him, and attempted to impose Christianity on people.   Erickson approached him in the hospital grounds and said, 'I understand you have had experience as a carpenter?'   The patient could only reply that he had.   Erickson involved the young man on a special project of building a bookcase and shifted him to productive labour.

It is not only the design of a paradoxical task that makes it potentially effective but also the way in which the task is given to the individual or family.   Haley (1976, p. 69) has commented that:

skill is required if this approach is used, because the therapist is communicating a number of different things at the same time. He is saying 'I want to help you get better' and he is saying 'I am benevolently concerned about you'.   He is saying things to the family that are on the edge of being insulting: he is saying he thinks the family members can really tolerate being normal, but he is also saying perhaps they cannot.   The dangers in this approach come about when the therapist does not communicate all these things at once.   If he does not, the family members may feel merely that he thinks they are hopeless.   Or they may feel that he is taking advantage of his position to be insulting.   Or that he does not really care if they change or not.

It is important, when framing a paradoxical intervention, to frame it in a way that is congruent with the individual's or family's ways of thinking and of viewing things.   For example, a

couple came into therapy for help with their thirteen-year-old
daughter who was defined as beyond their control.   Early on in
therapy the therapist found herself attempting to 'help' the father
see how his rigid, somewhat Victorian attitudes might be contributing to the continuation of the problem.   He rejected this viewpoint
and saw the therapist as a typical 'do-gooder' unable to appreciate
the difficulties he was experiencing in trying to bring up his
daughter correctly.   He adopted an increasingly entrenched position
until the therapist was advised to change direction by her colleagues.   She began to agree with him on how difficult it was to
bring up children, particularly female children, in this permissive
and undisciplined age.   She defined his rigid and over-intrusive
parenting as laudable concern for the well-being of his daughter.
The father relaxed and began to see the therapist in a more positive
light.   After a few minutes he suggested that perhaps he was too
strict and old-fashioned in his attitude and that perhaps this was
part of the problem.

I never explain the way in which a paradox works to an individual
or a family even after its use has produced a desired change.   Understanding or insight is not seen as a prerequisite for change nor
necessary during or after change.   It is of concern to many professionals that such a use of paradox involves 'trickery', is 'manipulative' and lacking in 'sincerity'.   I am in agreement with Watzlawick et al. (1974, p. xv) when they say:

'Sincerity' has lately become a catchword, a hypocrisy in its own
right, associated in a murky way with the idea that there is such
a thing as a 'right' view of the world - usually one's own view.
It also seems associated with the idea that 'manipulation' is not
only bad, but can be avoided.   Nobody, unfortunately, has ever
explained how this can be done.   It is difficult to imagine how
any behaviour in the presence of another person can avoid being a
communication of one's own view of the nature of one's relationship with that person and how it can, therefore, fail to influence that person....   The problem, therefore, is not how influence and manipulation can be avoided, but how they can best be
comprehended and used in the interest of the patient.

It is not easy for a therapist to make the jump from more
'straight' and traditional ways of working with problems to an approach that makes deliberate use of paradoxical dilemmas.   Such an
approach needs an ability to think in terms of 'games', to think
quickly, laterally, and to think tactically, often in situations involving high levels of pain and distress.   To work with paradox can
also mean dealing with colleagues, some of whom may express strong
feelings against what they see as 'insensitive', 'dishonest', 'in-
sincere', 'manipulative', and so on.   It requires that the therapist see himself as concerned with behavioural change and as responsible for devising ways of bringing about that change.   It requires
optimism about the capacity of people to change even the most seemingly entrenched of symptomatic behaviours.

REFERENCES

BATESON, G., JACKSON, D.D., HALEY, J. and WEAKLAND, J.H. (1956), Towards a theory of schizophrenia, 'Behavioural Science, vol. 1, no. 4.

EVANS-WENTZ, W.Y. (ed.) (1969), 'The Tibetan Book of the Great Liberation', Oxford University Press.

FRANKL, V.E. (1973), Paradoxical intention: a logotherapeutic technique, 'Psychotherapy and Existentialism', Penguin, Harmondsworth.

HALEY, J. (1963), 'Strategies of Psychotherapy', Grune & Stratton, New York.

HALEY, J. (ed.) (1967), 'Advanced Techniques of Hypnosis and Therapy: Selected Papers of Milton H. Erickson', Grune & Stratton, New York.

HALEY, J. (1973), 'Uncommon Therapy: The Psychiatric Techniques of Milton H. Erickson, M.D.', W.W. Norton, New York.

HALEY, J. (1976), 'Problem Solving Therapy', Jossey-Bass, San Francisco.

PALAZZOLI, M.S., BOSCOLO, L., CECCHIN, G. and PRATA, G. (1975), Paradox and counter paradox: a new model for the therapy of the family in schizophrenic transaction, 'Schizophrenia 75', proceedings of the Vth International Symposium on the Psychotherapy of Schizophrenia, Oslo, August 1975.

WATTS, A.W. (1962), 'The Way of Zen', Penguin, Harmondsworth.

WATZLAWICK, P., BEAVIN, A.B. and JACKSON, D.D. (1967), 'Pragmatics of Human Communication', W.W. Norton, New York.

WATZLAWICK, P., WEAKLAND, J. and FISCH, R. (1974), 'Change: Principles of Problem Formation and Problem Resolution', W.W. Norton, New York.

WEAKLAND, J., FISCH, R., WATZLAWICK, P. and BODIN, A.M. (1974), Brief therapy: focused problem resolution, 'Family Process', vol. 13, no. 2.

WHITEHEAD, A.N. and RUSSELL, B. (1910), 'Principia Mathematica', Cambridge University Press.

Chapter 5

NONVERBAL COMMUNICATION IN FAMILY THERAPY

Douglas Breunlin

INTRODUCTION

Students of family therapy as well as therapists experienced in work with individuals frequently report that their first encounters with families are overwhelming and exhausting. Several interrelated factors contribute to the taxing nature of family therapy. One is the enormous amount of sensory material with which the therapist is bombarded throughout a family therapy session. Second, this material is linked to several levels of systems organization to which the therapist must attend simultaneously. These levels range from organismic activity to the social life of the family group as a whole. The therapist is able to handle consciously only a fraction of this input. Some of it goes unnoticed, but a large fraction is also registered out of awareness and in a sometimes disturbing and confusing way. The experience of a family can, in fact, be overpowering.

Much of the action in family therapy takes place nonverbally. Family members are constantly shifting in their chairs, moving their limbs, altering their gaze, and emitting paralinguistic sounds. All of this occurs parallel with and in addition to the verbal content of the session. One is tempted to concentrate on the words alone, but one quickly realizes that the session only makes sense when the nonverbal activity is examined as well. Family therapists have always attributed major importance to nonverbal communication (NVC). Beels and Ferber (1969) reflect this importance by including NVC in their definition of family therapy. However, despite the overwhelming acceptance of the importance of NVC, there exists no unifying framework to enable the therapist to grasp the meaning and function of NVC in family therapy. Rather, the therapist is faced with a growing body of research and clinical information about NVC, which, if examined in isolation, can confuse more than clarify the relevance of NVC to family therapy.

This chapter is an attempt to grapple with the complex and fascinating role of NVC in family therapy. To organize the material, the framework afforded by systems theory is utilized. Viewed as a system, the family is seen to have several levels of organization. The individual's organization is one level in the hierarchy of a

family system.   A second is the interpersonal level of the dyad.
The group's organization as a whole is yet another.   The functions
and meaning attributed to NVC depend upon the level of organization
chosen to observe the system.   (See Table 5.1.)   Likewise, the diagnostic and therapeutic uses of NVC in family therapy also depend
upon the level of organization at which the therapist chooses to
intervene.   The reader who is looking for a checklist to interpret
NVC will be disappointed.   This simply is not possible because such
is not the state of the art.   Rather, an attempt will be made to
afford the reader a thorough look at NVC and its relationship to
family therapy in the hope that each therapist can then examine and
utilize NVC in a manner consistent with his own therapeutic style.

Before proceeding to describe the functions of NVC, it is necessary to clarify first the choice of the term nonverbal communication
for this chapter.   This is more than mere semantic wrangling, and
is necessitated by the wide variation in terminology found in the
literature on nonverbal interaction.   Other authors have used such
terms as visible behaviour (Kendon, 1967), bodily communication
(Argyle, 1975), body movement (Davis, 1973) and nonverbal behaviour
(Ekman and Friesen, 1968).   The choice of the term nonverbal communication is linked first to the central importance of communication
in family therapy, and second, to the definition of communication
adopted in this chapter.   A family is a natural system.   Its members live together more or less continuously.   As such, they share
intimate knowledge about each other and about their system.   When a
family member claims 'I can read him like a book' there is truth to
this statement in that every nonverbal behaviour emitted by one
family member is likely to have some shared meaning for the other
family members.   All behaviour, therefore, has shared communicative
value.   Communication may then be defined as 'any patterned interdependency of behavior between people' (Kendon, 1967, p. 354).   The
following statement by Scheflen adds clarity to this definition of
communication:

In communicational theory we say that the behaviour of each par-
ticipant is communicative;   that is, it is patterned and structured according to some tradition.   If so, it is potentially
recognizable and meaningful.   Therefore, behavior is the basis
for the social processes of communication.

I do not want to suggest an old dichotomy by such a statement.
I am not implying that some behavior is communicative and some is
not.   I do not believe it probable that anyone will behave in a
non structured way.   We learn to behave systematically in becoming socialized and enculturated, and it is very hard to behave in
any other way.   So it is redundant to speak of communicative behavior, when all behavior is patterned and capable of being recognized and comprehended, i.e. communicative (Scheflen, 1973,
pp. 14-15).

Family therapists find this broad definition of communication
most functional because their primary focus in therapy is on the
patterned interrelationships of the whole family system.   Further,
since all behaviour has communicative significance, the term nonverbal communication will be adopted for the purposes of this chapter.

Although every behaviour emitted by the family is potentially
communicative, some behaviours repeatedly function as nonverbal

TABLE 5.1 Functions of NVC in family therapy

Level of organization	Function	Subsystem within family	
Organismic or individual	Expressive of internal state	Individual family members	
Dyadic or interpersonal	Communicative about nature of relationship	Dyads	mother-father parent-child child-child grandparent-child parent-grandparent
Social or group	Communicative about regulation, maintenance and integration of group identity and security	Whole family group	

communication.   These behaviours are most often cited in the literature and bear mention at this point.
1 Body motion or kinesis: gestures and other body movements,
facial expressions, eye movements, posture and postural shifts.
2 Paralanguage: voice qualities, speech non fluencies, and non
language sounds such as laughing, yawning, and grunting.
3 Proxemics: the manner in which the family uses its personal
space.

FUNCTIONS OF NVC

The scientific study of NVC dates back to Darwin (1872) who then
published a classic and still respected work on the expression of
emotion.   Subsequently the subject received little systematic attention until after the Second World War.   Gladstein (1974) reviewed the literature on NVC relevant to counselling/psychotherapy
which appeared since the war, and noted that 75 per cent of the references had appeared during the past ten years.   Davis (1973) attributed this upsurge to a growing interest in group and family
therapy and in nonverbal therapy methods such as those used in encounter groups and in gestalt therapy.   It would be beyond the
scope of this paper to review completely the vast literature on NVC.
Rather we will use the literature to describe the main functions of
NVC, and to relate these functions to the arena of family therapy.
    A family is a natural social system.   Like any social system, it
consists of subsystems which are integrated hierarchically.   Each
subsystem constitutes a level of organization which can be isolated
conceptually and studied as a system in itself even though, in reality, all levels remain constantly in dynamic interrelationship
with one another.   In a family system, three levels of organization
can be identified: (1) the individual or organismic level; (2) the
dyadic or interpersonal level; and (3) the social or group level of
organization (see Table 5.1).   The functions ascribed to NVC depend
upon the level of organization chosen for observation.   Scheflen
(1967, p. 10) noted: 'It is not that some behaviors are communicative and others are expressive, but rather that behavior is expressive at the organismic level, and communicative at the social
level.'   Historically, NVC was first studied at the organismic
level.   Gradually interest shifted to the dyadic level, and most
recently the social level has received increasing attention.
Below, the functions of NVC will be considered using these three
levels of organization.

NVC at the organismic (individual) level of organization

If one focuses on the individual or organismic level of organization, NVC is viewed as a manifestation of some internal state of the
organism; that is, NVC is a function of individual expressiveness.
With respect to psychotherapy, three interrelated areas of expressiveness may be identified: (1) emotion; (2) intrapsychic processes; and (3) psychopathology.
    The nonverbal expression of emotion has received by far the most

attention.   The following authors report results of particular
relevance to family therapy.   Ekman and Friesen (1967) conducted
extensive research into the nonverbal communication of emotion.
They concluded that the face is a primary affect display system
while the body shows a person's adaptive efforts regarding affect.
They also concluded that the head is more informative about the
nature of an emotion while the intensity of an emotion is more accurately judged from the body.   Further, body position is superior
to body acts in conveying a full range of intensity.   Their experimental results showed that emotions judged from the face usually
differ from emotions judged from the body.   They proposed a hypothesis that conflict within the stimulus person may produce this
discrepancy.   Ekman and Friesen (1969) also postulated that some
nonverbal channels are less susceptible than others to conscious
control;   therefore, while one channel may communicate a censored
emotion, another may leak uncensored emotion, thus producing the
discrepancy in observable affect.   Dittman et al. (1965) found
similar discrepancies when they asked psychotherapists and dancers
to rate nonverbal expression of emotion.   The dancers responded
more to bodily cues and also noted more unpleasant affect.   Differences in training between dancers and therapists may account for
these results.   If this is the case, perhaps therapists over-
emphasize the face in judging emotion while missing valuable clues
communicated by the body.

Drag and Shaw (1967) and Thompson and Meltzer (1964) asked subjects to communicate emotions by facial expression.   Both studies
concluded that happiness was easiest to communicate while contempt
and related emotions were most difficult.   Thompson and Meltzer
also found that subjects varied considerably in their ability to use
facial expressions to communicate emotion.

Ellsworth and Carlsmith (1968) studied the effects of eye contact
and verbal content on affective responses in a dyadic interaction.
They found that the amount of eye contact influenced the subjects'
affective reactions to the situation and to the other person.   The
general direction of this influence, moreover, depended on whether
the verbal content was favourable or unfavourable to the subject.
Subjects responded positively when favourable content was accompanied by frequent eye contact.   They responded negatively when unfavourable content was accompanied by frequent eye contact.   These
results suggest that therapists should relate their use of eye contact to the verbal content (supportive v. confrontational) of their
interventions.   Their results also suggest that clients may be more
inclined to disclose negative material about themselves when the
therapist actually avoids eye contact.

Vande Creek and Watkins (1972) obtained results which suggest
that people differ in their responses to incongruent verbal and nonverbal emotional cues.   The subjects in their research were easily
classified as either verbal or nonverbal responders.   Nonverbal
responders also possessed some degree of sensitivity to the verbal
mode in contrast to verbal responders who responded only to verbal
emotional cues.

Psychoanalytically oriented clinicians and researchers consider
NVC to be expressive of intrapsychic processes.   Mahl (1968, p.
296) noted that 'Freud's main contribution to our topic was his pro-

posal that conflicted, repressed-unconscious impulses, wishful thoughts, emotions and memories, were often manifested in action instead of thought.' Reich (1949) greatly advanced the use of NVC in psychoanalysis. Ehlich (1970) noted that Reich ultimately concluded that the structure and form of communication were more important than meaning and content. Reich also advanced the thesis that an individual's stable defenses were manifested in the how of his skeletal behaviour (Mahl, 1968). Deutsch (1947) made thorough studies of postural variation during psychoanalysis, and Gostynski (1951) analysed the use of gestures. Loeb (1968) conducted a detailed analysis of a fist-like movement manifested during psychoanalysis, and concluded that this movement was directly related to the analysand's unconscious expression of anger.

Mahl (1967, 1968) researched the psychoanalytic implications of NVC. One of his most important findings was that transitory movements in interviews often have unconscious determinants, and anticipate spontaneous verbalizations which occur at a later point in the interview. Mahl (1967) cited an example of a woman who played with her wedding ring for some time before she disclosed marital difficulties. Mahl (1967) also argued that some nonverbal acts which have shared communicative meaning may, in fact, have unconscious determinants. He cited the example of an analysand who frequently gave other people the 'finger'. While this gesture has a commonly shared meaning, it was used primarily by the analysand because it gave him a feeling of being 'one-up'. Mahl further linked the gesture to a traumatic event in the analysand's life when he had been forcibly given an enema by his angry mother. Being 'one-up' meant something special for the analysand: he was the active administrator of enemas (symbolized by the 'finger') instead of a passive receiver. Scheflen and Scheflen (1972) applied the term 'transcontextual' to NVC which could not be explained within the context of an interaction. He hypothesized that such behaviours have unconscious determinants, but also cited Freud (1959) in arguing that all people perform such acts; thus, their occurrence in no way warrants psychiatric diagnosis.

Research on NVC has attempted to document the relationship between NVC and psychopathology. Two related questions have been examined: (1) Can NVC be used to determine mental status? and (2) If mental status alters in the course of therapy, is there an attendant change in NVC? Davis (1970a) studied the body movement of schizophrenic patients. She later commented on this research:

> I found that there are many different forms of disorganization, reduced mobility, rigidity or exaggeration observable in the movement of schizophrenic patients, even those whose manner is at first glance unremarkable. We could tell subtle shades of improvement over three weeks of intensive treatment as well as predict the differential diagnosis with notable success, all by seeing the patient behind a one-way screen without sound and without prior knowledge of the patient (Davis, 1973, p. 5).

Waxer (1974) and Hinchliffe et al. (1971) studied the NVC of depressed patients. Both found that depressives showed significantly less eye contact. In a film study of a family therapy session, Davis (1970b) found that changes in the way the identified patient gesticulated correlated dramatically with the degree of coherency and content of his speech.

Gladstein (1974) noted that several studies found that change in psychological functioning through psychotherapy are accompanied by changes in NVC.   For example, Ekman and Friesen (1968) found that the NVC of three depressed patients communicated significantly different impressions of their psychological functioning before and after treatment.   Condon et al. (1969) examined films of the original Eve of 'The Three Faces of Eve'.   They found that the rate and kind of eye strabismus correlated with Eve's various personality phases.   There was no eye divergence after she had improved.   It appears that NVC can be used to judge mental status, and to gauge changes in psychological functioning through psychotherapy.   Davis (1973), however, cautioned that some training may be required if this is to be done accurately.

NVC at the dyadic or interpersonal level of organization

At this level the focus shifts from the nonverbal expression of internal states of the individual to the communicative functions of NVC in dyadic interaction.   In any dyadic subsystem the participants continuously exchange information concerning the manner in which they perceive experience and define the relationship which exists between them.   Much of this information exchange occurs nonverbally.   Ruesch and Bateson (1951) and Bateson et al. (1956) pioneered the study of NVC in dyadic interaction.   Watzlawick et al. (1967) have built on this earlier work.   Their excellent discussion of the communicative functions of NVC in dyadic interaction is summarized below.

In any dyadic interaction, the interactants continuously exchange information.   Every message exchanged has both a 'report' and a 'command' function.   The 'report' function usually conveys the overt content of the message while the 'command' function contains information about the nature of the relationship between the sender and receiver.   Report and command functions are generally transmitted simultaneously, but usually via different channels of communication.   They may be either congruent or incongruent with one another.   These channels are labelled digital and analogic communication.   In digital communication symbols are used to represent things.   The most important form of digital communication for humans, of course, is language.   On the other hand, analogic communication can be more readily referred to as the thing for which it stands.   Watzlawick et al. postulate that analogic communication is virtually equivalent to NVC.   Digital communication is usually chosen to convey the content aspect of a message while the relationship aspect is conveyed predominantly via analogic communication.   Thus, at the dyadic level of organization the primary function of NVC is to communicate the nature of the relationship which exists between the interactants.

The following authors have reported research which supports this approach to NVC.   Beier (1974) found that happy couples created a more comfortable and supportive bodily environment with their NVC in contrast to couples experiencing the most conflict who sent the most distant vibrations.   Kahn (1970) found that dissatisfied spouses were more prone to misinterpret each other's NVC.   Navron (1967) found that happily married couples differ from unhappily married couples in that they communicate nonverbally to a greater degree via exchange of glances. Hersen et al. (1973) studied the NVC between alcoholic men and their wives. They found that these wives spent more time looking at their alcoholic husbands when the discussion involved alcohol. These results imply that the wives in this study nonverbally reinforce their husbands' drinking, and thus define alcoholism as a necessary part of the relationship. Finally, Speer (1972) reviewed several laboratory findings which support the hypothesis that individuals rely more heavily on nonverbal than verbal communication to convey their subjective moods to others.

NVC at the social or group level of organization

At this level of organization NVC is seen as a function of the group itself. Many nonverbal behaviours observable in a group combine to serve social purposes beyond the personal motivations of any one member (Scheflen, 1964). These purposes include the formation, mediation, correction, integration and maintenance of the group's relationships and activities (Scheflen, 1964). Moreover, at the group level NVC is viewed as patterned and synchronous activity shared and understood by each group member, and perpetuated by the group whether that group be a society, an institution or a family.

At the group level of organization, communication means more than the exchange of new information. It also involves the reduction of ambiguity and the regulation of group activity. Moreover, communication in general is seen as an altogether ordered and continuous process, occurring within a specific context (Birdwhistell, 1962) and consisting of an integrated arrangement of structural units which are organized hierarchically into larger and larger units (Scheflen, 1964). 'Just as language consists of a hierarchy of increasingly more inclusive units, so a communications system as a whole is an integrated arrangement of structural units deriving from kinesic, tactile, lexical and other elements' (Scheflen, 1964, p. 320). Thus communication involves more than spoken language. It also includes all behaviour which has common meaning for the group, regardless of whether the sender intended it to be perceived and responded to (Scheflen, 1963).

The understanding of NVC at the group or social level of organization has been greatly advanced by anthropological research on cultural patterns in societal groups. Using the natural history method of research, anthropologists have determined that, to a large extent, NVC is patterned within a culture and, thus, learned by each member of that culture. Much of the NVC observed in psychotherapy, therefore, may derive from the cultural heritage of the participants; consequently, the therapist must guard against naively imputing psychological significance to behaviours which are, in fact, culturally specified patterns. Likewise, since a family is a natural social group, communication within a family may be expected to exhibit properties similar to those described above.

The following authors have examined NVC at the group level of organization. La Barre (1964) has written a comprehensive survey of cultural differences in NVC. Trager (1958) examined cultural vari-

ations in paralanguage, while Hewes (1955) catalogued postural differences throughout the world.   Birdwhistell (1970) extensively
analysed kinesic behaviour.   He argued that kinesic patterns are
cultural and context specific, and have a structure similar to
spoken language.   Birdwhistell suggests that kinesic behaviour may
be an essential aspect of verbal behaviour, operating to clarify,
amplify or regulate the verbal content, or it may constitute a relatively independent channel of communication as in kinesic interchanges between intimates.   Hall (1963) developed a widely accepted
system of notation for recording proxemics.   Hall (1966) also suggested that the distance which separates interactants is partly related to the nature of the interaction.   Hall identified four types
of distance: intimate distance, casual personal distance, social-
consultative distance, and public distance.   At each distance NVC
and the senses operate differently.

Family therapy has been most influenced by Scheflen's research on
NVC at the group level of organization.   Some of his findings are
summarized below.   Scheflen (1963) found that NVC plays a vital
role in regulating group activity.   His research has shown that
once a group establishes a pattern, any deviation from that pattern
will be censured by the group until the deviation disappears or a
new pattern is established.   This regulatory function has several
characteristics:

(1) It is largely non-lexical, chiefly kinesic;   (2) relationship
and pace are regulated as well as deviant individual behaviours;
and (3) the operation is not conducted by a simple action and reaction sequence, but rather by mutual, often simultaneous, and
frequently complementary signals (Scheflen, 1963, p. 129).

The regulatory monitor is usually directed at a relationship or an
organization of behaviours rather than towards a single person's behaviour.   These regulatory activities appear to function to preserve the stability of the group and to insure that the group
achieves its aims.

Scheflen (1964) also found that postural configurations play a
vital role in structuring communication systems.   Posture and postural shifts mark both the duration and termination of hierarchically organized units of communication.   Thus, a speaker will maintain
head and eye positions while making a point, and change these positions when moving from one point to another.   Having made several
points, which combined constitute a point of view, the speaker
usually changes posture.   Not only do postural markers organize the
speaker's presentation, they also cue the listeners not to interrupt.   Moreover, if a listener wishes to speak, he will most often
use a postural marker to make this known to the group.

Postural configurations also provide valuable information about
the relationships which obtain between the participants of an interaction.   Thus, it is often possible to ascertain who is considered
part of a group or subgroup by noting the postural configurations of
the group members.   Members of a group may also place themselves in
vis-a-vis or parallel orientations.   The vis-a-vis orientation is
often confrontational while the parallel orientation is more often
marked by co-operation.   In a general way, postural congruence indicates similarity in views of roles in a group.   It may also be an
indication of status or rapport between the participants.   In a

group, the participants often split both their body orientation and their postural congruence.   These splits appear to give the group greater stability by linking several members together nonverbally.

NVC AND THE DYNAMICS OF FAMILY THERAPY

Virtually all family therapists, regardless of their approach to family therapy, consider NVC to be a vital factor in understanding the dynamics of a family therapy session.   One would expect, therefore, to find a thorough documentation of the place of NVC in family therapy.   The initial reaction to the dearth of literature relating to NVC and family therapy must be one of dismay; however, two factors afford a plausible explanation.   First, family therapists are sensitive to the enormous complexity of family systems.   This means they are also sensitive to the complexity of NVC in family therapy, and, therefore, have largely avoided NVC as an area of research. Riskin and Faunce (1972, p. 382), reviewing family interaction research, noted: 'Our impression is that body movement is generally considered so complex and unreliable to score that it is usually not utilized ....'   To grasp the effort required to research NVC in family therapy adequately, one need only consider how it took Bateson and Freida Fromm-Reichman one thousand hours to study just five minutes of family interaction (Framo, 1972).   Second, family therapists also recognize that every family system is unique;   consequently, a family's use of NVC is likely to be idiosyncratic.   Although every family therapist has innumerable anecdotes about NVC, this second factor has resulted in few of these experiences being reported in clinical papers.
    Despite the complexity of NVC in family therapy, some order can be obtained if the systems framework used to analyse the functions of NVC is applied to the dynamics of family therapy.   Using the systems framework, it was shown that the functions of NVC are related to three different levels of organization, any one of which could be chosen for observation.   In a family therapy session, the therapist is usually faced with all three levels of organization simultaneously.   Individually, each family member continuously emits nonverbal signals of an expressive nature.   At the dyadic or interpersonal level, family members constantly exchange nonverbal communications which define the nature of the relationships which obtain between the family members and between family members and the therapist.   Finally, at the groupllevel, patterns of NVC operate to maintain the stability and ongoing life of the family group.   Since these levels of organization are highly interdependent, NVC often serves more than one function: behaviour which is expressive for the individual may be communicative for the dyad and the group.   It should be noted that, when working and thinking within a systems framework, these distinctions between levels appear particularly arbitrary.   They do, however, make the process of conceptualization considerably more manageable.   Below, this systems framework is used to examine NVC at three levels of organization of the family system.

NVC at the organismic level of the family system

The person is a subsystem within the family.   During a family therapy session each person continuously emits nonverbal signals which
may be viewed as expressive in nature.   Three interrelated areas of
expressiveness have been discussed: emotion, intrapsychic processes
and psychopathology.
    Family life is an emotional experience.   Ackerman has emphasized
the importance of emotion in family breakdown:
    We believe that emotion is a bodily process, it is social;   it is
    contagious and circular in its effects.   The negative emotions,
    anxiety and rage, are infectious;   so too are the welfare emo-
    tions of affection, intimacy, and mutual caring.   In our view,
    deviant behavior and mental breakdown are largely a consequence
    of the contagion of disturbed emotion within the nexus of family
    relationships (Ackerman, 1972, p. 452).
    Since family members often do not verbalize their emotions, the
mechanism of this contagion is primarily nonverbal.   The family
therapist must obtain some sense of the locus of negative emotion
and the vehicle for its transmission.   This may be achieved directly by observing the expressive NVC of family members during a therapy session.   As we have seen, research has shown that the nature of
the emotion is most accurately read from the head, while the intensity is obtained from the body.   The following simple example illustrates this relationship of NVC to emotion.   A family came into
therapy because of the unruly behaviour of a seven-year-old boy.
While describing the boy's behaviour, the father also alluded to the
death of his own mother, and implied that certain extended family
members held the boy's behaviour to be responsible for the heart
attack which had caused her death.   As he said this, the boy's face
registered an expression of panic while his body went rigid, indicating the extreme intensity of the emotion.   This NVC alerted the
therapist to the implication of these events with respect to the
presenting problem.   By continuously monitoring the NVC of emotion,
the therapist is able to gauge the level of stress experienced by
each family member.   This information is vital because the therapist must be able to control the overall stressfulness of the session in such a way as to protect the most vulnerable member.
    Psychoanalytically oriented family therapists direct a consider-
able amount of attention to the interlocking intrapsychic processes
of family members and, for assistance in understanding these processes, rely heavily on the unconscious material produced in family
therapy.   Therapists using this approach generally see most NVC as
occurring outside the family's awareness and therefore as being unconscious.   Skynner (1976) hypothesized that much NVC is interna-
lized experience from one's family of origin.   When similar manifestations of NVC appear in the family of procreation, the adults
respond in a manner similar to the way they responded in their
family of origin.   Skynner succinctly expresses the psychoanalytically oriented family therapist's approach to NVC:
    If, therefore, the therapist becomes aware of the family's non-
    verbal expression and interactions, and makes the experience
    available to them by formulating these observations in the verbal
    mode, he gives them the possibility of making what is unconscious

conscious, at least to some degree.   The verbal mode brings
about the possibility of objectivity, of criticism, of standing
outside what is happening and correcting it ... (Skynner, 1976,
p. 94).

In short, the analytically oriented family therapist uses NVC to
help understand and interpret the unconscious processes of the
family.

Although family therapy defines the family as the patient, several considerations dictate that changes in the mental status of the
identified patient and of the other family members as individuals be
carefully monitored.   As mentioned earlier, research has shown that
such changes are often reflected in NVC.   Changes in the mental
status of the identified patient can be positive prognostic indicators of shifts in the family system.   Caution must be exercised,
however, because too rapid improvement in the identified patient can
alter the family homeostasis and produce panic and subsequent regression.   For example, a family came into therapy because of the
son's unusual facial tics.   After several sessions the tics had
subsided somewhat.   In the next session, the therapist explored the
marital relationship in greater detail.   At the outset of this session, the boy was relaxed and asymptomatic; however, as the session
became more stressful for the parents, the boy's facial tics became
progressively more pronounced.   As the identified patient improves,
a well family member often becomes symptomatic.   Indications of
this shift are often apparent from the NVC of the well family
member.   For example, a family came into therapy because of the extreme separation anxiety of a three-year-old girl.   After several
sessions, the girl's anxiety abated.   As the parents described this
improvement to the therapist, the six-year-old son, who had been
described as extremely well behaved and independent, curled up on
his mother's lap and complained of a stomach ache.   The therapist
was able to use this incident to help the parents recognize and
begin to meet the needs of their son.   By continuously assessing
the relationship between NVC and the mental status of individual
family members, the therapist can quietly remain one step ahead of
the family system, and regulate the pace of therapy in such a way as
to produce change without panic.

NVC at the dyadic or interpersonal level of the family system

At the dyadic or interpersonal level of organization, NVC has a communicative function.   More specifically, as a form of analogic communication, NVC carries 'command' or 'relationship' messages exchanged by participants in an interaction.   Sometimes the nonverbal
message stands alone.   More often, it accompanies a verbal message.
The verbal and nonverbal messages may be congruent or they may be
incongruent, in which case the NVC invariably carries the more accurate message about the relationship.   For example, a family came
into therapy because the father claimed he hated his young son.
However, while he professed this hatred in the first session, he
also smiled warmly at the boy who was playing at his feet.   The boy
reciprocated the smile and remained close to his father throughout
the session.   Obviously, the two levels of communication were in-

congruent in this instance, and, as later events in therapy confirmed, the nonverbal rather than the verbal communication defined the nature of the father-son relationship.

In dysfunctional families, members frequently refuse to define the nature of the relationships in the family.   This is accomplished by the repeated disqualification of any member's attempt to define the relationship.   This disqualification often occurs nonverbally.   Silence is a simple but effective nonverbal disqualification of a relationship message in that the receiver of the message neither affirms nor denies the message.   The nonverbal disqualification may also accompany a verbal message which appears to affirm or negate the relationship message.   In dysfunctional family systems, relationships are frequently rigid and inflexible.   While family members may profess a desire to alter the nature of relationships in the family, their NVC often betrays the underlying rigidity.   For example, a husband, who was described by his wife as a chronic alcoholic, professed to her his desire to improve the marriage by altering his drinking habits.   Throughout this discussion, the wife listened to what her husband said, but sat slouched in her chair at right angles to her husband and with her hand shielding him from her view.   Nonverbally she was either rejecting his suggestion or communicating that she had better shield herself from the hopelessness of his attempts to stop drinking.

The concept of the double bind has contributed enormously to the understanding of dysfunctional relationships.   The general characteristics of the double bind are summarized below:

1. When the individual is involved in an intense relationship; that is, a relationship in which he feels it is vitally important that he discriminate accurately what sort of message is being communicated so that he may respond appropriately.

2. And, the individual is caught in a situation in which the other person in the relationship is expressing two orders of messages and one of these denies the other.

3. And, the individual is unable to comment on the messages being expressed to correct his discrimination of what order of message to respond to;   i.e., he cannot make a metacommunicative statement (Bateson et al., 1956, p. 254).

One of the incongruent messages described above may be delivered nonverbally.   Double bind messages are difficult to demonstrate with practical examples because they become apparent only over long periods of observation.   They are, however, sometimes apparent in the interactions of those involved.   A family was referred because of the promiscuous acting out of an adolescent girl.   The mother repeatedly professed her displeasure about the girl's sexual behaviour, but on one occasion giggled when she described the fancy underwear she had purchased for her daughter.   Both the giggle and the behaviour of purchasing the underwear conveyed the injunction that the mother wanted, on one level, the daughter to be promiscuous.

Families also use NVC to define their relationship with the therapist.   Such nonverbal ploys as who comes to the sessions and the dropping of sessions are commonly used.   Each family member also uses NVC to define his/her relationship with the therapist.

In one session a mother constantly winked at the therapist while
her husband described the ramifications of her agoraphobia on the
family.   Family members may also assume congruent postures with
the therapist or mimic other aspects of his nonverbal behaviour in
order to convey their need to be approved of by him.

NVC at the social or group level of the family system

At this level of organization NVC has a communicative function which
regulates and maintains the security and identity of the family
group.   These nonverbal behaviours ensure that, during a family
therapy session, members will predictably follow a 'programme' which
will preserve the homeostasis of the family.   The nature of a
family programme is described below:

> A program is a pattern of behavior enacted by a group in a rela-
> tively stereotyped and (under recurring circumstances) repetitive
> way.   It may be learned from the culture or, in the case of
> families, from long association of the participants;   that is,
> it may be a piece of the particular culture of that group.   It
> may have rich variations, but it always has limits of variation,
> and members of the group will monitor each other's behavior to
> keep it from deviating too far from the program.   They also cue
> each other to begin new parts of the program (Ferber and Beels,
> 1970, p. 30).

These authors state further that 'the ultimate structure of
family relationships is in shared programs of communicative behavior, in accordance with which all members act, but some of which
are outside of awareness' (Ferber and Beels, 1970, p. 30).

As Ferber and Beels go on to point out, when a family comes into
therapy, it confronts the therapist with two very different programmes.   The first is an 'official programme' which the family
performs in order to save face and maintain self-esteem.   The official programme will contain the family's explanation for its distress.   The second is an 'unofficial programme' through which the
family monitors its emotional network.   Clues about the dysfunctional properties of the family system may be derived from the unofficial programme.   During a family therapy session, NVC is vital
to both programmes.   Family members will use NVC to monitor other
members who deviate from the official programme.   Family members
will also constantly leak nonverbal clues which highlight discrepancies between the official and unofficial programmes.   The
therapist must not only grasp the nature of both programmes, but
must also find a way to move between programmes in order to achieve
a shift in the family system.   The following example illustrates
both the regulatory function of NVC in family therapy and the pitfalls a therapist encounters when moving from the official to the
unofficial programme.

A family came into therapy because of the daughter's rebellious
behaviour.   In the first few sessions, the focus remained on
parent-child interactions.   As the daughter's behaviour improved,
hints of marital difficulty crept into the sessions.   The family
was being treated by a team of therapists, one of whom interviewed

the family while the others observed.   Following a consultation
with the observers, the therapist took back a message to the family
that the observers were impressed with the parents' hard work and,
based on the daughter's improvement, felt the parents deserved a
chance to talk about their own needs.   As the message was given,
the daughter shifted her chair so as to turn her back to the observation screen.   This nonverbal rejection of the observers was
wrongly interpreted as expressive of the daughter's anger that the
focus had been shifted from her.   In fact, subsequent events suggest that it was a regulatory monitor.   Each time the therapist
offered the parents an opportunity to discuss themselves, the
daughter engaged in a flurry of nonverbal activity - taking off her
hat (which she otherwise wore continuously) and shifting about
violently in her chair.   Each time the therapist noticed this
activity, she turned her attention away from the parents and back
to the daughter.   The sequence occurred twice.   When the therapist
turned to the daughter the first time she provocatively stated that
she was thinking of committing suicide.   The second time she
stated her desire to be a boy.   These two ploys preoccupied the
group for the remainder of the session.   Thus the daughter's NVC
appeared to function as a monitor which drew the session back to
the family's official programme (the daughter's behaviour) and away
from the crucial unofficial programme which the therapist was
trying to approach prematurely.

Regulatory monitors are not always so easy to detect.   They can
be disguised by a torrent of words or can be as fleeting as a
raised eyebrow.   Obviously, the use of observers or video tape
greatly facilitates their detection.

THE THERAPEUTIC USE OF NVC IN FAMILY THERAPY

How the therapist chooses to intervene with respect to NVC depends
on his orientation to family therapy, and the treatment goals he
is helping the family to achieve.   Some family therapists focus
more attention on the expressive functions of NVC for the individual, while others focus more attention on the interpersonal or
regulatory functions of the dyad and group.   Family therapists
have developed a variety of techniques to make therapeutic use of
NVC in family therapy.   While these techniques often incorporate
a verbal mode, they have in common a reliance upon NVC for their
effectiveness.   One may distinguish between those techniques which
give the family insight into its NVC and those which use NVC but
without attempting to increase the family's awareness.   The purpose of the insight-oriented techniques is to make the family more
aware of its NVC so that members may have a better understanding
and awareness of themselves and the processes of their family and
so enable them to behave more functionally.   The non-insight-
oriented techniques, which may be labelled as structural or strategic, use NVC to achieve a purposeful shift in the family system
by changing the communicative or structural patterns within the
family.

Below, some of the nonverbal techniques used in family therapy

are discussed under two headings: (1) those which are insight-
oriented;   and (2) those which are structural or strategic.
Neither the techniques nor their suggested applications are exhaustive.   There are unlimited ways to use NVC in family therapy,
and the following discussion is offered only as a guideline.

Insight-oriented techniques

This approach is well described by Bell and Ackerman.   In his
exposition of family group therapy, Bell (1975) argued that the
method depends on talking with words rather than with muscles.
He stated:
> For the therapist to understand what is going on, the family
> has to interpret, help put private language into public words.
> The therapist advises that he will try to help the family ver-
> balize things being said nonverbally, or things he cannot under-
> stand so the meaning will become clearer.   This, of course, is
> not only for the sake of the therapist, but for the sake of the
> family as a whole, toward the aim of improving communication
> (Bell, 1975, p. 116).

Bell believes that a therapist cannot comprehend the richness
of meaning in NVC;   therefore, he does not ascribe meaning to NVC,
but aims simply to make the family aware of it, leaving the actual
verbalization to the person or persons engaging in the NVC.   Such
neutral observations prevent the family members from feeling that
the therapist is accusing them or taking sides.

Ackerman was a master at using NVC to highlight for the family
its interpersonal processes.   He used NVC to stir spontaneous
interaction within the family itself and between the family and the
therapist.   He would call pointed attention to facial expressions,
body postures, movements, and other NVC in order to expand and shar-
pen the perceptions of relevant family conflicts (Ackerman, 1961).
Sherman et al. (1965) have examined Ackerman's use of NVC with respect to conflict in family therapy.   They note:
> There are various cues, verbal and non-verbal that prompt each
> family to re-enact the traumas and conflicts that led the family
> to seek treatment.   We see the family drama re-lived in minia-
> ture scenes, each of which reproduces the family conflict and
> the members' place in it.   The therapist may then be seen as a
> kind of director or stage manager, who sets the scene and eli-
> cits the dialogue and stage action (Sherman et al., 1965, p.
> 275).

These authors state further that NVC must be judged within the
context of the total family structure and alongside verbal communication.   NVC may 'dramatize, deceive, disguise, express or
betray;   and each expression must be evaluated accordingly' (Sherman
et al., 1965, p. 276).

Sometimes family therapists concentrate in depth on a specific
aspect of NVC.   To do so they may utilise special techniques,
some of which are borrowed from other forms of therapy.   For instance, gestalt therapy techniques, with their emphasis on the nonverbal presentation of self, may be used to explore more fully the

expressive functions of NVC in family therapy (Perls, 1973).   For
example, a couple came into therapy because the wife was uncertain
whether she wished to continue the marriage.   In one session, the
therapist observed the wife gripping her left hand tightly with
her right.   It was suggested to the wife that she exaggerate this
grip, and then give her hands an identity of their own and create a
dialogue between them.   She quickly labelled the right hand as the
'strong, repressive and punitive' one and the left hand as the
'submissive, repressed and sad' one.   As the dialogue progressed
she found that she was describing conflicting aspects of herself
and also the two protagonists in the marriage.   Previously she had
been unable or unwilling to face these issues.

A basic requirement of family life is the ability to express
one's needs effectively.   When a family member is unable to express himself, one frequently notices that the nonverbal components
of his presentation do not support and may even hinder his speech.
In such cases, it may be appropriate to use assertiveness training
techniques consciously to modify that family member's NVC (Lehman-
Olson, 1976).   For example, a single-parent family came into
therapy because a six-year-old boy seldom obeyed his mother.   It
soon became apparent that the grandmother, who lived with the
family, subtly undermined the mother's efforts to discipline the
boy.   The therapist invited the grandmother to the next session,
and noted that whenever the mother spoke to the grandmother about
the boy's behaviour, her voice trembled and she sat slouched in her
chair with her eyes cast downward.   In a subsequent session, the
therapist pointed out to the mother the futility of her communication with the grandmother, and proposed to teach her to communicate
more effectively.   Using behavioural rehearsal, the mother learned
to maintain eye contact while speaking, to lean forward and gestic-
ulate when appropriate, and to speak with a firm tone of voice.
When the therapist was satisfied with her progress, he invited the
grandmother to another session at which time the mother confronted
her on several issues relating to the discipline of the boy.   Although the grandmother was furious, subsequently she became less
interfering, and the boy's behaviour steadily improved.

The presence of young children in family therapy places a responsibility on the therapist to integrate them into the treatment
process.   Since children rely heavily on NVC, the therapist must
be prepared to listen and respond to them at this level.   Play
materials constitute a vital nonverbal medium through which children communicate in family therapy.   Most family therapists provide age appropriate materials to enable children to express themselves through play.   A doll's house, for instance, offers
excellent opportunities for a child to express his internal world
or his perception of the family.   For example, a four-year-old
boy set up a battle between two sets of grandparent dolls.   He
viciously banged the dolls together until the therapist inquired
about the row taking place in the doll's house,   The ensuing discussion not only allowed the boy to express his fear of violence,
but also exposed the intense jealousy between the two sets of
grandparents.   Drawing materials and clay also afford children
opportunities to express themselves.   For example, a family came

into therapy because an eleven-year-old boy had set alight two
fires which had caused considerable damage.   The parents believed
the three younger children knew nothing of the fires or their
brother's involvement.   During the initial session, however, each
of the younger children drew pictures of houses on fire.   Some
skill is required on the part of the family therapist if he is to
maintain his nonverbal work with young children as an integral part
of the family therapy session, but unless these opportunities are
given much of the richness of the young child's contribution is
lost.

Family therapy can be particularly constraining of NVC if too
much emphasis is placed by the therapist on verbal content.   In
order to grasp clearly the function of NVC in defining relationships, the therapist must at times generate some physical activity.
Role play, simulation and psychodrama are related techniques which
provide such physical activity.   In one session, for instance, a
depressed woman described her desire to avoid her husband when he
arrived home from work.   The therapist asked the couple to roleplay this situation.   During the roleplay the husband made a half-
hearted gesture to touch his wife in greeting her to which she reacted by abruptly withdrawing and bursting into tears.   Initially,
she claimed she hated to be touched but later admitted that she resented her husband's physical contact because it was always done
in jest rather than intimacy.

When treating relationships in which a sexual dysfunction constitutes the presenting problem, a heavy emphasis is placed on
tasks of a largely nonverbal nature being completed by the couple
between sessions (Masters and Johnson, 1970).   By focusing on
specific sexual behaviours, these tasks force the couple to communicate nonverbally about their sexual relationship.   Not only
do the tasks help the couple move toward the elimination of their
specific sexual dysfunction, but also, the manner in which the task
is completed or not completed offers important information about
sources of resistance to the therapy.   The treatment of sexual dysfunctions is discussed in detail by Crowe in Chapter 7.

Family sculpting is a powerful tool for enhancing the family's
awareness of its relationship system.   Walrond-Skinner (1976,
p. 87) defines sculpting as a 'technique whereby the relationships
between family members are recreated in space, through the formation
of a physical tableau'.   The sculptor makes a pictorial statement
about the family system by consciously specifying the proxemics,
postures, gestures, facial expressions, and physical contact of the
family members.   Some therapists allow the family sculpture to
speak for itself while others invite the family to discuss it.
A more thorough discussion of sculpting is given by Papp et al.
(1973) and Simon (1972).

Papp (1976) more recently argued that emotional relationships
are always in motion;   therefore, sculpting must be an instrument
of movement.   Papp, therefore, prefers to refer to her use of
sculpting as choreography.   Her use of choreography is summarized
below:

My own use of this technique ... is based not so much on experiencing or understanding the system to which one belongs as

on creating new patterns and thus changing the system.   Choreography is used as a method of actively intervening in the
nuclear and extended family by realigning family relationships.
This realignment is done through exploring alternative transactional patterns in terms of physical movement and positioning
(Papp, 1976, p. 466).
Papp's use of choreography, as described above, may be viewed also
as a structural intervention.   Sculpting and choreography may be
used with families who are excessively verbal or when a session has
become dull or unproductive.

Video tape playback has become a more commonly used device in
family therapy.   It may be used to augment any of the techniques
described above.   Video tape playback may be used simply to afford
the family a visual impression of itself, or, more specifically, to
call pointed attention to some aspect of the family's NVC.   Alger
(1976), reported several examples of the latter use of playback.

Finally, the genogram constitutes a nonverbal medium for gather-
ing information and helping the family become more aware of its
system, by mapping relationships between several generations on a
board or piece of paper (Guerin and Pendagast, 1976).

Strategic and structural techniques

The second basic approach to the therapeutic use of NVC in family
therapy is taken by those therapists who elect not to reveal their
awareness and understanding of the family's NVC, but to use their
own understanding of it to assist the family in moving toward its
treatment goals.   This group hypothesizes that to help the family
to understand its NVC better only leads to a redefinition of the
'official programme' by the family, and to a more careful protection
of the 'unofficial programme'.   These therapists focus primarily on
the communicative functions of NVC, and use it as a medium for defining the repetitive patterns of interaction within the family
system.   Once these patterns are understood, the therapist can intervene at the dyadic or group level of the family system to shift
the pattern.   The interventions, which are usually strategic or
structural, are frequently directed at some aspect of NVC.   This
use of NVC is illustrated by the following examples.

A family came into therapy because of the hostile and rebellious
behaviour of an adolescent daughter.   They were seen by a male
therapist and a team of observers.   The observers noted that the
following sequence occurred quite frequently.   Each time the therapist directed attention to the father, the mother would initiate
quasi-courtship behaviour (Scheflen, 1965).   She would begin to
preen her hair and arch her back.   This behaviour would catch the
therapist's attention, and he would divert his attention to the
mother.   As the therapist altered his attention, the father crossed
his arms and ankles and began to pout.   This sequence was symbolic
of the family's characteristic pattern of interaction in that every
attempt made by the father to assert control over the daughter was
ultimately undermined by the mother, with the father in turn becoming even more angry at the daughter.   The observers pointed out

this sequence to the therapist and advised him to congratulate
the father on his strength in maintaining a patient silence while
his wife 'sorted out' their daughter.   When the therapist delivered this message, the father uncrossed his limbs and became more
animated and involved in the session.   As he spoke, the wife
placed her hand over her mouth.   Moreover, she did not use the
quasi-courtship manoeuvre to interrupt him for the remainder of the
session.

The second example highlights the strategic use of seating arrangement.   A family was referred by the school authorities because of
the behaviour of an adolescent son.   In several consecutive sessions the seating arrangement shown in Figure 5.1 was used.

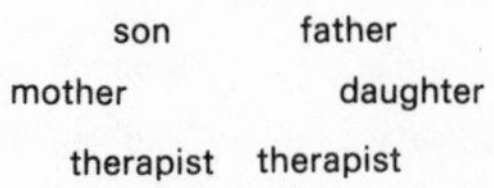

son   father

mother   daughter

therapist therapist

Figure 5.1

A central problem in the family was the son's inability to accept
his stepfather;   however, whenever the therapists encouraged the
males to explore this difficulty the mother would deflect attention
from the topic.   The therapists decided to change the seating arrangement for the following session to the configuration shown in
Figure 5.2.   The family was simply informed that the therapists had
grown tired of the old seating arrangement and wished to try a new
one.

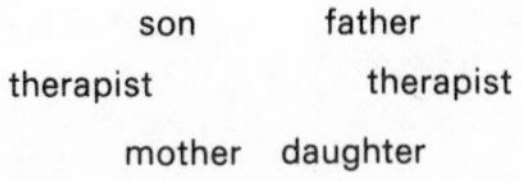

son   father

therapist   therapist

mother daughter

Figure 5.2

In the next session, the mother again attempted to block constructive discussion between the males;   however, the therapist seated to
the left of the mother merely shifted his posture forward to create
a subtle but effective barrier between the mother and the two males.
This small shift reduced her effectiveness and allowed the son and
stepfather productively to resolve a long-standing issue.

Structural family therapists change a dysfunctional family system
by restructuring family patterns of relationships (Minuchin, 1974).
This approach is predicated on a belief that family dysfunctions are
frequently caused and maintained by the formation of alliances
across generational boundaries.   Such is the case when a parent
sides with a child against the other parent.   This restructuring
may be done through tasks which force the family members to relate
in a different way, or it may be accomplished during a family therapy session through a symbolic restructuring of the family relation-

ships.   In the latter case, the therapist relies heavily on the
nonverbal media available to him.   He may ask one family member to
sit next to another member to emphasize the relationship between the
two, or he may move a member behind a one-way screen to symbolize a
separation.   The following example illustrates the use of restructuring techniques.

A family came into therapy because Karen, a ten-year-old girl,
refused to go to school.   It soon became apparent that the grandmother undermined not only the mother's attempts to get the girl
back to school, but also her parenting in general.   There were two
other daughters in the family.   The session to be described opened
with the seating arrangement shown in Figure 5.3.

```
                        Karen
            mother            grandmother
         daughter               daughter
            therapist    therapist
```

Figure 5.3

During the session, one of the therapists encouraged a disagreement
between the mother and grandmother about Karen while the other therapist invited the other two daughters to watch the discussion from
behind the one-way screen.   This manoeuvre produced the seating
arrangement shown in Figure 5.4.

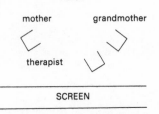

```
                        Karen
            mother            grandmother
            therapist

              ──────────────
                 SCREEN
              ──────────────

        daughter, daughter, therapist
```

Figure 5.4

From behind the screen it was easy for the daughters to see that the
grandmother sided with Karen.   The therapist, however, suggested
that Karen seemed uncomfortable between her mother and grandmother,
and asked one of the daughters to invite Karen to change her seat.
When this suggestion was made, Karen moved to the empty chair next
to her grandmother, thus making the alliance overt.   At this point
the mother burst into tears, and one of the daughters rushed from
behind the screen to comfort her, making overt another alliance.
Shortly thereafter the remaining daughter and therapist rejoined the
family.

Having made the alliance between Karen and grandmother overt, the
therapists tried to break it symbolically by inviting the grandmother to join one of the therapists behind the one-way screen.   As
the therapist and grandmother rose to leave the room, Karen jumped

up to join them.   The grandmother attempted to restrain the girl,
but she refused and went directly behind the one-way screen.   This
left the grandmother standing in the middle of the interviewing room
furious because Karen had defied her.   To make this loss of power
even more overt, the therapists invited the grandmother to attempt
to persuade Karen to return.   The grandmother tried for ten minutes
but without success.   Meanwhile, one of the therapists sympathized
with the mother's growing awareness of the grandmother's interfer-
ence, and supported her determination to regain control over her
daughter.

When Karen and grandmother were invited to rejoin the family,
Karen returned first.   A deadly serious game of 'musical chairs'
followed.   Karen chose a seat as shown in Figure 5.5.   Mother immediately moved to sit next to her (Figure 5.6).   Karen then moved
over one chair, and mother, determined to sit next to her, also
moved (Figure 5.7).   Grandmother then returned and chose her original chair (Figure 5.8).   It is significant that Karen remained next
to mother (Figure 5.8) even though, in the final seating arrangement
there was an empty chair next to grandmother.   The exclusive alliance between grandmother and Karen had been broken and the beginnings of a new alignment introduced.

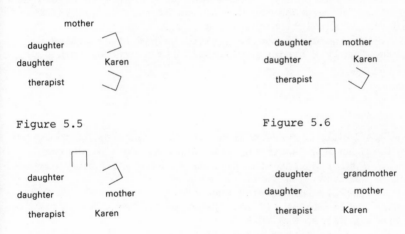

Figure 5.5   Figure 5.6

Figure 5.7   Figure 5.8

Structural family therapists may also concentrate specifically on
getting the family to recreate its presenting symptomatology in the
session.   Symptoms may be thought of as powerful pieces of NVC.
The choice of the symptom itself and the symptom bearer are eloquent
comments on the family system.   Minuchin, for example, in his work
with anorectics, frequently invites the family to eat with him
during the first session, thereby enabling the family to 'describe'
the conflicts and interpersonal patterns which develop around and
are expressed nonverbally and directly by the symptom.   Minuchin
then makes use of the data which the nonverbal activity affords to
prepare a set of tasks to begin restructuring the family pattern of
relationships (Aponte and Hoffman, 1973).

CONCLUSION

Family therapy is about changing family systems.   The growing body
of knowledge about family dynamics and family therapy attests that
this change may be produced in a number of ways.   In fact, one of
family therapy's strongest advantages is its technical flexibility.
The therapist can intervene at any one of several levels of organization within the family system.   This paper has attempted to examine the functions of NVC at three such levels: the individual,
the dyad and the group.   Table 5.1 summarizes this multi-level view
of NVC in family therapy.   A range of techniques which make use of
NVC have also been discussed.

    Family therapy is a challenging, exciting, and sometimes fright-
ening method of work.   The experience is somewhat like encountering
a new culture.   The visitor immediately registers an awareness of
great difference, but he cannot articulate what it is.   The
strangeness lies largely out of sight, within the nonverbal components of the culture.   Hall (1966) has referred to these nonverbal
components as the hidden dimension.   Only those visitors who are
willing to observe carefully and ask questions are ever able to feel
at home in the new culture.   So also is each family a unique experience when the therapist first encounters it.   Only with time does
the therapist begin to grasp the dimensions of the family system:
its individuals, its relationships, and its life as a group.   To
achieve this, the therapist can be greatly helped if he learns to
understand the family's hidden dimension: its nonverbal communication.

REFERENCES

ACKERMAN, N.W. (1961), A dynamic frame for the clinical approach to
family conflict, in N.W. Ackerman, F.L. Beatman and S.N. Sherman
(eds) (1961), 'Exploring the Base of Family Therapy', Family Service
Association of America, New York.
ACKERMAN, N.W. (1972), The growing edge of family therapy, in C.J.
Sager and H.S. Kaplan (eds) (1972), 'Progress in Group and Family
Therapy', Brunner/Mazel, New York.
ALGER, I. (1976), Integrating immediate video playback in family
therapy, in P. Guerin (ed.) (1976), 'Family Therapy: Theory and
Practice', Gardner Press, New York.
APONTE, H. and HOFFMAN, L. (1973), The open door: a structural
approach to a family with an anorectic child, 'Family Process', vol.
12, no. 1, pp. 1-44.
ARGYLE, M. (1975), 'Bodily Communication', Methuen, London.
BATESON, G., JACKSON, D.D., HALEY, J. and WEAKLAND, J.N. (1956),
Toward a theory of schizophrenia, 'Behavioral Science', vol. 1, no.
4, pp. 251-64.
BEELS, C.C. and FERBER, A. (1969), Family therapy: a view, 'Family
Process', vol. 8, no. 2, pp. 280-332.
BEIER, E.G. (1974), Nonverbal communication: how we send emotional
messages, 'Psychology Today', vol. 8, no. 5, pp. 52-6.
BELL, J.E. (1975), 'Family Therapy', Jason Aronson, New York.
BIRDWHISTELL, R. (1962), An approach to communication, 'Family Pro-
cess', vol. 1, no. 2, pp. 194-201.

BIRDWHISTELL, R. (1970), 'Kinesics and Context: Essays on Body Motion Communication', University of Pennsylvania Press, Philadelphia.

CONDON, W.S., OGSTON, W.D. and PACOE, L.W. (1969), Three faces of Eve revisited: a study of transient microstrabismus, 'Journal of Abnormal Psychology', vol. 74, no. 5, pp. 305-15.

DARWIN, C. (1872), 'The Expression of the Emotions in Man and Animals', reprinted by the University of Chicago Press (1965).

DAVIS, M. (1970a), Movement characteristics of hospitalized psychiatric patients, in 'Proceedings of the Fifth Annual Conference of the American Dance Therapy Association'.

DAVIS, M. (1970b), 'An Effort-shape Movement Analysis of a Family Therapy Session', Dance Notation Bureau Publication, New York.

DAVIS, M. (1973), Clinical implications of body movement research, 'International Mental Health Research Newsletter', vol. 15, no. 1, pp. 3-7.

DEUTSCH, F. (1947), Analysis of postural behavior, 'Psychoanalytic Quarterley', vol. 16, pp. 195-213.

DITTMANN, A.T., PARLOFF, M.B. and BOOMER, D.S. (1965), Facial and bodily expression: a study of receptivity of emotional cues, 'Psychiatry', vol. 28, no. 3, pp. 239-44.

DRAG, R. and Shaw, M. (1967), Factors influencing the communication of emotional intent by facial expression, 'Psychonomic Science', vol. 8, no. 4, pp. 137-8.

EHRLICH, M.P. (1970), The role of body experience in therapy, 'Psychoanalytic Review', vol. 57, no. 2, pp. 181-95.

EKMAN, P. and FRIESEN, W.V. (1967), Head and body cues in the judgement of emotions: a reformulation, 'Perceptual and Motor Skills', vol. 24, no. 3, pp. 711-24.

EKMAN, P. and FRIESEN, W.V. (1968), Nonverbal behaviour in psychotherapy research, in J.M. Schlien (ed.) (1968), 'Research in Psychotherapy', American Psychological Association, Washington, DC.

EKMAN, P. and FRIESEN, W.V. (1969), The repertoire of nonverbal behavior: categories, origins, usage and coding, 'Semiotica', vol. 1, pp. 49-98.

ELLSWORTH, P.C. and CARLSMITH, J.M. (1968), Effects of eye contact and verbal content on affective responses to a dyadic interaction, 'Journal of Personality and Social Psychology', vol. 10, no. 1, pp. 15-20.

FERBER, A.S. and BEELS, C.C. (1970), Changing family behavior programs, in N.W. Ackerman (ed.) (1970), 'Family Therapy in Transition', Little Brown, Boston.

FRAMO, J. (ed.) (1972), 'Family Interaction: A Dialogue between Family Researchers and Family Therapists', Springer, New York.

FREUD, S. (1959), 'Psychopathology of Everyday Life', New American Library, New York.

GLADSTEIN, G.A. (1974), Nonverbal communication and counseling/psychotherapy: a review, 'Counseling Psychologist', vol. 4, no. 3, pp. 34-57.

GOSTYNSKI, E. (1951), A clinical contribution to the analysis of gestures, 'International Journal of Psycho-Analysis', vol. 32, pp. 310-18.

GUERIN, P. and PENDAGAST, E.G. (1976), Evaluation of family system and genogram, in P. Guerin (ed.) (1976), 'Family Therapy: Theory and Practice', Gardner Press, New York.

HALL, E. (1963), A system of notation of proxemic behavior, 'American Anthropologist', vol. 65, pp. 1003-26.
HALL, E. (1966), 'The Silent Language', Fawcett, Greenwich, Conn.
HERSEN, M., MILLER, P.M. and EISLER, R.M. (1973), Interactions between alcoholics and their wives: a descriptive analysis of verbal and non-verbal behavior, 'Quarterly Journal of Studies of Alcohol', vol. 34, no. 2, pp. 516-20.
HEWES, G. (1955), World distribution of certain postural habits, 'American Anthropologist', vol. 57, pp. 231-44.
HINCHLIFFE, M.K., LANCASHIRE, M. and ROBERTS, F.J. (1971), A study of eye contact changes in depressed and recovered psychiatric patients, 'British Journal of Psychiatry', vol. 119, no. 549, pp. 213-15.
KAHN, M. (1970), Non-verbal communication and marital satisfaction, 'Family Process', vol. 9, no. 4, pp. 449-56.
KENDON, A. (1967), How people interact, in A. Ferber, M. Mendelsohn and A. Napier (eds) (1967), 'The Book of Family Therapy', Houghton Mifflin, Boston.
LA BARRE, W. (1964), Paralinguistics, kinesics and cultural anthropology, in T. Sebeok, A. Hayes and M.C. Beteson (eds) (1964), 'Approaches to Semiotics', Mouton, The Hague.
LEHMAN-OLSON, D. (1976), Assertiveness training: theoretical and clinical implications, in D.H.L. Olson (ed.) (1976), 'Treating Relationships', Graphic, Lake Mills, Iowa.
LOEB, F.F. (1968), The microscopic film analysis of the function of a recurrent behavioral pattern in a psychotherapeutic session, 'Journal of Nervous and Mental Diseases', vol. 147, no. 6, pp. 605-17.
MAHL, G.F. (1967), Some clinical observations on non-verbal behavior in interviews, 'Journal of Nervous and Mental Diseases', vol. 144, no. 6, pp. 492-505.
MAHL, G.F. (1968), Gestures and body movements in interviews, in J.M. Shlien (ed.) (1968), 'Research in Psychotherapy', American Psychological Association, Washington, DC.
MASTERS, W. and JOHNSON, V. (1970), 'Human Sexual Inadequacy', Little Brown, Boston.
MINUCHIN, S. (1974), 'Families and Family Therapy', Tavistock Publications, London.
NAVRON, L. (1967), Communication and adjustment in marriage, 'Family Process', vol. 6, no. 2, pp. 173-84.
PAPP, P., SILVERSTEIN, O. and CARTER, E. (1973), Family sculpting in preventive work with well families, 'Family Process', vol. 12, no. 2, pp. 197-212.
PAPP, P. (1976), Family choreography, in P. Guerin (ed.) (1976), 'Family Therapy: Theory and Practice', Gardner Press, New York.
PERLS, F. (1973), 'The Gestalt Approach and Eyewitness to Therapy', Science and Behaviour Books, Ben Lomond, California.
REICH, W. (1949), 'Character-Analysis', Noonday Press, New York.
RISKIN, J. and FAUNCE, E.E. (1972), An evaluative review of family interaction research, 'Family Process', vol. 11, no. 4, pp. 365-456.
RUESCH, L. and BATESON, G. (1951), 'Communication: The Social Matrix of Psychiatry', W.W. Norton, New York.
SCHEFLEN, A.E. (1963), Communication and regulation in psychotherapy, 'Psychiatry', vol. 26, no. 2, pp. 126-36.

SCHEFLEN, A.E. (1964), The significance of posture in communication systems, 'Psychiatry', vol. 27, no. 4, pp. 316-31.
SCHEFLEN, A.E. (1965), Quasi-courtship behavior in psychotherapy, 'Psychiatry', vol. 28, no. 3, pp. 245-57.
SCHEFLEN, A.E. (1967), On the structuring of human communication, 'American Behavioral Scientist', vol. 10, pp. 8-12.
SCHEFLEN, A.E. and SCHEFLEN, A. (1972), 'Body Language and Social Order: Communication and Behavioral Control', Prentice Hall, Englewood Cliffs, New Jersey.
SCHEFLEN, A.E. (1973), 'Communicational Structure: Analysis of a Psychotherapy Transaction', Indiana University Press, Bloomington, Indiana.
SHERMAN, M.H., ACKERMAN, N.W., SHERMAN, S.N. and MITCHELL, C. (1965), Non verbal cues and reenactment of conflict in family therapy, 'Family Process', vol. 4, no. 1, pp. 133-62.
SIMON, R.M. (1972), Sculpting the family, 'Family Process', vol. 11, no. 1, pp. 49-57.
SKYNNER, A.C.R. (1976), 'One Flesh: Separate Persons', Constable, London.
SPEER, D.C. (1972), Nonverbal communication of affective information: some laboratory findings pertaining to an interactional process, 'Comparative Group Studies', vol. 3, no. 4, pp. 409-23.
THOMPSON, D. and MELTZER, S. (1964), Communication of emotional intent by facial expression, 'Journal of Abnormal and Social Psychology', vol. 68, no. 2, pp. 129-35.
TRAGER, G.L. (1958), Paralanguage, a first approximation, 'Studies in Linguistics', vol. 13, no. 1, pp. 1-12.
VANDE CREEK, L. and WATKINS, J.T. (1972), Responses to incongruent verbal and nonverbal emotional cues, 'Journal of Communication', vol. 22, no. 3, pp. 311-16.
WALROND-SKINNER, S. (1976), 'Family Therapy: The Treatment of Natural Systems', Routledge & Kegan Paul, London.
WATZLAWICK, P.J., BEAVIN, J. and JACKSON, D.D. (1967), 'Pragmatics of Human Communication', W.W. Norton, New York.
WAZER, P.H. (1974), Therapist training in non verbal communication: 1. Nonverbal cues for depression, 'Journal of Clinical Psychology', vol. 30, no. 2, pp. 215-18.

Chapter 6

COUPLE THERAPY

Anthony Ryle

To work with married couples in crisis is to face two people suffering pain and disappointment. The wedding photographs which, however posed and public, were once the expression of private hopes and
intentions, stand as a rebuke or have been put away. If there are
children who were conceived in joy or, at least, with a shared commitment, they may have become a source of guilt or a focus of conflict. The future, once certain, if only in being a shared one,
has become threatening and clouded with anticipated loss. Whatever
skills we have to offer as professionals to people in such a situation must seem small in relation to this central pain; and yet the
brief assistance of therapists of many different temperaments and
persuasions can, in many cases, enable couples to live better, often
together, sometimes apart. It is the purpose of this chapter to
examine the nature of such therapeutic interventions, confining
attention to those approaches that are transactional in Olson's
(1970) sense; that is to say, where the couple are treated together, with the attention being on their relationship.

NON-SPECIFIC FACTORS IN THERAPY

In aiming to describe what constitutes effective therapy, one is
hampered by the paucity of, and difficulty in carrying out, effective research; it must also be acknowledged that, whatever particular skills we bring as therapists, much of what we provide is not
specific to our training and knowledge, even though it may be related to our personality and role. These non-specific features need
to be considered first; and their presence as an ingredient in most
of the methods described in detail later in this chapter needs
always to be borne in mind.
 1 The installation of hope: couples accepting conjoint therapy
will have a small residue of hope in most cases, and this is likely
to become focused, not always realistically, on the helper or helpers. To be accepted for professional help conveys the possibility
that something might be done, and provides some relief for the feelings of debilitating helplessness which long-standing, unresolved
conflict can engender. Seligman's (1975) concept of 'learned helplessness' is relevant here.
132

2 The provision of support: unhappy people whose lives are going
badly are likely to feel dependent, child-like, and often ashamed.
Most professionals, through a matter-of-fact acceptance of people
and their difficulties, will meet, in some symbolic way at least,
this need for care and acceptance without judgment.

3 Clarification: the account given by a couple of their difficulties will be, in most instances, confused; in the course of telling
it, and through the professional's picking out the essential content
of the story, especially the feeling content, some clarification
will be achieved. In so far as some explanatory patterns may be
discerned by the couple, the difficulties may seem less arbitrary
than before.

4 Communication: an important part of this process of clarification will be listening carefully to the different accounts and different perceptions of the two people involved. The therapist, by
concentrating on the differences in these accounts, by naming accurately what seems to be said or seen by one in relation to the
other, and often by attending directly to the modes of contradictory
communication going on between the couple, will restore communication in a situation where it has often been largely blocked.

5 Learning: whether by instruction, through behavioural programmes aiming to change behaviour between the couple, or by the
example of the way that the therapist or therapists conduct the interviews, or by explanation and interpretation of what is said and
done, therapists offer a learning experience which alters for the
couple the meanings attached to the interactions between them, and
hence opens up the possibility of change.

6 Giving permission: the professional, by his non-judgmental
stance, by his willingness to listen, and to discuss what is usually
held back and felt shameful or private, and by the implicit authority he holds (and also by the inflated authority he is likely to be
invested with by the couple), is likely to relieve the couple of
some of the pressures of social opinion and personal self-accusa-
tion. In this way, the couple may be able to move in the direction
of voicing feelings, especially negative ones, and so become less
tied down by unspoken resentment and unproductive guilt.

7 The encouragement of different behaviours: whether the therapist acts directly, by encouraging changes, or indirectly, by aiding
communication and helping each individual reconsider and reconstrue
the ways in which the other is seen, the therapist will be freeing
the couple from their habitual set patterns of interaction, and encouraging new attempts and explorations between them.

Before considering in more detail how these different processes
may be carried out, it would be best to consider the size of the
problem and the selection of couples suitable for joint therapy.

THE SIZE OF THE PROBLEM

Direct provision for marital therapy is relatively scanty in Britain, but the potential size of the problem is vast. Dominian
(1972) quotes estimates that between one-sixth and one-quarter of
contemporary marriages are likely to fail. He also summarises the
evidence for an association between marital disruption and suicide,

and notes the importance of marital problems in the commonly presenting emotional problems treated by family doctors, and he reviews
the evidence showing the importance of the parents' marital relationship as a cause of psychological disturbance in children (see
also Ryle, 1967 and Rutter, 1971).   It seems likely that a large
part of the present vast and escalating consumption of tranquillising and sedative drugs is consumed by people whose essential emotional problems are centred upon the marriage relationship.   Taking
account of this evidence, it is clearly an urgent task to see how
far therapeutic interventions into the marital relationships may be
effective.

SELECTION

The request for help with the marriage relationship may come direct
from the couple, and this is particularly likely to be true where
the agency approached has a public commitment to working in this
way, like, for example, the Marriage Guidance Council, and often the
clergy.   In other cases, a breakdown in the relationship, or a
crisis of some sort, may lead to the involvement of agencies coping
with families or individuals in crisis, notably the Probation Service and the Social Services Department.   Sometimes the presentation will be through the disturbance of a child, who is affected by
the bad relationship between the parents.   If there is a clear relationship between the marital problem and the request for help, it
is becoming increasingly likely that such agencies will offer some
counselling help to the couple.   However, in many less acute situations, the first sign of marital stress will be through the consultation of one individual, with the family doctor or a psychiatrist,
complaining of anxiety or depression or the somatic effects of
these.   Whatever the agency, the provocation, or the presenting
problem, the decision to offer conjoint marital therapy rather than
individual therapy or whole family therapy, needs to be based upon a
careful assessment.
   In choosing whether to work with a couple rather than with one or
other individual, the connection between the symptoms and the relationship problems must be determined.   It could happen that, in a
crisis presentation of a couple with marital problems to an agency
offering joint counselling help, the underlying difficulty was in
fact caused by an acute mental illness in one member, and here individual psychiatric treatment would be the appropriate form of help.
Psychopathic personality disorders and schizophrenia are particularly likely to lead to marital breakdown, while the more common, relatively mild, endogenous depression, with associated loss of sexual
interest, can lead to secondary marital conflict.   Conversely, it
may be that an individual complaining of long-established and elaborated psychological symptoms could, in fact, be presenting these
largely or exclusively because of difficulties in the marriage relationship, the symptoms being either a communication, a form of controlling behaviour, or a response to stress.   If it is ascertained
that a significant proportion of the stress complained of is related
to issues between the couple, and if both individuals recognise that
fact, or come to do so, and can accept the desirability of exploring

their relationship, then conjoint work will usually be the treatment of choice, at least initially.   The possibility of subsequent individual treatment for one or both always remains open, but work on the couple should take precedence.   It is important to establish the joint focus of the work early on, before one or other has been designated as the ill or responsible one in a way which blocks exploration of the interaction.

The decision to offer joint treatment will usually require one or more joint interviews, in the course of which the professional will be making his assessment of the nature of the problem, and the couple will be having some opportunity to see the kind of help which is being offered.   It is important, therefore, that the basic stance of the professionals is conveyed at this time as being accepting, inquiring, and non-judgmental, and that the kind of approach being offered is made clear to the couple.   It is further desirable that, after the initial interview, a clear contract is made with the couple, in which the aims, methods, frequency and duration of the treatment are agreed between those concerned.

The choice between couple therapy and family therapy is most likely to be an issue when the family problem is manifest in the disturbance of a child or of children, who are being affected by the dispute or unhappiness between the couple, either as a scapegoat or go-between, or ally of one or other parent.   In so far as the family is one system, many workers would argue for the inclusion of the children as being the norm, at least during the diagnostic stage.   Just as to take on an individual patient for treatment can ignore the way in which his difficulties are a reflection of a marital problem, so taking the couple on for treatment may ignore the way in which their difficulty is part of a family problem (Whitaker, 1975).   However, against this, it may be argued that children are not always deeply enmeshed in their parents' problems, and may have some right to be spared such involvement.   In so far as the parental difficulties are usually the source of family difficulty, the parents, once helped, can become in turn a source of recovery, without the children being directly involved in treatment.   This decision, however, is likely to be made most often on grounds of preference or ideology or available resource as, at the present time, there is little evidence in favour of one or other course.

CLASSIFICATIONS

Although the complexity of this issue means that, in many cases, each marital problem that presents will seem unique, it is clearly important for understanding and intelligent decision-making to have some classificatory system at work.   Berman and Lief (1975) have provided a useful review of this issue and they suggest that there are four main types of classificatory system.   The first are those which are based upon the rules for defining power; this they see as yielding three groups, the symmetrical marriage (which this author has categorised as the cosy-collusive); the complementary marriage; and the co-operative marriage.   This classification resembles the three groups identified by Collins et al. (1971) in a study of the marriages of sixty neurotic males and sixty controls.   Their groups

were identified as segregated, husband-dominated, and co-operative,
the proportion of segregated and husband-dominated marriages being
significantly higher in the neurotic group.

The second classificatory system described by Berman and Lief is
by parental stage, being based upon the presence or absence, and the
age-span, of the children.

The third classification is by the level of intimacy, and here
they list the conflict-habituated, the devitalised, the passive-con-
genial, the vital, and the total marriage, the titles being on the
whole self-explanatory.

Finally, there are the psychiatric or personality style descriptive categories, particularly favoured in psychiatric literature.
Here the following patterns are described: the obsessive-compulsive
husband and the hysterical wife; the passive-dependent husband and
the dominant wife; the paranoid husband and the depression-prone
wife; the depression-prone husband and the paranoid wife; the oral
dependent relationship, and the neurotic wife and the omnipotent
husband. Each of these combinations may represent some kind of
stable complementary fit, although some are far more likely to break
down than others.

The descriptive categories described by Berman and Lief can be
related, in turn, to the formulations of the marital relationship in
terms of object-relations theory, in which different combinations,
based upon parent-child patterns, are seen to occur. The relationship between the partners can be described in terms of various combinations of an idealised, rejecting, or authoritarian parent, in
the one partner, and the dependent, compliant or rebellious child,
in the other.

An alternative classification, based upon psychodynamic concep-
tions of the developmental stage or maturity of the individuals, is
offered by Skynner (1975). He describes three developmental
levels: at the infantile level, the individual is more or less insensitive to the existence of the other, except in so far as he or
she is seen as a potential supplier of need. Marriages at this
level are seldom helped by interpretive treatment, but may respond
to firm management and instruction. Marriages at the childish
level are marked by anxious, over-dependent behaviour, with either
clinging to or flights and escapes from the relationship. The individual is either complaining of suffocation, or embarking upon
infidelities. The psychotherapeutic goal in such marriages is to
increase the level of responsibility and individuation of each
member of the pair, so that the relationship can be recreated on a
different basis. The third level would be the reasonably mature
and adult relationship. The emphasis upon individuation as a
necessary, but often problematic, stage in the history of the marriage was eloquently described in a neglected article by Jung
(1928). This task of individuation, and the stages of maturity
described by Skynner, suggest that, within the marital relationship,
there is a kind of recapitulation of the infant's development, a
fact which is understandable when one considers Dicks's (1967) observation that individuals coping at a mature, adult level every-
where else can behave in the marital relationship at extraordinarily
infantile levels. The descriptions of Mahler et al. (1975) of the
infant's individuation can be compared to Skynner's classification;

his infantile stage corresponds to the symbiotic phase in their
terms.   The childish stage has two equivalent substages in Mahler's
account of infancy, the first marked by 'practising and refuelling'
in which the child essays independence but has to return to mother
for recharging at intervals, and still regards the mother as primarily a source of safety; and the second stage which she calls 'ambi-
tendency', which is marked by a combination of clinging and coercion.   Both these descriptive categories seem applicable to disturbed marital relationships.

THE AIMS OF COUPLE THERAPY

Although therapy is conducted exclusively with the couple, one of
its first aims will be to enhance the individuality of each partner,
enabling them to recognise and state more clearly their feelings and
needs, and to distinguish more clearly the degree to which it is
themselves, and the degree to which it is their partners, who are
responsible for their difficulties.   Beyond this, the aim of therapy will be to free the partners from painful and unrewarding interactions in order that they can live together more happily; or alternatively to enable them to free themselves from the relationship,
if they find it impossible or intolerable to resolve.   In all
cases, but especially in those cases where one or other of the partners is reluctant to embark upon therapy, perhaps having already
lost hope, or already being involved in some extra-marital relationship, it is important to make clear that the aim of the intervention
is not the preservation of the marriage at all costs, but rather
restoration of choice and possibility to the couple.   In 'last
ditch' consultations of couples on the point of separating, joint
treatment during 'structured separation' as described by Toomin
(1972) enabled 6 out of 18 couples to stay together, and 11 of the
remaining 12 to separate without legal battles.   In this approach,
the couple had to agree to defer decisions about child-care and
access or finance for the three months of the counselling intervention, during which time they met only if both wished to do so.

DIFFERENT APPROACHES TO COUPLE THERAPY

The different approaches to couple therapy include the non-specific
elements listed above, with particular emphasis being placed upon
one or other of the ingredients by different practitioners.   Little
is known about the specific indications for different approaches,
and ideological commitment and polemic still characterise many workers and writers in this field.   This is unfortunate, as the common
ground is considerable.   Therapists of all persuasions aim to alter
the unhappy experience of the couple, and recognise that this involves modifying their behaviour together.   The behavioural therapist will do this by focusing directly on mutually rewarding or
hurting behaviours, an approach involving alterations in the meanings the couple place upon their behaviours in the first instance.
If successful, this will, in turn, alter their experience of, and
the meanings accorded to, the relationship between them.   The dyna-

mic psychotherapist will first reconsider the meanings the couple
place upon their relationship, and their perceptions of each other.
He will aim to define and make manifest these meanings and perceptions, and the discrepancies between them, in order to free the
couple for a more positive and rewarding set of mutual behaviours.
The communications approach will focus especially upon the couple's
meanings and perceptions, and particularly upon those meanings conveyed behaviourally, with the aim of achieving accurate understanding and improving the ability to express needs and feelings, in the
belief that this will free the couple to behave more rewardingly together.   The system of mutual perception, mutual communication or
mis-communication, and of mutual behaviour, can be entered into by
the therapist at any point, and modification at any point will
effect the whole system;   however, the methods and theories of different practitioners are sufficiently different to require separate
consideration.

PSYCHOANALYTIC APPROACHES TO COUPLE THEORY

The base from which psychoanalytic theory and practice was built up
was the individual relationship of analyst and patient, and the
therapy depends, above all, upon the use of transference, that is,
of the constructions placed by the patient upon this relationship.
In the transference, the patient's phantasy becomes manifest, and
this provides a central route to understanding and treatment.
Early marital work in this tradition tended to be no more than the
parallel analytic treatment of the couple with, perhaps, communication between the analysts of the couple.   The move from this approach, to working centrally or exclusively with the couple together, with one or two therapists, was due largely to the work of
Dicks (1967).   This move was based upon the recognition of the fact
that the problem of disturbed marriages represented essentially the
disruption of the conscious, intentional aspects of the marriage relationship by the same kinds of distortion of perception as are manifest in the transference during analytic treatment.   Separate
treatment might, in the long run, diminish the power of each individual's phantasy and distorted perceptions, but in the short, and
often long, run, would leave the interaction between the couple un-
touched, especially as this interaction is essentially collusive so
that the consciously unwanted responses of the other are usually
being provoked or maintained by some action or attitude of the self.
At this point, a case may be given in illustration.

Case-history 1

A couple, considering divorce after five years of marriage, reported
that, despite large areas of shared interest and contentment and a
good sexual relationship, they faced a recurrent cycle of rows in
which the wife would be bitchy and demanding and the husband withdrawn and silent.   After periods of trial separation in the past
they had always found themselves drawn together again.   They came
for help at the point of again considering divorce, the wife saying

she could stand no more coming and going, and insisting that the
husband must either commit himself to staying or go for good.
After two sessions, the husband said that he felt able to make a
firm commitment, but a few days later, after a further cycle of
rowing, he changed his mind once again.   The wife moved out, saying
she would have no more contact, but he wrote to her and recontacted
her, being overcome with sadness.   During the first two interviews,
he had put forward a view of relationships as essentially the matching or mismatching of preformed, unchangeable personalities, and had
been very reluctant to explore interactional patterns.   Now, however, he had been able to see how his withdrawal from his wife's
angry or dependent behaviours was a reflection of his horror of any
kind of fighting, and he related this to his childhood memories of
noisy quarrelling from behind his parents' bedroom door.   At the
same time, his wife recognised how her bitchiness was her response
to a sense of anticipated rejection.   She noted how cross she was
if people were late for appointments with her, and also how angry
she got if she found that the larder was deficient in any kind of
food which she needed;   and was able to link these feelings with her
recollection of her mother as a cold, largely unavailable person.
In situations when she sensed the fact or possibility of deprivation
she would fear rejection and either become clinging and demanding
or, more often, angry.   These were the two behaviours to which her
husband was quite unable to respond.   Both then saw how, in these
spirals, their relationships represented a re-enactment of the pattern of relationships they had seen in their own parents, in which
essentially nice fathers had been diminished and suppressed by
rather cold and powerful mothers.   Under stress, their own marriage
fell under the shadow of this shared image of the rejecting mother.

   Dicks worked on the basis of the later developments of object-
relations theory, as described by Fairbairn (1952) and Guntrip
(1968).   This is important, for these later developments in psycho-
analysis pay far more attention to the infant's seeking of relationship with the mother than, as in classical psychoanalysis, seeking
of instinctual gratification.   By replacing concepts of superego,
ego, and id with internal 'objects' representing early (real or
phantasised) relationships between the child and his parents, their
theory has much clearer application to the study of how adult relationships are influenced by the early parental relationship.   In
these inner representations of parent-child relationships, parents
are often polarised as either caring and idealised, or harsh or rejecting, relating to needy, often greedy, rebellious or crushed
children.   In the disturbed marriage relationship, the public, consciously desired aspects of the relationship, as reflected in the
patterns of mutual dependency and care, and of agreed role perfor-
mances and expectations, are threatened or disrupted by forces
coming from these parent-child remnants.   These patterns, which are
unconscious, or anyhow only partially accessible and recognised,
often turn out to have played an unrecognised part in the process of
mate-selection, often acting in ways opposite to that which is consciously sought and desired.   Thus, in the couple already described
(case-history 1) at the conscious level it is likely that the wife
sought a warm, accessible man like her father was, but stronger, and
the husband sought an emotional and caring woman who would not do to

him what his mother had done to his father.   At the unconscious
level, however, it seemed that each had chosen a partner ready to
play the exact role that would repeat the feared parental pattern of
interaction, for the strength the wife sought in her husband would
always disappear at the precise moment she most sought after it as,
in her fear and dependency, she would behave like both their mothers
did, so provoking in the husband the withdrawal which she feared.

The therapist using an object-relations model aims to explain the
couple's interaction by noting discrepancies between the relationship that is sought after and intended and the one that is actually
happening.   He will usually note, in the undesired interactions,
elements of dependency or coercions which point to childhood origins, and in pointing these out, he will often provoke some exploration of those origins.   Often the therapist will find matching patterns in the pair, as in the couple described above, where the 'alternative script' of the marriage was a shared one, and therefore
available for replaying over and over again.   The identification of
these inappropriate perceptions and behaviours opens the way for
their abandonment, and reduces the force of actions based upon them.
The couple themselves can usually do this on their own, but the
direct suggestion of possible alternative behaviours, not based on
parent-child remnants, would be considered appropriate by all but
the strictly psychoanalytic therapist.

As in any therapy, transference on to the therapist may occur,
but as a general rule in work with couples it is best to interpret
the transference only if it obtrudes or if it can be related to the
unconscious reiterative processes going on between the couple.
This statement is at variance with the views of some of the earlier
work in the field in the analytic tradition.   An example may be
given at this point.

Case-history 2

A couple in their mid-thirties consulted in crisis, after infidelity
by both partners.   The wife had slept with a mutual friend, and the
husband with an ex-girlfriend of his from before the marriage.
Their own sexual relationship had more or less ceased for some
months.   The wife was an expressive, active, controlling and obsti-
nate character, with a fair amount of dependency.   The husband was
meticulous, efficient, and ambitious at work, but in the home tended
to be slow and passively resistant;   for example, the house was
always full of half-completed carpentry jobs which remained in that
state for months at a time.   Both felt frightened of the threat to
their marriage, and had consulted urgently, at first separately,
then together.   At the first of a regular series of joint sessions,
they had almost immediately become almost entirely silent.   This
silence was interpreted as passive-resistance to the therapist (a
transference interpretation), but this interpretation was linked
with comments on the husband's behaviour in terms of his excessive
drives at work, and his resistance to work at home, and to the
wife's choice of a husband whom she saw as a powerful person who
would control her, against whom she was now in rebellion.   It
seemed that both husband and wife had set high ideals for, and high

demands upon, themselves. In this session they had put the therapist into this demanding role and responded to this by withholding.
In the marriage, the demanding aspects of the self were projected by
each into the other, and then rebelled against, actively through infidelity, and passively through emotional muteness and withdrawal.
This interpretation, therefore, of a transference manifestation, was
used to name more accurately the withdrawn, ungiving behaviours as
hostile, and to start upon the task of separating out, for the partners, how much of the demandingness they resisted in the other was
actually in the other, and how much was a projection from themselves. This led on to a consideration of how the 'black script'
of their bad marital interaction was essentially a replaying of the
resentful child in relation to the demanding parent, rather than a
relationship between an adult man and a woman.

The object-relations theory therapist aims to diminish the amount
of fantasy and to increase the reality of the perceptions of the
other, using interpretation as his primary method. However, the
fact that the theory is psychoanalytically based does not in my view
necessarily confine the practitioner to interpretation as his only
therapeutic tool. Another example may illustrate this point.

Case-history 3

This couple had decided upon a period of trial separation during an
interruption in therapy. At the first resumed sessions, they gave
a very grumpy account of their interactions since the separation.
The wife had almost immediately become ill, the week after starting
a new job, and the husband had therefore spent virtually every evening at home, yet had none the less been upbraided by the wife for
lack of help and sympathy. The therapists, in this case, were
quite unable to deduce from the couple's account what the terms of
the separation had been. The pattern of interaction suggested, as
it had previously, that each wished for some needs to be met by the
other, but resented that wish in the self, and also resented the
other for failing to meet the need. The parent-child nature of
this interaction was noted, but the main point taken up was the neb-
ulousness of their present arrangements. Against some resistance,
it was suggested very firmly that they should spend time before the
next session in negotiating, as two adults, an exact agreement about
responsibility for the children and for each other.

As in this example, marital therapists working in the psychoanalytic tradition are tending to widen the range of methods used in
couple therapy in the direction of being more present and transpar-
ent as therapists and more prepared to use challenge, confrontation
and modelling as techniques. Skynner (1975), for example, argues
that couples showing the common pattern of a self-effacing, unasser-
tive husband whose wife rejects him because he has given control
over to her may be helped by assertive managing behaviour on the
part of the male therapist. Some might feel that his adherence to
traditional sex-role models goes too far; this would certainly be
so for Laws (1975) who writes vigorously and critically of the excessive influence of conventional sex-role stereotypes on the practice and theory of marital work. Quite apart from sociocultural

and ideological issues, a therapist's own views on marital patterns,
and his own experience and historical role in relation to his parents, are likely to provoke, consciously or unconsciously, powerful
responses to the marital dramas he meets in his work.   Although the
research evidence does not show any advantage for two therapists
over one (Gurman, 1973), many workers feel that a therapist pair, of
opposite sexes, is more effective, or anyway more comfortable.   In
so far as therapists need to be open, and to get drawn to some
extent into the feelings being exchanged between the couple, the
counter-transference reactions need to be monitored.   The hectic
nature of some conjoint sessions, and the fact that the therapist is
more exposed, and less defended than in individual therapy, means
that therapists may easily get confused or over-involved; but, with
a colleague present who is likely to show different patterns of personal involvement and defence, no great harm can come from this;
(for a further discussion of the use of co-therapy see Dowling,
Chapter 8).

SYSTEMS THEORY AND COUPLE THERAPY

The assumptions underlying the systems theory and the communications
approach to couple therapy is that counselling ending in improved
communication will free self-correcting behaviours and attitudes between the couple (Bolte, 1975).   Behind this is the more general
assumption or recognition of the fact that any behaviour occurring
between a couple is produced and maintained by both of them.   Systems theory represents the best developed conceptualisation of this
assumption.   This theory would regard the marital dyad as a system,
often a sub-system of a larger family one, which demonstrates system
characteristics, namely that change in one part of the system (for
example, in one partner) has inevitable effects on the rest of the
system; that there are homeostatic mechanisms maintained by feedback, tending to stability, and that there is a system of rules, implicit or explicit, governing the system.   Any given act by one
partner represents both a response to previous acts of the other and
a stimulus to subsequent acts.   Watzlawick et al. (1967) identified
three aspects involved in any communication: the conveying of information, the giving of meaning, and the naming of behavioural implications (the latter being influenced by both the content and the
context of the communication).
     Conflict can arise when one member of the pair fails to confirm
the other.   Confirmation can be given by agreement or opposition,
disconfirmation representing rather the failure to recognise that
concept of the self being offered by the other.   Any communication,
as well as conveying information, conveys behavioural expectations,
and any behaviour, including, for example, symptomatic behaviour,
has a communication element.   Symptoms can be particularly powerful
instruments which the individual may use while, at the same time,
denying responsibility or agency for the message being given.
     Conflict may arise, also, because the implicit rules governing
interaction are not agreed, or because there is not agreement about
who makes these rules, or because conflicting rules or demands are
issued simultaneously, as in the double-bind situation.   Counsel-

ling based upon this theoretical structure will aim to improve the couple's skill and accuracy in sending out and receiving messages, and will tend to pay particular attention to discrepancies, notably between verbal and non-verbal modes of communication, the latter including posture, expression and tone of voice.   Emphasis will be placed upon the feelings and personal meanings of communication, both those claimed for the self, and those attributed to the other in any given interaction.   Wells et al. (1975) report their experience with a group programme, training couples in accurate empathy and warmth on Rogerian lines, in which a brief didactic exposition was followed by modelling exercises and a group experience over eight sessions.   They found that, according to three criteria, improvement occurred in the majority of participants.   Hurvitz (1975) emphasised one aspect of the communications approach, by distinguishing between what he calls 'terminal hypotheses' and 'instrumental hypotheses'.   Terminal hypotheses are those explanations of the problem offered by the couple or, he would say, often by the therapist (of other schools), that have no implication for change in their interaction.   Examples would be, 'It's his nerves' or 'He is just like his father, of course'.   Instrumental hypotheses, on the other hand, offer a model which has behavioural consequences.   The counsellor's function, as he sees it, is to help the couple generate and act upon instrumental hypotheses to the greatest possible extent.   The husband, in case-history 1 was helped to move from terminal to instrumental hypotheses about his marriage relationship.

BEHAVIOURAL METHODS IN COUPLE THERAPY

The essential principles underlying behavioural treatment of marital problems have been summarised by Liberman (1975).   The behavioural sequences characterising the undesirable interactions between the couple are identified, and the therapist, in alliance with the couple, designs and supervises the implementation of a programme whereby each learns to reinforce the desired rather than the maladaptive or symptomatic behaviour of the other.   Goals are specified through a chain of intermediate goals, and appropriate reinforcing behaviour from the other is applied, at first in relation to the desired behaviour, and later more generally.   Bancroft (1975) writes rather more eclectically than do many behaviourists, and he would include in his programme the identification of attitudes responsible for failure to carry the programme out, and he would add, to the treatment programme, the modification of such attitudes. This would be achieved by discussion and by the encouragement of direct expression of feeling; by means, in fact, which show much overlap with the behaviour of the dynamic therapist.   In the treatment of sexual disorders, the work of Masters and Johnson (1970) is based on essentially behaviourist principles, depending upon initial instruction and encouragement of the 'give to get' principle.   This represents a self-reinforcing programme of desired behaviour, which focuses upon the seeking and giving of pleasure, leaving sexual performance to take care of itself.   For major problems, for example, severe frigidity or impotence, behavioural programmes will specify intermediate goals which will exclude in the early stages any attempt at genital contact.   (See Crowe, Chapter 7.)

In the course of identifying the problem and identifying the re-
inforcers available to a couple embarking on a behavioural programme, some kind of contract may be drawn up between the couple.
Bancroft considers that sexual behaviours should be excluded from
such trade-offs, on the grounds that such bargaining around sex is
all too often a problem area between distressed couples.   Not all
writers in the behaviourist tradition, however, show this delicacy.
Hickok and Komechak (1974), for example, report a token economy programme between a couple in which the husband was rewarded one token
for each hour for which he allowed his wife out of the home.   One
token bought him the right to light petting, two tokens to heavy
petting.   Many writers in this field, for example Laughren and Kass
(1975) and Stuart (1975), seem prone to a heady enthusiasm in advance of research evaluation.   I cannot find any enthusiasm for
those approaches that indicate an entirely mechanistic model of
sexual behaviour and of the marriage relationship.   What quality of
relationship between therapist and couple, and between the couple
themselves, is implied, for example, by the kind of programme described by Lobitz and Piccolo (1975), which is based upon the use of
'phantasy and pornography in combination with a 9-step masturbation
programme to enhance sexual responsiveness', and which includes a
'refundable penalty fee deposit' to ensure client co-operation?
Readers anxious for further accounts of thorough-going behavioural
approaches of this sort must consult the sources direct.   Such
models seem peculiarly unsuited to apply to the unhappy and sensitive people who, in my experience, seek help with marital problems;
but it is, of course, always possible that clients seek out the
agency which suits them.
     It should be emphasised that not all behavioural work is open to
these criticisms and, in the hands of a sensitive therapist, behavioural techniques clearly have a very important part to play.
While, in some sense, more didactic and authoritarian than the interpretive approaches, they also clearly enlist the co-operation of
the couple in their own treatment, sometimes more effectively than
is the case in the vaguer, apparently more permissive, dynamic
therapies.

GROUP COUPLE THERAPY

The use of group methods of treatment for marital problems is increasingly popular, and this approach may be the method of choice,
especially for the longer-term problems not requiring crisis intervention.   Three to four couples are usually treated together, and
the emphasis is upon the marital interaction observed in the group
between the couples, rather than on the general group process.   In
the work of Framo (1973) each couple is allotted an appropriate proportion of the group time.   Framo, in starting groups, was originally motivated by his own difficulty in coping with difficult
couples in conjoint therapy, but on the basis of two-hundred such
couples treated in a group situation, now considers it to be the
method of choice in most cases.   He instructs couples, at the
start, in the value of free expression of feeling and in the desirability of making criticism as constructive as is possible.   Like

Leichter (1975) he recommends a reasonable match of couple groups in terms of life-stage, but prefers a mix of socio-economic status, finding particularly the presence of working-class couples breaks through the intellectualisation often used as a defence by the more educated.   Skynner (1975) concludes that:

> Couples groups thus combine the advantages of conjoint therapy (i.e. continued 'homework' between the formal sessions, which is of course not possible in a therapy group composed of people who are strangers to each other) with the advantages of the artificially constituted therapy group (which includes a variety of roles, social skills, attitudes and values which complement or interact with, and alter, each other, rather than the collusive, defensive system in shared rigid values which inevitably characterise disturbed couples and families).

THE RELATIONSHIP BETWEEN DIFFERENT TREATMENT APPROACHES

It is inevitable, in a review of this sort, that the author's preferences and experiences influence the account given, and the reader is likely to realise by now my preference for the framework provided by object-relations theory as giving the fullest account of the nature of marital conflict.   Psychiatric classification, based upon descriptions of personality and concepts of illness, can be linked with object-relations formulations, and these dual perspectives are of importance in identifying those cases where the problem is primarily in the illness of one individual rather than in their interaction.   The evaluation of a couple's suitability for joint therapy should, in my view, be based upon an assessment taking account of psychiatric and object-relations models.   Approaches based upon systems theory and behaviourism do not seem to pay any sustained attention to issues of personal illness or personal maturity, and tend to discuss selection rather infrequently.   However, though psychiatric and object-relations formulations are important in selection, it is probable that a large proportion of cases selected as suitable for joint therapy will be capable of responding to therapies in which the focus of the therapist is primarily upon communication or upon behaviour.

The rejection of psychoanalytic models, which is included, almost ritually, in the writings of those of other orientations, tends to refer in general to outmoded, classical theoretical formulations, and to forms of treatment which no longer characterise practitioners of this persuasion.   Later in its development, object-relations theory provides an appropriate model around which to explore and modify the misperceptions and communications failures of couples, and a model to which behavioural change can be also usefully related.   The marital therapist of the future, whether working with couples, or with groups of couples, can, with advantage, draw upon the work of all these schools, and should not, in my view, abandon the contribution of any of them.

RESEARCH INTO COUPLE THERAPY

As in the whole field of psychotherapy, the contribution of research
to understanding the process, or evaluating the effectiveness of
different couple therapies, has been scanty and confused.   Gurman
(1973) has contributed a valuable review of the outcome research in
this field.   He concluded with some caution that studies of varied
patient groups and different therapeutic methods suggested an overall improvement rate of about two-thirds, similar to the rate found
in most psychotherapy research.   He argued, however, that the spontaneous improvement rate in disturbed marital situations is almost
certainly lower than the spontaneous improvement rate in individual
cases.   In line with recent writers in the fields of research into
group therapy (Yalom, 1970) and individual psychotherapy (Bergin and
Strupp, 1970) he points to the need for controlled comparative
studies for the effects of well-defined treatments, and argues that,
in the assessment of change, multi-dimensional measurements are
essential.   He also argues for the important contribution to be
made by what he describes as 'n = 1 experimental case-studies', in
which case-material of the sort familiar to clinicians is subjected
to quantitative evaluation.
    From the behavioural standpoint, with its concern for the careful
setting of serial goals, the recording of achieved change can be
seen as an integral part of the treatment process, and research and
therapy need be in no kind of conflict.   This being the case, it is
surprising that the research record of behavioural therapists in
this field is little better than that of the dynamic therapists
whose goals are often less clearly defined, and whose criteria of
change are more difficult to express in measurable terms.   For the
dynamic therapist, concerned particularly with the couple's mutual
perceptions and how these are modified, developments in repertory
grid techniques derived from Kelly's personal construct theory
(Kelly, 1955) offer a relatively new and powerful research tool.
It would, however, be a pity if research methods were necessarily
tied to the orientation of the therapists, and ideally research into
behavioural, or systems theory, or psychoanalytic therapies, would
include measures of change in all three areas.   There seems little
doubt that successful behavioural treatments alter how couples perceive each other, and little doubt that successful psychotherapies
alter how couples behave towards each other.   The development of
flexible research methods in recent years brings this ideal of
evaluation across the spectrum of change into the realm of the possible.   It seems likely that small-scale studies (n = 1 and up-
wards), using methods of measurement constructed around the couple's
specific difficulties, will play an increasing role in future research.   Serial ratings of progress towards specific behavioural
goals (e.g. Levy and Meyer, 1971) and serial ratings in relation to
specific target problems (e.g. Battle et al., 1966 and Candy et al.,
1972) are methodologically feasible and have been used in individual
psychotherapy research;   to these, repertory grid methods add a way
into the issues of mutual perception.   A short account of these
methods, as applied to marital research in my own work, will therefore be given at this point (a fuller account is given in Ryle,
1975, chapter II).

In the basic repertory grid method, the subject compares and contrasts a number of people (the elements of the test) against a
number of descriptions (the constructs).   Both the people and the
descriptions can be supplied by the tester, but more is learned if
the subject himself provides them under the tester's guidance in so
far as the test has a specific purpose.   These comparisons are obtained by rating or ranking all the elements against all the constructs, and are then subjected to mathematical analysis.   Analysis
can yield a number of measures of psychological interest;   in particular, the overall similarity of any two elements, in terms of the
constructs used, is expressed as an element distance;   and, similarly, the degree to which any two constructs are used similarly in relation to this range of elements is expressed as a correlation.
This latter figure provides evidence of the implications of given
descriptions for the individual;   for example, for one subject,
loving and weak, or feminine and passive, might show high intercor-
relations.   In Slater's principal component analysis of the grid
(carried out by the MRC Unit for the processing of repertory grids),
the relationships of elements and constructs are also expressed in
terms of their loadings upon the principal components obtained from
the analysis of the mathematical grid expressing construct-element
interaction.   Each element and each construct is located by its
loadings upon each of these components.   By plotting out elements
and constructs in terms of the first and second principal components, which together usually account for some three-quarters of the
total variance of the grid, a simplified map of conceptual space is
derived.   On this map, elements are located in different regions,
and their location can be described in terms of their fellow elements in that area, and in terms of the meaning given to that area
by the construct loadings.

A modification of this basic repertory grid technique, of particular interest in the field of couple research, is the dyad grid
(Ryle and Lunghi, 1970).   In this form of the test, the elements,
rather than being individuals, are the relationships between individuals, i.e. self-to-other, other-to-self.   A grid made up in this
way can contain a number of couples, or the relationship between a
couple and each partner and his or her parents, and can include
their own relationship under different conditions, for example, when
it is going well and when it is going badly.   In a study comparing
seven maladjusted couples and seven control couples (Ryle and Breen,
1972a) this latter method was used, and the findings were of some
interest.   Maladjusted couples showed a greater tendency for the
role of the self to be construed as more childlike, and the role of
the other as less parent-like.   This difference was also found between the 'going badly' and 'going well' conditions.   This finding
is very much in line with the emphasis placed in psychoanalytically
derived models of marital conflict, and in line with the case-histories quoted earlier in this chapter, in which a crucial element of
distress and conflict in the marriages was characterised by the increasingly childish behaviour of each partner, exacerbated by the
diminishing ability of the other partner to meet these childish
demands.

Case-histories, with repertory grid data, describing the effects
of couple therapy are given in Ryle (1975), Ryle and Breen (1972b)

and Ryle and Lipshitz (1975 and 1976).   The reconstruction grid
(Ryle and Lipshitz, 1975) is a form of dyad grid in which the elements are successive ratings of the relationship of self-to-spouse
and spouse-to-self, recorded serially through the course of therapy.
Two methods of recording change are described;   in one, all the
serial ratings are included in a single grid, and the elements self-
to-other and other-to-self are plotted out against the components of
the grid to form a graphic representation of change through time.
An additional analysis investigates the changes in the implications
of certain descriptions, or judgments, by separating the first and
last half of therapy, and comparing construct correlations in the
grids made up of ratings on these two periods.   In the case reported there were marked shifts in the implications of dominating and
attacking behaviours, which became less dangerous and more positively evaluated, while helpful and comfort-seeking behaviours became
less valued in the course of therapy.   In a second study of therapy (Ryle and Lipshitz, 1976) the causes of an impasse in therapy
were demonstrated, from grid data, to be the result of what, in psychoanalytic terms, would be called projective identification.   In
this case, when the husband saw the marriage to be going well, he
saw himself as caring and his wife as depressed and hopeless;   when
he saw the marriage as going badly, this relationship was reversed.
The wife's somatic and depressive symptoms, which had provoked consultation, were thus the condition of the husband's contentment in
the marriage which, not surprisingly, did not endure.

CONCLUSION

A recent newspaper article reported a suggestion that couples should
take out insurance policies to cover the cost of separation and divorce, an idea turned down by an insurance spokesman as impracticable on the grounds that it would be like issuing fire policies when
you could already smell the smoke.   The idea cannot be dismissed as
entirely cynical, however, in view of the instability of marriage in
contemporary society.   The changes in sexual mores and the general
questioning of traditional frameworks of behaviours are reflected in
the current interest in alternative life-styles, in which people experiment with all kinds of different contracts and patterns of relationship under the banners, variously, of consciousness raising,
liberation, hedonism or, often, simple confusion.   The situation
still bears many traces from the past, however;   while I was working
on this chapter, a cheerful young man living half-a-mile away from
me was murdered by his lover's husband, a scene that could come
straight from a Hardy novel.   Neither the old nor the new morality
has resolved the painful paradoxes inescapably present in that centrally important relationship of marriage;   a relationship at once
calling for the most adult and mature behaviours, and calling forth
the most primitive and childish ones.   Too often, the outcome is
that described in the bitter poem by C. Day Lewis, The Marriage of
Two:

   What is the marriage of two?
   The loss of one,
   By wounds or abdication: a true

Surrender mocked, an unwished victory won:
Rose, desert - mirage too.

What can we do, this motley crew of clergymen, counsellors, social-workers, psychologists and doctors, working with couples, for a society where no such marital unhappiness exists?   There is clearly no way in which the high prevalence of conflict and break-down can be reduced in the short run.   In this chapter I have out-lined the ways in which help can be provided for couples who do con-sult.   In this work I believe we often witness the emergence from extreme personal pain, of resource and growth; and I believe we see this above all when, out of crisis, the individuality of each part-ner is enhanced.   The emergence of a more developed consciousness, of the capacity to tolerate more uncertainty, of the acceptance of more individual responsibility and the letting-go of a comfortable adherence to provided solutions, and of coercive dependency upon the other, represent real human gains.   As counsellors we often have to provide hope for our clients through their most difficult times, but we are often also given hope by the evidence we see of resilience and creativity.   Perhaps this can enable us to act also as guardi-ans of hope about human relations for a society that has lost con-fidence in itself in so many ways.

REFERENCES

BANCROFT, J. (1975), The behavioural approach to marital problems, 'British Journal of Medical Psychology', vol. 48, pp. 147-52.
BATTLE, C.C., IMBER, S.D., HOEHN-SARIC, R., STONE, A.R., NASH, E.R. and FRANK, J.D. (1966), Target complaints as criteria of improve-ment, 'American Journal of Psychotherapy', pp. 20-184.
BERGIN, A.E. and STRUPP, H.H. (1970), New directions in psychother-apy research, 'Journal of Abnormal Psychology', vol. 73, p. 13.
BERMAN, E.M. and LIEF, H.I. (1975), Marital therapy from a psychia-tric perspective: an overview, 'American Journal of Psychiatry', vol. 132, no. 6, p. 583.
BOLTE, G.L. (1975), A communications approach to marital counsel-ling, in 'Couples in Conflict - New Directions in Marital Therapy' (eds) A.S. Gurman and D.G. Rice, Aronson, N.Y.
CANDY, J., BALFOUR, H.G., CAWLEY, R.H., HILDEBRAND, H.P., MILAN, D.H., MARKS, I.M. and WILSON, J. (1972), A feasibility study for a controlled trial of psychotherapy, 'Psychological Medicine', vol. 2, no. 4, p. 345.
COLLINS, J., KREITMAN, N., NELSON, B. and TROOP, J. (1971), Neuroses and marital interactions, III family roles and functions, 'British Journal of Psychiatry', pp. 119-233.
DICKS, H.V. (1967), 'Marital Tensions', Routledge & Kegan Paul, London.
DOMINIAN, J. (1972), Marital pathology - a review, 'Postgraduate Medical Journal', vol. 48, p. 517.
FAIRBAIRN, W.R.D. (1952), 'Psychoanalytic Studies of the Personali-ty', Tavistock, London.
FRAMO, J.L. (1973), Marriage therapy in a couples group, in 'Tech-niques of Family Psychotherapy' (ed.) D.A. Bloch, Grune & Stratton, New York.

GUNTRIP, H. (1968), 'Schizoid Phenomena, Object-Relations and the Self', Hogarth Press, London.

GURMAN, A.S. (1973), The effects and effectiveness of marital therapy - a review of outcome research, 'Family Process', vol. 12, p. 145.

HICKOK, J.E. and KOMECHAK, M.G. (1974), Behaviour modification in marital conflict: a case report, 'Family Process', vol. 13, no. 1, p. 111.

HURVITZ, N. (1975), Interaction hypotheses in marriage counselling, in 'Couples in Conflict - New Directions in Marital Therapy' (eds), A.S. Gurman and D.G. Rice, Aronson, N.Y.

JUNG, C.G. (1928), Marriage as a psychological relationship (trans. Baynes and Baynes), in 'Contributions to Analytical Psychology', Kegan Paul, London and N.Y.

KELLY, G.A. (1955), 'The Psychology of Personal Constructs', Norton, N.Y.

LAUGHRAN, J.P. and KASS, D.J. (1975), Desensitisation of sexual dysfunction - the present status, in 'Couples in Conflict - New Directions in Marital Therapy' (eds), A.S. Gurman and D.G. Rice, Aronson, N.Y.

LAWS, J.L. (1975), A feminist view of marital adjustment, in 'Couples in Conflict - New Directions in Marital Therapy' (eds), A.S. Gurman and D.G. Rice, Aronson, N.Y.

LEICHTER, E. (1975), Treatment of married couples in groups, in 'Couples in Conflict - New Directions in Marital Therapy' (eds), A.S. Gurman and D.G. Rice, Aronson, N.Y.

LEVY, R. and MEYER, V. (1971), New techniques in behaviour therapy, 'Proceedings of Royal Society of Medicine', vol. 64, p. 1115.

LEWIS, C. DAY (1954), 'Collected Poems', Jonathan Cape and Hogarth Press, London.

LIBERMAN, R. (1975), Behavioural principles in family and couple therapy, in 'Couples in Conflict - New Directions in Marital Therapy' (eds), A.S. Gurman and D.G. Rice, Aronson, N.Y.

LOBITZ, W.C. and PICCOLO, J.L. (1975), New methods in the behavioural treatment of sexual dysfunction, in 'Couples in Conflict - New Directions in Marital Therapy' (eds), A.S. Gurman and D.G. Rice, Aronson, N.Y.

MAHLER, M.S., PIRIE, F. and BERGMAN, A. (1975), 'The Psychological Birth of the Human Infant', Hutchinson, London.

MASTERS, W.H. and JOHNSON, V.E. (1970), 'Human Sexual Inadequacy', Churchill, London.

OLSON, D.G. (1970), Marital and family therapy: integrative review and critique, 'Journal of Marriage and the Family', vol. 32, p. 501.

RUTTER, M. (1971), Parent child separation: psychological effects on the children, 'Journal of Child Psychology and Psychiatry', vol. 2, p. 233.

RYLE, A. (1967), 'Neurosis in the Ordinary Family', Tavistock, London.

RYLE, A. (1975), 'Frames and Cages: The Repertory Grid Approach to Human Understanding', Chatto & Windus, London.

RYLE, A. and BREEN, D. (1972a), A comparison of adjusted and maladjusted couples using the double dyad grid, 'British Journal of Medical Psychology', vol. 45, p. 375.

RYLE, A. and BREEN, D. (1972b), The use of the double dyad grid in the clinical setting, 'British Journal of Medical Psychology', vol. 45, p. 383.

RYLE, A. and LIPSHITZ, S. (1975), Recording change in marital therapy with the reconstruction grid, 'British Journal of Medical Psychology', vol. 48, p. 39.

RYLE, A. and LIPSHITZ, S. (1976), Repertory grid elucidation of a difficult conjoint therapy, 'British Journal of Medical Psychology', vol. 49, p. 281.

RYLE, A. and LUNGHI, M. (1970), The dyad grid: a modification of repertory grid technique, 'British Journal of Psychiatry', vol. 117, p. 323.

SELIGMAN, M.E. (1975), 'Helplessness: on Depression, Development and Death', Freeman, San Francisco.

SKYNNER, A.C.R. (1975), Some approaches to marital therapy, 'Proceedings of the Royal Society of Medicine', vol. 68, p. 405.

STUART, R.B. (1975), Behavioural remedies for marital ills: a guide to the use of operant interpersonal techniques, in 'Couples in Conflict - New Directions in Marital Therapy' (eds), 'A.S. Gurman and D.G. Rice, Aronson, N.Y.

TOOMIN, M.K. (1972), Structured separation with counselling: a therapeutic approach for couples in conflict, 'Family Process', vol. 11, no. 3, p. 299.

WATZLAWICK, P., BEAVIN, J.H. and JACKSON, D.D. (1967), 'Pragmatics of Human Communication', Norton, N.Y.

WELLS, R.A., FIGUREL, J.A. and MCNAMEE, P. (1975), Group facilitated training with conflicted marital couples, in 'Couples in Conflict - New Directions in Marital Therapy' (eds), A.S. Gurman and D.G. Rice, Aronson, N.Y.

WHITAKER, C.A. (1975), A family therapist looks at marital therapy, in 'Couples in Conflict - New Directions in Marital Therapy' (eds), A.S. Gurman and D.G. Rice, Aronson, N.Y.

YALOM, I.D. (1970), 'The Theory and Practice of Group Psychotherapy', Basic Books, N.Y.

Chapter 7

THE TREATMENT OF SEXUAL DYSFUNCTION

Michael Crowe

In a volume such as this, devoted to family spychotherapy, the position occupied by sexual function and dysfunction is a powerful but ambiguous one. When family therapy is discussed, the immediate image is of a therapist dealing with family members of at least two generations - typically the nuclear family with young children and two parents. Such a family could not exist unless sexual intercourse had taken place, and clearly all family members have their own sexual wishes and fantasies. On the other hand, sex is not a subject easily talked about between members of different generations, and can thus remain a hidden but powerful force influencing family dynamics. It seems to me that to formulate a family's problem without finding out the degree of sexual satisfaction in the parents' marriage is leaving out an important source of information. One could even postulate that a good sexual relationship, along with a sensible attitude to sex, between the parents is an indispensable prerequisite to the rearing of children in a balanced way. Again, one can cite many examples of families where sexual frustration or inhibition in the parents has led to sexual dysfunction in later years in the children.

It is, however, difficult to put sexual function into a comfortable perspective in family life. Some parents seem quite unable to 'close the bedroom door' either literally or figuratively, preferring the exclusive role of parent to that of husband and wife; and the problem is compounded when only one parent has this attitude and imposes it on the other (see Aponte and Hoffman, 1973). Such a pattern is often accompanied by an excessively close relationship between one parent and a child, which effectively absorbs all that parent's energy and emotion to the exclusion of the other, and usually to the disadvantage of the child. In such a situation it may be a difficult, but necessary, task for the therapist to try and explore the sexual relationship between the parents, perhaps excluding the children from sessions or parts of sessions in order to discuss the sexual difficulties in more detail. It is sometimes legitimate to ask general questions like 'are there any problems in the physical relationship?' while children are present, but any detailed inquiry should probably be carried out in their absence.

Not all cases of sexual dysfunction, of course, present in family

therapy.   It is much commoner for them to present either as individuals complaining of impotence, anxiety, tiredness, etc., or, more
commonly these days, as couples referred together for sexual dysfunction.   In recent years, as public discussion of sexual matters
has increased, there has been a concomitant increase in the demand
for treatment of sexual problems.   If we accept Kinsey's estimate
that 50 per cent of marriages are sexually unsatisfactory, the
potential demand is very large indeed.

The rest of this chapter will be devoted to a more detailed description of the types of sexual dysfunction encountered, causative
factors, treatment approaches and outcome research.

CLASSIFICATION OF THE SEXUAL DYSFUNCTIONS

The simplest and most satisfactory classification of sexual dysfunction is a behavioural one, according to which aspect of sexual intercourse is disturbed.   A list of types of sexual dysfunction is
given in Table 7.1.

TABLE 7.1   Types of sexual dysfunction

---

1   Male conditions:

   (a)   Primary erectile impotence (potency never achieved in the
         heterosexual act).
   (b)   Secondary erectile impotence (potency previously achieved
         but lost).
   (c)   Premature ejaculation (variously defined, but perhaps most
         satisfactorily as a man ejaculating before he wants to).
   (d)   Failure to ejaculate or delayed ejaculation.
   (e)   Low sex drive or libido (lifelong or secondary to physical
         illness, marital problems, depression, etc.).

2   Female conditions:

   (a)   Total anorgasmia (orgasm never experienced).
   (b)   Situational anorgasmia (orgasm experienced with other part-
         ners, or in masturbation, but not with present partner).
   (c)   Secondary anorgasmia (orgasm previously experienced but not
         at present).
   (d)   Vaginismus (involuntary contraction of pubococcygeal muscles
         so as to render penetration painful or impossible).
   (e)   Dyspareunia (pain on intercourse, superficial or deep: also
         occasionally found in males).
   (f)   Fear or refusal of sex.
   (g)   Low sex drive or libido (lifelong or secondary to physical
         illness, depression, etc.).

To begin with erectile impotence, this is habitually divided into
primary and secondary types, according to whether it has been present throughout the man's heterosexual experience or has begun after
previous successful intercourse.   This is not an absolute distinction, in that some men have had one or two successful attempts at
intercourse in their lives but are essentially suffering from pri-

mary impotence.   Impotence has been found by Ansari (1976) to have
a better prognosis if the onset is sudden and accompanied by anxiety
than if it is insidious.   Masters and Johnson (1970) found that
primary impotence was a more difficult condition to treat by their
approach than secondary impotence.   Some cases which are termed
impotence really relate to reluctance of the husband to initiate
sexual activity, and come more into the category of marital problems.   Impotence may be total or partial, and in the latter case
erection is often lost during, or soon after, penetration.

The definition of premature ejaculation is a very difficult one.
Arbitrary figures such as ejaculation within one minute of penetration are not satisfactory, as they seem to impose universal criteria
which may not be applicable.   Similarly, definitions such as satisfying the sexual partner less than 50 per cent of the time are
vitiated by the fact that a man with an anorgasmic wife would be
automatically defined as a premature ejaculator.   Perhaps the most
satisfactory, if oversimple, definition is that the man ejaculates
before he wants to;   that is, he has insufficient control of ejaculation.   Most men with this condition are able to have intercourse
fairly soon after a previous ejaculation, and can often delay ejaculation more successfully on the second occasion.   In any case, this
condition responds quite well to conjoint treatment (Masters and
Johnson, 1970;   Crowe et al., 1977).   But in couples who have continued to have the problem for some years, secondary impotence often
occurs.

Failure to ejaculate or delayed ejaculation (sometimes called
impotentia ejaculandi) is a much rarer condition than premature
ejaculation.   In most such men, wet dreams occur, and those who can
ejaculate in masturbation have a better prognosis than those who
cannot.   Paradoxically, their sexual partners rarely complain, as
the long-continued intercourse usually brings considerable physical
satisfaction to the woman.   The complaint is either one of infer-
tility, or one of dissatisfaction in the male partner, who never
achieves the release of ejaculation during intercourse.   Occasionally men present with 'dry orgasms', either due to delayed puberty
or to an incompetence of the internal sphincter resulting in retro-
grade ejaculation into the bladder.   Such orgasms can also occur in
elderly men, but the mechanism is not clear.   A more disturbing
condition is ejaculation unaccompanied by pleasurable feelings:
this usually presents after a successful sexual relationship has
been experienced, and can be accompanied by hypochondriacal or depressive features.   In rare cases, ejaculation may be accompanied
by pain: here a physical cause is often suspected, but is very hard
to confirm or treat.

Low sexual drive or interest may be lifelong, as judged by in-
frequent sexual urges or outlets in adolescence or later life.   Alternatively, loss of a previously active sexual drive may accompany
all sorts of life stresses, from job anxiety and marital problems to
depression or physical illness.

The classification of problems occurring in the female partner is
beset by the use of the word frigidity.   Apart from its male chau-
vinistic connotations, this term is unsatisfactory because it can be
used to describe most kinds of female sexual dysfunction, from anorgasmia and vaginismus to fear of sex or low sex drive.   It is probably best avoided for both reasons.

Anorgasmia, or failure to reach an orgasm, can be primary (total), secondary or situational.   Because it is easy with manual or vibrator stimulation to achieve an orgasm, Barbach (1974) has termed women with primary anorgasmia 'pre-orgasmic'.   Secondary anorgasmia refers to the condition where it was possible in the past to achieve an orgasm but it is now no longer possible.   Situational anorgasmia refers to the case where the woman can experience an orgasm by masturbation or with other partners, but not with her husband or regular sexual partner.   This last condition seems harder to treat than the other two, because marital difficulties are often found in these couples underlying the sexual problem.

Vaginismus is a condition often associated with fear of sexual intercourse, and most commonly presents as a referral for non-consummation.   The basic mechanism is a spasmodic contraction of the muscles surrounding the vagina such as to prevent penetration, and this is accompanied in severe cases by adduction of the legs and arching of the back.   Usually it is primary, in that intercourse has never taken place: but occasionally it is found in women who have had successful intercourse and may even have been pregnant. In vaginismus with non-consummation, there is often a characteristic marital relationship.   The wife is very ladylike and has a close relationship with her mother, while the husband is placid, non-demanding and very anxious to avoid giving pain or disturbing things in any way.   If these characteristics can be overcome, and some enthusiasm for change engendered, vaginismus is not a difficult condition to treat.

Dyspareunia, or pain with intercourse, is often divided into two types, superficial and deep.   Superficial dyspareunia may be associated with vaginismus, or with various vaginal infections, or may be psychogenic: the pain is felt in the vagina itself.   Deep dyspareunia, which is usually connected with uterine or ovarion pathology if the cause is physical, is felt deep in the pelvis.

Quite commonly women present with a complaint that they are afraid of sex, or they 'can't bear their husbands to touch them'. There is often an accompanying anorgasmia, and sometimes the patient will experience a panic attack if intercourse is attempted.   In other cases, the reluctance to have sexual relations is a kind of weapon in the marital power struggle: there is no sexual dysfunction as such, but the wife's resentment and anger are such as to make her unwilling to give her husband what he wants.   Another, more subtle, variant of this problem is the wife who cannot tolerate foreplay, or any display of emotional involvement on her husband's part, but will accept, and experience an orgasm with, intercourse.

Low sex drive in the woman is a very similar condition to low sex drive in the man.   It may be lifelong, or at least have begun at the age (later than in boys) when most girls become sexually active. Alternatively, loss of sexual interest may have accompanied life stresses, such as mental or physical illness, marital difficulties or financial problems.   A common antecedent to loss of sexual interest is childbirth; this may affect sexual drive in many ways, for instance trauma to the vagina or clitoris during delivery, hormonal changes, increased responsibility, loss of a satisfying career or marital difficulties.

CAUSATIVE FACTORS IN SEXUAL DYSFUNCTION

Sexual dysfunction is almost always multifactorial in origin.   When
one considers the complexity of the sexual act, involving as it does
two people going through an elaborate physiological and behavioural
sequence of events together, and when one considers that each person
has his or her own history of parental attitudes, masturbation and
guilt, previous sexual encounters, current anxieties and areas of
sexual ignorance, it is not surprising that at times things go
wrong.   Add to this the fact that sex is a subject that most people
feel sensitive about, that they do not communicate freely or honestly about, and that society creates great expectations for and makes
jokes about, and the existence of sexual dysfunction becomes very
easily understood.
    Some of the major causes of sexual dysfunction are shown in Table
7.2.   It is rare to find a case in which there seems to be a single
cause: more commonly there is a combination of marital difficulties, unhelpful parental attitudes, pressures of life and perhaps
ageing, and all of these should be taken into account when planning
treatment.

TABLE 7.2   Common causes of sexual dysfunction

---

1 Physical.

   (a)   Causing impotence: spinal injuries, neurological diseases
       including diabetic and alcoholic neuropathy.
   (b)   Causing dyspareunia: local vaginal inflammation, pelvic
       infections, tumours, cysts, and occasionally injuries to
       ligaments.
   (c)   Endocrine disorders: menopausal changes in females, and
       rare conditions (e.g. Fröhlich's syndrome) in males.
   (d)   Drugs, especially antidepressants and antihypertensives.

2 Poor technique and ignorance (especially about female response).

3 Neurotic and phobic reactions, deriving often from parental attitudes or previous unpleasant sexual experiences, such as rape,
  and resulting in guilt and rejection of physical pleasure.

4 Anxiety about current situations, e.g. problems with career or
  children, or simple anxiety about sexual performance.

5 Loss of libido (physical or mental illness, pressures of life,
  depression, drug dependency, advancing age, etc.:   in some cases
  low sex drive is lifelong).

6 Marital problems (communication difficulties, resentment, overprotection with dependency or continual fighting).

    Some comment is needed to supplement the list of physical causes
given in Table 7.2.   First, there are only a few types of dysfunction known to have a physical cause: erectile impotence is the best
known, although some of the drugs which cause impotence may also
cause failure of ejaculation and possibly anorgasmia in the woman.
No physical causes of premature ejaculation are known, and physical

causation of anorgasmia in the woman is excessively rare.   In impotence, it has been estimated by Johnson (1968) that 5 per cent of
men presenting at a psychiatric clinic had a physical cause for
their problem.   These are usually spinal lesions or neuropathy
(Table 7.2).   While diabetes mellitus can cause impotence through
damage to pelvic nerves (diabetic neuropathy) this is not necessarily the case, and it has been shown by Campbell et al. (1974) that if
deep testicular pain sensation and vascular reflexes are preserved,
impotence in a diabetic patient should be treated as psychogenic -
i.e. caused by the invalid role, the effect of a chronic illness,
loss of confidence, etc.   The effects of alcohol, too, are somewhat
complex.   A small amount of alcohol can increase sexual desire and
release inhibitions: acute intoxication will cause impotence, and
chronic alcoholism can cause both neuropathy (leading to impotence)
and a decrease in the attractiveness of the patient for his wife, so
that her lack of co-operation can make an erection less easy to
obtain.   The effect of antidepressant drugs on sexual function is
also complex: they may reduce depression and therefore increase
sexual desire, while at the same time making it less easy to achieve
erection and orgasm.

Many local conditions in the woman can cause pain in sexual intercourse.   Vaginal infections such as candida (thrush) and tricho-
monas vaginalis can cause superficial dyspareunia, and atrophic
vaginitis occurring at the menopause can cause thinning of the vaginal wall and consequently pain and loss of lubrication.   Deeper
dyspareunia can be caused by pelvic infections (e.g. gonorrhoea);
and by tumours, cysts and other conditions in the uterus, ovaries,
Fallopian tubes and other pelvic and lower abdominal organs.   A
rare condition following pelvic trauma (e.g. forcible rape) has been
described in which rupture of the broad ligament causes unusual
mobility of the uterus and pain on intercourse (Masters and Johnson,
1970).   It should be emphasised that not all cases of pain on intercourse can be explained by physical disorders, but it is important, as in any other condition, to exclude these by a competent
gynaecological opinion before treating the pain as psychogenic or
functional.

Probably the most important thing to be emphasised in discussing
physical causation of sexual dysfunction is that the physical cause,
however serious, is usually not the only cause.   Even in cases of
paraplegia in the male, some kind of sexual interaction is usually
possible, although it needs considerable co-operation from both
partners to overcome some of their inhibitions over unusual activities.   An example of the interaction of physical and emotional factors is given by the case of the inhibited and intellectual school-
master who developed partial impotence and multiple sclerosis at
about the same time.   He and his wife were taken on for treatment,
and work was being done on the marital interaction and psychogenic
causes for the impotence, including his lack of confidence and
drive.   He made little progress, but one week he developed some
anaesthesia in the pubic region and consulted a neurologist, who
told him that multiple sclerosis undoubtedly caused impotence and
that he should look no further for the cause.   That night he experienced the best erection he had had for months - but in discussion
he could not understand the irony of the situation.   In any event,
his erectile problems were much less troublesome after that time.

Of the non-physical causes of sexual dysfunction, perhaps the most common one affecting the individual is anxiety, which can relate to many current life problems such as extra responsibilities at work, sickness in a child, financial strains or any of the other situations which make people worried. In addition, as Masters and Johnson pointed out, 'performance anxiety' can spoil the sexual performance itself: the more the impotent man thinks and worries about his erection, the less likely is the erection to occur. Often both types of anxiety occur together, as in the man with diabetes (without neuropathy) who had a high level of sexual drive but had been impotent for three years. He was always an anxious man with low self-confidence, and he was rather dominated by his more confident, outgoing wife. He worried excessively about meals and insulin injections, and when it came to an attempt at intercourse he worried about whether he could get an erection and whether his wife would reject him if he did. A very short course of relaxation, sensate focus and genital focus therapy resulted in good erections, and his increased confidence in his sexual powers helped him to be a little more assertive (with the therapist's approval) toward his wife. The mixture of marital and anxiety factors in this case is, of course, quite typical (although not universal).

Neurotic and phobic reactions as causal factors in sexual dysfunction appear to be more common in women, although many men experience these as well. Typically, the patient has experienced an unpleasant sexual approach either as a young girl or an adolescent, and sometimes with the unpleasantness she had had some guilty enjoyment of part of the experience. An example is a girl who was in a cinema at the age of eleven when a man put his hand on her leg and tried to put a finger into her vagina. She was frightened, but did nothing until he became too insistent, and then she asked her older sister to take her out. She then avoided theatres and buses and, when seen for treatment at the age of seventeen, she reported total lack of feeling during sex play with her fiance. It was only after a fairly intensive course of desensitisation and some less intensive work with the couple that she began to experience orgasms with her fiance stimulating her manually.

Another female patient, who became panicky when her cohabitee made any sexual advances to her, had had a very bad relationship with her mother. Her mother had never had a good sexual relationship with her father, who had left her when the patient was fifteen; she was in the habit of calling the patient a whore when she put on lipstick, and predicting an unwanted pregnancy whenever the patient set foot outside the house. In fact the patient remained a virgin until her marriage at twenty-two, and this was annulled because of non-consummation. In the present relationship, sex had gone well until the relationship became 'respectable' - i.e. mother knew about it and did not disapprove. At that time, the patient began refusing sex and becoming panicky, and it was not until the relationship with mother was explored in a kind of abreaction with her that she began to be able to co-operate with sensate focus and eventually accept intercourse.

I have listed parental attitudes in Table 7.2 separately from ignorance about sexual approaches, but often the two go together: there is no one so ignorant as one who is afraid to learn, and this

seems often to be the result of parental prohibition.   Certainly it
is surprising how many quite confident and socially acceptable men
are in ignorance of the function of the clitoris, to take only one
example.   Many women, too, are unaware of the nature of the female
orgasm, and some expect a kind of ejaculation to take place, as in
the male.

Loss of libido is a very common occurrence in all sorts of illness, both physical and mental.   In a sense, sexual appetite may be
seen as an affirmation of health, and it seems one of the most vulnerable factors to any reduction in physical or mental well-being.
It has been found in various studies (e.g. Crowe et al., 1977) that
the occurrence of psychiatric illness, whether psychotic, neurotic
or personality disturbance, adversely affects the prognosis in a
case of sexual dysfunction.   Similarly, adverse living conditions
make treatment harder, as in the case of the couple living in a
basement flat where the landlord had to have access in order to get
to the back yard;   their problem of impotence did not improve until
they found a house of their own.

Again, the effect of age on libido is important.   Both men and
women seem to require less frequent sexual gratification as they
become older.   Sometimes this is not appreciated by the couple,
and they are expecting to have intercourse in their fifties as often
as in their twenties: simple discussion about unrealistic expectations is often sufficient to clear the situation, and results of
conjoint therapy with middle-aged couples are surprisingly gratify-
ing.

I have left till last the most pervasive and frequent cause of
sexual dysfunction, namely marital problems.   It was estimated at a
clinic dealing with sexual dysfunction (Crowe et al., 1977) that
over 60 per cent of the couples seen had marked or severe marital
problems in addition to their sexual ones.   These may take many
forms, such as simple communication difficulties, difficulty in expressing emotions, resentment expressed as arguments or hostile silences, dependency in one partner combined with overprotection in
the other, continual fighting between the partners and many other
combinations.   In many cases of sexual dysfunction, sex can be
seen as a weapon in the power struggle between the spouses, as in
the case of the woman with a high sexual drive married to a man who
preferred intellectual pursuits.   She would complain about various
aspects of his behaviour including his lack of sexual interest,
while he would retaliate by retiring to his books and not initiating
sex.   When in therapy he decided to change his ways and initiate
sex more often, while she agreed to reduce her nagging, she lost her
sexual drive completely, and it took considerably more conjoint
therapy to remove sex from the battle front and help them to co-
operate rather than compete in this way.

Occasionally the marital difficulties can be seen as directly
caused by the sexual problems (for instance frustration and irrit-
ability in the wife of the man with premature ejaculation), but more
often the marital problem appears to be primary, while in a considerable number of cases the two problems seem to have developed in
parallel.   When anorgasmia is situational, that is when the woman
can achieve orgasms in other situations but not with her husband, a
marital difficulty normally underlies the sexual problem.   This is

illustrated by the case of the female company director married to a man who worked as a plumber in the same firm: their marriage was threatened by her anorgasmia and by his 'excessive' sexual demands, and also by the reversal of their roles by which the husband did most of the housework and the wife travelled the world.   Marital contract therapy was begun, in which in return for the husband's reduction in complaints the wife would be more tidy around the house; and, after a successful holiday together, the wife's sexual desire returned and their sexual and marital relationship became mutually satisfactory.

A case with features in common is that of a man with impotence married to a very competent, motherly woman who looked after his every need, bought presents for them both at Christmas time, and worked full time while her husband studied.   In marital therapy her protective behaviour had to be challenged repeatedly, and eventually the husband was able to stand up and look after her at times, as well as being more independent himself.   This cleared the path for sensate focus treatment (see below) which was eventually fairly successful.

A case illustrating the admixture of marital and sexual problems is that of a couple in their thirties with two children in which the wife had begun to hate both foreplay and any expression of tenderness on her husband's part, while at times (though much too rarely for him) allowing sexual intercourse.   She had come from a family where physical contact was almost unknown, and he from a family where such contact was frequent - indeed he had often avoided his mother's embraces rather than welcoming them.   In this case, neither marital nor sexually orientated therapy altered the situation. He said he could not live without emotional warmth, and she said she loved him but could not show it in her behaviour.

Sometimes all that is required is a simple instruction to the couple to talk about sex.   One such couple, who had never before discussed sex, and presented with anorgasmia and refusal of sex in the wife, returned for their second appointment to say that talking about it had brought about a complete change, that the husband had completely altered his approach and they did not now need to go through the complicated hierarchy of exercises in order to achieve intercourse.

APPROACHES TO TREATMENT

The case reports given in the previous section, while mainly illustrating aspects of causation, have also contained some suggestions as to the effective variables in treatment.   In this section, I want to deal more systematically with the treatment of sexual dysfunction.   If one looks at the various causes listed in Table 7.2 and takes into account the multiplicity of causes operative in most cases, it becomes clear that any treatment programme must be either flexible or extremely comprehensive.   In particular, it is important to have the capability of dealing with physical causes, emotional or psychiatric causes and interpersonal or marital causes of sexual problems.   Clearly in the past, when cases of 'frigidity' were seen by gynaecologists and cases of 'impotence' by psychia-

trists, and partners were usually excluded from treatment, there
were some successes.   However, it seems that the more recent approaches, especially those offering conjoint therapy, have the pot-
entiality of dealing with a greater range of problems in the same
therapeutic milieu, and should therefore be more successful overall.
I will be dealing first with the more widely used conjoint approaches, and then with some of the more recently introduced individual
and group approaches.

Conjoint therapy

At about the same time that conjoint family therapy was developing
in the USA and Britain (Beels and Ferber, 1969), Masters and Johnson
(1970) were formulating their conjoint approach to the treatment of
sexual dysfunction.   This approach recognised, almost for the first
time, the importance of the marital relationship in the causation of
sexual problems.   The approach consists very much of a therapeutic
'package' which is comprehensive but relatively inflexible.   The
couple are asked to stay in a hotel away from family and business
commitments for the full two-week period of treatment.   They attend
the clinic every day during the two weeks, including Sundays, and
can phone the therapists (always a male-female pair) at any time.
     The first two or three days comprise the introductory phase.   A
full medical, sexual and psychiatric history is taken from both
partners, and this is supplemented by a full physical examination of
both partners alone, and sometimes also in each other's presence.
Physical pathology, if found, is dealt with by referral to physi-
cians, surgeons or gynaecologists.   During the physical, the couple
are reassured on anatomical variations in size and shape of the gen-
italia.   After this, a series of 'round table conferences' between
the couple and the co-therapists begins, and continues daily
throughout therapy.   At these conferences, the couple are encouraged to communicate freely on sexual matters, aud to tell the therapists about their difficulties and successes.   A considerable
amount of marital counselling takes place, and Masters and Johnson
make the rather rigid rule that the male therapist never looks at
the female partner, or answers her question directly, and similarly
with the female therapist and the male partner: this is supposed to
avoid seduction, but its main advantage seems to be that it avoids a
possible alliance between both therapists and one partner against
the other partner.   A considerable emotional crisis often builds up
between husband and wife during the fortnight of therapy (see 'The
Couple', by Mr and Mrs K, 1972, which recounts the experiences of a
couple treated in this way).   A marital relationship could hardly
be unaffected by this intensive therapy experience.
     Regarding the specific aspects of the Masters and Johnson ap-
proach, instructions are given from the fourth day on for various
techniques for the couple to use in private in their own hotel room.
At first, there is a ban on intercourse, which is a great help to
those suffering from 'performance anxiety' (Table 7.2).   Instead of
intercourse, the couple practise the sensate focus technique:
mutual body massage, using a special scented skin lotion, and covering every part of the body except the breasts and genitals, with the

aim of rediscovering the sensations of touch, smell and body contact, and of learning how to obtain pleasure by giving pleasure.
The lotion is used partly to help those with rough hands, but also
to accustom the couple to the feel of secretions such as vaginal
lubrication and semen.   The emphasis is on physical communication
via the hands of the 'masseur' and the recipient's body, with verbal
feedback as to whether the pressure and movement of the hands is
producing the desired feelings of relaxation and being cared for.
Sexual arousal is not discouraged but is an unimportant aspect at
this stage - an example perhaps of paradoxical intention, in that it
often occurs when it is not being sought.   In the absence of any
demand for intercourse, the dysfunctional partner can relax with
physical contact, often for the first time for years.

After sensate focus, the couple proceed to genital sensate focus.
Starting with the non-genital technique as above, they proceed to
handle and stimulate the genitals, not with the object of producing
sexual climax or ejaculation, but in order to continue giving pleasure.   Often a 'teasing' technique is recommended, whereby if a partial erection or some female arousal is obtained, stimulation ceases
for a few minutes and then begins again, resulting in further sexual
excitement.   The purpose of this is to dispel the myth that once an
erection or lubrication is lost, it can never be regained on that
occasion.   As in the non-genital sensate focus, there is an alter-
nation between husband and wife being the active partner.

When intercourse is attempted, after some days of training with
the sensate and genital focus techniques, it is recommended that
this should be in the female superior position.   There are various
reasons given for this, such as the association of the traditional
position with repeated failures, the increased freedom of movement
in the dysfunctional female partner, and the difficulty for the dysfunctional male partner in penetrating in the traditional male superior position without ejaculating or losing the erection.

The non-genital and genital sensate focus techniques are the
basic ones for impotence and female anorgasmia, but for other conditions, specific techniques are recommended.   For premature ejaculation the 'squeeze' technique is used, whereby the wife stimulates
an erection in her partner, and when the urge to ejaculate is felt,
but before the point of 'ejaculatory inevitability' she squeezes the
glans penis firmly between her fingers and thumbs, from dorsal to
ventral (upper to lower) surface, thus inhibiting the desire to
ejaculate.   If, despite squeezing, ejaculation should still occur,
the couple have to learn by this experience to apply the squeeze a
little earlier in the reflex cycle.   This technique, which can be
varied as the 'stop' technique (simply stopping stimulation at the
same point in the cycle) can then be included in the couple's sexual
practice during intercourse.

For failure to ejaculate, Masters and Johnson recommend a 'superstimulation' technique, whereby the female partner tries by mutual
masturbation to produce an ejaculation, and once it can be done in
this way, she inserts the penis at the point of ejaculation in her
vagina.   Again, the couple can learn to incorporate the technique
in their usual sexual practice.

The treatment of vaginismus also involves special techniques.
During the physical examination of the female partner, the therapist

carries out a vaginal examination and passes a small dilator; the
husband, who has been watching, repeats the process, and is then
asked to pass larger dilators in sequence during the sensate focus
sessions in their hotel room.   After passage of the larger dilators, the wife is asked to keep them in position for several hours.
In addition, of course, the couple go through the usual series of
exercises as for other dysfunctions, and the dilator treatment is an
important, but relatively short, aspect of their total management.

Masters and Johnson are reticent on the subject of the treatment
of dyspareunia, although very firm in their recommendation that physical causes must be excluded before the pain is identified as psychological in origin.   Presumably, in the cases thought to be psychogenic, the sequence of sensate focus training should be followed,
as for anorgasmia.

The treatment offered is a very comprehensive one, as mentioned
above, and it might be questioned how much of it is strictly necessary in all cases.   In particular, the two-week residential course
of treatment and the insistence on two therapists for each couple
seem to be expensive items which might be dispensed with if found to
be unnecessary.   They themselves suggest that it is possible to do
without the residential commitment, but in that case they recommend
a three-week course of daily treatment.   They are adamant about the
use of two therapists.   However, recent research work (Mathews et
al., 1976) has suggested that no significant advantage is gained by
using co-therapists compared with one therapist.   The last word has
not been spoken on this point, but various modifications of the
technique are now being used in rather different settings.

In this country, for example, a number of clinics have now been
in existence for three to four years, treating sexual dysfunction by
conjoint therapy based on the Masters and Johnson model (Bancroft
and Coles, 1976; Duddle, 1975; Crowe et al., 1977).   A brief description of the work at the last of these clinics should suffice, as
all of them function in a basically similar way.

The patients attend as couples, and at this clinic referrals of
single patients are not taken.   Treatment consists of an initial
visit of about three hours, followed by weekly or fortnightly visits
lasting about 30-45 minutes, to a total of six to ten visits in all.
Before their first visit, the couple are asked to complete and return a biographical, psychiatric and medical history questionnaire.
In the clinic itself, each partner is seen separately at first, by
one therapist and then the other (if in co-therapy) or by the one
therapist only (if in single therapy).   History-taking focuses on
presenting problems, sexual and marital history, current sexual
practices and attitudes, social and personal circumstances (including sources of anxiety, such as career or children) and any illness
or medication which might interfere with sexual function.   Patterns
of behaviour and problems in the marital relationship are explored,
with a view to a contract or operant-interpersonal approach to marital therapy (Stuart, 1969; Crowe, 1977).   After a case discussion
with the supervisors and therapeutic team the first conjoint interview takes place, in which goals for therapy are carefully checked
with the couple.   After this, the interview consists mostly of explanations of the sensate focus technique, of instructions for relaxation by the technique of Jacobson (1938) and of negotiation of

any marital contracts for the following week (see below).   They
take home typed sets of instructions as a reminder of the relaxation
and sensate focus techniques.

On the second visit, usually a week later, a physical examination
of both partners is done, usually in each other's presence, both to
exclude pathology and to educate the couple in sexual anatomy and
physiology.   Progress is then variable according to the couple's
response to the original instructions.   They may proceed quickly
through experimentation with self-stimulation (again with typed instructions) and genital sensate focus, and on to the various techniques used by Masters and Johnson (see above) such as 'teasing' for
impotence and anorgasmia, the squeeze or stop technique for premature ejaculation, the superstimulation technique for delayed ejaculation and the use of dilators for vaginismus.   Alternatively, more
attention may be paid to anxiety reduction, to the control of depression (perhaps with antidepressant drugs), to the resolution of
marital or communication difficulties or any other approaches that
seem indicated, such as assertiveness training or exploration of individual psychological difficulties with sex.   For couples with low
interest or low sex drive, books, magazines or films dealing explicitly with sex may be recommended as an aid to sex interest and to
their communication on sexual matters (Gillan and Gillan, 1976).
In most cases the initial goals worked out with the couple are ad-
hered to, and this means resolution of the sexual dysfunction as the
primary aim.   However, in other cases, where progress towards the
main goal is slow or non-existent, it may still be possible to improve marital interaction by conjoint therapy, and anxiety symptoms
by relaxation or tranquillisers;   often in such cases it is necessary to conclude that progress is unlikely to be made, and that they
must accept the status quo or even make a decision to separate.

The importance of marital problems in sexual inadequacy has been
mentioned in an earlier section.   It might be said that one of the
most important aspects of both the Masters and Johnson approach, and
those based on it, is the conjoint interview situation, with its
potential for clearing up misunderstandings in the marriage, encouraging freer communication, adjusting power struggles and increasing
tolerance.   A specific approach to marital problems has been advocated by Stuart (1969) and Liberman (1970) and has recently been
shown by the author (Crowe, 1976) to be superior to a control procedure and compatible with a Masters and Johnson approach.

The simple hypothesis behind the Stuart approach is that couples
with marital problems wish to change each other's behaviour but have
not been employing effective means to do so.   In particular, they
do not carry out enough behaviour which is rewarding to the partner,
but instead use negative means to control each other - such as nagging, threats, punishment, hostile silences or lack of co-operation
in the sexual area.   The remedy for this situation is that each
partner should set certain tasks for the other, and that an equal
exchange of these tasks (similar to the Masters and Johnson 'give-
to-get' principle) would result in a more harmonious marital relationship.   In another sense, the tasks are seen as a kind of mutual
reward: the husband carrying out his task as a reward for the wife
carrying out hers and vice versa.   The wishes for changed behaviour
on both sides, which are translated into tasks, have to be phrased

in certain ways, and the therapist is involved in this process.
Thus, the tasks must be positive, specific and repeatable. 'Showing more affection' is positive and repeatable, but has to be rephrased for instance as 'kissing me before going out in the morning
and on return from work' to increase specificity. 'Nagging less
often' is not suitable because it is a negative goal, and might be
rephrased as 'listening to what I have to say and giving a pleasant
and constructive reply'. Other examples of specific, positive and
repeatable behaviour might include gardening, cooking meals, house
repairs, more frequent sexual intercourse, specific behaviour in the
sexual relationship, etc. The expectation is that, as a result of
the positive interchange of behaviour, the couple become more attractive to each other, the whole relationship is improved, and the
exchange of more rewarding behaviour becomes automatic.

Clearly the simple instruction to increase rewarding interpersonal behaviour is not sufficient in all cases, although in a surprisingly high proportion of couples this simple and easily taught
approach produces worthwhile improvements. If there are major conflicts deriving from past family experiences, unrealistic expectations or constellations of dependency and overprotection in which
one partner is infantilised, the simple approach above may not be
sufficient to alter the relationship. In those cases, a more
searching approach to the marital difficulties involving analysis of
the system and perhaps the individual dynamics may be necessary,
always keeping in mind the stated goal of the couple (in this case
the restoration of sexual function). Paradoxical task setting and
structural manipulation of the system may be in order, as well as
more traditional interpretations designed to give insight. In some
cases what is needed is a task that will introduce movement (physical or psychological) such as an instruction for back-to-back wrest-
ling before tackling the sensate focus exercises.

In some cases, the communication between the partners is the
major problem, and here another approach is useful, as described by
Liberman et al. (1976). While the conjoint therapy continues, the
therapist checks with each partner the effect that the other partner's remarks are having. If misunderstandings seem to occur, for
instance if remarks intended as neutral or friendly are being interpreted as hostile, the therapist asks the speaker to rephrase the
remark until it is accepted by the hearer in the spirit in which it
was meant. Again, the rephrasing is usually in more positive and
specific terms: perhaps 'you showed me up in front of our friends
again' might reappear as 'I felt rather uncomfortable in the car
with George and Barbara when you criticised my driving'. The difference is in several aspects: the complaint is more specific, it
is centred on the speaker's feelings rather than the hearer's behaviour, and the word 'again' is omitted. Frequently the word 'angry'
in this sort of exchange evokes hostile feelings in the hearer and
leads to an irresistible escalation of angry exchanges: if the word
'hurt' or 'sad' can be substituted this often avoids such results
and enables constructive communication to continue.

A case example may be useful here to illustrate the combination
of Masters and Johnson technique, anxiety reduction and marital
therapy. The husband, aged 55, presented initially with partial
impotence. No physical cause had been found by the referring

doctor, but he noted in his letter that the wife, aged 51, was
'aggressive and abusive' towards her husband.   When asked individually about their complaints, the husband mentioned tiredness and
his wife's criticism, and the wife complained of quarrels and unhappiness, in addition to the sexual problem.

At first, the wife was reluctant to enter into conjoint therapy,
and it took the therapist some time to persuade her to be treated
with her husband 'for his sake'.   However, she soon became more co-
operative, and explained that her husband had, until three years
before, been a quiet, kind, helpful man, who had 'put his family
first'.   He had then undertaken the direction of a new company,
providing night security, to which he had become 'married': he now
spent many nights working and others receiving phone calls in the
early hours.   He described his wife as a good cook and a good
mother.   When asked what they would like of each other, he asked
her to stop nagging and criticising; this was interpreted as 'listen to what he says in the evenings about work' and 'give him the
soft answer in talking about work'.   She asked him to kiss her
goodbye in the morning and let her know what time he would be home
in the evenings; her tasks were specific enough to be used as they
stood.   They were also given instructions for sensate focus technique, with a ban on intercourse.

The next week they reported that their marriage had been better
than at any time in the previous three years, with hardly a cross
word spoken.   The sensate focus technique had particularly pleased
them, as it had not been their previous practice to have intercourse
without their nightclothes on: they had broken the ban on intercourse twice, and the husband had had a good erection on each occasion.   He said in particular that he found his wife more sexually
attractive when she did not nag him.   A new task was negotiated,
that the husband would arrange for a new roster at work so as to
leave him free on some weekends and some evenings, while his wife
would leave the whole question of dealing with the staff to her
husband.

The following week when genital contact was permitted, the husband reported that when his wife went to touch the penis, it would
shrink, and his impotence had been worse, although the marital relationship continued to improve.   They were reassured on the sexual
problem and told to expect no improvement, but to continue the ban
on intercourse.   The impotence fluctuated; sometimes the husband
was able to achieve intercourse, sometimes not.   It emerged that
his expectations were that he should be able to have full intercourse six times a week, and thought his wife expected this too: on
questioning, she said that once a week would be quite enough.   At
one stage, the husband found that taking a drink of sherry and playing with the penis after urinating helped him to sustain an erection.   At another point in treatment, it seemed that the husband
could not relax in sex play because their seventeen-year-old son
might come into the bedroom; the wife volunteered to have a word
with the son, and that problem was solved.   The wife remained quite
outspoken to the end of treatment, and the husband more shy and defensive.   He valued the therapy as a means of allowing him to speak
his mind towards his wife, and she valued it as a means of controlling her husband's behaviour.   Both were apprehensive at the break

after ten sessions, although by that time the sexual relationship was very successful about once a week and the marital relationship remained quite good.   Two years later, they continued to be successful sexually, and ironically the wife's desire began to lessen as she knew her husband could perform adequately.   Arguments occurred, but did not reach a very acrimonious level, and the security firm was running well, with the wife making no complaints about it.

There is now a small body of literature and experience in the treatment of sexual and marital problems in couples' groups.   Burbank (1976) has reviewed the area, and the general impression is that such groups function in a similar way to stranger groups, but with the added complication of paired relationships between the members.   Some therapists find a group of couples easier to handle than a couple, because of the dilution of the extreme dependency on the therapist.   Certain guidelines for behaviourally oriented groups have been suggested by Liberman et al. (1976) including warmth and support from the leader, an encouragement of cohesiveness (i.e. the leader praises any group member who supports another) and an emphasis on task orientation.   The group tasks might include Masters and Johnson techniques for couples to practise at home or 'love days' in which hostility is temporarily laid aside and the partners specifically do things that each other would want.   As yet couples groups for sexual dysfunction have not been widely adopted, but economic considerations commend them.

Kaplan's approach (Kaplan, 1974) is widely recognised as useful. She usually sees couples, and carries out a combination of Masters and Johnson technique and dynamic psychotherapy, with considerable flexibility in seeing the couple or the individual.

Individual and group therapy

While it is my view that conjoint therapy is the most appropriate approach for the couple with sexual dysfunction, such an approach is not always possible, either because the patient is single or separated, or because the spouse is unwilling or unable to attend.

Individual approaches can be divided into those which aim at anxiety reduction, those which aim at teaching skills and those which aim at increasing sexual interest.   The basic anxiety reduction techniques are desensitisation either for the individual (Friedman, 1968) or the group (O'Gorman et al., 1975);   and the administration of tranquillising drugs, which was found in a somewhat poorly controlled study by Ansari (1976) to be equivalent in efficacy to conjoint treatment.   Ellison (1968) described a treatment for vaginismus which combined anxiety reduction, supportive psychotherapy and physical examination of the female partner by a female therapist, and reported very good results.   The broad-spectrum behavioural approach of Annon (1976) includes anxiety reduction techniques, individual and couple psychotherapy, marital contracts and orgasmic conditioning;   no results are reported, but case reports suggest a good success rate.

Treatment approaches which aim at teaching skills include some aspects of anxiety reduction too, but divide into two types, those aimed at achieving orgasm and those aimed at social skills acquisi-

tion.   Lobitz and Lopiccolo (1972) described a programme for
achieving orgasm in anorgasmic women, which was successful in all
their patients.   Methods used to achieve orgasm included vibrator
applied to the clitoris, running water over the clitoris or manual
stimulation of the clitoris.   The technique was then gradually combined with the normal intercourse patterns of the women.   Barbach
(1974) has described a similar programme for women in a group, combining discussion and the viewing of films of female masturbation in
the group with self-stimulation exercises at home.   Zilbergeld
(1975) has described similar groups for dysfunctional men.   Clearly
some of these groups also involved the learning of social skills,
but for some single male patients with impotence, social skills are
the main deficit for which they need help.   Social training groups
may be of some help to these men, but in reality not much improvement is to be expected in sexual function from social skills training.

Various techniques designed to increase sexual interest in those
with a low sex drive have been advocated (Gillan and Gillan, 1976).
These include the recommendation to read magazines and books dealing
explicitly with sex, or the viewing of films showing sexual intercourse, masturbation and similar activities.   There is evidence
that such activities increase sexual activity in the short-term, and
this may be sufficient to restore the patient's confidence with a
partner and thus reverse a sexual dysfunction.   However, there is
no real evidence that the main standby of traditional approaches,
namely testosterone, has any effect at all on sexual function or
desire, except in rare cases of androgen deficiency.

The use of surrogate partners was recommended by Masters and
Johnson, more for male than for female patients, but there are ethical difficulties with this practice, and it is difficult to endorse
it except in rare cases.   Unattached male patients whose main difficulty is with confidence in the heterosexual situation might benefit from sexual training with a sympathetic surrogate partner; but
it is difficult to justify their use in other situations such as
that of a male patient whose wife refuses to attend for treatment.
In this case, one can sometimes give the partner who attends the
same kind of instructions as if both were there, and ask him or her
to communicate them to the absent partner.   This is not often successful, the difficulty being that a partner who is not motivated to
attend the hospital is probably equally unmotivated to improve the
sexual relationship.   Occasionally however, as in cultures such as
the Indian, where the wife is not expected to take part in talk
about sexual matters, she may be prepared to co-operate with sensate
focus treatment without attending the hospital, and good results
have been obtained with couples from this culture with the husband
attending alone.

One must not dismiss interpretative psychotherapy, which may be
useful in some cases, and which Kaplan (see above) has combined with
the Masters and Johnson approach.   However, such psychotherapy is
very broad-spectrum treatment, and as such is difficult to evaluate
as an approach to specific sexual dysfunctions.

THE RESULTS OF TREATMENT

As in most areas of treatment which have been developed recently and with enthusiasm, there is as yet very little evidence as to the efficacy of the treatment.   On the other hand, the nature of sexual dysfunction is such that it can be relatively easily evaluated by self-report, in that the target of treatment is usually an all-or-none event.   Because of this, one can put a certain amount of faith in the totally uncontrolled reports which most workers in the field have produced.   Thus Masters and Johnson consider that between 59 and 100 per cent of 500 couples (varying according to the type of dysfunction) have, during the two weeks of treatment 'initiated reversal of the basic symptomatology of sexual dysfunction for which they were referred' (1970, p. 352).   This is a rather vague criterion of improvement, but the fact that after five years follow-up the figures are basically similar reinforces the reliability of this assessment.   Using similar criteria, though more clearly spelled out, with 75 cases, Crowe et al. (1977) found a figure of 62.7 per cent overall improvement, or (if 13 couples who defaulted in the first two sessions are omitted) 75.8 per cent improvement.   In both studies, primary and secondary impotence were the least easy conditions to treat, and vaginismus and premature ejaculation the easiest.   Among the cases of orgasmic dysfunction, Crowe et al. found that those with situational dysfunction (i.e. occurring only in the marital relationship) were least easy to treat.   Masters and Johnson found difficulty in couples who held orthodox religious views of any type, in couples with severe marital problems, and with couples in whom one or both partners had had psychiatric treatment. These latter two findings were confirmed by Crowe et al., who also found a significantly greater defaulting rate in couples where the male partner was the presenting patient.

Controlled trials are very few in this area.   Kockott et al. (1975) reported that conjoint therapy was effective in eight out of twelve couples who had failed to improve in systematic desensitisation treatment of the impotent husband.   Mathews et al. (1976) reported no advantage of two therapists over one therapist administering the Masters and Johnson approach, but also found that neither approach was superior to a method in which instructions for sensate focus etc. were sent to the couple by mail.

Some uncontrolled reports by Lobitz and Lopiccolo (1972) suggest very good results (thirteen out of thirteen improved) for primary anorgasmia with their orgasmic conditioning approach;   secondary anorgasmia was not as successfully treated.   Barbach (1974) reported a 92 per cent improvement, but only with masturbation techniques, in 83 'pre-orgasmic' women.

Thus we are given some indications as to overall efficacy of the various techniques, of some factors in clients or patients predicting good response, and of some specific dysfunctions with better response to treatment than others.   We can only await the results of further surveys and controlled trials as the treatment methods become more established.

TRAINING FOR SEXUAL DYSFUNCTION THERAPY

This is not an appropriate setting for an exhaustive account of training in this area; however, some points of a very general nature should be made.   The first is that many types of professional may be suitable to undertake therapy of this kind: medical practitioners of all kinds, but especially psychiatrists, gynaecologists and general practitioners;   psychologists and social workers;   nurses and other paramedical professionals;   and marriage guidance counsellors.   In setting up a clinic, the ideal arrangement is that there should be a medical person in the team of therapists, especially if direct referrals or self-referrals are accepted.   However, if this cannot be done, some regular contact should be available with a hospital, a general practitioner or a family planning clinic to cover for physical disorders and to allow physical examinations to be performed.

The training of sexual dysfunction therapists is as yet not systematised, but a start has been made at the National Marriage Guidance Council, where six counsellors were trained in an eighteen-month period by treating cases in co-therapy with the supervising psychologist.   These counsellors are now taking part under supervision in the training of other counsellors, still under the general control of the NMGC.   In many hospitals throughout the country conjoint therapy is being offered for sexual dysfunction, sometimes through the family planning clinic, sometimes through the gynaecology department, but most often through the psychiatric department.   Generally the workers, who are drawn from various professions as above, devote one or two sessions a week to this work, and are trained through supervision with patients.

While there is room for workers of many disciplines in this field, it is clearly an area open to abuse and exploitation, and it is to be hoped that in the very near future some guidelines will be laid down as to a code of practice and minimum necessary qualifications for the work.   It is my own opinion that it would be reasonable for members of the 'helping professions' to be free to practise in the area, although cover by some official body such as a hospital or clinic would be desirable.   It would seem that bodies such as the National Marriage Guidance Council or the Catholic Marriage Advisory Council would be able to provide suitable cover, but anyone wishing to practise independently should subscribe publicly to a code of ethical practise as strict as that covering medical practitioners, and those without an appropriate professional background should be asked to go through a fairly stringent training course before seeing cases of sexual dysfunction.

The provision of theoretical teaching on the subject is still minimal in this country, and is provided mainly through workshops, put on for instance by the British Association for Behavioural Psychotherapy or the Association of Sexual and Marital Therapists. The kinds of teaching given include lectures and case reports, videotapes of couples being treated, and roleplay in which members of the group take the part of couple and therapist(s) for the purpose of training.   In addition, it has been found useful for therapists new to the field to see some of the films specially made for treatment and training, which involve explicit scenes of inter-

course, masturbation, etc.   The films are normally shown to a
group, who then discuss the films and their own attitudes to the
experience.

If one had to pinpoint the two most important skills to be
learned by a therapist beginning in this field, I would suggest
first, the ability to talk openly and in a relaxed way about sexual
matters and second, the ability to work with a couple in conjoint
marital therapy.   Regarding the first of these, there is a kind of
myth in existence that it is difficult to persuade clients to talk
about their sexual experiences in therapy.   In fact, most of the
problems are on the therapist's side: when the therapist is sufficiently relaxed and confident in talking about sex, whether with a
couple or an individual, the client usually has no difficulty in
being open and honest about it.   Regarding the second, the most
important step is to be able to get away from thinking in terms of
individuals with diseases and think instead about relationships and
systems - in exactly the same way as one has to change attitudes in
starting conjoint family therapy.

Having said this, however, one is left with the hardest problem
in the whole field, namely the man or woman with a sexual dysfunction who has no partner, or whose partner is unwilling to enter conjoint therapy.   As yet in this country there are very few centres
offering treatment for such clients, or any kind of training in the
individual or group methods available.

With this exception, however, there are now perhaps many thou-
sands of people with sexual dysfunctions who are capable of being
helped, and this may be of assistance not only to the couple but
also indirectly to their children, for whom, as I said in an earlier
section, a healthy sexual relationship and sensible attitudes to sex
in the parents may be an essential prerequisite in a good and balanced upbringing.

REFERENCES

ANNON, J.S. (1976), 'Behavioural Treatment of Sexual Problems, Brief
Therapy', New York, Harper & Row.
ANSARI, J.M.A. (1976), Impotence: prognosis, a controlled study,
'British Journal of Psychiatry', vol. 128, pp. 194-8.
APONTE, H. and HOFFMAN, L. (1973), The open door: a structural
approach to a family with an anorectic child, 'Family Process', vol.
12, pp. 1-44.
BANCROFT, J.H.J. and COLES, L. (1976), Three years' experience in a
sexual problems clinic, 'British Medical Journal', vol. i, pp. 1575-
7.
BARBACH, L.G. (1974), Group treatment for pre-orgasmic women, 'Jour-
nal of Sex and Marital Therapy', vol. 1, pp. 139-45.
BEELS, C.C. and FERBER, A.S. (1969), Family therapy: a view, 'Fam-
ily Process', vol. 8, pp. 280-318.
BURBANK, F. (1976), The treatment of sexual problems by group thera-
py, in S. Crown (ed.), 'Psychosexual Problems', London, Academic
Press.
CAMPBELL, I.W., EWING, D.J., CLARKE, B.F. and DUNCAN, L.J.P. (1974),
Testicular pain sensation in diabetic autonomic neuropathy, 'British
Medical Journal', vol. ii, pp. 638-9.

CROWE, M.J. (1976), Evaluation of conjoint marital therapy, Oxford, DM Thesis.

CROWE, M.J. (1977), 'Sexual Dysfunction Today', Update, London, pp. 21-8.

CROWE, M.J., CZECHOWICZ, H. and GILLAN, P. (1977), 'The Treatment of Sexual Dysfunction: a report of 75 cases',

DUDDLE, C.M. (1975), The treatment of marital psycho-sexual problems, 'British Journal of Psychiatry', vol. 127, pp. 169-70.

ELLISON, C. (1968), Psychosomatic factors in unconsummated marriage, 'Journal of Psychosomatic Research', vol. 12, pp. 61-5.

FRIEDMAN, D. (1968), The treatment of impotence by brietal relaxation therapy, 'Behaviour Research and Therapy', vol. 6, pp. 257-61.

GILLAN, P. and GILLAN, R. (1976), 'Sex Therapy Today', London, Open Books.

JACOBSON, E. (1938), 'Progressive Relaxation', University of Chicago Press.

JOHNSON, J. (1968), 'Disorders of Sexual Potency in the Male', Oxford, Pergamon Press.

MR and MRS K (1972), 'The Couple', London, W.H. Allen.

KAPLAN, H. (1974), 'The New Sex Therapy', New York, Brunner/Mazel.

KOCKOTT, G., DITTMAR, F. and NUSSELT, L. (1975), Systematic desensitisation of erectile impotence: a controlled study, 'Archives of Sexual Behaviour', vol. 3.

LIBERMAN, R. (1970), Behavioural approaches in family and couple therapy, 'American Journal of Orthopsychiatry', vol. 40, p. 106.

LIBERMAN, R.P., LEVINE, J., WHEELER, E., SANDERS, A. and WALLACE, C.J. (1976), Marital therapy in groups: a comparative evaluation of behavioural and interactional formats, 'Acta Psych. Scand. Suppl.', p. 266.

LOBITZ, W.C. and LOPICCOLO, J. (1972), New methods in the behavioural treatment of sexual dysfunction, 'Journal of Behaviour Therapy and Experimental Psychiatry', vol. 3, pp. 265-71.

MASTERS, W.H. and JOHNSON, V.E. (1970), 'Human Sexual Inadequacy', London, Churchill.

MATHEWS, A., BANCROFT, J. et al. (1976), The behavioural treatment of sexual inadequacy: a comparative study, 'Behavioural Research and Therapy', vol. 14, pp. 427-36.

O'GORMAN, E., MACALLISTER, J., QUINN, J.T., GRAHAM, P.J. and HARBISON, J.J.M. (1975), Treatment of frigidity by group desensitisation, in 'Progress in Behaviour Therapy', (ed. J.C. Brengelmann, Berlin, Springer Verlag.

STUART, R.B. (1969), Operant-interpersonal treatment for marital discord, 'Journal of Consulting and Clinical Psychology', vol. 33, p. 675.

ZILBERGELD, B. (1975), Group treatment of sexual dysfunction in men without partners, 'Journal of Sex and Marital Therapy', vol. 1, pp. 204-14.

Chapter 8

CO–THERAPY: A CLINICAL RESEARCHER'S VIEW

Emilia Dowling

There are three broad types of co-therapy or multiple therapy as it is sometimes called. The first consists of two therapists working together 'in vivo' with the family group; second, a team of therapists working together, one of whom is directly involved with the family in the therapy room while the others, although equally committed as therapists to the family, work from behind an observation screen; third, a team of therapists who work in different combinations with a family, intensively over a short period of time, as in multiple impact therapy.

For the purposes of this chapter, the term co-therapy refers to a team of two workers who simultaneously conduct 'in vivo' the treatment of an individual, an artificial group, a couple or a family group. The chapter will be devoted to examining the rationale of co-therapy in family and conjoint marital treatment, and will describe the way in which some basic assumptions frequently stated in the clinical literature have been empirically examined. A few of these studies will be discussed and my own work in this area will be reported.

Although co-therapy has been widely used when both individuals and artificial groups, Davis and Lohr (1971), Whitaker et al. (1951), McGee and Shuman (1970), and Yalom (1970), it has achieved popularity in the treatment of families and couples only in recent years. Early reports of its use in family therapy are given in Haley (1962) and Framo (1962). Although its use has been encouraged in training as well as in clinical practice, there have been few studies that actually look at the co-therapy team's behaviour. Rice, Fey and Kepecs (1972) refer to the lack of careful empirical studies of co-therapy. They surveyed the literature on the subject, finding that most authors discuss the method from a clinical point of view; of those who offered research studies only three use a large enough sample for statistical purposes. They report a control procedure used by Rabin (1967) comparing the feelings of the therapist about co-therapy with his feelings about a single therapist in the treatment of groups. Rabin found general agreement among therapists regarding the value of co-therapy. Co-therapy is, in fact, frequently cited in the clinical literature of family therapy as the preferred mode of work. Holt and Greiner (1976) found

five benefits of co-therapy referred to by different groups of clinicians: (1) security and protection for the therapists;   (2) the
possibility of more objective evaluation of family dynamics;   (3)
exposure of the family to a functional relationship which they could
use as a model;   (4) the increased effectiveness of a heterosexual
team in dealing with parenting and marital issues;   and (5) a
greater degree of satisfaction and pleasure on the part of both
family and therapist deriving from the co-therapy experience.   However, none of these assumptions have been tested out through empirical research.

In order to examine some of the issues underlying co-therapy,
Rice et al. (1972) carried out a study at the University of Wiscon-
sin, Department of Psychiatry, which involved twenty-five experienced and twenty-five inexperienced therapists, who had treated a
total of forty-eight married couples in co-therapy.   The instrument
used was a questionnaire including questions regarding the therapist's own therapeutic style, his co-therapist's style, as well as
feelings about the effectiveness of therapy and preferences of co-
therapist.   The therapists' style variable was examined using self-
descriptive statements in which therapists had to rate themselves on
a five-point scale ranging from 'never' to 'always'.   The responses
by all fifty therapists were factor analysed, yielding six clusters
of self-descriptive therapy factors which were subjectively labelled
as reflecting six therapeutic styles or orientations: blank screen,
paternal, transactional, authoritarian, maternal, idiosyncratic.

The main statistically documented conclusions of the study were:

1 The experienced therapists as a group differed from the inexperienced, both in personal style and in style desired for a co-
therapist.

2 Subjectively rated effectiveness of co-therapy is related to the
therapists feeling comfortable in the relationship and accepted by
their co-therapists.

3 A negative correlation was found between number of couples seen
and satisfaction in co-therapy.

Subjective ratings of the effectiveness of therapy were obtained
from the three groups of co-therapists, i.e. experienced, inexperienced and experienced/inexperienced.   Although the analysis of variance indicated no significant inter-group differences, the authors
point out the fact that the lowest ratings corresponded to the ex-
perienced/inexperienced group.   This finding, they suggest, has implications for the hypothesis that co-therapists must be of equal
status if therapy is to be effective.   (This finding seems particularly relevant for the training of family therapists and may call
into question the use of co-therapy teams of student/supervisor,
widely employed as a technique in 'live supervision' (Walrond-
Skinner, 1974).)   Regarding the point of 'diminishing returns' in
co-therapy satisfaction, which came with increased experience, this
may relate to the fact that experienced therapists have a more definite style and find it increasingly difficult to adjust appropriately to their working partners.

Gurman (1974a) studied and measured attitudes of twelve couples
in conjoint therapy with male and female co-therapists and compared
these results with their therapists' attitudes.   The study replicates Beutler's study (1971) of attitude change in couples therapy,

but also extends it to research into the treatment of the couple by co-therapists, which Gurman considers 'an essentially unstudied clinical practice and training modality'.   The instrument used was an attitude questionnaire in which both patients and therapists reported attitudes towards two areas of behaviour, along nine-item scales.   Outcome assessment was carried out using improvement ratings on three dimensions: change in marital relationship, change in husband, change in wife, which were rated independently by both co-therapists and spouses on nine-point scales from 'very negatively changed' to 'very positively changed'.   Gurman concluded that the 'relationship between attitude convergence in the marital dyad and rated outcome varies depending on who is evaluating change and what change is being evaluated'.   His study shows a negative relationship between co-therapists' different levels of experience and attitude convergence in the marital dyad which corroborates Rice, Fey and Kepecs' findings in this respect.   Finally, the study suggests that the nature of the co-therapists' relationship with one another is of extreme importance to the outcome of marital co-therapy.

WHY CO-THERAPY?

Before discussing the role of the co-therapist in treatment, it is worth considering the rationale for this method of therapeutic intervention.   Skynner (1976) sees it as a consequence of the 'changed views of human functioning and of therapy that conjoint family therapy has brought about'.   The new values of openness, confrontation and exposure of feelings by the therapists within the family therapy framework has made co-therapy a useful and popular technique for those working with the family group.

In the psychoanalytic model the therapist does not share his counter-transference with the patient;   it is only in the privacy of his own 'therapeutic' or 'training' analytic session that his feelings are disclosed.   In the co-therapy model, the relationship between the therapists as whole human beings with their weaknesses and feelings is experienced and shared by the family.   It is the exposure of this live struggle of human interaction in the therapeutic setting which provides a new and richer tool for growth and change in the treatment process.

FUNCTIONS OF THE CO-THERAPY TEAM

Modelling

This seems to be widely accepted as one of the most useful functions of the co-therapy team.   The interactional pattern of behaviour between the co-therapists will hopefully provide a model of more functional ways of relating, in the following areas:

1 Dealing with hostility and aggressive feelings: one of the most commonly shared phantasies in relationships is that expressed aggression, because it is perceived as being omnipotent, can destroy the other person.   This leads to various ways of hiding the aggressive feelings, either through repression or suppression, through

displacement (often onto another member of the family), through reaction formation, or through turning the aggression against oneself
with the consequent feelings of self-depreciation and guilt that
predominate in depression.   The functional co-therapy team is able
to disagree about different points of view in front of the family.
This helps to dispel the myth that the relationship will be des-
troyed if differences are expressed.   It is the wholeness of the
relationship with its 'good' and 'bad' aspects that will survive,
and it is the good aspects of trust, care and respect that will make
it possible to work through the difficulties and develop.

2 Clear communication patterns: the co-therapy team can make use
of their relationship to show the family how clear communication
makes for more functional relationships.   In order to do so, they
will avoid giving each other or the family 'double binding' or mixed
messages (unless employed as a particular technique for a special
reason, as described by Cade in Chapter 4); they will test their
understanding of each other and make sure they ask for clarifica-
tions when necessary, rather than assume that a meaning is clear.
An excellent description of this kind of communication modelling by
the therapists can be found in Satir (1967).

3 Healthy differentiation: in allowing each other to be different
and yet finding a way of functioning together, the therapists will
be providing a healthy model of differentiated marital interaction.

In evaluating these modelling functions of the therapeutic team,
clinicians and writers have sometimes used the term 'therapeutic
marriage' to describe some of the central features of the co-therapy
relationship.   Skynner (1976), for example, considers that

a pair of co-therapists of opposite sex can also provide more
adequate gender role models for spouses and children in families
where these have been confused or conflicting, and the relationship between the co-therapists can demonstrate principles - even
though these are expressed within the context of their professional cooperation - which also govern successful marital and
sexual interaction.

There are inevitably some similarities in the way co-therapists
interact with one another during the course of treatment and the way
married couples function.   However, it seems important also to
stress some of the basic differences between the relationships in
order to avoid the danger of falling into an 'undifferentiated therapeutic mass' (to paraphrase Bowen, 1971), where differences in
roles are denied and the couple's projection of an ideal and omnipotent relationship onto the 'therapeutic marriage' is unconsciously
fostered by the therapists.   Unlike a real marriage, the 'therapeutic marriage' has to find a way of operating together with regard
to one task only: the treatment.   The relationship has very clear
boundaries both in time and space.   The levels of communication and
the degree of intimacy are far more limited than with the married
couple.   Physical contact is usually very limited and carefully
avoided.   Expression of basic emotions, like aggression, is usually
rationalised, verbalised and worked through rather than acted out.
Likewise, loving and sexual feelings are sublimated through socially
acceptable non-physical means of expression.

In terms of their modelling role, the co-therapy pair should be
capable of providing a paradigm for functional interaction in terms
of:

a   clear communication, with sufficient openness to express differ-
    ences;
b   healthy expression of feelings, both positive and negative;
c   sufficient room for individuality and therefore creative auton-
    omy in the relationship;
d   above all, a model of whole object relationships (to use
    Kleinian terminology), in which the 'good' and 'bad' parts of
    the partner are integrated and accepted.

There is however an implicit danger in employing this metaphor of
marriage in describing the co-therapy relationship.   The therapists
may indulge in a phantasy whereby real differences between the therapeutic marriage and the real marriage are denied, thereby preventing the emergence of behavioural patterns in the couple that may be
appropriate for them though not necessarily similar to those expected and perhaps unconsciously presented by the therapists.

To try to mitigate against this happening, each member of the co-
therapy team must spend time looking at his needs and expectations
of his partner in their working relationship, and must carefully and
continually examine the meaning of their behaviour to one another,
especially in terms of their unconscious and perhaps unacceptable
needs.   Gurman (1974) comments in this respect that

    If one of the likely potential therapeutic values of marital co-
    therapy is its offering to patients a model of a workable human
    relationship, it is imperative that co-therapists confront and
    resolve discrepant expectations of their own roles.

The question of modelling, however useful in bringing about behavioural change, raises a philosophical issue, or, more precisely,
an ethical one.   Modelling is an active process by which we are
encouraging new patterns of behaviour to replace older ones, promoting imitation of the behaviour presented by the model, and enabling
successful replication of the model to be positively reinforced and
rewarded.   Therefore, through the modelling process are therapists
imposing their own values of 'better behaviour' on their clients?

This issue not only applies to family therapy; it is part of
the argument that concerns psychotherapy in general and the extent
to which therapists may be manipulating their clients' behaviour.
It poses a particular problem when evaluating outcome of therapy.
Who decides what is good for the family? If it is the therapists,
it can be argued that it becomes a question of value judgment, and
therefore it will be difficult for different therapists to agree on
this point.   In behaviourally oriented treatment, outcome criteria
can be related to the goals established at the beginning of treatment between the family and the therapists.   However, it is inevitable that in the course of treatment the priorities given to these
goals will be influenced by the therapist's beliefs regarding the
family's needs.   For example, the identified patient's symptomatic
relief seen by the family as a first priority may be considered by
the therapists to be a side-effect of the marital dysfunction which
has to be explored first.   The ultimate goal - the disappearance of
the symptom - remains the same, but the therapists and the family
may differ in the ways they think this should be achieved.

Division of labour

Like modelling, this is considered by practitioners to be one of the
main advantages of co-therapy.   Co-therapy makes it possible for
the therapists to cope better with the diverse and complex material
presented by the family by dividing attention and skill and responding with different and often opposite types of behaviour to a given
situation.   This task is usually more difficult for the single
therapist to achieve.
   It is assumed in clinical practice that co-therapists will vary
their therapeutic interventions to counterbalance the partner's behaviour, as a result of the complementarity function of the co-
therapy relationship.   This is achieved through displaying opposite
behaviours during a family therapy session.   For example, one therapist plays the supportive, nurturing role, while the other therapist displays the more confronting, challenging behaviour.   Another way in which co-therapists can complement each other is by increasing the time spent in a certain therapeutic intervention when
the partner is devoting less time to it.   In a research study reported later in this chapter, it was found that although therapists
have a 'permanent' therapeutic style regardless of co-therapist or
client families, the actual time they spend in specific interventions does vary according to the co-therapist with whom they are
working, as a result of this complementarity function.
   Skynner (1976) describes the way in which one therapist allows
himself to be sucked in to the family pathology and to manifest the
family disorder while the other stays detached as 'observing ego'
and ensures that the total situation remains constructive.
   When working with families where there are young children, the
therapeutic tasks can be divided so that one of the therapists
attends to the children's subsystem while the other one attends to
the adults.   The therapist dealing with the children can get involved in their play and help to interpret their phantasies and nonverbal messages back to the adults, thus bridging the gap between
the two levels of communication.

Mirroring families' behaviour

This is a commonly observed phenomenon in which the dysfunctional
pattern of behaviour displayed by the family is unconsciously repro-
duced in the co-therapy relationship.   It is important to stress
the word 'unconscious' because it is only when the therapists become
aware of this that it becomes a therapeutic tool to share and work
on with the family or the couple (Rubinstein and Weiner, 1967).
This unconscious mirroring of behaviour, which can be seen as the
result of projective identification, is different from the conscious, wilful replicating of a certain situation in which the therapists are simulating a specific pattern of behaviour in order to
demonstrate to the family what they are doing to each other.
   Object relations theory with its notions of projective identification, split, collusion and shared phantasy can throw some light on
the mirroring role of the co-therapy team.   These ideas and their
implications for marital and family therapy have been discussed by

Stewart et al. (1975).   The term projective identification was
first coined by Melaine Klein who became aware that her patients
were 'putting things into her' and then trying to destroy them.
The term was defined by her in 1946 as 'a process in which the
patient seemed to envy some projected aspect of himself and wanted
to destroy it'.   In interpersonal behaviour one partner may project his split-off undesirable aspects on to the other, and by collusion the partner acts as he is expected to.   Projective identification takes place in co-therapy when the team mirrors the
family's behaviour, replicating the split-off projected and undesirable aspects of the family's relationship system.

Some examples may clarify the way in which this process operates.
A male and female team were treating a family made up of a husband,
wife and three children.   It was a second marriage for both partners, with the oldest boy being mother's son by her first marriage
while the two younger children were from father's previous marriage.
The marital relationship revealed a clear pattern in which the wife
carried all the anxiety and therefore expressed all the aggression,
whereas the husband appeared as a vague, passive procrastinator who
expected solutions to their problems to come from external sources.
The interviews were always observed through a one-way screen and in
discussion after the sessions it gradually became apparent how the
female therapist was sensitive to any criticism, always reacted
strongly and even aggressively to justify the co-therapy team's interventions when challenged, and very angrily denied that there were
any difficulties in the co-therapy relationship.   In contrast, the
male therapist listened and smiled very passively leaving all the
anger and anxiety to his colleague.   Feedback from the observers
made it clear how the co-therapists were unconsciously replicating
the problems within the marital dyad.

In this example it was only the 'third eye' of the observers
which enabled the co-therapists to gain an understanding of what was
happening.   Just as a family group makes use of the more objective
observations of the therapists, so the co-therapy team requires an
outside reference point - either a team or a single consultant - who
can help them to understand the way in which family members are influencing their relationship.

Another example - in a family with two adolescents where the
splitting process made one the 'good' one and the other the 'bad'
delinquent one, the therapists were turned likewise into 'good' and
'bad' by the family, and through projective identification colluded
in this shared phantasy.   The 'bad' therapist was the aggressive
one who confronted the family with the way in which they scapegoated
one of the girls.   This made him the hated persecutor.   By collud-
ing with this projection, the whole system preserved the other therapist as the 'good' gentle one to which he responded by being inef-
fectual and placating, thereby perpetuating the splitting.   The
therapists had to work through this split in their relationship and
in doing so they were able to show to the family in the 'here and
now' how this relational pattern was replicating the split between
the two girls in the family.   As Walrond-Skinner (1976) points out:

> The most powerful and subtle use of co-therapy as a treatment
> technique is the use of the relationship to internalise the prob-
> lems of the family group itself; to work them through and ulti-

mately to resolve them during the course of the treatment step by step alongside the family.

DEVELOPING THE CO-THERAPY RELATIONSHIP - DIFFICULTIES

The idea of co-therapy is especially appealing when dealing with the family group.   Faced with such a powerful system, with its history, alliances, and defences, the possibility of a partnership seems an attractive proposition.

However, the co-therapy team itself is bound to encounter difficulties and, as in any new relationship, time has to be allowed for trust to develop sufficiently for the partners to feel safe enough to express their negative feelings and confront each other with honesty.   It is in the early development of the relationship that the danger of falling into fixed roles has to be fought.   It is easy to become dependent on an active partner and let him or her express the more confrontational aspects of therapeutic behaviour. Likewise, it may be difficult for a therapist of either sex who is predisposed towards carrying a nurturing, maternal role, to be able to express any other.   This rigidity of roles can be rationalised by the therapeutic team in terms of the family's needs, but the family also needs to experience the way in which both the roles and functions of a relationship can be flexibly exchanged and developed.

Skynner (1976) points out an interesting parallel between therapist's needs and Freudian stages of development.   He suggests that therapists who have strong oral dependent needs tend to be passive and rely on their partners to take the lead, while therapists with anal characteristics tend to engage in struggles for control and hold on to their theories in a rather obsessional and rigid manner. At the phallic level, the need for competition predominates particularly regarding sexual roles.   At the genital level, by contrast, the team is able to be different but mutually supportive and their experience is enriched by the complementarity of their different roles.

TYPES OF CO-THERAPY

The co-therapy team may be homogeneous or heterogeneous regarding discipline, sex, experience and style.   We will attempt to look at the implications that these similarities or differences between the pair have for their working relationship.

The sharing of authority and control

As a relatively new model of intervention, co-therapy has flourished in various therapeutic settings bringing professionals from different disciplines together to form a direct therapeutic partnership face to face with their clients.   In the classical child guidance setting, for example, the tradition has been for the psychiatrist to take responsibility for the treatment of the child, while the social worker is assigned the role of 'supporting' the parents.

When this team decides to embark upon treating the whole family, the decision to make use of the co-therapy model may arise.   The most logical move is to 'pool' resources and in the same way that the subsystems in the family are brought together for treatment, so are the workers.   So psychiatrist and social worker, for example, may constitute the co-therapy team.   However, unless they work at the definition of their new roles in their partnership, there is a danger of remaining in fixed roles regarding authority, control and decision-making.   In their co-therapy experience they have to step outside the hierarchy which may have been inherent in their profes-sional status, and begin to function as a partnership with equal power and responsibility regarding the family they are treating. Problems arise when professionals of different disciplines doing 'co-therapy' together have not been able to recognise their change of roles, and one of them makes most of the decisions while the other one colludes by doing the 'donkey' work.   This can be dan-gerous for the family as well as for the co-therapy pair.   The family will perceive a clear inequality of roles and may uncon-sciously identify this pattern of relationship as healthy.   On the other hand, members of the family may split the therapeutic team, investing the 'over-zealous' one with all goodness and turning the more detached partner into a persecutor.

The splitting process can also occur the other way when the family invests the powerful controlling partner with all goodness, while invalidating the weaker one, thus identifying with the aggres-sor and in phantasy internalising his power.   Similar problems may arise in training situations where co-therapy is done by supervisor and student, and the needs for dependency and nourishment on the part of the student may 'fit' with the need for power and dominance on the part of the supervisor.   As Rice and Rice (1974) comment, 'Many co-therapy relationships falter because of the inability of the therapists to work through the issue of control and achieve a comfortable sharing of power and dominance.'

Professionals from different disciplines who engage in co-therapy together have to iron out the difficulties that may arise regarding the aims of therapy.   Diverse views regarding goals, method and priorities in the treatment process will have to be reconciled and integrated towards a therapeutic strategy planned by a team rather than by two individuals.   This move from the individual therapist to the co-therapy relationship system replicates the conceptual leap that has to take place when the family system becomes the focus of treatment instead of the individual client.

Dual sex co-therapy

Rice and Rice (1974) point out the implications of status and sex role equality both from the point of view of the therapeutic rela-tionship and of society's expectations of the therapists' roles. They see therapists as agents of social change who have the opportu-nity to present to their clients new models of human interaction. Male/female co-therapy teams are regarded as particularly useful in dealing with marital difficulties, especially those relating to sexual dysfunction (Bancroft, 1974;   Crowe, Chapter 7).   Masters

and Johnson (1972) consider dual sex co-therapy as essential in
treating sexual difficulties: 'The primary purpose of a male/female
team is to provide full and fair clinical representation for both
members of a marital unit undergoing treatment.'   They see each
therapist as responsible for facilitating communication and helping
the partner of the same sex to express his or her needs and difficulties.   However, they point out some of the difficulties that may
arise in the dual sex co-therapy team.   For example, the tendency
on the part of the male therapist to take control and the collusion
on the part of the female therapist by failing to assert herself and
share equal responsibility.   They report evidence of this observation as being constant for each of four trained teams.   Interestingly, they report the display of 'masculine' responses in the
female therapist which they interpret as part of the therapist's
professional adolescence.   They consider such responses as harmful
and confusing for the female client!

Obviously it is essential that psychotherapists dealing with
sexual dysfunction be comfortable with their own sexuality; but
where a male and female therapist are working together, there is the
added requirement of being comfortable dealing with the most intimate sexual material in front of each other.   Moreover, it is the
fact of being comfortable or otherwise that is itself 'on show' to
the therapeutic partner.

Masters and Johnson, whilst recognising the occurrence of transference phenomena in their work, do not make the use of transference
a feature of their technique.   However, other family and marital
therapists place great importance upon the way in which the dual
sex co-therapy team take on the roles of parents for the family.
Skynner, for example, describes the way in which the projection of
the family's phantasy can cast the co-therapists into paternal and
maternal roles.   Behind this allocation of roles lies the related
phantasies surrounding the parental couple particularly regarding
intercourse, each family member's unconscious phantasies being related to his own particular developmental stage.   Markowitz and
Kadis (1972) emphasise the use of dual sex co-therapy teams because
of their use in eliciting parental transferences and thereby facilitating the resolution of basic conflicts.   They also feel that
'with male and female co-therapists present, sex syntonic identifi-
cations are more easily evoked'.   Another advantage they see in the
use of co-therapy with marital dyads is the fact that in a foursome
setting triangular types of difficulties are avoided, particularly
those relating to pre-oedipal and pre-genital regressions which are
likely to occur as a defence against more mature types of relationships.

Sonne and Lincoln (1965) provide a detailed description of the
struggle and working through of difficulties in a heterosexual co-
therapy pair during the course of treatment.   Their comments are
useful regarding the underlying feelings of the therapists and
their effects on the family they were treating.   However, they also
illuminate one of the pitfalls inherent in making generalisations
from their personal value judgments regarding the male/female roles
and needs.   Here is an example:

   The therapists, by working through various misunderstandings and
   differences of communication between them, arrived at an agree-

ment, which colored the therapy, that being loved to a woman is most important, and it is only when she feels she is not loved that she places undue stress on such things as status and responsibility.   Moreover, she feels happiest when her husband is a winner even though she may fight hard to beat him in an argument. This may be an accurate appraisal of the male/female relationship in both the client couple and the co-therapy pair in that particular case.   But the immediacy of the primitive feelings aroused by sexual role relationships can, if not carefully checked and monitored by the co-therapists, lead to the danger of projecting their own value system on to the therapy situation.   Rice and Rice (1977) refer to the ways in which the therapists' own marital experience as well as the presence of sex-role stereotyped behaviours and expectations can limit their ability to deal with marital conflict especially when it is related to disenchantment about the 'traditional marriage'.   They suggest specific helpful experiences for the therapists - such as working with a co-therapist of the opposite sex - and discuss a general therapeutic goal of equal power sharing, giving attention to social and political as well as intra-psychic forces.

An interesting variation of dual sex co-therapy is the professional husband-wife team (Rice and Rice, 1974; Lazarus, 1976; Skynner, 1974).

Same sex co-therapy

It is important to realise that, although co-therapists may be of the same sex, the family members may invest them with 'feminine' or 'masculine' characteristics according to their unconscious needs and phantasies in spite of the actual sexes of the therapists.   The therapists need to be aware of these projections whether they choose to make explicit use of them with the family or not.   If these transferences are not recognised, the therapists may spend a lot of unnecessary energy trying to avoid being cast into the role of the opposite sex.   Hall and Taylor (1971) present a beautiful example of a co-therapy team of the same sex treating a family with a blind child.

THE BEHAVIOUR OF CO-THERAPISTS - A RESEARCH STUDY

So far the advantages and disadvantages of using co-therapy as a treatment technique have only been clinically assessed.   No empirical evidence has been offered which suggests convincingly that co-therapy produces better results in terms of treatment outcome.   An important first step in this direction might be to examine the specific behaviour exhibited by pairs of co-therapists during a therapy session.   This has been a particularly unexplored theme in family and marital therapy (Gurman, 1971) in contrast with individual psychotherapy (Truax and Carkhuff, 1967) where efforts have been made to establish specific dimensions of the therapist's behaviour and their relationship to the outcome of treatment.   Truax and Carkhuff's work has been criticised regarding the limited evidence supporting the effectiveness of the three Rogerian conditions of empathy, warmth and genuineness related by Truax and Carkhuff to the outcome of treatment.   However, their contribution represents the first substantial step towards the specification of variables that can be manipulated in order to increase effectiveness in psychotherapy (Shapiro, 1969).   It is obviously not possible to assume that the same qualities that favourably affect the outcome of individual treatment should necessarily be the same for family or marital therapy, since there are many major differences between the goals and techniques of individual psychotherapists and family therapists (Haley, 1971).

Although various descriptions of family therapists' styles can be found in the literature (Beels and Ferber (1969), Ferber and Ranz (1972)), no empirical studies of their actual behaviour during therapy are available.   As mentioned earlier, Rice et al. (1972) present the only study that focuses on co-therapist style as distinct from the style of working alone and comment on its relevance as a factor contributing to the outcome of treatment.   However, their study is based entirely on subjective data such as self-descriptions of therapists' own style and subjective ratings by therapists on the outcome of treatment.   It was the lack of empirical material in this field that prompted our decision at the Family Institute in Cardiff to examine in a systematic manner the behaviour of co-therapists in family therapy.*

The project consisted of a comparative study of therapists' behaviour as it occurred in various combinations of co-therapy pairs. Five therapists, two female and three male, comprised the subjects of the study, providing ten possible combinations of co-therapy pairs.

The aims of the study were:

1 to develop profiles of each individual family therapist's behaviour and patterns of behavioural flexibility/stability when working with different family types and with different co-therapists;
2 to develop profiles of the various co-therapy pairs' behavioural patterns;
3 to test the hypothesis, frequently asserted in clinical practice, that one of the main functions of co-therapists is to counterbalance each other's behaviour by playing complementary roles to each other, e.g. supportive/provocative, passive/active, etc. (Bardill and Bevilacqua, 1964).

The basis for analysis was hour-long audio-tape recordings of family therapy sessions, with each co-therapy pair.   These data were compared with questionnaires completed by each therapist about his working relationship with his co-therapists.   Spontaneous statements written by each of the therapists about their working relationship with each other were also obtained.   Three types of

---

* The Family Institute, Cardiff, was established in 1971 to practise, teach and study family therapy.   Since its exclusive concern is with family therapy, and as co-therapy is a regular method of work amongst the staff, the Family Institute provided an ideal setting for undertaking this research project.

information were therefore assembled: analysis of taped verbal behaviour;   structured questionnaire responses;   unstructured personal
statements.

DESIGN

Audio tapes

A sample of three tapes, representing the beginning, middle and end
of treatment, for each co-therapy pair was selected.   In the event,
only twenty-three tapes were available, three each of seven co-
therapy pairs, one each of two co-therapy pairs.   Due to the fact
that one member of staff left before the project was completed, the
missing data were impossible to obtain.
   The rating procedure was undertaken with a digital event recor-
der.   This apparatus made it possible to categorise each therapist
behaviour;   the time spent in each intervention;   the silences
during the session;   and the time spent in family interaction.   It
was decided to rate the whole of the sixty-minute tapes rather than
to select excerpts from them, in order to obtain the most accurate
picture possible of the therapists' range and sequence of interventions.   Mintz and Luborsky (1971) have shown the relevance of
rating whole sessions in order to avoid distortions of the psychotherapeutic interaction.   They found in their analysis of four-
minute segments of therapy sessions that the judgments of therapist
empathy cannot be generalised to whole sessions.
   The instrument used was a category system consisting of fifteen
identifiable, operationally defined and mutually exclusive verbal
behaviours.   A modified version of the Developing Interactive
Skills Category System (as used by the British Air Transport and
Travel Industry Training Board, Staines, Middlesex)* was adapted for
rating the audio tapes.   Its main advantage was that it was highly
specific and, therefore, all verbal behaviours could be classified,
avoiding 'dustbin' categories, such as 'miscellaneous', 'other',
etc., which tend to distort the picture of the behavioural sequence.
The adapted version consisting of fifteen categories with their operational definitions appears in Table 8.1

TABLE 8.1 Developing interactive skills - therapists
_____

PROPOSING - a behaviour which puts forward a new concept, suggestion
or course of action (and is actionable).
BUILDING - a behaviour which extends or develops the actions, proposals, comments, and/or contributions of self or another.
SUPPORTING - a behaviour which involves a conscious and direct dec-
laration of support or agreement with another person or his concepts.

* The Training Board were running a course aimed at teaching members how to distinguish these behaviours and become more flexible in
their use of them.   They hoped to provide their members with a tool
for monitoring their own behaviour in order to achieve a more efficient interactive style.

DISAGREEING - a behaviour which involves a conscious and direct dec-
laration of difference of opinion, or criticism of another person's
concepts.
DEFENDING/ATTACKING - a behaviour which attacks another person or
defensively strengthens an individual's own position. Defending/
attacking behaviours usually involve overt value judgments and often
contain emotional overtones.
OPEN - a behaviour which involves self-exposure of the individual by
disclosure of personal experiences or feelings or admitting mistakes
or inadequacies, providing that these are made in a non-defensive
manner.
TESTING UNDERSTANDING - a behaviour which seeks to establish whether
or not an earlier contribution has been understood.
INTEGRATING - a behaviour which summarises and integrates the content of previous discussions or considerations.
ELICITING - a behaviour which seeks facts, opinions, or clarification from another individual or individuals.
GIVING INFORMATION - a behaviour which offers facts, or clarification to other individuals.
SHUTTING OUT - a behaviour which excludes, or attempts to exclude,
another group member (e.g. interrupting; talking over).
BRINGING IN - a behaviour which is a direct and positive attempt to
involve another group member.
CHALLENGING - a behaviour which is intended to provoke the expression of a response at a feeling level (e.g. anger, sadness) which
otherwise would remain unexpressed.
ENLARGING - a behaviour which expands or enlarges the meaning of a
previous contribution by interpreting or providing awareness of
underlying dimensions.
POINTING OUT - pin-pointing a specific verbal or non-verbal dimension of another's behaviour that is taking place without being commented upon.

Questionnaires

The next set of data were provided by the therapists' responses to
structured questionnaires which were later correlated with the
ratings of the therapists' performance on the tapes. The questionnaire consisted of five parts which had to be completed by using
ranking orders so that the data could be correlated with that generated by the tapes.
    Part I asked the subjects to rank their four co-therapists from
one to four according to the frequency with which they perceived
them using each of the fifteen categories of the Developing Interactive Skills - Therapists system. This question was intended to
obtain the therapists' perception of each other's therapeutic behaviour.
    Part II asked the subjects to rank the categories from one to
fifteen in order to make a profile of the subjects' 'ideal' co-
therapy partner. This question was intended to elicit what sort of
behaviours are most desirable in a co-therapist. It also provided
an indicator of the priority given by experienced therapists in
using the categories.

Part III asked the subjects to rank the categories in the order that would reflect most accurately their own therapeutic style. This question was intended to elicit the therapists' self-perceptions of their own style of working.

Part IV asked the subjects to rank their co-therapy experiences with each other in order of merit.   These data could then be compared with the profiles of 'ideal' co-therapists, thereby providing cross-validation measures between sub-sections of the questionnaire.

Part V consisted of a short description of five 'typical' families who might be referred for family therapy, and which roughly corresponded to the actual families with which the therapists had been working at the point when the audio tapes of their sessions were collected.   The subjects were asked:

a   to rank the categories in the order of merit they would like them to be used by their co-therapist with the five different families;

b   to rank their colleagues in order of preference as a co-therapist when working with each family.

This part was designed to see if there was agreement between therapists as to what type of behaviour is most desirable in dealing with each type of family.

Personal statements by the therapists

The therapists were asked to write freely about their working relationship with each other.   This exercise was undertaken prior to the completion of the questionnaires.   For the purpose of this chapter, the discussion of findings will be limited to the first two sets of data, namely the tapes and the questionnaires.

DISCUSSION OF FINDINGS

The analysed data provided a wealth of material that would be beyond the scope of this chapter to discuss in detail.   However, an attempt will be made to present some of the main findings in the hope that they will be of interest to the clinician as well as to the researcher.

What do family therapists do?

The analysed data from the audio tapes provided the material for looking at this issue.   The proportion of the session spent by the therapists using the various categories was represented by calculating the total intervention time per category for each one of the five therapists.   These data show that intervention time for all five therapists represents one third of the total time of the tapes, that is 7.19 hours out of 23 hours.   All the therapists spend three-quarters of their total intervention time using five of the categories, while the other ten categories are distributed in small proportions in only a quarter of the total time.   Four out of these top five categories are common to all five therapists: 'Enlarging', 'Integrating', 'Eliciting' and 'Pointing Out'.

Table 8.2 shows the hierarchy (descending from 1 to 5) in the use of the categories according to the total times spent by the therapists operating within each of them.

TABLE 8.2   Use of categories by five therapists

	Highly used categories	Moderately used categories	Rarely used categories
1	Enlarging	Giving Information	Open
2	Integrating	Challenging	Disagreeing
3	Pointing Out	Supporting	Bringing In
4	Eliciting	Building	Defending/Attacking
5	Proposing	Testing Understanding	Shutting Out

If we regroup the highly used categories into a logical order in terms of therapeutic behaviour, a process frequently witnessed in a family therapy session clearly emerges.   The therapist will point out an event, 'I notice that X is happening', integrate it in the general context, 'This has happened before', enlarge it with his own interpretation, 'It seems to me that this means ...', elicit any additional information needed, 'Is this the way it is at home?' and finally make a proposal that will promote a new behaviour 'How about doing Y?'

The next question that seemed important to ask refers to the therapists' consistency in style:

Do therapists have a permanent style or does their behaviour vary according to co-therapist?

This question was designed to explore two clinical issues.   First, the degree to which therapist's behaviour is consistent on different occasions and with different co-therapists.   Second, the extent to which the therapist's style varies according to the co-therapist with whom he is working as a result of 'complementarity' in the co-therapy pair.   A Coefficient of Concordance (Kendall W) was calculated for each of the five therapists in the study in order to gain a measure of their consistency in the ranking order of their use of categories across pairs.   The results can be seen in Table 8.3

TABLE 8.3   Therapists' consistency in style

Therapists	Coefficient of concordance	Significance level
B	.85	$p < .001$
E	.85	$p < .001$
A	.76	$p < .001$
D	.62	$p < .01$
C	.75	$p < .01$

These results indicate a high degree of consistency in style for

each of the five therapists despite variations in the co-therapist
with whom they worked or the families they were treating.
     This picture of consistency in style must be interpreted in terms
of the ranking orders of the therapists' use of the categories, that
is, the order of priority they give to different interventions in
family therapy.   However, it was found that although the order remains the same, the amount of time they spend operating within a
certain category does vary according to co-therapist, as a result of
the complementarity function.   For example, the amount of time
spent Proposing by Therapist A decreased with Therapist B who used
Proposing more but increased with Therapist C who spent less time
using this type of intervention.   These results therefore indicate
that although therapists may vary in the actual amount of time they
spend using each category according to their co-therapist, each
therapist has a consistent trans-situational profile of behaviour
unaffected by co-therapist or client family.

What sort of behaviours do therapists consider more desirable in
family therapy?

This information was obtained from the responses to Part II of the
questionnaire administered to the therapists.   They were asked to
rank the categories in order to make a profile of a co-therapist
with whom they would feel most comfortable, and to describe the profile of an 'ideal' partner in a co-therapy relationship.   Their
responses were classified into 'Highly Desirable', 'Moderately Desirable' and 'Least Desirable', in order to make a parallel with the
'Highly Used', 'Moderately Used' and Rarely Used' categories in
their performance on the tapes.   The grouping was done by entering
the categories ranked by the therapists from one to five as 'Highly
Desirable', the categories ranked from six to ten as 'Moderately
Desirable', and those ranked from eleven to fifteen as 'Least Desirable'.   In order to scrutinise the level of agreement by the
therapists, a scoring procedure was employed by which the highly
desirable categories scored three points, the moderately desirable
scored two points, and the least desirable scored one point.   These
scores were multiplied by the number of therapists who rated the
category in that particular bracket, giving a highest possible score
of fifteen.   (See Table 8.4.)

TABLE 8.4

Highly used categories	Least used categories
Enlarging (11)	Open (12)
Integrating (9)	Disagreeing (11)
Pointing Out (14)	Bringing In (13)
Eliciting (9)	Defending/Attacking (7)
Proposing (12)	Shutting Out (5)

We can see from these results how 'Pointing Out', a behaviour
that simply highlights what is taking place verbally or non verbal-

ly, is both highly used and considered to be highly desirable in
family therapy.   'Proposing' is also highly used and highly desirable, again confirming the proposition that many family therapists
promote change in an active manner by suggesting new patterns of
behaviour.   ('Conductors', as defined by Beels and Ferber, 1969.)
In contrast, the fact that 'Enlarging' is highly used and highly
desirable would confirm some family therapists' belief that reflective, insight-promoting interpretations are necessary in order to
produce change.   ('Reactors' as described by Beels and Ferber,
1969.)   Since both theoretical orientations were represented
amongst the subjects, it is not surprising that these two contrast-
ing behaviours should receive high regard.   In fact, the diversity
of opinion among family therapists on this matter is clearly reflected in the sample, and the 'Enlarging' category was rated quite in-
consistently by our five therapists: highly desirable by two therapists, moderately desirable by two therapists, and least desirable
by one therapist.

Categories like 'Shutting Out' and 'Defending/Attacking' are
least desirable and rarely used by the therapists, which suggests
that they are not considered useful behaviours in family therapy.
The two categories 'Integrating' and 'Eliciting' were highly used
by the subjects, but felt to be moderately required behaviours in an
ideal co-therapist - possibly because they are behaviours that most
family therapists would feel comfortable in exhibiting themselves.

However, if we look at categories like 'Bringing In', 'Open' and
'Disagreeing', these are least used by the subjects but are felt to
be highly desirable in a co-therapist.   One could argue that family
therapists may find these three behaviours difficult to exhibit and
that they therefore would hope that their co-therapist would have
greater facility in this respect.   This would support the hypothesis regarding the role of complementarity in a co-therapist, in
other words that therapists tend to look for certain behaviours in a
co-therapist that they do not practise to a high degree themselves.
If this were the case, negative correlations would be expected between the therapists' behaviour on the tapes and their profile of
ideal co-therapists in the questionnaires.   In fact, only one of
the five therapists showed a negative correlation ($r = -.11$) and
this result was not statistically significant.   On the other hand,
the data also reveal categories which are both highly used by the
therapists themselves and felt to be highly desirable in a co-therapist, i.e. 'Pointing Out', 'Enlarging' and 'Proposing'.

The study shows a high degree of agreement amongst the five therapists regarding the characteristics desired in a co-therapist (Kendall $W = .72$ $p < .01$).   Therefore the therapists in our sample co-
incided in preferring some behaviours to be similar and some to be
complementary in a co-therapist.   Referring back to the earlier
discussion of functions, it can be hypothesised that, in terms of
division of labour between two therapists, some behaviours will be
more frequently and intensively required on the part of the therapists than others.   Thus it is reasonable to expect that these behaviours would be found to be highly used by the subject and considered to be highly desirable in a co-therapist simply because 'more'
of the particular behaviour is needed during a family therapy session.   If this hypothesis is correct, the subjects in this sample

imply that more 'Enlarging', 'Proposing' and 'Pointing Out' are required in family therapy and conversely less 'Disagreeing', 'Bringing In' and 'Openness', even though these behaviours are still considered to be highly desirable.   However, it is relevant to note
that 'Bringing In' and 'Open' types of interventions are considered
particularly useful therapeutic behaviours in family therapy theory,
therefore they might be expected to be highly used as well as highly
desirable by therapists.

With what sort of person do therapists prefer to work when treating
different types of families?

This question will be discussed using the therapists' preferences in
co-therapist behaviour for each of the families sketched in Question
V of the questionnaire.   This question was designed to explore the
behaviours that were felt by the subjects to be desirable for a particular type of family and a Coefficient of Concordance (Kendall W)
was calculated for each family in order to determine the degree of
agreement between the therapists.   The results are shown in Table
8.5.

TABLE 8.5

Family	Coefficient of concordance	Significance level
A	.49	p < .01
B	.31	p < .10
C	.54	p < .001
D	.39	p < .02
E	.37	p < .05

These findings suggest that the levels of agreement between the
therapists vary according to different types of families.   It
seemed relevant to determine the extent to which therapists wanted
consistent characteristics in a co-therapist for the five families,
that is, regardless of the particular problems or systems structure
of the family being treated.   A Coefficient of Concordance (Kendall
W) was calculated using the consensus of ideal co-therapist for four
out of the five families.   (Family B was not used since the consensus was not significant, as shown in Table 8.5.)   A Coefficient of
Concordance (Kendall W) of .79 (p < .001) was obtained.   This shows
a high degree of agreement in the characteristics desired by all
therapists for the different families.   In other words, there is an
overall consistency for the behaviours desirable in a co-therapist
regardless of the different types of families.
    There are three categories that are considered highly desirable
for all families: 'Supporting', 'Bringing In' and 'Eliciting'.
'Pointing Out' is desirable for three out of the four families.
This finding suggests that empathic, information-seeking behaviours
as well as interventions intended to draw in the more passive members and to highlight what is taking place verbally or non verbally

are desirable in a co-therapist regardless of the type of family.
Three categories were ranked amongst the least desirable for all
families: 'Disagreeing', 'Defending/Attacking' and 'Shutting Out'.
This confirms our earlier finding that these are not considered
useful behaviours in family therapy.

Two categories that vary the most as to how desirable they are
for different families are 'Building' and 'Testing Understanding'.
It is interesting to link these variations to the types of families.
'Building', for example, is a highly desirable behaviour for two of
the families: Family A is a depressed low-keyed family who probably
would need a lot of encouragement and active intervention from the
therapists. The therapists are likely to have to 'build' on their
proposals in order to motivate the family towards change.   Family E
is a multi-problem family facing both internal and external difficulties.   Like Family A, this type of family is likely to need the
therapists to 'build' on any positive suggestion in order to encourage change. It is interesting to note that in both these families
father is disabled and out of work.   It could be suggested that
perhaps the therapists feel that these families need extra encouragement from them in order to move towards change.

'Testing Understanding' is considered by the subjects to be a
highly desirable behaviour when working with Family E.   This was
the most disorganised of the sample families sketched in the questionnaire.   They have five children between the ages of three and
thirteen.   In contrast, this category is considered least desirable
by the therapists for Family D.   This is an older family and all
its members are adults.   This contrast could suggest that perhaps
'Testing Understanding' is a more useful therapeutic behaviour when
there are young children in a family.   However, since the ranking
order of desired behaviours is so similar for the various families,
it is not possible to conclude from the present data that there are
specific patterns of behaviour desirable for specific types of families.   Nevertheless, these findings do suggest that there is a
basic hierarchy of behaviours which therapists agree are useful for
a co-therapist to display in general.

How accurately do therapists perceive their own behaviour?

The degree of accuracy in the therapists' self-perceptions of their
own behaviour was considered an important dimension to measure for
two reasons:
a The clinical implications - it is assumed that the more accurately therapists perceive their own behaviour, the more reliable their observations about the family will be.
b The teaching implications - students can be taught to monitor
   their own behaviour and their self-perception can be examined
   before and after training.
The hypothesis at the beginning of the study was that the therapists' perceptions of their own behaviour obtained through Part II
of the questionnaire and their performance on the tapes would be
highly correlated.   It was hypothesised that experienced therapists
would have highly accurate perceptions of their own behaviour.
Spearman (rho) correlations were calculated for each therapist

between the ranking order of their use of categories in the tapes and the ranks used to describe their own therapeutic style in Part II of the questionnaire.   The results are shown in Table 8.6.

TABLE 8.6 Comparison between therapists' behaviour (tapes) and self-perception (questionnaire Part II)

Therapist	Spearman rho
B	$r = .38$ Non significant
A	$r = .19$ Non significant
D	$r = .21$ Non significant
C	$r = .22$ Non significant
E	$r = .63$ $(p < .05)$

As Table 8.6 shows, only one therapist (myself), shows a significant correlation between these two dimensions.   That is, only one of the five therapists has a highly accurate perception of her own behaviour.   I was familiar with my own behaviour through the rating of the tapes.   However, all the other therapists are used to listening to themselves on audio-taped recordings of the sessions, as it is the normal practice at the Family Institute to tape record all sessions and for therapists to listen to the tapes in between sessions. The discrepancy, therefore, can be attributed to my familiarity with the behaviour category system, through using it in rating my own and the other therapists' behaviour.

The discrepancy between the degree of accuracy of perception in the therapist who rated the tapes (myself) and the other therapists suggests that familiarity with a system of specifically defined behaviours makes it easier to conceptualise one's own behaviour in a more accurate manner.   The implication is that in order for therapists to become more accurate in their perception of their own behaviour, they have to practise the recognition and categorisation of their interventions.   The implications for training would be that students should be taught to monitor their own behaviour using a behaviour category instrument in order to recognise and identify their interventions.   Trainees can learn to identify the desirable behaviours as well as the ones used by experienced therapists and, as the gap between self-perception and behaviour closes, improvement can be achieved in more specific areas of behaviour.

How accurately do therapists perceive the other therapists' behaviour?

In order to examine this issue it was decided to establish a consensus of opinion on each of the five therapists' behaviour by the other therapists.   This consensus was obtained by calculating a Co-efficient of Concordance (Kendall W), in order to ascertain the degree of agreement between the five therapists regarding each subject's use of the categories.   However, as shown in Table 8.7, the consensus of opinion was only significant for three out of the five therapists.

TABLE 8.7   Consensus of opinion on each of the five therapists (as assessed by the views of the remainder)

Therapist	Kendall W
A	.52 (p < .01)
B	.46 (p < .05)
C	.47 (p < .05)
D	.34 Non significant
E	.27 Non significant

Therefore, therapists' consensus of opinion could only be compared with performance on tapes for three of the therapists, i.e. the ones for whom the consensus was statistically significant.   The results of this comparison are shown in Table 8.8.

TABLE 8.8   Correlation between consensus of opinion and behaviour on tapes

Therapist	Spearman rho
B	.45 (p < .05)*
A	-.32 Non significant
C	.36 Non significant

* one tailed test

It can be seen from this table that only one out of the three therapists shows a significant correlation between the consensus of opinion of her colleagues about her and her behaviour on the tapes. Although the other two results do not reach a level of statistical significance, it is interesting to note that in the case of Therapist A there is a negative correlation which would point to an inverse relationship between what Therapist A actually does and the way he is perceived.   In fact, the consensus of opinion amongst the other therapists about Therapist A was the highest (Kendall W = .52, p < .01) as shown in Table 8.7.   This means that the other four therapists reached the highest level of agreement between them regarding Therapist A's behaviour.   Nevertheless, though consistent as a group in the way they perceive him, there is a negative (inverse) relationship between their perception of Therapist A and his actual behaviour on the tapes.   This finding is particularly striking in our sample since Therapist A is the one therapist who differed most radically from the others in his style.

As described before, only for three out of the five therapists was the consensus of agreement statistically significant, and of those three, only for one therapist was there a significant correlation between the way she was perceived and the way she actually behaved.

These results reveal that the therapists in our sample are not as accurate as would be expected of experienced therapists in their perceptions of each other's behaviour.   Moreover, they have only a moderate degree of agreement regarding their colleagues' behaviour

and in two of the cases this agreement is not statistically significant.

These findings bear special importance for the clinical practice
of family therapy. What evidence is there that this group of therapists perceive their client families accurately if this is not the
case with one another? It could be argued that they found it difficult to conceptualise their colleagues' behaviour in terms of the
behaviour categories used in this project. However, findings discussed earlier do not support this hypothesis. When they were
asked to define a profile of the ideal co-therapist in terms of the
use of categories, they found no difficulty and, in fact, they were
highly consistent in doing so. There was a high degree of agreement between the five as to what behaviour categories were desirable
in a co-therapist. Could it be that therapists' behaviour is always changing and that therefore they found it difficult to think in
terms of their colleagues' behaviour at the time when they worked
together but instead could only visualise them in terms of their
current style? (For some co-therapy pairs, there was a gap of two
years between the time their work together was recorded on the audio
tapes and the completion of the questionnaire, while other pairs
were working together at the time they completed the questionnaire.)
In order to test that hypothesis, audio tapes recorded at the time
when therapists completed the questionnaires would have to be rated
and these data compared with their answers.

We could regard this team of five therapists, working closely and
intensely together, as an emotional system with similar emotional
pressures and interrelationship difficulties to those experienced by
a family system. Therefore, it is possible that, like a family,
they found accurate intra-group perceptions very difficult. If
this is the case, the perceptual inaccuracies of the therapists
within this group regarding each other's behaviour would not necessarily mean that they are unable to perceive families more objectively.

An alternative explanation could be the fact that therapists,
when practising or observing family therapy, focus their attention
mainly on the family's behaviour and the interactions that take
place within the family-plus-therapists system. It is possible,
therefore, that in this context therapists may fail to develop an
accurate knowledge of each other's therapeutic interventions.

SUMMARY AND CONCLUSIONS

Several clinical issues regarding co-therapy as a method of therapeutic intervention have been explored. The rationale for this
modality of treatment, as well as the various types of co-therapy
and the main functions of the co-therapy team have been described.
Some research findings related to the behaviour of co-therapists
have been discussed.

At the beginning of this study, I faced a dilemma between re-
searching into a natural situation which was difficult to fit into
an ideal experimental design, and, on the other hand, losing the
richness that such a situation provided in an attempt to recreate it
in an artificial experimentally controlled manner. It was decided

that the advantages of a natural situation - the retrospective study
of the behaviour of a group of therapists - outweighed its limita-
tions, as it provided a genuine picture of what therapists did in
family therapy.

One of the problems encountered at the beginning of this investigation was the lack of an adequate instrument to classify therapist
behaviour.   It was necessary to find and adapt an instrument that
could categorise accurately all therapists' verbal behaviours with
sufficiently clear definitions so that there would be no ambiguity
when the actual rating of the behaviours took place.   The question
of adequate instruments of measurement not only applies to therapists' interventions, but it is also a problem when attempting to
evaluate family therapy outcome.   What are the dimensions of the
family's behaviour that an instrument should include in order to
provide an accurate index of the results of treatment?   This is a
very complex question and a detailed discussion of how to evaluate
family therapy is far beyond the scope of this chapter.   Gale provides an exhaustive checklist of questions to be asked in studies of
outcome research in family therapy in Chapter 10.   As he points
out, the task of designing an instrument to measure the effectiveness of therapy becomes very difficult when there are no clear criteria regarding the behaviour of 'normal' families.   Family therapy
theory is lacking in taxonomies of both normal and dysfunctional
families' behaviour, which makes it difficult to establish concrete
criteria for the evaluation of therapeutic outcome.

In this study it was found that the therapists were consistent in
their personal style of intervention.   They behaved in a similar
manner with different therapists and different families.   This
similarity refers to the priorities they give to the use of certain
types of intervention not to the actual amount of time spent in different interventions which, as pointed out earlier, does vary according to co-therapist.   The therapists also expressed that they
would want similar characteristics in a co-therapist regardless of
the type of family.

The hierarchy of behaviours used by all five therapists in the
study was found to be highly similar despite their different theoretical orientations.   This finding suggests that apparent differences at a theoretical level are not necessarily present when therapeutic approaches are compared.

In this study, it was found that the therapists' perceptions of
their own and each other's behaviour was not as accurate as was expected.   It was found that the author who was familiar with the
category system through the rating of the tapes had a higher accuracy in self-perception.   An interesting research development based
on this finding would be to train family therapy students to use the
behaviour category system listed in this study to monitor their interventions.   Their perception of their own behaviour could be
tested before and after training and compared with their actual
therapeutic behaviour.

Finally, another major issue that requires empirical study is the
value of co-therapy itself as compared to single therapist intervention.   So far there is no evidence that families treated in co-
therapy achieve better results than those treated by a single therapist.   This subject is inextricably linked with outcome evaluation,

the most complex but perhaps most vital aspect of research in the field of family therapy. Which of the therapist's interventions promote change in families? Although family therapy research has a long way to go before the answer to that question is found, hopefully, the present study moves a small step in that direction by establishing the sort of therapeutic behaviours that actually take place in family therapy.

ACKNOWLEDGMENT

The author's research reported in this chapter was made possible by a special grant from Dr Barnardo's.

REFERENCES

BANCROFT, J.H.J. (1974), The behavioural approach to marital therapy, paper presented at British Psychological Society Conference, Bangor.
BARDILL, D.R. and BEVILACQUA, J.J. (1964), Family interviewing by two caseworkers, 'Social Casework', vol. 15, no. 5, May.
BEELS, C.C. and FERBER, A. (1969), Family therapy: a view, 'Family Process', vol. 9, p. 280.
BELVILLE, T.P., RATHS, O.N. and BELVILLE, C.J. (1969), Conjoint marriage therapy with a husband and wife team, 'American Journal of Orthopsychiatry', vol. 39, pp. 373-483.
BEUTLER, L.E. (1971), Attitude similarity in marital therapy, 'Journal of Consulting and Clinical Psychology', vol. 37, pp. 298-301.
BOWEN, M. (1971), The use of family theory in clinical practice, in J. Haley (ed.), 'Changing Families, Grune & Stratton, New York.
DAVIS, F.B. and LOHR, N.E. (1971), Special problems with the use of co-therapists in group psychotherapy, 'International Journal of Group Psychotherapy', vol. 21, pp. 143-58.
FERBER, A. and RANZ, J. (1972), How to succeed in family therapy - set reachable goals - give workable tasks, in A. Ferber (ed.), 'The Book of Family Therapy', Science House, New York.
FRAMO, J. (1962), The theory of the technique of family treatment of schizophrenia, 'Family Process', vol. 1, no. 2.
GURMAN, A.S. (1971), Group marital therapy: clinical and empirical implications for outcome research, 'International Journal of Group Psychotherapy', vol. 21, pp. 174-89.
GURMAN, A.S. (1974), Attitude change in marital co-therapy, 'Journal of Family Counseling', vol. 2.
HALEY, J. (1962), Whither family therapy?, 'Family Process', vol. 1, no. 1.
HALEY, J. (1970-1), Family therapy, 'International Journal of Psychiatry', vol. 9, pp. 233-42.
HALL, J. and TAYLOR, K. (1971), The emergence of Eric: co-therapy in the treatment of a family with a disabled child, 'Family Process', vol. 10, no. 1, pp. 85-96.
HOLT, M. and GREINER, D. (1976), Co-therapy in the treatment of families, in P. Guerin (ed.), 'Family Therapy', Gardner Press, New York.

LAZARUS, L.W. (1976), Family therapy by a husband-wife team, 'Journal of Marriage and Family Counseling', vol. 2, no. 3, pp. 225-33.

MASTERS, W.H. and JOHNSON, V.E. (1972), The rapid treatment of human sexual dysfunctions, in C.J. Sager and H.S. Kaplan (eds), 'Progress in Group and Family Therapy', Butterworth, London, pp. 553-63.

MARKOWITZ, M. and KADIS, A.L. (1972), Short term analytic treatment of married couples in a group by a therapist couple, in C.J. Sager and H.S. Kaplan (eds), 'Progress in Group and Family Therapy', Butterworth, London, pp. 463-82.

MINTZ, J. and LUBORSKY, L. (1971), Segments versus whole sessions: which is the better unit for psychotherapy process research?, 'Journal of Abnormal Psychology', vol. 78, pp. 180-91.

MCGEE, T.F. and SHUMAN, B.N. (1970), The nature of the co-therapy relationship, 'International Journal of Group Psychotherapy', vol. 20, p. 25.

RABIN, H. (1967), How does co-therapy compare with regular group therapy?, 'American Journal of Psychotherapy', vol. 14, pp. 550-65.

RICE, D.G., FEY, W.F. and KEPECS, J.G. (1972), Therapist experience and 'style' as factors in co-therapy, 'Family Process', vol. 11, no. 1, pp. 1-12.

RICE, D.G. and RICE, J.K. (1974), Status and sex role issues in co-therapy, in A.S. Gurman and D.G. Rice (eds), 'Couples in Conflict: New Directions in Marital Therapy', Aronson, New York.

RICE, D.G. and RICE, J.K. (1977), Non-sexist 'marital' therapy, 'Journal of Marriage and Family Counseling', vol. 3, no. 1, pp. 1-10.

RUBINSTEIN, D. and WEINER, O.R. (1967), Co-therapy teamwork relationships in family therapy, in G.H. Zuk and I. Boszormenyi-Nagy (eds) (1967), 'Family Therapy and Disturbed Families', Science and Behaviour Books, Palo Alto, California.

SATIR, V. (1967), 'Conjoint Family Therapy', Science and Behaviour Books, Palo Alto, California.

SHAPIRO, D.A. (1969), Empathy, warmth and genuineness in psychotherapy, 'British Journal of Social and Clinical Psychology', vol. 8, pp. 350-61.

SKYNNER, A.C.R. (1976), 'One Flesh: Separate Persons', Constable, London.

SKYNNER, P.E. (1974), Family therapy with co-therapists - a husband and wife team, paper presented at Tavistock/Ackerman Conference, London, July.

SONNE, J.C. and LINCOLN, G. (1965), Heterosexual co-therapy team experiences during family therapy, 'Family Process', vol. 4, no. 2, pp. 177-97.

STEWART, R.H., PETERS, T.C., MARSH, S. and PETERS, M.J. (1975), An object-relations approach to psychotherapy with marital couples, families and children, 'Family Process', vol. 14, no. 2, pp. 161-77.

TRUAX, C.B. and CARKHUFF, R.R. (1967), 'Toward Effective Counseling and Psychotherapy: Training and Practice', Aldine, Chicago.

WALROND-SKINNER, S. (1974), Training for family therapy, 'Social Work Today', vol. 5, no. 5.

WALROND-SKINNER, S. (1976), 'Family Therapy, The Treatment of Natural Systems', Routledge & Kegan Paul, London,

WHITAKER, C.A., WARKENTIN, J. and JOHNSON, N.L. (1951), A comparison

of individual and multiple psychotherapy, 'Psychiatry', vol. 14, p. 415.
YALOM, I.D. (1970), 'The Theory and Practice of Group Psychotherapy', Basic Books, New York.

Chapter 9

EDUCATION OR TRAINING FOR FAMILY THERAPY?: A reconstruction

Sue Walrond-Skinner

The purpose of this chapter is to look at developing ideas regarding education and training for family therapists. Two models will be examined in detail and some research findings will be presented relating to outcome evaluation of a limited area of the training experience. Some ongoing problems in the field will be considered and suggestions for future research will be offered.

The family therapy literature is replete with statements regarding the enormous differences between family therapy and the various forms of individual treatment. 'Conceptual leap' and 'discontinuous change' are phrases that are frequently found in assessments of the place of family therapy amongst other treatment modalities. Bell (1963, p. 3) speaks of having to 'wipe clean the blackboard of my mind and find a fresh piece of chalk to write large "the family is the problem"'; whilst Bowen (1971, p. 163) believes that family therapy proposes 'a completely new order of theoretical models for thinking about man and his relationship to nature and the universe'.

Compared with the quantity of literature on family therapy itself, the training of family therapists has received rather limited attention. What writing there is, however, indicates that workers in this field are aware of the need to produce a shift of orientation in their students commensurate with the perceived differences existing between family therapy and other treatment modalities. Erickson (1973, p. 13) for example, writes as follows:

The goal of the teacher is to assist the learner in shifting his orientation toward new ways of perceiving, thinking and behaving in at least three related areas:

1) From perceiving individual behaviour to perceiving a larger context of behaviour.

2) From bringing about change through a professional relationship to bringing about a systems change.

3) From passivity to activity within the social situation of the interview.

Put another way, Cleghorn and Levin (1973, p. 444) point out that 'being an agent of change is very different from being a helper of human suffering' and they go on to classify three types of learning objectives, towards which the beginning family therapist must strive. They describe these as involving the development of per-

ceptual skills, conceptual skills and executive skills, and suggest
that significant areas of difference exist on each level between the
development of family therapy skills compared with those required
for individual therapy.

As these considerations are generally agreed upon throughout the
field of family therapy, it is not surprising that considerable attention has been devoted to the development of teaching techniques
that express within themselves some of the shifts in focus required
in family therapy training.   Teaching is a reflexive process and
its methods are necessarily governed by the same general principles
as the subject matter that is being taught.   Hence, if the learning
of family therapy is to be effective, a model that is congruent with
that which is being taught is an essential feature of any training
programme.   Some of the features which underly the rationale of the
family therapy approach itself are thus routinely incorporated into
training programmes organised for trainees.   For example, group
supervision replaces individual supervision, since the trainee must
learn to work within a group situation.   To mitigate what Erickson
(1973, p. 12) calls a '"trained incapacity" to move into a family
therapy method', the family therapy teacher provides a learning situation centred around the group rather than the individual.
Second, he will try to foster a culture of openness within the
learning situation which will hopefully enable the student to foster
the same sort of trusting openness in the families he treats.
Family therapy demands an ability to struggle with working on intimate areas of pain in the presence of one's intimate others.   The
student, therefore, needs help in assisting family members to
achieve this difficult task, and can best do so if he himself is
helped to share his work with families openly with his student colleagues and supervisor, through the use of group meetings, audio-
visual aids, and a one-way viewing screen.   Third, whilst most
family therapy training programmes offer a mixed experiential/di-
dactic approach, they lay greater emphasis on the experiential aspects of the learning process.   Simulated family role play and
sculpting are used to replicate the treatment situation and engage
trainee and teacher in a mutual, active learning process around
selected clinical material (Ferber and Mendelsohn, 1969).

TWO MODELS OF SUPERVISION

These are some general features which normally form part of a
family therapy training programme whatever its orientation.   However, as the methodological approaches within the overall modality
have developed, so different technical approaches to teaching have
been adopted.   Sub-models have been developed within both therapy
and teaching, and useful attempts are being made to continue the
search for congruence between clinical practice and the teaching of
trainees.   Because family therapy is still young, it is too early
to speak of 'schools' of work in the strict sense, even though an
attempt to delineate some was made in the introduction to this book.
The most realistic distinction that can safely be made at present
is between insight-focused family therapists on the one hand and
behaviourally focused therapists on the other.   Neither group can

be tied very strictly to the psychoanalytic or group analytic approaches, or (in terms of the behavioural orientation) to the learning theory approach - though both these are of course included. But many other different orientations can also be included within these two broad subdivisions.   Based on this subdivision in therapy, there have grown up subdivisions in teaching methods which can be distinguished from each other, in some cases quite sharply, in terms of their model, focus and highlighted teaching areas.   Table 9.1 sets out a comparison between the two models.   As will be noted, the philosophy behind the teaching method adopted reflects that which underlies the therapeutic approach.

The insight-oriented family therapist who uses a more reflective, interpretative approach, adopts a reflective model of case supervision whereby clinical material is discussed or worked on after the therapy session has been completed.   The behaviourally oriented supervisor who uses a more task-oriented approach to treatment, engages in 'live' supervision whereby he guides the trainee therapist during the trainee's therapy session and corrects mistakes as they occur.   Thus, the reflective therapist maintains in his teaching a clear boundary between the functions of therapist and teacher, and is non-intrusive into his trainee's therapy;   the behaviourally oriented therapist blurs the boundary between therapy and teaching, moving in and out of the therapy session as he or his trainee sees the need arising.   The two approaches work from different models which can be broadly summarised as analogistic compared with algorithmic.   The reflective supervisor (analogistic) will extrapolate from the learning which he tries to promote through trainees' work on their own families of origin, to the trainees' work with other families in treatment.   Simulation and sculpting will be used in the supervision group in order to help the trainee to understand how his own areas of dysfunction may be blocking his work with the family (Skynner, 1976, ch. 14).   Personal growth is emphasised and, as Allen (1976, p. 188) points out, the goal of group supervision

is not unlike that of family therapy.   In the group the members develop techniques for dealing with each other that will help in achieving insight and promoting professional growth.   Many of these techniques are valuable not only within the peer group, but within the family therapy setting.

Moreover, the processes of the supervision group itself are used reflectively to throw light upon aspects of the clinical material under discussion.   As Walrond-Skinner (1974, p. 151) says:

Different members [of the group] become 'identified' as being vulnerable, troublesome or even sick by the processes within the group and this gives everyone the opportunity to reflect on the dynamic properties of the group's emotional system.   Roles can become fixed or fluid, task orientated or dysfunctional within the supervision group as in the family.

Thus, the examination of the group's processes and the application of this learning to the way in which family groups function, together with the development of the trainee's self through an attention to the counter-transferential aspects of his work, forms a central core from which to draw analogies with the trainees' work with families in treatment.   (Gosling et al., 1967.)   In addition, the reflective supervisor (Dowling, unpublished paper, 1974) 'considers

TABLE 9.1 Two supervision models in family therapy

Therapeutic approach	Insight-oriented	Behaviour-oriented
Teaching approach	Reflective Supervision. Supervisor reflects on case material with trainee after therapy session and is non-intrusive.	'Live' Supervision. Supervisor guides the therapist while he works and is intrusive.
Model	Analogistic	Algorithmic
Focus	Education of therapists	Training of technicians
Teaching techniques	1 Emphasises personal growth of trainee.	1 Emphasises executive skills in therapy
	2 An emphasis on learning to assess and diagnose dysfunctional patterns of family dynamics	2 Little emphasis on learning techniques of assessment as such.
	3 Supervision group used as a model for family therapy session. Use of sculpting, genograms and Bowen's 'detriangulation' techniques to develop therapist's understanding of own family. Use of group process.	3 Supervision group used as a laboratory for trying out treatment techniques. Group becomes therapy team working with each treatment family.
	4 One-way viewing screen used to observe trainee's work. Maintenance of the screen's membrane function by using the two sides as discrete entities.	4 One-way viewing screen used as semi-permeable membrane, whereby trainee can come for feedback or supervisor can move in.
	5 Audio/video tape monitoring of therapy to play back to supervisor and supervision group.	5 Audio/video tape monitoring of both sides of the supervisory gestalt.
	6 Delayed feedback of 'results'.	6 Immediate feedback of 'results'.
	7 Preparedness to train professionals.	7 Preparedness to train pre-professional students, para-professionals and laypeople, as well as professionals.

that it is particularly helpful for family therapy trainees to undergo some type of personal therapeutic experience himself.   The more the family therapist knows about himself, the more resources he will have available to work with his families'.   Many family therapy trainees are encouraged to undertake some individual or (more appropriately) group psychotherapy themselves during the time they are in training.   Alternatively, trainees may be encouraged to 'detriangulate' themselves from their family of origin, by visiting distant relatives, writing letters to those with whom they have lost contact, and setting up family meetings, in which unresolved issues can be worked through (Bowen, 1971; Anonymous, 1972).

For the behaviourally oriented family therapist, all this would seem at best vague and at worst irrelevant and therefore as interfering with what should be the main preoccupation of a training course.   As Haley (1976, p. 181) points out:

a therapist can only learn about [therapy] by doing it.   All other training activity is peripheral, if not irrelevant.

Ideally he learns to do therapy by doing it while guided by a supervisor at the moment the therapy is happening.

The behaviourally oriented family therapy supervisor, using 'live' supervision, emphasises the way in which the supervision group can become a laboratory for trying out treatment techniques.   Working from an algorithmic model, whereby meaning is structured in a progressive and ordinal manner, the supervisor aims to give his trainees a blueprint which can be directly transposed into the treatment situation.   Technical skills are emphasised and developed through the simulation of critical phases in the treatment process, whilst personal growth in terms of the trainees' own self is considered to be of marginal importance.   Moreover, the behaviourally oriented supervisor would see personal growth versus the development of executive skills as a straight either or choice: as Haley (1976, p. 173) points out: 'training a student therapist can be conceived of as providing him with a rich philosophical life and helping him to grow as an individual.   Or it can be conceived of as teaching specific skills'.

The 'live' supervisor sets himself the task of welding his group of trainees into a therapy team and the one-way viewing screen is used as a semi-permeable membrane through which the trainee working with the family can stay in contact with the supervisor and team. As the therapy session progresses, the observing team behind the screen assists the trainee by maintaining his task-oriented impetus and redirecting his course should he move too far away from the treatment goals.   Contact between the two sides of the screen is maintained either through the trainee coming out to consult with his colleagues or by the supervisor moving in.   The supervisor can choose either to enter the therapy session physically;   or to telephone in and speak to the trainee;   or to speak to the trainee via a 'bug in ear' device (Birchler, 1975).   These three possibilities are stated in descending order in terms of the open availability of communication to the family members.   With the third, only the trainee therapist receives or is aware of the communication from behind the screen.   An exception to this is described by Birchler (1975) in a vivid verbatum transcript.   As well as illustrating how the supervisor guides and reinforces the trainee's efforts, it shows

how he can use the 'bug in ear' device to speak to one or more of
the family members direct, thus considerably altering the dynamic
pattern of the interview.   A similar effect can be obtained by the
supervisor sending a carefully contrived message in to a family
member from behind the screen.   In both cases, the supervisor becomes part of the therapeutic process.

Because of the complexity of the interactional dynamics which are
set up by this model, the teacher needs to maintain control of the
total situation.   In particular he maintains responsibility for
monitoring any messages that get sent into the therapy room and en-
suring that the trainee working with the family (and hence the
family itself) does not get caught into some competitive triangle
vis-a-vis the two sides of the screen.   Just as therapeutic work
for the behaviourally oriented teacher consists in changing the
family's behaviour patterns (with or without insight following), so
the teacher working from within this model sees his task as shaping
his trainee's behaviour in such a way that they are able to become
effective in using the technical skills that they have learnt.
Like the reflective model, audio-visual aids are used so that the
trainee can play back the session to himself and/or the supervision
group afterwards;   but because the two sides of the screen have, in
the behavioural model, been engaging in a more or less continuous
process of interaction during the session, both sides may need to
'catch up' on what has been happening in the part of the process
where they have not been directly involved.   The trainee who has
been treating the family may need to hear more details of the discussions that took place while he was interviewing the family;   or
both trainee and observer may need to tune in (via video playback)
to the work that the family was continuing whilst the therapy team
was engaged in the consultation sessions.   In this model, the development of assessment skills is treated somewhat warily and the
emphasis is placed squarely on the encouragement of executive skills
in treatment rather than in diagnosis - the latter being viewed as
being very difficult to distinguish from the 'labelling' processes
inherent in traditional psychiatric nosology.

Just as the reflective model seems vague and irrelevant to the
behaviourally oriented teacher, so the behaviourally oriented model
usually appears manipulative and infantilising to the reflective
supervisor.   There are obviously sharp differences in philosophy
and aims behind each of the two approaches to teaching, stemming
from quite different approaches to therapeutic practice.   In the
reflective model, we might summarise the general intention as being
the education of therapists, contrasted in the behavioural model
with the training of technicians.   (Whilst both groups would, I
think, be happy with this description of themselves, both would
probably use the description of the other in a pejorative sense.)
The former would on the whole be more comfortable with the idea of
teaching professionals who are already qualified in their basic
mental health disciplines, whereas the latter would be more prepared
to train pre-professional students off undergraduate courses or to
embark on the training of para-professionals (Umbarger, 1972).

It would be simplistic to link the two teaching models described
here with any one educational system (the pedagogic versus the an-
drogogic dichotomy might, for example, spring to mind).   It is not,

however, my intention to make a comparison based on a division in educational thought whereby one system may carry pejorative connotations when compared with the other.   On the contrary, both approaches described above seem to embody valuable insights into good teaching practice.   The reflective model obviously encourages a greater degree of autonomy on the part of trainees and is more broadly based.   The behaviourist model, however, incorporates important principles in terms of its greater immediacy.   Feedback of results occurs almost instantaneously and opportunities for immediate reinforcement of a trainee's effective work by the supervisor are more readily available.

Clearly we do not all practise family therapy in the same way, nor do we share common beliefs about what families are for, how problems arise or how to help bring about change when things have gone wrong. Similarly, we do not share a common view as to the learning areas which need to be emphasised in the training of family therapists. Moreover, some highly challenging comments have been made regarding the effectiveness of one therapeutic model as compared with the other. Haley (1969) has delineated the characteristics of the unsuccessful therapist and then shown how this model is linked to what in his opinion is an equally unsuccessful model of training (Haley, 1976), the main area of debate concerning the relative emphasis which should be placed on executive skills compared with the development of the therapist's self. It seemed that it might be interesting to test out some of the basic assumptions behind these ideas, since, as I have noted elsewhere (1977) this current tendency to dichotomise between models may not ultimately be conducive to the development of the modality and may simply show evidence of the rigid, pre-emptive type of construing to which Kelly (1955) for example, has called attention.   Since Haley has been the most specific in selecting out one area for attack, the development of the therapist's self, it seemed of interest to evaluate the degree to which this variable alters after training, within a behaviourally oriented training programme.   The expectation would be that as specific encouragement for trainees to engage in personal growth is not given, significant change on this variable during training would not occur.   On the other hand, if it could be shown that changes did occur on this variable, despite no active interventions on the part of the supervisor, several issues would be called into question:

1 The claim made by the behaviourists that training occurs 'successfully' without the trainee engaging in any personal growth. Since personal growth would have been shown to occur after a behavioural training programme, this variable could not be discounted in their evaluation of an effective family therapist.

2 The claim made by the reflectives that training received according to a behaviourist model is defective because it does not bring about change on what they would consider to be the all important variable, personal growth.   This criticism would obviously be unsubstantiated if personal growth is found to occur.

3 The claim made by the reflectives that family therapy training must include an active programme directed towards personal growth.   This might seem to be redundant if personal growth occurs anyway.

The choice of dependent variable for this study was also influ-

enced by the fact that one of the training programmes at the Family
Institute had moved from an essentially reflective model (as described in Walrond-Skinner, 1974) to an exclusively behaviourist
model.   It was therefore decided to select that aspect of training
which might be expected to be most influenced by this change - the
trainee's personal growth - and to evaluate it in terms of outcome
measures applied to this particular training programme.   The concept of personal growth is an elusive one and in order to allow some
hypotheses to be rigorously tested, a rather limited definition of
personal growth had to be taken.   Personal growth was defined as
involving

1   a greater degree of integration within the individual's self-
    identity system (see below) and between various aspects of his
    self and his significant others;
2   a greater degree of cognitive/emotional complexity in the way in
    which he evaluated crucial relationships within the family
    therapy gestalt;   and
3   less perceived difficulty in handling various aspects of the
    therapeutic situation.

Specifically, it was hypothesised that changes would occur in terms
of the student's self-identity system;   construct system;   and his
own perceptions of various aspects of the therapeutic situation.
The hypothesis was formulated that, despite no active encouragement
on the part of supervisors and teachers, personal growth, as outlined above, would nevertheless occur after a behaviourally oriented
family therapy training programme.

Subjects were drawn from the social work student unit which functions within the Family Institute, and the experimental group comprised the total population of students (fourteen) from three consecutive intakes.   Their experience at the Institute constituted
part of their fieldwork practice on a professional social work
training course.   The first two intakes remained at the Institute
for three months and the third for six months.   All fourteen members of the experimental group received a behaviourist training approach to family therapy as outlined above - the sole teaching emphasis being on the development of executive therapeutic skills with
families via the use of 'live' supervision.   No 'personal' work was
undertaken with any of the students during the placement.   A control group was assembled consisting of six untrained social workers
who were nevertheless engaged in a variety of ongoing professional
work with families.   This group was used to control for the possible personal learning effect contributed by ongoing exposure to
professional work with families.   Members of this group were tested
in exactly the same way as the experimental group but they received
no formal training in family therapy of any kind between testings.
As various writers (Runkel and Darwin, 1961;   Philip and McCullogh,
1968;   Tully, 1976, and others) have shown, repertory grids have
successfully been used to evaluate change after training.   Repertory grid technique was therefore adopted for this study also.
(For a comprehensive discussion of repertory grid technique, see
Fransella and Bannister, 1977.)

CHANGES IN THE SELF-IDENTITY SYSTEM

In order to evaluate the amount of personal growth which might have
occurred during the course of training, two repertory grids were
administered to students at the beginning and end of the training
course, and in the case of the third group which was at the Institute for six months, at the mid-point of their training experience
in addition.   A repertory grid is a form of sorting task which enables the relationships between a subject's constructs and elements
to be assessed (Kelly, 1955).   The raw data is yielded in the form
of a matrix whereby elements are ranked or rated against bi-polar
descriptive constructs.   After analysis by hand or by computer, a
finely textured 'map' of the subject's intra-personal psychological
space is revealed (Bannister and Fransella, 1971; Fransella and
Bannister, 1977).   For the purpose of this study, a modified form
of Kelly's original repertory grid was used, whereby the elements
supplied to the subjects took the form of dyadic relationships.
This modification, introduced by Ryle and Lunghi (1970), enables the
investigator to evaluate the subject's perception of interpersonal
relationships, and hence is especially relevant to understanding the
changing construing processes and element organisation of a family
therapist in training.   Dyadic elements were selected to include
salient relationships from the subject's family of origin and current emotional world, those used by Ryle and Breen (1974) providing
the basis for this selection.   Three individuals, the subject's
father, mother and current significant other were chosen as being
highly personalised; and to this was added the subject's supervisor
during his training experience, so that changes occurring in both
modelling and transference phenomena could be tested.   Finally,
three aspects of the subject's own self in relation to client families were included.

These generated twelve different combinations of relationships,
the element dyads being formed by splitting the two aspects of each
relationship and considering, for example, how the self relates to
father (first element) and then how father relates to the self
(second element).   (See Table 9.2.)   Subjects were therefore asked
to construe each relationship from both aspects, first describing

TABLE 9.2

A	Self to Father
B	Self to Mother
C	Self to Current Most Significant Other
D	Self to Client Family
E	Self to Supervisor
F	Father to Self
G	Mother to Self
H	Current Most Significant Other to Self
I	Client Family to Self
J	Supervisor to Self
K	Ideal Self to Client Family
L	Social Self to Client Family

how the subject relates to his father and then how he perceives his
father as relating to him.   In doing this, subjects would, amongst
other things, be indicating the extent to which they were viewing
the relationships in their own emotional world as being essentially
symmetrical, complementary or unrelated within themselves.

In order to focus very specifically on personal change occurring
in the subject's internal world, the three aspects of the self were
considered to be particularly important elements.   Taken together,
they make up what Norris and Makhlouf-Norris (1976) have called the
self-identity system.   Whilst the concept of 'self' remains an elusive one, for practical purposes we can be reasonably certain that
three ways of viewing the self are of major importance: the individual's perceptions of his 'actual' self in relation to others;   his
perception of how he would like to be - his 'ideal self';   and his
perceptions of how others view him - his 'social self'.   The way in
which the individual perceives the relationship between these three
aspects of the self, and the way in which he views his significant
others in relation to each aspect provides a detailed reading of an
intimate and probably only partly conscious area of his internal
world.   In this study it is of course the 'professional' self that
is being examined in the sense that it is the way in which the subject views his actual, ideal and social self in relation to client
families.   But, as the detailed analysis which follows will show,
the fact that each subject is describing the way in which he con-
strues his intimate others in relation to himself as a professional
person gives us a reasonably accurate picture of whether or not
change is occurring in terms of personal growth after training.   We
are able to begin to test an assumption which is made by the 'reflectives' regarding training that (Skynner, 1976, p. 287) 'one
cannot continue to engage in conjoint therapy, and strive to improve
one's skill, without some growth also taking place in one's own general maturity in relationship to oneself and others'.   More specifically, if personal growth is occurring during training, we would
expect there to be (a) some lessening in the 'gap' between the student's perception of his actual self and his ideal self;   (b) between his ideal self and the expectations he perceives the agency
having of him (social self);   and (c) between his actual self and
the agency's expectations of him (social self).   In this way,
intra-personal and intra-professional conflict would be reduced
after training.   Moreover, it would be expected that there would be
a greater integration of the professional and personal self-identity
system after training.   These, then, were the hypotheses which were
tested in relation to the student's self-identity system.

A mixture of supplied and elicited constructs were used, since
both offer certain advantages to the experimenter (see for example
Isaacson and Landfield, 1965;   Bannister and Mair, 1968;   and Adams-
Webber, 1970).   Eight constructs were elicited from the subject for
the first grid using the normal triadic method, whereby the subject
is asked how two elements seem to him to be alike and different from
the third.   This yields a bi-polar construct having both an emer-
gent and implicit pole.   For the second grid eight constructs were
supplied, derived from Ryle and Breen's study (1974).   (See Table
9.3.)   These were felt to be representative of some basic emotional
positions experienced in family therapy both by family members and

by the therapist himself in relation to the family with which he is
working.   Subjects were asked to rank the elements along each set
of constructs to give a completed grid matrix.   Tied ranks were
disallowed.   The completed grids were analysed by computer using
Slater's INGRID programme (1972).

TABLE 9.3

---

1   Is made anxious by
2   Feels hostile towards
3   Feels affectionate towards
4   Feels sexually attracted towards
5   Is made angry by
6   Feels discouraged by
7   Is controlling towards
8   Is dependent on

The INGRID programme shows the distance between each pair of elements in the grid as a ratio of the expected distance between all
pairs.   The possible distance runs from 0 through 1 to more than 1,
where 0 is the minimum and 1 is the mean.   The closer the distance
between the element pair to 0, the more closely similar they are
perceived by the subject;   whilst the bigger the distance between
them, the more dissimilarly they are viewed by the subject.   Element distances close to 1 represent those which are seen as being
neither similar nor dissimilar.   Using Slater's GRANNY programme
(1974) as a control (capable of generating random number matrices)
Norris and Makhlouf-Norris (1976, p. 83) showed that there existed a
'central indifference area between 0.8 and 1.2 on both variables'
(i.e. the actual and the ideal self).   Thus a grid composed of
random numbers generates 92 per cent of its element distances within
this central indifference area.   This being the case, we can assume
that element distances placed outside this area give a meaningful
account of a subject's self-identity system;   and that an inspection
of the pattern shown before and after training will reveal whether
or not changes have occurred both within the internal relationship
of the self-identity system itself and in the relationship between
the three aspects of the self and the way other relationships are
viewed.   A method of evaluating the degree of integration within
the self-identity system has been suggested by Norris and Makhlouf-
Norris (1976) and they have offered operational definitions of four
types of non-integration which can be perceived by visual inspection
of a subject's self-identity plot:
  a)   Actual-self-isolation.   There are no non-self elements
       within a distance of 0.8 from the actual self.
  b)   Ideal self-isolation.   There are no non-self elements within
       a distance of 0.8 from the ideal self.
  c)   Social alienation.   There are not more than two non-self
       elements within a distance of 0.8 from either the actual self
       or the ideal self.
  d)   Self alienation.   The actual self is separated from the
       ideal by a distance greater than 1.2, and not more than two
       non-self elements are closer to the ideal than is the actual
       self.

Figures 9.1 and 9.2 compare Bill's self-identity system before
and after training, using his elicited construct grids.   Although
the actual self and ideal self are plotted orthogonally, this is
merely an artifact of convenient graphic presentation and does not
imply any assumptions about the orthogonal relationship of the two
elements.   Table 9.4 gives the distance between Bill's perception
of his actual self and ideal self with all the other elements before
training.   The element distance between Bill's actual self and
ideal self before training is 1.08 and thus the two elements are
seen as being neither like nor unlike each other.   What we can note
from the plot is the way in which the actual self is in the 'unlike
ideal self' quadrant and vice versa.   Because the elements being
used are dyadic elements, it is important to remember that it is
relationships, not individuals, which are being plotted.   Thus we
can note from Figure 9.1 that Bill perceives his relationship with
the supervisor and vice versa (elements 5 and 10) as being like the
way he sees himself relating to client families (element 4).   A
good deal of phantasy must enter into Bill's perceptions at this
stage because his relationship with the supervisor is only a week
old.

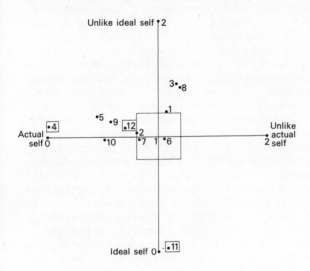

FIGURE 9.1

Similarly, he also views the way in which the client family relates to him (element 9) as being similar to the way in which he relates to the client family - thus indicating that he expects this
professional relationship to be a symmetrical one.   He seems to be
using a concretist method of making comparisons, resting on a somewhat superficial split between, on the one hand, his relationships
with his supervisor and his client families which he perceives as
being 'professional', and, on the other hand, those relationships
which are obviously 'personal'.   The degree of concretism in a student's construing of elements is of interest in itself as Lifshitz
(1974) found 'a developmental pattern of concept internalisation,
from the more concrete to the more abstract' when she compared the

TABLE 9.4 Distance of all elements from the actual professional
self (E. 4) and ideal professional self (E. 11) (elicited
constructs)

Elements	Actual professional self	Ideal professional self
1	1.10	1.20
2	0.80	1.01
3	1.18	1.45
4	0	1.08
5	0.44	1.18
6	1.06	0.98
7	0.83	0.93
8	1.21	1.44
9	0.56	1.10
10	0.52	0.95
11	1.08	0
12	0.73	1.06

superordinate constructs of social work students in training with
those of their experienced supervisors. At the beginning of his
training, Bill perceives his relationship with his wife (elements 3
and 8) as something that is quite unlike the way in which he actually relates or would like to relate to his client families, thus
helping to define his professional relationships by their dissimilarity from this personal one. His relationships with both parents
fall within the central area of indifference (elements 1 and 6; and
2 and 7) and thus do not contribute to the way in which he under-
stands either his actual or ideal self as a professional person.
  This splitting of professional and personal self is induced by
the content of the elicited constructs used by Bill as well as by
the structure of the element organisation, most of Bill's relationships being described by specifically 'professional' or specifically
'personally' related constructs. Element 12, the social self, is
comparatively isolated from both the other self elements, although
there is less distance from the actual self than from the ideal
self. It is, however, not far off the central area of indifference
whereby it would fail to play any significant part in defining the
quality of the other two self elements. For this student it may
simply have been out of his psychological reach to phantasise what
the agency's expectations of him might be at this early stage in his
training. Finally, we may note that the ideal self is very isolated. No non-self element relationship is seen as being similar to
Bill's ideal self or is within a distance of 0.8 from it on the
self-identity plot. Thus the plot reveals a picture of ideal self
isolation according to Norris and Makhlouf-Norris' operational definition cited above. At the beginning of training, Bill is clearly
more able to perceive relationships in terms of how he does not want
to be as a family therapist, rather than in terms of a desired
positive identification. This can be seen as a natural and indeed
useful psychological stance for a student at the beginning of training, feeling that a great deal has to be learned before his own
standards for himself can be met.

Figure 9.2 outlines Bill's self-identity system at the end of his three-month period of training. The element relationships are now 'scattered' much more generally instead of being confined in the non-ideal self half of the graph as before. There has been a con- siderable degree of convergence between the three aspects of self, which are now all viewed as residing in the actual self/ideal self quadrant. Clearly, Bill experiences considerably less conflict be- tween how he perceives his actual relationship with client families, the way in which he would like to relate to client families, and the way in which he perceives the Agency's expectations of his re- lationships with client families. Elements 9, 10 and 5 have moved to the 'positive' quadrant whereby they are seen as being both how Bill actually relates professionally and how he would like to relate professionally. Elements 1 and 6, his relationship with his father, have moved out of the central area of indifference and are now more clearly defined. Only Bill's relationship with his mother (elements 2 and 7) is not contributing to his definition of a 'pro- fessional self'. Whilst Bill continues to divide his 'personal' relationships from his 'professional ones' the division is now based on a greater convergence between how he feels he is in reality and what he and the agency requires of him.

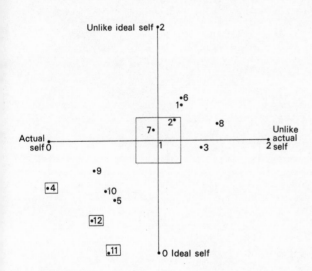

FIGURE 9.2

Bill was at the Family Institute for only three months. Fred, on the other hand, was trained for six months and was re-tested once after three months and again at the end of his training. Figures 9.3, 9.4 and 9.5 show Fred's self-identity plots through his train- ing period using elicited constructs. Like Bill, Fred's first grid (Figure 9.3) shows a complete isolation of the ideal self and relatively little convergence between the three aspects of self. Again, 'professional' and 'personal' relationships are carefully distinguished. Figure 9.4 shows an interesting development, with the three aspects of self, far from becoming more convergent, polar- ising quite sharply. His perceptions of how he actually relates to

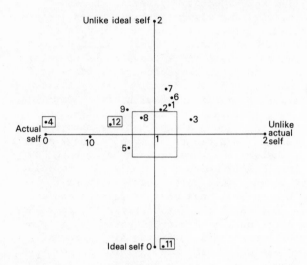

FIGURE 9.3

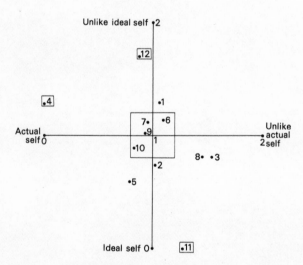

FIGURE 9.4

client families have moved further from how he would like to relate
to them and both his actual and ideal self are now seen quite differently from the demands he perceives the agency making on him.
Interestingly, he distinguishes the agency's expectations very
strongly from those of his supervisor, for he sees his relationship
with his supervisor as being quite close to both his actual and
ideal professional self.   Obviously this student was experiencing
considerable conflict midway through his training in terms of the
three aspects of his professional self.   By the end of his training, a considerable degree of convergence has occurred between
Fred's three 'selves' as is shown in Figure 9.5, and his personal

and professional worlds are not as sharply polarised.   He has now
rejected his supervisor as being an exclusive model for his professional work and is moving into an appropriate phase of disengagement
from the Agency.

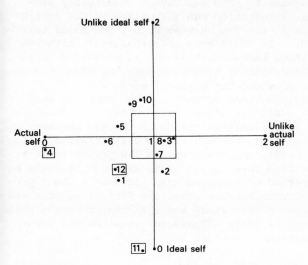

FIGURE 9.5

    Aspects of the two patterns of development demonstrated by Bill's
and Fred's grids were found to occur in the experimental group as a
whole.   With regard to the relationship of ideal and expected self,
after three months' training there was a significant lessening in
the gap between the students' ideal selves and what they perceived
as the agency's expectations of them (p = < .01, 1 tailed, N = 26,
T = 82, Wilcoxon matched pairs signed ranks).   Contrariwise, the
results are non-significant when the third group's third testing
(after six months) is compared with their second testing (after
three months), suggesting that no measureable advantage is gained in
relation to this dimension from prolonging training to six months.
The control group shows no significant diminution in the gap between
their ideal self and their perception of their agency's expectations
of them when re-tested and in fact the trend was in the reverse
direction.   Thus we may conclude that, despite the sole emphasis
of the training programme on the acquisition of technical skills in
working with families, students nevertheless experienced positive
changes in terms of internal integration between two aspects of
their professional self.   This type of integration would normally
be associated with some direct work on the self undertaken either
individually with the supervisor or, more usually in the family
therapy field, in the supervision group.
    In terms of the relationship between the actual self and the
ideal self, a different pattern emerged.   After three months'
training, there was no significant lessening of the gap between the
students' perception of how they actually function with client families and how they would like to function and the trend was in the
reverse direction.   However, when the results of the third group's

third testing are considered, there is a significant reduction in
the gap between their real and ideal self (p = < .05, 1 tailed, N
= 9, T = 6, Wilcoxon matched pairs signed ranks) suggesting that
progress is only made along this dimension after a longer period of
training and that an increase in this gap may be a necessary prerequisite before eventual integration can take place.   The control
group showed no reduction in the gap between actual and ideal self
when re-testing occurred.   It would seem therefore that, although
it takes longer, integration between actual and ideal self does take
place after a strictly behaviourist training programme even when no
formal opportunities are provided for personal work.

    Finally the relationship between actual self and expected self
was examined for change.   Neither after three months nor after six
months training was any significant lessening of the gap between
these two variables revealed.   However, when the experimental group
was retested after six months, the trend was in the predicted direction.   We must conclude from this result that, although it could be
the case that a longer period of training than six months might produce a significant convergence between these two variables, this was
not shown to have occurred in this study and that therefore the null
hypothesis (that no change in terms of personal growth would occur)
was confirmed in this instance.

CHANGES IN THE CONSTRUCT SYSTEM

Next, the amount of personal growth taking place after training was
examined by an inspection of changes occurring in the students'
construct system.   Researchers using repertory grid technique to
evaluate changes that may occur after treatment or training have
offered various different techniques for examining the structure of
the subject's construct system.   As Kelly (1963, p. 56) pointed out
in his organisation corollary: 'Each person characteristically
evolves, for his convenience in anticipating events, a construction
system embracing ordinal relationships between constructs.'   If one
or more of a person's core constructs are altered as a result of
treatment or training, whole areas of the system of interrelated
subordinate constructs will show evidence of change.   Obviously, a
behaviourist training programme in family therapy would be disinterested in bringing about this sort of change, but a 'reflective'
teacher such as Skynner (1976, p. 285) would view this internal reorganisation of the 'therapist's psyche [as constituting] the main
difficulty for one beginning the technique'.   Skynner goes on to
assert (p. 286) that 'if this dynamic interaction is coped with, it
leads, inevitably, to a more integrated personality in the professional, as well as more successful family therapy'.   It was, therefore, felt to be of interest to see if some sort of internal structural changes in the students took place even though their training
programme would not have actively promoted this kind of personal
growth.

    One useful measure of change in construct structure is that of
cognitive/emotional complexity.   Bieri et al. (1966) defined cognitive complexity as '... the capacity to construe social behaviour in
a multidimensional way.   A more cognitively complex person has

available a more differentiated system of dimensions for perceiving others' behaviour than does a less cognitively complex individual.' Adams-Webber (1969) makes a similar inference: 'relatively cognitively complex persons infer the personal constructs of others in social situations more efficiently than do relatively cognitively simple persons'. Although the development of cognitive complexity is a severe test of personal growth to apply to a twelve- or sixteen-week training period, it was nevertheless felt to be an important area to investigate.

Various measures have been used to compute the relative degree of complexity revealed by a subject's grid (Epting, 1972; Honess, 1976). The method adopted in this study was to examine the comparative size of percentage variance accounted for by the first two principal components generated by the INGRID analysis. Complexity of the construct system increases in inverse proportion to the increase in percentage variance accounted for by the first two principal components. The aim of this part of the study was to ascertain whether or not students developed different ways of looking at the interpersonal relationships occurring between the family group and family therapist gestalt, by examining whether or not changes were revealed in the students' construct systems after training. Two grids were administered, using dyad elements taken from a video-taped family therapy interview. Relationships between the therapist, father, mother and a small child in the interview were used to generate twelve element dyads. (See Table 9.5.) Eight constructs were elicited from each subject for the first grid, and eight were supplied as before for the second grid. (See Table 9.3.) Table 9.6 lays out a comparison between the percentage variance revealed in the grids before and after training for all the students. It can be seen that for grid 1, although the results did not reach significance, changes occurred in the predicted direction for nine out of the fourteen students on the first retest after three months' training. The mean value for the first test was 79.84 compared with 77.09 after three months, showing a small increase in cognitive complexity. When the third group was tested again after six months' training, changes occurred in the predicted direction and were significant at p = < .05 level (Wilcoxon matched pairs signed ranks, 1 tailed). The mean values for the third group's three

TABLE 9.5 Element dyads derived from video-taped family therapy session

A	Father to Mother
B	Father to Child
C	Mother to Child
D	Father to Therapist
E	Mother to Therapist
F	Child to Therapist
G	Mother to Father
H	Child to Father
I	Child to Mother
J	Therapist to Father
K	Therapist to Mother
L	Therapist to Child

TABLE 9.6 Percentage variance accounted for by the first two principal components

| | Elicited constructs | | | | Supplied constructs | | |
Subjects	T1	T2	T3	Subjects	T1	T2	T3
A	77.86	59.73	58.80	A	67.27	76.93	68.81
B	69.79	66.30	56.00	B	64.34	65.74	60.16
C	90.35	80.96	73.31	C	72.07	75.39	74.75
D	74.52	80.16	71.79	D	56.44	78.78	67.83
E	89.00	80.11	81.48	E	67.53	74.15	60.92
F	71.43	80.85	–	F	63.57	69.61	–
G	81.93	75.23	–	G	82.23	73.31	–
H	68.66	73.90	–	H	71.38	67.38	–
I	70.33	81.15	–	I	61.24	75.88	–
J	78.67	75.09	–	J	75.95	67.74	–
K	81.26	71.28	–	K	69.32	77.94	–
L	93.94	88.91	–	L	73.94	66.71	–
M	82.22	87.59	–	M	60.67	76.09	–
N	87.86	78.02	–	N	65.55	63.50	–

testings were 80.30, 73.45, 68.28 respectively, showing a marked decrease in percentage variance, and thus a marked increase in cognitive complexity after six months' training.   The control group, on
the other hand, showed no increase in cognitive complexity, the mean
value for the group's test and retest being 82.80 and 87.38 respectively.   Thus, our hypothesis regarding personal growth was confirmed in this instance, and the results indicated that a six-month
training period produced an important development in terms of increased cognitive complexity.

The second grid, using supplied constructs, did not however
reveal the same pattern.   After three months' training the percentage variance accounted for by the first two principal components
had increased from 67.96 to 76.89 for the group as a whole (group
means).   The mean values for the third group's three testings were
65.53, 74.10 and 66.49 respectively.   The pattern here is interesting as it replicates the one which was found by Ryle and Breen
(1974), using a similar group of supplied constructs.   When retest-
ing their sample after three months, they found an increase in variance and consequent decrease in cognitive complexity.   It was only
after twelve months' training, using these supplied constructs, that
Ryle and Breen found a statistically significant increase in complexity.   It is important to note here that the training course
being tested by Ryle and Breen for change was an MSc social work
course, which could reasonably be expected to engage students directly in issues relating to personal growth - yet even so, when supplied constructs germane to various affective positions were employed, a year's training was required to increase the complexity of
the students' construct system.   What seemed surprising in terms of
the present study was that so much development in cognitive complexity had however occurred for students when their own construct
system was tapped via eliciting constructs on each testing occasion.
When their personal construct systems were investigated, a picture
of tight, pre-emptive construing was revealed at the outset of
training.   By the end of training the picture had become much more
multidimensional for most of the students, indicating that the way
in which they assessed the interpersonal relationships between
family members and therapist as they occurred in a family therapy
session had developed into a richer and more complex picture.

CHANGE IN STUDENTS' PERCEPTIONS

The third method of testing personal growth was to gather information about the students' own perceptions of change.   In order to
determine the degree to which the students consciously altered their
perceptions of various aspects of the therapeutic situation, a questionnaire was administered before and after training in which they
were asked about the difficulty which they perceived in tolerating
various interpersonal situations within a family therapy session.
Eighteen questions called for the subject to mark his opinion along
a line proceeding from 'very difficult' to 'not at all difficult'.
Table 9.7 shows the way in which the students' responses changed
after training on eight of the 'situations' which they were asked to
consider, and it shows nine situations which did not indicate any

TABLE 9.7 Degree of change shown in students' perceptions regarding various family therapy situations before and after training (group scores)

	T	Before*	After*	Significance level (one tailed)
Toleration of anger	21	371	461	p = < .05
Toleration of approval	20	501	434	p = < .05
Toleration of depression	25	289	386	p = < .05
Toleration of hostility	26	302	402	Non-significant
Toleration of sexual attraction	13	306	366	p = < .05
Toleration of affection	26.5	449	498	Non-significant
Toleration of dependence	37.5	327	391	Non-significant
Toleration of being controlled	40.5	177	204	Non-significant
Fear of damaging families	22.5	391	488	p = < .05
Fear of being damaged	31	544	514	Non-significant
Toleration of silence	11	369	536	p = < .025
Comfort in co-therapy	52	431	397	Non-significant
Anxiety regarding confidentiality	25	425	514	p = < .05
Anxiety regarding audio-visual aids	18	402	529	p = < .025
Toleration of discouragement	49	338	343	Non-significant
Clarity of effects of own family of origin on performance as a family therapist	29	344	284	Non-significant
Clarity of effects of own current family on performance as a family therapist	17.5	275	365	p = < .05
Difficulty in sharing feelings and experiences with family when appropriate	45.5	467	501	Non-significant

Using Wilcoxon matched pairs signal ranks test, p.= < .05 when the values of T = < 25.

* The rating scales were scored using low numbers to represent a
  greater degree of difficulty.

significant change after training.   One question: 'How difficult would it be for you to tolerate approval from family members?' showed an increase in perceived difficulty, significant at p = < .05.   When the control group's testings were compared, no significant change was found to occur on any of the eighteen questions.   This fact clearly increases the importance considerably of the otherwise somewhat meagre findings.   The fact that the stu-

dents' feelings about eight of nineteen 'situations' changed significantly in a favourable direction takes on a different perspective
when we compare this with nil for the control group. Some of the
differences in this change between 'situations' are interesting to
examine. Fear of damaging families, for example, recedes much-more
quickly than fear of being damaged by families, reflecting what
would seem to be an internal reassessment on the part of the student, after his period of supervised practice, of the power imbalance within the family therapy gestalt. Toleration of anger, depression and sexual attraction experienced in the family group in
treatment increases, but what might perhaps usually be more veiled
emotions - hostility, affection, dependence and control do not
become less difficulty for the students to tolerate, although the
students' increased tolerance of hostility and affection almost
reach significance. What might be considered to be more superficial anxieties, surrounding silence in the family therapy sessions,
issues of confidentiality and the self-exposure necessitated by the
use of audio-visual aids all recede quite quickly. Interestingly,
despite no 'personal' work being undertaken, their perceptions of
the way in which their relationships within their current family
situation affect their performance as a family therapist, have
become significantly clearer. Predictably this increased clarity
does not occur regarding the influence of their family of origin -
this being a more remote area of change, presumably requiring active
interventions to promote personal growth and development along this
dimension. Likewise, students do not find it easier to share their
own feelings openly within a family therapy session - but again one
would expect this type of intervention, almost completely un-utili-
sed within a behaviourist approach, to be one of the most difficult
areas for a student to develop, without active 'personal' work
being undertaken.

CONCLUSION

This chapter has set out to describe two different approaches to
the training or education of family therapists and to present some
research findings which challenge the validity of the basic dichotomy between these two approaches to teaching. The findings suggest that a considerable amount of personal growth takes place in a
student even after a short behaviourally oriented training programme. No claim is, of course, being made by such a statement
that the measures used in this study adequately or comprehensively
measure personal growth, but in terms of the definition adopted, a
considerable amount of change along this dimension was found to
occur. Some may feel that the descriptions of the two approaches
to teaching given here are somewhat caricatured and that many training programmes lie somewhere in the middle, combining methods of
'live' supervision with those designed to increase the trainee's
self-awareness. However, the move to develop teaching programmes
in many agencies based on the broad subdivision between insight and
behaviourally focused therapies, increases the danger of rigid de-
marcation lines being perpetuated.
        Almost every question pertaining to the outcome of family therapy

teaching remains unanswered and there would at present be no way of
knowing whether either training model is effective, or whether one
model is more effective than the other in accomplishing what it sets
out to do.   Matarazzo (1971) noted that when she and her colleagues
reviewed the status of research into the teaching of psychotherapeutic skills in 1966 (Matarazzo, Wiens and Saslow, 1966), the situation could be succinctly summarised by repeating a statement made by
Carl Rogers in 1957 to the effect that although 'we would expect
that a great deal of attention might be given to the problem of
training individuals to engage in the therapeutic process.... For
the most part this field is characterised by a rarity of research
and a plenitude of platitudes' (quoted in Matarazzo, 1971, p. 895).
Matarazzo goes on to point out that 'today this state of affairs has
begun to change, apparently in teaching programs of all theoretical
persuasions, although progress is uneven among them'.   Matarazzo
was solely concerned with research into the teaching of individual
psychotherapy.   The situation regarding research into the teaching
of family therapy is still much more akin to the description given
by Rogers in 1957.   One can only describe it as being entirely em-
bryonic.   No properly validated behaviour category instruments
exist by which a student's audio- or video-taped interviews with
actual families can be rated - thus no work has been done on the
degree to which student family therapists develop their mastery of
executive therapeutic skills after training.   Likewise there has
been no evaluation made of the correlation of change in trainee
therapists' behaviour in therapy with outcome measures designed to
examine the families they have treated.   Many questions remain unanswered.   What are the significant variables of family therapist
behaviour which should be taught to trainees?   Which teaching techniques are most effective in enabling students to learn them?   Who
should be trained as family therapists and what prior knowledge and
experience base should they have?   How should theory and supervised
practice be integrated and in what setting and for what duration of
time should training take place?   (See Gale, Chapter 10).

The present writer could find not one single piece of published
research into any of these aspects of family therapy training.
Thus it would seem that, as has been the case with the teaching of
individual psychotherapy in its various forms, research into the
effectiveness of family therapy teaching must wait its turn at the
end of the queue of priorities.   Hopefully, the present study will
serve a purpose in drawing attention to a large and completely un-
filled gap in the family therapy literature and, further, will move
a small step towards helping forward differentiation without demar-
cation and integration without fusion between the various different
approaches to teaching being developed within the field as a whole.

ACKNOWLEDGMENT

The author's research reported in this chapter was made possible by
a special grant from Dr Barnardo's.

REFERENCES

ADAMS-WEBBER, J. (1969), Cognitive complexity and sociality, 'British Journal of Social and Clinical Psychology', vol. 8, pp. 211-16.
ADAMS-WEBBER, J. (1970), Elicited versus provided constructs in repertory grid technique: a review, 'British Journal of Social and Clinical Psychology', vol. 43, pp. 349-54.
ALLEN, J.D. (1976), Peer group supervision in family therapy, 'Child Welfare', vol. LV, pp. 183-9.
ANONYMOUS (1972), Toward the differentiation of a self in one's own family, in J.L. Framo (ed.), 'Family Interaction - A Dialogue between Family Researchers and Family Therapists', Springer, New York.
BANNISTER, D. and FRANSELLA, F. (1971), 'Inquiring Man', Penguin, Harmondsworth.
BANNISTER, D. and MAIR, M. (1968), 'The Evaluation of Personal Constructs', Academic Press, London.
BELL, J.E. (1963), A theoretical position for family group therapy, 'Family Process', vol. 2, pp. 1-14.
BIERI, J., ATKINS, A.L., BRIAR, S., LEAMAN, R.L., MILLER, H. and TRIPODI, T. (1966), 'Clinical and Social Judgment: the Discrimination of Behavioural Information', Wiley, New York.
BIRCHLER, G.R. (1975), Live supervision and instant feedback in marriage and family therapy, 'Journal of Marriage and Family Counseling', vol. 1, pp. 331-42.
BOWEN, M. (1971), The use of family theory in clinical practice, in J. Haley (ed.), 'Changing Families', Grune & Stratton, New York.
CLEGHORN, J.M. and LEVIN, S. (1973), Training family therapists by setting learning objectives, 'American Journal of Orthopsychiatry', vol. 43, pp. 439-46.
DOWLING, E. (1974), The training of family therapists, unpublished paper delivered at Tavistock/Ackerman Conference on Principles and Practice of Family Therapy, London.
EPTING, F.R. (1972), The stability of cognitive complexity in construing social issues, 'British Journal of Social and Clinical Psychology', vol. 11, pp. 122-5.
ERICKSON, G. (1973), Teaching family therapy, 'Education for Social Work', Fall 1973, pp. 9-15.
FERBER, A. and MENDELSOHN, M. (1969), Training for family therapy, 'Family Process', vol. 8, pp. 25-32.
FRANSELLA, F. and BANNISTER, D. (1977), 'A Manual for Repertory Grid Technique', Academic Press, London.
GOSLING, R., MILLER, D.H., TURQUET, P.M. and WOODHOUSE (1967), 'The Use of Small Groups in Training', Codicote Press.
HALEY, J. (1969), The art of being a failure as a therapist, in J. Haley, 'The Power Tactics of Jesus Christ and other Essays', Grossman, New York.
HALEY, J. (1976), 'Problem Solving Therapy', Jossey-Bass, San Francisco, California.
HONESS, T. (1976), Cognitive complexity and social prediction, 'British Journal of Social and Clinical Psychology', vol. 15, pp. 23-31.
ISAACSON, G.I. and LANDFIELD, A.W. (1965), Meaningfulness of personal and common constructs, 'Journal of Individual Psychology', vol. 21, pp. 160-6.
KELLY, G. (1955), 'The Psychology of Personal Constructs', vols 1 and 2, Norton, New York.

KELLY, G. (1963), 'A Theory of Personality', Norton, New York.
LIFSHITZ, M. (1974), Quality professionals: does training make a difference?   A personal construct theory study of the issue, 'British Journal of Social and Clinical Psychology', vol. 13, pp. 183-9.
MATARAZZO, R.G. (1971), Research on the teaching and learning of psychotherapeutic skills, in A.E. Bergin and S.L. Garfield (eds), 'Handbook of Psychotherapy and Behaviour Change', Wiley, New York.
MATARAZZO, R.G., WIENS, A.N. and SASLOW, G. (1966), Experimentation in the teaching and learning of psychotherapy skills, in L.K. Gottschalk and A. Auerbach (eds), 'Method of Research in Psychotherapy', Appleton-Century-Crofts, New York, pp. 597-635.
NORRIS, H. and MAKHLOUF-NORRIS, F. (1976), The measurement of self-identity, in P. Slater (ed.), 'Explorations of Intra-personal Space', Wiley, London.
PHILIP, A. and MCCULLOUGH, J. (1968), Personal construct theory and social work practice, 'British Journal of Social and Clinical Psychology', vol. 7, pp. 115-21.
RUNKEL, P. and DARWIN, D. (1961), Effects on training and anxiety upon teachers' preferences for information about students, 'Journal of Educational Psychology', vol. 52, pp. 254-61.
RYLE, A. and BREEN, D. (1974), Change in the course of social work training: a repertory grid study, 'British Journal of Medical Psychology', vol. 47, pp. 139-47.
RYLE, A. and LUNGHI, M.W. (1970), The dyad grid: a modification of repertory grid technique, 'British Journal of Psychiatry', vol. 117, pp. 323-7.
SKYNNER, A.C.R. (1976), 'One Flesh: Separate Persons - Principles of Family and Marital Psychotherapy', Constable, London.
SLATER, P. (1972), 'Notes on INGRID 72', St George's Hospital Medical School, London.
SLATER, P. (1974), 'The Reliability and Significance of Grids', St George's Hospital Medical School, London.
TULLY, T.B. (1976), Personal construct theory and psychological changes relating to social work training, 'British Journal of Social Work', vol. 6, pp. 481-99.
UMBARGER, C. (1972), The paraprofessional and family therapy, 'Family Process', vol. 11, p. 147.
WALROND-SKINNER, S. (1974), Training for family therapy, 'Social Work Today', vol. 5, pp. 149-54.
WALROND-SKINNER, S. (1977), 'Theoretical Frameworks: Synthesis and Antithesis', Proceedings of the Association for Family Therapy Conference, 1976.
WELLS, R.A., DILKES, T.C. and BURCKHARDT, N.T. (1976), The results of family therapy: a critical review of the literature, in D.H.L. Olson, 'Treating Relationships', Graphic Publishing Co., Inc., New York, pp. 499-516.

Chapter 10

PROBLEMS OF OUTCOME RESEARCH IN FAMILY THERAPY

Anthony Gale

This chapter is an attempt to summarise the main issues involved
in the evaluation of outcome research in family therapy.   A
checklist is provided against which individual studies may be
assessed and to provide a basis for future research.   It is
argued that for a number of reasons, family therapy is in danger
of going the way of all other therapies, unless steps are taken
to curb blind enthusiasm and to ensure a more rigorous approach.
Several key reviews indicate that we have little knowledge of the
true patterns of interaction in normal or abnormal families, or
that there is little evidence that family therapy and/or marital
therapy actually have any beneficial effect.   Indeed the burden
of evidence is that they do not work.   However, it is difficult
to pose the question 'Does family therapy work?' since there is
no unitary theory or common set of specified practices.   Research done so far has been sloppy and ill-controlled and characterised by a common bias that the outcome will be favourable.
Of the many problems which abound a few instructive examples are
dealt with in detail.   It is concluded that family therapy research has a long way to go before it can make a useful contribution to our body of knowledge concerning human behaviour.

INTRODUCTION

According to Glick and Kessler (1974), family therapy
    might broadly be thought of as any type of psychosocial in-
    tervention utilising a conceptual framework that gives pri-
    mary emphasis to the family system, and which in its thera-
    peutic strategies aims for an impact on the entire family
    structure.   Thus any psychotherapeutic approach that
    attempts to understand or to intervene in an organically
    viewed family system might fittingly be called family ther-
    apy.   This is a broad definition and allows many competing
    points of view, both in theory and in therapy, to be placed
    under one heading.
    They go on to say that the primary goals of family therapy are

first, the facilitation of the communication of thoughts and feelings within the family; second, to shift disturbed roles and co-
alitions within the family; and finally, for the therapist to serve
as a role model, educator and demythologiser.

These definitions seem to be innocent, fair-minded and straightforward.   However, as we shall see, their apparent simplicity masks
a host of problems which are easily revealed by asking simple questions of the following sort.   What is the meaning of 'family',
'therapy', 'psychosocial', 'intervention', 'system', 'therapeutic
strategy', 'impact', 'entire family structure', 'psychotherapeutic',
'understanding', 'intervention' and 'organic'?   Indeed Glick and
Kessler devote their excellent book to a detailed and balanced discussion of these key terms.   It is clear from their account that
there is in fact little agreement among the experts as to what these
key terms mean.   Thus the generality of their general definition is
somewhat reduced.

The aim of the present chapter is to set out, in as straightforward a manner as possible, the criteria to be used for the evaluation of the outcome of family therapy.   This is not a detailed
catalogue of successes and failures, because a number of excellent
reviews are already available.   My intention, rather, is to lay
bare the underlying logic of the examination of change in individuals and groups as the result of therapy.   There is not space for
a consideration of individual studies and this chapter is therefore
largely a review of reviews.

FAMILY THERAPY AS A SOCIAL MOVEMENT

Interest in family therapy has grown from trickle to flood over the
last fifteen years.   This vigorous growth is reflected in the zest
and enthusiasm shown in the earlier contributions to this volume.
Enthusiasm is of course essential for the initiation and promotion
of change, but for some purposes it has to be guided, channelled and
even restrained; otherwise it can dominate and corrupt.   Quite
often, enthusiasm is no friend of science, for the enthusiast can
lose contact with reality.

The truth is that the family therapy movement has become something of a social movement with a quasi-evangelical flavour.   The
frequent existence of social movements for the creation of change
and reform is an historical and socio-psychological fact.   Indeed
such phenomena are themselves worthy of study, for social movements
are not limited to politics, social reform and religion; they frequently invade science and are certainly not unknown to medicine and
to therapy.   They have a common life-cycle which begins with enthusiasm and ends with doubt and denial.   The present fervour and financial and commercial commitment to the transcendental meditation
and biofeedback movements, in the absence of any scientific evidence
of note in favour of their efficacy, stands as a warning to us all.

There seems to be in men of goodwill a potent desire to achieve
some utopia on this earth and to strive toward an ego ideal which
history so far may have told us is impossible.   The paradox is that
without this desire for change there would be no change.   But
desire and reality often dwell in different domains of experience.

One purpose of this chapter is to dash a little cold water in the eyes of the enthusiasts in the hope that they will stop in their tracks, wipe their eyes, and engage in a little reality testing.

May I declare at the outset a bias in favour of the notion of family therapy, particularly where it is combined with other forms of therapy. Family therapy appears to be a sensible and ecologically valid way to tackle the problem of mental stress. People are born into, and live and develop in, families, and families live and develop because of the people in them. The family is therefore the cradle and the web of our emotional development and the origin of our basic patterns of social interaction and interpersonal adjustment. Not only is the family the origin, but also a powerful source for the sustenance of our unique and eccentric behaviours and beliefs. There is, therefore, a prima facie case for suggesting that the family might be an appropriate vehicle and even the primary medium for the promotion of change within the individual. The system which creates and supports patterns of behaviour may be the means of describing, assessing and changing the behaviour.

Certainly, therapeutic techniques which derive from an emphasis on intra-psychic and individual factors are notorious for their failure to promote long-lasting and beneficial changes in the individual. Family therapy represents a shift from an historical approach, based upon dubious interpretations of intra-psychic data, to an examination of the here-and-now and an observation of current behaviour in a potentially objective manner. Thus recognition of the importance of family process to the functioning of the individual could constitute a major theoretical advance.

But history is in danger of repeating itself. The promise which family therapy bears may be denied if the errors so often made in relation to individual therapy are repeated yet again in the case of family therapy. For much of this chapter I shall be drawing upon the lessons learned in the history of the evaluation of the effects of individual therapy in the hope that they may be recognised as cautionary warnings. Unfortunately, there is already evidence that this caution comes too late for a proper foundation to be laid for family therapy. In ten years' time, family therapy may be looked back upon as little more than a will-o-the-wisp, something which came and passed too quickly, and then was gone.

I am therefore making an appeal, which perhaps contrasts strongly with the content of some of the other contributions to this volume, in the hope that my depressing prophecy might be proved wrong. Family therapists must recognise that a scientific and objective evaluation of their therapeutic activity is the only way in which that activity can be shown to be well spent. None of us likes to be subjected to detailed scrutiny, least of all in our professional activities, which are the source of our self-esteem and proper feelings of competence. But therapists, like politicians, must lose certain rights enjoyed by private individuals; the therapist has the professional obligation to cause his own competence to be examined. The declared objective of therapy is to benefit the client. In the search for truth, the therapist may suffer, for there are of course three logically possible outcomes to any examination of the efficacy of a therapeutic procedure. Therapy may be shown to lead to improvement (as so many therapists believe and declare that it

does);   it may achieve nothing at all (as is indicated by so much
research into the effects of traditional psychotherapies);   or finally, it may even be shown to be harmful and personally destructive, reinforcing those behaviours which it sets out to eliminate
(as some have claimed are the effects of psychoanalytic procedures).

A large proportion of the studies designed to examine the efficacy of family therapy have been biased from the outset with the
desire to show that they do in fact work.   Investigations have not
been disinterested in the way which true scientists must be.   Quite
often, the investigators have been out to show that they are not
wasting their professional time or dissipating their sponsors' funds
in idle self-indulgence.   But even in spite of this bias on the
part of researchers, to the notion that family therapy is beneficial it appears that as yet there is little objective evidence that
family therapy actually does work.   It will therefore be immediately apparent to the reader that if I am to talk about outcome studies, it is likely that I shall have many critical things to say and
some of them will be very harsh indeed.   But my hope is that the
therapist, in becoming more aware of research problems, may learn to
incorporate this awareness into his daily working life and benefit
from the creative hygiene of objectivity.

FAMILY THERAPY: A PROBLEM IN APPLIED PSYCHOLOGY

Whilst I can focus on only a handful of important problems, it is
important to recognise that there are dangers in emphasis and selectivity.   In the present section, therefore, I set out a checklist
of questions to be asked in this field.   I shall address myself to
only a few of these, but hope that the remainder will serve to guide
the reader either in further explorations of the field or in terms
of the evaluation of his own therapeutic activity.

Imagine that an applied psychologist were asked by a government
agency to conduct an evaluation study of family therapy.   Where
could he begin?   What questions could he ask?   No such investigation can be carried out at random.   The investigator must have certain specific questions in mind to which he will require specific
answers, or at least some indication that he might be asking the
wrong questions.   I provide here some specimen questions under a
number of heads: theoretical considerations, methods of training for
therapists, pre-treatment characteristics of clients, techniques of
treatment, and evaluation of outcome of treatment.   Since the data
which the applied psychologist will examine will also include existing research into family therapy, we require also a heading, quality
and character of research.

A CHECKLIST OF QUESTIONS TO BE ASKED IN RESEARCH INTO FAMILY THERAPY

Theoretical considerations

What exactly is family therapy?
Is there one form or several?
If there are several forms, what do they have in common?

If they have little in common (other than a commitment to treat the
family) is it legitimate to ask questions about family therapy per
se?
What is the theoretical rationale for family therapy?
Is it based on a particular view of the nature of man?
Has it arisen historically from the clinical tradition, or does it
have roots within scientific psychology?
Are the various theories of family therapy in any sense comparable;
for example, are they stated in such a common language that we might
compare them?
For example, do different theories yield practices which might come
into conflict with each other?
What are the agreed objectives of therapy?
Are those objectives stated in precise forms (so that we can test to
see whether they are achieved in practice) or are they vague and un-
specifiable?
Do the practices of family therapy actually arise directly from
theory or is the logical link between theory and practice illusory?
In what ways does family therapy differ from other forms of therapy
(assuming that family therapy and other forms are well enough defined to allow for such comparison)?
What are the similarities with other forms of therapy?
Are the factors common between therapies responsible for beneficial
effects rather than the difference i.e. are general (non-therapy-
specific) factors responsible?
Has family therapy theory anything to offer to general psychological
theory?

Methods of training for therapists

Who practises family therapy?
Are there standardised procedures for training?
Are there specified objectives for training?
How are therapists selected for training?
Have they undergone prior forms of training which include or do not
include training in therapeutic techniques?
Is there a formal system of qualifying examination?
Is there some central body which surveys, evaluates, co-ordinates
and controls courses for the training of family therapists?
Are there identifiable minimal standards of professional qualifica-
tion and experience?
Are there mechanisms of ethical control?
Are there formal limits for possible abuse?
Does training include training in methods of evaluating the efficacy
of treatment?

Pre-treatment characteristics of clients

Who comes for family therapy?
Why do some families come and others not come?
Is there some symptomatic, occupational, ethnic or any other bias in
the sample of families undergoing family therapy?

Are some families refused therapy?
Which agencies are involved before a family comes for family
therapy?
How do families come to learn that family therapy is available?
Is family therapy the last resort when all else has failed?
Do family therapists believe there are different types of family?
What is the basis of such beliefs?
Do they include taxonomies for normal family types and types of
family in need of treatment?
To what extent have the medical model or concepts of individual
pathology, influenced the ways in which families are classified?
Is it believed that families with no apparent symptomatology could
benefit from family therapy?
Are some families considered suitable for family therapy and others
not?
Do families have different expectations of family therapy?
Do some therapeutic agencies consider themselves to be experts in
only a particular type or class of family problem?

Techniques of treatment

Are there agreed objectives for therapy?
How are the objectives influenced by theory?
How is the duration of treatment determined?
By what procedures are particular therapists matched with different
families?
What considerations are incorporated into decisions concerning the
duration of 'contracts' for therapy?
What is alleged to happen during family therapy?
What actually happens during family therapy?
What techniques are employed by family therapists?
Do family therapists actually do what they say they do or believe
they do?
What sort of information do therapists take about their clients?
What records do therapists keep of what occurs during therapeutic
sessions?
Do therapists make case notes?
What sorts of statement are included in case notes?
Do therapists confer with other therapists?
Does the theoretical persuasion of the therapist influence his
formal therapeutic approach?
Does formal training predominate in the determination of therapist
behaviour, or is personal style more influential?
Are there agreed patterns of behaviour for therapists during
therapy?
Do patterns of behaviour vary when more than one therapist is
present?
Do they vary as a function of family behaviour?
If so, what is the taxonomy of family behaviour which is employed to
make decisions about the appropriateness of the therapists' behaviour?
Does the therapist's behaviour vary as a function of time into
treatment or of time into treatment session?

Are individual therapists consistent in their behaviour, whatever
the behaviour of the family?
Are different techniques of therapy considered to be appropriate at
different times in the life-cycle of families?
Does the presence of very young children influence the behaviour of
family therapists?
How broad is the conception of 'family' employed in the determination of who participates in therapy?
What do families do during family therapy?
Is the behaviour of families in any sense representative of their
behaviour when they are not in therapy?
If not, how can the therapist assume that his observations of family
interaction are in any sense valid?
What instruments have been developed to measure the behaviour of the
family?
Have such instruments undergone the accepted procedures of standar-
disation and validation desirable for measures of complex behaviour?

Evaluation of the outcome of treatment

How do family therapists evaluate outcome?
Who decides to terminate treatment?
What criteria are employed?
Is follow-up a normal part of therapy?
Do some families drop out of treatment and why?
Do therapists expect all families to improve or only some?
What are the criteria of success and failure accepted by family
therapists?
What success rate would be regarded as acceptable?
What is the estimate of the incidence of 'spontaneous remission'?
What are the criteria of success and failure adopted by families?
Do families and therapists agree in their evaluation of outcome?
Is it acceptable if one problem disappears after therapy only to be
replaced by another?
Is there sufficient agreement about criteria of improvement for a
meaningful comparison of treatments or of treatment centres?

The quality and character of research

The questions relating to research are of two types.   First, what
is the formal quality of the research in terms of the form of the
questions asked and the methods chosen to ask them?   Second, what
exactly are the questions to which research has been addressed?
Virtually all the questions already listed are worthy of research
investigation and therefore some issues raised in the present section merely repeat problems already alluded to.
Who has conducted research into family therapy?
Was such research well-designed?
Was it free from bias?
Have control groups been incorporated within the design, to examine
differences (i) between types of family therapy, (ii) between family
therapy and other forms of therapy, and (iii) between family therapy
and no therapy at all?

Have controls been incorporated which enable us to distinguish the
effects of the therapist, independent of the type of treatment employed?
Do the case records maintained by family therapists contain data
that may be crucial to the comparison of studies?
Do they provide basic data on the characteristics of families and
each of their members, thus enabling comparisons between therapeutic
agencies?
Do we have basic data on the duration of therapy?
What are the common criteria of outcome employed to evaluate the
success or failure of therapy?
Where multiple criteria are employed do they intercorrelate?
Have there been follow-up studies of families who have completed
family therapy?
If so, do they demonstrate that the effects of therapy (whether good
or bad) are persistent over time?
Is there evidence that family therapy can do harm as well as good?
Has anyone set out to demonstrate that family therapy is harmful and
then failed to do so?
Is there evidence of spontaneous remission of symptoms in families
in the absence of treatment, which can therefore be employed as a
baseline for the evaluation of treatment?
Does research tell us what characteristics of families are associated with the success or failure of therapy?
What reasons are given for success or failure?
Does research tell us what characteristics of therapists are associated with the success or failure of therapy?
If family therapy were shown to have an equal level of success to
other therapies or forms of treatment, could it be because there is
common feature to the treatments or therapies which has little to do
with the identified treatment per se?
If so, what is the comparative cost in terms of time and specialist
expertise, of family therapy?
What is the estimated cost to the community in financial and other
terms of failing to provide financial support for family therapy?
Are there organisations and/or learned journals which disseminate
knowledge about family therapy research?

SOME COMMENTS ON THE CHECKLIST

The reader may well feel weary after plodding through this list.
The questions raised are a distillation of the questions and issues
which have been raised in the literature relating both to individual
therapy and to family therapy.   It must already be clear that the
question 'does family therapy work?' is an improper question to
which no general answer can be given.   Rather, the aim of the researcher should be to focus on the specific problems outlined in the
checklist while bearing in mind the awful possibility that, because
of the multivariate nature of the exercise, issues which he is not
investigating might have a crucial influence upon the issues he is
investigating.   But such considerations should not deter us from
the proper pursuit of truth in this important field.   Knowledge increases by small increments, and much of research activity is repe-

titive, conservative and tedious. There is often little drama or
romance in discovery and quite often the key lesson to be learned
from research is that we must do the research better on the next
occasion. Unfortunately, as with a tedious opera, only the arias
are memorable.

I shall now briefly describe the findings of a number of key
papers in the field of research into family therapy, and then proceed to discuss some of the fundamental problems.

RISKIN AND FAUNCE (1972)

Riskin and Faunce provide us with an extensive review of ten years
of research into family interaction and conclude with a most useful
glossary or compilation of terms used in the field. In many ways
their paper is an appeal to researchers to behave in a more responsible manner, since duplication of effort and failure to learn from
other people's mistakes lead to a costly dissipation of precious resources. They are harsh critics. They show how family therapy
has grown from a variety of sources, living in isolation one from
the other, employing an eccentric terminology and devising sloppy
research. They identify in particular the bad habit of using high
prestige words like 'communication' in order to create the illusion
of clarity denied by ill-considered theory. In this context they
point out that this term 'sometimes seems to be synonymous with
"behaviour" and at other times appears to refer specifically to
verbal messages.... One wonders, if these expressions were stric-
ken from the vocabulary, would hard thinking be encouraged, or would
other terms immediately fill the vacuum?' They show how the basic
assumptions of the researchers have dominated the choice of variables to be studied and the context within which the family is observed, making most of the available literature incoherent and fragmented. They review problems of sampling, bias, selection of units
of measurement, family classification (which they regard as the most
serious problem), case-history data and methods of measuring family
interaction. Few studies at that time had examined interaction of
groups of more than two or three, which therefore provides an inadequate technology for the study of most families. Nevertheless,
they identify certain areas of common interest and comparability between studies. Having discarded much of the research of the 1960s
they make recommendations for the future, appealing for a retreat
from the bad practices of the past and urging greater collaboration
between disciplines. Unfortunately, this review came just at the
time when the flood of research funds was beginning to dry up, with
the impending economic crises of the mid-1970s.

The Riskin and Faunce review is as depressing as it is impressive. It obliges us to acknowledge that the study of family interaction, let alone family therapy, really is in its infancy. This
point is of great importance for the present chapter, for in the
absence of reliable information on how families behave, we have no
indication of what is normal even in the statistical sense. Nor
indeed have we any guarantee that our observation of the abnormal
will be trustworthy or that we can reliably describe changes or
shifts to apparent normality as the result of treatment. Thus

Riskin and Faunce kick away one of the keystones to outcome research.

WELLS, DILKES AND TRIVELLI (1972)

This is a review of twenty years of family therapy research with particular reference to outcome.   After discussing possible research designs and having identified a factorial group design with no-treatment controls as the only design which is stringent enough to allow for confident inference, they concede that they are obliged to limit their review either to case studies where some form of measurement was employed, or to non-factorial group designs, without no-treatment controls.   It is thus a sad reflection of the research literature that they can find no study which allows for adequate evidence.   They select studies involving a minimum of three families and incorporating some explicit form of outcome measure.   This modest requirement was met by only eighteen studies of which fifteen were seen to be inadequate since no control of any sort was included.   The common failings of these fifteen inadequate studies were: absence of pre-treatment evaluation of the family, failure to follow-up families after treatment, follow-up but absence of multiple criteria for outcome, different types of data for different families in the sample, use of unvalidated tests and inclusion of illogical controls.   For example one study compared families with a delinquent child under treatment, with families not in treatment but without a delinquent child!   Of the three final studies in their sample only two are classed as adequate and these were carried out by the same research group.   Even so, they include an other-treatment rather than no-treatment control and use a self-devised questionnaire which is unstandardised and lacks norms.   Wells, Dilkes and Trivelli also examine clinical studies, which of course have no controls and were not designed with research purposes in view.   Of 238 studies they claim some 79 per cent show 'improvement' or 'some improvement' by their criterion.   However they fail to examine the possibility that the baseline for no-treatment controls might be near this figure.   We shall discuss this point below.   The authors admit that the results of their investigation are disappointing.

GURMAN (1973)

Gurman has devoted his attention to marital therapy, which as he points out covers a multitude of approaches including behaviour modification techniques, concurrent treatment of both spouses separately, conjoint treatment, Rogerian conjugal therapy directed at clarification of feelings in relation to marital problems, individual therapy of a single spouse and group therapy of several couples. He says: 'Relatively little about marital therapy has been established empirically and ... what has been learned is based on methodologically weak studies.'   Gurman reviews all the work from 1950 to 1972 and finds only twenty-six studies which satisfy the weak criteria adopted by Wells, Dilkes and Trivelli, i.e. a minimum of three couples in the sample under study and provision of some explicit outcome criteria.

Even so, Gurman finds his studies defective in several respects. Samples are small, the research is generally carried out by the therapist himself, only one-third employ no-treatment controls, only one-quarter measure outcome not only in each spouse but also within the marital pair, only one half employ multidimensional criteria, generally the outcome criterion is a global rating, clients are rarely described in detail, therapists have broad and unspecified training and experience so that we have no guarantee that they have a common view of what they are doing, and finally few studies indicate the level of drop-out from treatment.   Gurman concludes that for the 253 couples in the survey there was some 66 per cent improvement, which as he points out, is the figure Eysenck (1960) gives for spontaneous recovery without treatment in individual therapy.   Gurman argues quite cogently that there are grounds for believing that since couples interact in a manner which probably helps to sustain and reinforce their difficulties, spontaneous recovery for couples will be lower than for Eysenck's estimate for individuals.   Nevertheless, Gurman urges caution in interpretation of these data, pointing out that they do not demonstrate that family therapy does not make couples worse!   One thing is clear, and that is that within his data there is no evidence that co-therapy is superior to other techniques.   We should note that the large sample is no indication of the mean sample size for these studies, for one study alone contained 211 couples.   Since Gurman admits that he is able to find no estimate anywhere in the literature of spontaneous remission in marital therapy we must conclude, as he began, that little has been established empirically about marital therapy.   My view is that Gurman's suggested spontaneous recovery rate of 16 per cent for marital therapy (as opposed to 64 per cent for individual therapy) is a gross underestimate.   If, according to family therapy theory, all disorders in individuals are a result of membership of a malfunctioning system, then one cannot argue that marital pairs are more at risk than individuals.   For individuals are also members of families and also live within a system which promotes their disorder.   Gurman cannot both have his cake and eat it.

The three studies which have been summarised are important because they represent a shift in strategy and the beginnings of a recognition of the need for rigorous evaluation of outcome research. All may be seen as watersheds in the history of family therapy research.   These are not the only reviews drawing such conclusions and the reader should refer to Haley (1972) and Olson (1970).

SOME MAJOR ISSUES

We come now to some major issues which have been referred to several times both in our checklist and in the three reviews of research into family interaction, family therapy and marital therapy.   I shall consider one or two issues from each of the main headings of the checklist: the problem of theory, the view of man in family therapy theory, family taxonomy and the retreat from the medical model, the problem of control in outcome research, objectives for training and curriculum design, and the evaluation of change.   I shall conclude with an appeal to applied psychologists to become more involved in family therapy and family therapy research.

The problem of theory

The principle criterion against which theories are judged is their
usefulness.   In the case of theories in family therapy, usefulness
would be evaluated in terms of the generation of techniques for the
description of families, their treatment and the evaluation of the
effects of treatment.   A good theory would also absorb other theories as special cases or cause them to be dismissed as inadequate
and unsatisfactory.   In other words a good theory in family therapy
must cover the domain of family behaviour.   A theory is not just a
set of loosely stated 'ideas' about something, or a job lot of
jargon designed to be impressive but uninformative.   Theories have
to have certain formal properties if they are to do their job and
many philosophers of science have asked the question?   'What exactly
is it which makes a theory a useful theory?'   Clearly this is a
contentious issue and we have space only for a skeletal answer.
However, the reader should be warned that the answer will not be the
answer to the question: 'How can I write a good theory?' for that
is another issue.
     The formal characteristics of theory in family therapy are impor-
tant since theory is the source of hypotheses about what makes the
family function normally, what causes dysfunction, what might restore function, and indeed what functions are important, should be
sampled and assessed.   Let us take an analogy the problem of theories in personality.   Hall and Lindzey (1970), in their classic
account of the basic requisites of theory, point out that a theory
must be explicit and lack ambiguity.   To achieve this, the following formal characteristics are essential: (a) there must be clearly
stated assumptions which identify the key features of the theory;
(b) there must be guidelines for relating these key assumptions
theoretically;   (c) there must be rules for deriving empirical predictions;   finally (d) logical consistency within the theory will
ensure that derived predictions are coherent and non-contradictory.
These are the characteristics which enable the theory to describe
and account for events which occur within the domain to which it
refers.   Now such requirements may appear to be quite trivial and
obvious.   Unfortunately, it is Hall and Lindzey's conclusion in
their review of theories of personality that no theory comes near to
satisfying these requirements.
     One might argue that if this applies to the relatively simple
problem of accounting for individual behaviour, then ipso facto it
follows that it is likely to apply even more regrettably to theories
about family behaviour, since families contain individuals and are
therefore by definition more complex than the elements of which they
are composed.   This must be a primary problem in assessing outcome
of family therapy, since there are many theories of family interaction and many theories of family therapy, all of which seem to
lead to different therapeutic strategies.   It follows that since
there are many family therapies no general statement can be made
about the outcome of family therapy per se.   In the absence of a
formal analysis of their content, it is unsafe to assume that theories of family therapy have more in common than the trivial fact
that they purport to refer to families rather than individuals.
Moreover, the various theories vary in their formal rigour and their

capacity to generate clearly testable hypotheses.   What do we mean
by this?   Let us take the homely and humble analogy of the baking
recipe.

A good theory is something like a good recipe for baking cakes.
It tells you what you wish to make, what ingredients to use, what
quantities to use, how and when to mix them, when to place them in
the oven, when to take them out and how to test when they are ready
for consumption.   If by misfortune, the cake goes wrong, the cook
should be able to go back to the recipe and find out why.   What was
it she did wrong?   Indeed a dozen cooks should be able to take the
recipe to a dozen separate and independent kitchens and all produce
the same cake.   So it should be with theories.   For example, one
of the standard criticisms of Freudian theory is that it is stated
in such vague terms that it is impossible to determine exactly what
it says and what it predicts.   It is claimed that Freudian theory
contains so many logically contradictory propositions that one is
led to make contradictory predictions about what might happen in
certain circumstances.   The experts become confused.   One produces
a jam sponge and the other a plumduff!

Such a state of affairs would clearly be unsatisfactory for the
family therapist, since he demands a great deal of his theory, ante
hoc and not post hoc.   In particular, he wants the theory to tell
him what sort of strategy to adopt with a particular family and how
he is to know that the strategy has been successful.   The theory
must provide the recipe for achieving these deceptively simple-look-
ing goals.   It is improper to condemn without presenting the evidence, but it is my view that no theory purporting to be relevant to
family therapy is precise enough or unambiguous enough, or general
enough enough, or where necessary, specific enough, to help the
family therapist in any practical manner.   The general notion of
family therapy may be helpful as we indicated earlier, but practical
men can do little with general notions.   A new idea might serve to
shift us away from humbug and self-deception, and in this respect
the notion of treating the family has succeeded in raising questions
about many traditional forms of individual therapy.   However, the
final verdict may be that in this respect family therapy will have
done more harm than good, since it has acted as a life-giving blood
transfusion to patients for whom there could be little argument over
the virtues of euthanasia.   The shift of focus from individual to
family has been a welcome deus ex machina for several therapeutic
approaches which have long outlived any semblance of usefulness.
The reader is invited to examine the theory of family therapy he
knows best and see how easily he can use it to provide concrete
advice for the therapist.

The view of man in family therapy theory

The person appears to have become lost in family therapy.   There
are several related reasons for this; the desire to consider the
family as an integrated system, the shifting of blame for symptoms
away from the identified patient, the retreat from a medical model
which sees deviance as a disease within the individual and the emphasis placed on communication which in turn is seen as interactions

between people rather than confusion within the person.   Now, I do not wish to say that this approach is incorrect, but rather that the emphasis has gone too far to the extent that the therapist might be obliged by theoretical alliance and dogma to deny the extent of the variance for family difficulty attributable to the problems of an individual, or might similarly believe that it is improper to treat the individual in any other medium than within the family, or with any other treatment but family therapy.   Playing down the role of the individual raises several practical problems.   In the assessment of outcome do we only look at the functioning of the family as a whole or do we also examine the behaviour of indivudals, and where is the operational dividing line?   Have we succeeded if one family member improves in functioning and another deteriorates?   Again, if we improve the functioning of an individual within the family, do we reduce the possibility of efficient functioning when he becomes independent from the family?

There is a general problem here, for personality theorists are not yet decided what exactly a person is and whether there is a constellation of persisting and intact traits which describe the individual or whether his varied responses to environmental pressures and stimuli provide us with a more useful set of parameters which will in fact enable prediction of behaviour.   If one tends to the latter view, then the family context is an appropriate context for the description of the person since it provides a relatively constant pattern of stimuli and responses to the person's responses to stimuli.   But I suspect that in rejecting the medical model, the family therapist has perhaps overshot in the right direction.   If we limit our observations merely to the family as a group, we might be taking the wrong observations, since the most informative data may be bound within the functioning of one member.   This is a good example of how theoretical persuasion determines the variables chosen for study.   The question is whether family therapy can manage without an adequate theory of personality, for psychology at large has yet to produce one.

Family taxonomy and the retreat from the medical model

How shall we classify families?   To label them as 'schizophrenic', or 'neurotic', merely compounds the errors made for so long in individual psychopathology.   It is worth reminding the reader of several unfortunate features associated with traditional psychiatric nosology.

1 The nosology was devised not on the basis of systematic observation or any other scientific means, but merely on the basis of the accumulated wisdom of psychiatrists, who, when controversy arose, were obliged to classify a piece of abnormal behaviour as this or that largely on the basis of committee vote.

2 Several studies have shown that psychiatric diagnosis is unreliable both within and between psychiatrists.

3 If the classification system represented reality then one might expect to find similar distributions of disorders in different populations;   in fact, the distribution varies from area to area, hospital to hospital and even from ward to ward, reflecting the partic-

ular biases of the psychiatrist, the facilities available both within and outside the hospital, and the attitudes towards deviance held by the community at large.

4 Diagnosis is based on a brief interview under stressful circumstances and rarely involves prolonged observation of the individual in his natural habitat.

5 The undue representation of different groups within particular categories (for example the association of higher income groups with neurosis but lower income groups with psychosis) has not yet been adequately explained and therefore could be more to do with aspects of diagnostic procedures and psychiatric expectation than with the true state of affairs.

6 Patients who behave in certain ways when interacting with psychiatrists are more likely to be released. This may indicate that such behaviours are of good prognostic value, or it could be that psychiatrists respond unwittingly to certain responses to their own behaviour.

In circumstances like these, the use of labels to describe disorders is perhaps the only thing to do if one wishes to convince oneself that one is doing the correct thing. Such findings indicate that psychiatry in its traditional form may have as little to offer to family therapy as has psychology. However, the retreat from the medical model may again lead us away from the truth. It is more than likely that the predisposition to respond to stress in inadequate ways is largely determined by biological factors and that to deny this is to deny appropriate help to the client. The family therapist may be observing the precipitating rather than the predisposing factors. This does not mean that psychological treatment rather than biological treatment is inappropriate. But talk of 'systems', 'communication', 'ego boundaries' and so on may be just as blithe an oversimplification as talk of 'genes', 'amine deficiency', 'autonomic reactivity', or 'loss of hippocampal inhibitory control over memory banks'. The truth is that we know so little about how families behave that we are far from devising a taxonomy of abnormal families. This again is an important problem since if we cannot describe families, if we do not possess an adequate terminology, how can we compare families or studies of families and how can we describe meaningful shifts in the behaviour of families?

The problem of control in outcome research

Why do scientists worry so much over controls? Why is it not sufficient for a family therapist to report that five families underwent family therapy and that after a period of six months, in his judgment, treatment was successful in four cases? Would this not be an adequate demonstration of the efficacy of family therapy? Let us consider an extension of the example. Say five additional families had been awaiting family therapy during this period, and three of these families appeared no longer to require treatment. What could we say then? We could say that treatment appeared to have a slight advantage but that, given the size of our sample, this could have been due to factors of which we can only guess. Indeed some of those factors which brought about change in the untreated families may have operated upon the treated families, in spite of the therapist. Now say a fellow therapist, in a different centre, with different views, claims to have an equal level of success merely by dealing with the identified patient. What brings about the cure? Could there be something which is common to both types of treatment, for example, the clarification of feelings, or the encouragement of positive affect statements about the self? And again, since family therapy differs in so many ways from traditional treatments, what aspects are in fact beneficial? May it not be the case that simply succeeding in getting a family together to discuss a problem, however it is discussed, has a beneficial effect? Or could it be that the novelty and notoriety of the procedure invest this treatment with an allure which will dissipate over the years but which has great potential at this point in time for inducing faith in the clients? And what about faith within the therapist, particularly if he has been following false trails in the past; may not his enthusiasm imbue his efforts? And say the effects are only in the short term? Must the treatment not be shown to be long-lasting in comparison with other treatments, once novelty or other effects have worn off? What if there is something about a particular therapist that makes him an agent for change, whatever the treatment he uses? Should we not compare a number of therapists, each trying a number of techniques with a number of different families and should we not compare each of these techniques against a no-treatment group which has waited for treatment as long as the treated groups have been treated? This is what Wells, Dilkes and Trivelli mean when they talk of factorial designs with no-treatment controls. And do we need a no-treatment control period even for the families which receive treatment, just to ensure that they would not have adjusted without treatment. Would this not also provide us with a baseline against which to compare their behaviour both during treatment and during the follow-up period following treatment?

What this all amounts to is that any observed effects might be due to a number of possible factors. We eliminate such factors by incorporating them into our research design just so that we are free to demonstrate that their effects are negligible. The view now held of individual psychotherapies is that they work, if they do work, first because they happen to be appropriate to the patient in question, second because the client (as well as the therapist) has for one reason or another some faith in the procedure, and third, that the treatment makes sense to the client and puts the responsibility for himself partially at least in his own hands, reducing dependence upon the mysteries exercised by the 'expert'. It also appears to be the case that certain aspects of therapist behaviour (whatever the particular brand of treatment) may be associated with a higher rate of success. At the same time it is clear that a certain proportion of clients cease to have treatment because they recover, or recover without treatment. This latter effect is called 'spontaneous recovery'. The term 'spontaneous' is really a misnomer or a confession of ignorance. The point is that some factor or combination of factors beyond the therapist's control, life events of some sort or another (which could include a therapeutic relationship with a non-professional), bring about the change.

If such things do happen, then it is important to estimate how often they happen, so that we can use that datum as our baseline against which to measure true therapy effects.   There is controversy in the psychological literature as to the exact extent of this phenomenon.   Estimates for individual therapy have ranged between 30 and 64 per cent.   Thus, to show that his treatment is effective, the therapist must exceed this rate by a healthy percentage.   However, we should remember that family therapy varies from individual therapy in many ways.   Two essential characteristics of individual therapy are that the client recognises his distress and wishes to eliminate the discomfort which it causes.   Families are often unwilling to attend for treatment as a group and do not recognise that there might be anything amiss with the group, pointing instead to the deviance of the identified patient.   The absence of such elements, if we follow the individual therapy example, is likely to make the spontaneous recovery rate very much lower, thereby enabling us to be more confident of our recovery rates after treatment. There is an excellent discussion of this problem in Gurman (1973), although as we have argued above, his estimate is more conservative than our own.

Objectives for training and curriculum design

If there are no agreed objectives for training, then it is likely that there is little in common in the behaviour of practising therapists.   It may also indicate that theory is too vague to allow for a precise brief for the instructor.   Curriculum design involves a number of basic elements: (a) the objectives of the course must be agreed;   (b) the means of achieving the objectives must be specified;   (c) the content of the course may be identified;   (d) the appropriate medium must be devised which gives the student the best experience of course content;   finally, (e) there must be methods of assessing the course to ensure that the objectives have been reached.   Without this sort of approach, research in family therapy is likely to be confounded by the fact that what is called 'family therapy' is in fact a large family of therapies, each conducted in different ways by therapists who have had different types of experience and training.   If this is the case then it is virtually impossible to conduct comparative studies between therapists and between therapy centres.   Chalk and cheese may taste delicious but they are difficult to digest together.

The evaluation of change

We have already seen that the ideal design compares families before, during and after treatment.   But what are we to compare?   Which aspects of behaviour point to the true and valid aspects of family life?   Can we trust just one measure, or should we employ several? It is generally agreed that individual criteria of outcome are unsatisfactory.   First, there is no guarantee that we have chosen the right criterion and thus there is safety in numbers.   Second, in the case of individual therapy, multiple measures have tended not to

intercorrelate.   This may indicate that particular measures are
indeed inappropriate for particular clients, or that in fact no real
change has occurred.   Criteria which have been used in individual
therapy are: subjective evaluations by the client (which may range
from global ratings to the use of standardised scales), ratings by
the therapist, ratings by intimates and peers of the client, objective measures of the behaviour of the client (e.g. verbal utteran-
ces, behaviour at work, non-verbal behaviours and so on), frequency
of interaction with social agents (social workers, police, medical
practitioners), changes in score on psychometric instruments (personality tests, achievement tests), changes in physiological responsiveness and disappearance or reduction in the frequency of specific
symptoms or patterns of behaviour.   The question to be asked in the
present context is whether we should use all these measures or some,
and whether these should be taken both for individual members of the
family, and for the family acting as a group.   So far, very few
studies of the efficacy of family therapy have used multiple outcome
criteria and the evidence from individual therapy is not too encouraging, since correlations between criteria are rarely high.   Thus,
there are studies which show the therapists' estimate of success to
be twice as high as that of their clients.   Of course, if the
theory upon which the therapy is based is clear, then there should
be no difficulty in identifying those aspects of the client's behaviour which warrant our attention.

CONCLUDING COMMENTS

I declared at the outset that I was in favour of the use of family
therapy, as there appears to be a sensible prima facie case for its
use.   I also suggested that this brief review might be depressing,
but that it would at the same time be constructive.   The guidelines
which I have set out for research into outcome in family therapy are
not impossible guidelines.   The difficulties are technical rather
than logical.   It would be possible to conduct large-scale studies
which were so designed as to allow for only a limited set of interpretations.   The assessment of research is not merely in actuarial
terms, and one good study of quality is worth many mediocre ones.
Applied psychologists are particularly well trained to conduct such
research and it is to be hoped that therapists will have the courage
to invite them to help evaluate their work.   At present the number
of psychologists engaged in family therapy is easily outweighed by
the number of members of other professions.   This is possibly the
psychologist's fault.   The field of family therapy is a proper
place for the psychologist to exercise his skills of clarifying concepts, defining therapeutic objectives and setting up criteria for
the evaluation of change.
   An excellent example of the possible contribution which psychologists might make is an article by Cromwell, Olson and Fournier
(1976) entitled Tools and techniques for diagnosis and evaluation in
marital and family therapy.   It sets out to provide a comprehensive
and evaluative survey of objective and subjective methods of describing both the therapist's view of the family and the family's view
of itself.   At the same time it explains, in straightforward

language, why certain techniques are appropriate and methodological-ly sound and why others are not.   Such a contribution is of great benefit to the future development of family therapy.

But the psychologist himself might also benefit from an involve-ment with family therapy, for it will provide him with the opportu-nity to study the individual within his natural ecology.   Psycho-logists have, for the most part, limited their study of human beings to relatively artificial and contrived situations.   These situa-tions have not only placed bias upon particular types of investiga-tion but have influenced psychological theory as well.   We have studied individuals, as individuals, in the laboratory, or adminis-tered psychometric tests from the other side of the desk, neglecting the social context within which the individual develops, lives, and gains his view of himself.   Similarly, studies of social inter-action have been conducted upon experimentally constructed groups which exist for an hour or two and rarely more, and whose members meet each other for the first time, or whose reasons for being mem-bers of the group are different from the reasons for their member-ship of most other groups.   I would like to suggest that as the idea of treating families rather than individuals gains more force, becomes more fashionable and socially acceptable, then psychologists will find it also becomes easier to gain access to the family for the purposes of psychological investigation.   Here is a group which is a primary social group, which has a predictable life-cycle within the culture, to which qualification for membership follows certain well-defined criteria, and in which membership is highly valued and protected.   The detectable influence of the family appears to be lifelong.   Here, then, is a basis for a body of ethological data which would breathe new life into psychology, which compared with anthropology and sociology has neglected the family.   This has dis-torted our view of individual differences and our explanations of the ways in which individual behaviour is sustained.   Access to family data could help psychology to resolve many key issues con-cerning trait and state.

A final problem.   It is often claimed that it is unethical to withhold treatment merely for the benefit of the researcher.   There are several replies to this criticism.   First, many clients go without treatment simply because treatment is not available. Second, it is common practice in other forms of treatment to with-hold treatment just in order to demonstrate that the treatment in question does actually work.   Finally, it is unethical to apply treatments for which there is no evidence of positive benefit.   The only way to demonstrate such benefit is to conduct scientific re-search.

The problems facing outcome research in family therapy today are captured in a quotation from Tolstoy.   In the opening lines of 'Anna Karenina', Tolstoy declares:

All happy families resemble one another, every unhappy family is unhappy after its own fashion.

This is a fine beginning to a superb novel and the evaluation of Tolstoy's statement must be a literary evaluation.   A scientist would point out that Tolstoy has no grounds for this generalisation! It is most probably false, but more important, we do not have at our disposal at this point of time any means of determining how this statement could be shown to be either true or false.

Eternal verities are no substitute for unromantic fact.   Family therapy must decide whether family therapy is to be an art or a science.

REFERENCES

CROMWELL, R.E., OLSON, D.H.L. and FOURNIER, D.G. (1976), Tools and techniques for diagnoses and evaluation in marital and family therapy, 'Family Process', vol. 15, pp. 1-49.
EYSENCK, H.J. (1960), The effects of psychotherapy, in H.J. Eysenck (ed.), 'Handbook of Abnormal Psychology' (1st edn), Pitman, London.
GLICK, I.D. and KESSLER, D.R. (1974), 'Marital and Family Therapy', Grune & Stratton, New York.
GURMAN, A.S. (1973), The effects and effectiveness of marital therapy: a review of outcome research, 'Family Process', vol. 12, pp. 145-70.
HALEY, J. (1972), Critical overview of the present status of family interaction research, in J.L. Framo (ed.), 'Family Interaction: A Dialogue Between Family Researchers and Family Therapists', Springer, New York.
HALL, C.S. and LINDZEY, G. (1970), 'Theories of Personality' (2nd edn), John Wiley, New York.
OLSON, D.H. (1970), Marital and family therapy: integrative review and critique, 'Journal of Marriage and the Family', vol. 32, pp. 501-38.
RISKIN, J. and FAUNCE, E. (1972), An evaluative review of family interaction research, 'Family Process', vol. 11, pp. 365-455.
WELLS, R., DILKES, T. and TRIVELLI, N. (1972), The results of family therapy: a critical review of the literature, 'Family Process', vol. 11, pp. 189-207.

INDEX